The Best
AMERICAN
SPORTS
WRITING
1991

The Best AMERICAN SPORTS WRITING 1991

EDITED AND WITH
AN INTRODUCTION BY
David Halberstam

Glenn Stout, SERIES EDITOR

HOUGHTON MIFFLIN COMPANY
BOSTON · 1991

This book is dedicated to
  W. C. Heinz — D. H.
  and
  Shelby Strother — G. S.

ISSN 1056-8034
ISBN 0-395-57043-3
ISBN 0-395-57044-1 (pbk.)

Printed in the United States of America

AGM 10 9 8 7 6 5 4 3 2 1

"Pure Heart" by William Nack. First published in *Sports Illustrated*. Copyright © 1990, The Time Inc. Magazine Company. All rights reserved. Reprinted courtesy of *Sports Illustrated* from the June 4, 1990, issue.

"Bo Knows Fiction" by David Racine. First published in *The New Yorker*. Copyright © 1990 by David Racine. Reprinted by permission of the publisher.

"The Sports Fan" by Peter Richmond. First published in *The National Sports Daily*. Copyright © 1990 by *The National Sports Daily*. Reprinted by permission of the publisher.

"Pride and Poison" by Linda Robertson. First published in *The Miami Herald*. Reprinted by permission of the publisher.

"Let the Games Begin" by Duane Noriyuki. First published in *The Detroit Free Press Magazine*. Reprinted by permission of the publisher.

"The Fight of His Life" by Gary Smith. First published in *Sports Illustrated*. Copyright © 1990, The Time Inc. Magazine Company. All rights reserved. Reprinted courtesy of *Sports Illustrated* from the October 22, 1990, issue.

"Wild and Crazy Hombres" by Franz Lidz. First published in *Sports Illustrated*. Copyright © 1990, The Time Inc. Magazine Company. All rights reserved. Reprinted courtesy of *Sports Illustrated* from the January 8, 1990, issue.

Contents

Foreword

AT A RECEPTION this past winter in honor of his retirement after forty-four years as a sportswriter, *Boston Herald* columnist Tim Horgan remarked that he is often approached by students asking, "How can I become a sportswriter?" Horgan said he generally responds by posing his own question: "Why do you want to be a sportswriter?" Invariably, said Horgan, the student responds, "Because I love sports."

"Wrong," admonishes Horgan. "You have to love the writing."

Precisely.

That is why this book is entitled *The Best American Sports Writing* and not *The Best American Sportswriting.* Though many contributors are full-fledged sportswriters, others are not. All are, however, *writers,* some well known and some not so well known but all immensely talented writers who have chosen to apply their sizable talents to sports, with some remarkable results.

As long as human beings have played games and as long as human beings have been able to scratch out a written language, some of those scratches have been about those games. This should come as no surprise, for the first lesson any writer learns is: write what you know. In this society there are perhaps two subjects about which it is possible to speak with any stranger: the weather and sports. This is why the poet writes about the rain and why the writer so often writes about sports.

There is a long tradition of sports writing in American literature. Many of our most acclaimed writers either began as sportswriters or found themselves inexorably drawn to the subject later.

Ernest Hemingway first wrote for newspapers in Chicago and Toronto about boxing, hunting, and fishing. These activities would later appear in his own short stories and novels. Ring Lardner was a famous baseball writer before he wrote his first short story. As a child Jack Kerouac penciled his own "Daily Racing Form." His first byline appeared on the sports page of the *Lowell Sun.* Arthur Daley, Red Smith, and Jim Murray have earned Pulitzers for their work as sports columnists. All of these writers share a similar biography. Through their love of sports each learned to love the language, and through writing each learned to explore and discover the subject they loved.

It is odd, given the enormous amount of sports writing appearing each year, that no comprehensive history of the genre has been compiled. The genealogy of sports writing is as murky as that of many of the games that we lump together as "sports." One hundred and fifty years ago there was little identifiable sports writing per se, although that didn't stop Walt Whitman from writing about ballplaying on the Boston Common. Not until the 1880s did the sports page become a staple of the American newspaper. For years thereafter the bulk of sports writing was either pure reportage, or florid, self-conscious displays of how not to write, or works of pure fancy. Yet just as American literature evolved and developed its own tradition, so too did American sports writing. As sports became a recognized part of the American scene, sports writing helped create that recognition and expand upon it.

Today, the sports section often makes up as much as one quarter of some daily papers. There are hundreds of sports magazines, and hundreds of other magazines for which the subject of sports is a significant part of the editorial landscape. Millions upon millions of words are penned each year about sports. Yet only a small percentage are worthy of a second glance. For while there are more words written about sports today and more places for them to appear, there seems, somehow, less space for them. Despite the attention we pay to sports, I notice a disturbing trend: more and more people see sports as simply a collection of numbers or a simple description of victory and loss.

There are many reasons this has happened. Newspapers are still reeling from the impact of television and seem eager to substitute their own version of the ten-second bite. The climate of American magazine writing has changed drastically over the past thirty years. Once, magazines actually existed for the writing instead of the marketplace. The quality of the articles attracted the readers, instead of a demographically selected audience determining the subject of the writing. Years ago, it was not rare for a magazine writer to be given several weeks, plus expenses, to fully explore a subject, craft a story, then be paid enough to put a down payment on a house. That doesn't happen much anymore. The accent, both in the daily press and in magazines, is too often on speed, brevity, and appeal to some hazy, preselected "readership." The writing itself is an afterthought.

A good number of the writers recognized in this collection are not, by profession, sportswriters. This does not reflect a bias on the part of this anthology against sportswriters or an infatuation with other kinds of writers. The fact is that many publications, both newspapers and magazines, seem far more eager to allow a "writer" the space and freedom for a more thoughtful story than someone perceived of as a "sportswriter." Newspapers seem increasingly less likely to allow *any* story to run more than seven or eight hundred words. This seems foolish to me, as a good number of sportswriters I know hew to Horgan's edict far more than some "writers." As demonstrated herein, given the opportunity of space and time to craft a story, the background of the writer is insignificant. What ends up on the page is what counts.

The unfortunate demise of *The National Sports Daily* notwithstanding (economics, not the lack of good writing, forced it to fold), there are still plenty of writers and editors with the ability and desire to buck these trends. The social and political upheavals of the past several decades have allowed sports writing to leave the narrow confines of the field of play and follow sports out into the world. The writer, by his or her very nature, is driven to create, and in spite of conditions that sometimes conspire to subvert good writing, still manages to create remarkable, memorable work. For good writing can do what other media cannot: offer a bottomless well of ideas and imagery from which an experience is born. The best writing never diminishes, never exhausts, a subject. Rather, the subject seems continually replenished and made

new. We can watch, for example, a videotape of the wonder horse
Secretariat rumbling across the finish line at Belmont and marvel
at his physical majesty. But after several screenings the message
of the tape is depleted. It has spoken all it can. In his superb story
"Pure Heart," William Nack of *Sports Illustrated* reinvigorates those
images in a poignant tribute to the horse that lets us see Secretariat, not just as a wonderful animal, but as a living being that
brought wonder into the world that surrounded it. In "Bo Knows
Fiction" by David Racine, and "Personal Best" by Richard Cohen,
the worlds of writing and sports are intermingled with intriguing
and amusing consequences. The late Shelby Strother of the *Detroit News,* in the story "An American Tragedy," manages to allow
the reader to share his subject's athleticism while at the same time
empathize with his lamentable plight. The inside and outside views
combine to create an entirely new vision. At its best, this is what
writing can do. In their own way each of the stories in this collection demonstrates that truth.

If there is one thread that ties these stories together, apart from
the quality of writing, it is the fact that they elicit an emotional
response that is not peculiar or specific to athletics. The subject
may be a particular game, event, or athlete, but those games,
events, and athletes matter, if not to ourselves, then to someone
else. The writer accepts the responsibility to take us there, by
whatever means he or she can. Some of the stories in this collection are amusing, others quite tragic, but each calls for the reader
to feel and reflect. I am not someone who necessarily adheres to
the notion of sports as a metaphor for society, but I do believe
whatever makes us human beings, for better or worse, can be
found in the games we play.

For that reason the reader of this book need not be a hard-core
sports fanatic, some caricature glued to ESPN, a subscriber to *Sports
Illustrated* and a half-dozen daily papers, the mind a swirling mess
of statistics and endless replays. That reader, if he or she really
exists, should find *The Best American Sports Writing* absolutely irresistible. But I am convinced the casual fan, who may see sports
more as recreation than religion, will likewise find pleasure in
this anthology. As Tim Horgan stated best, "You have to love the
writing." My wish with *The Best American Sports Writing* is that
Horgan's admonition is made obvious and that the reader does,
indeed, love the writing.

*

The process that resulted in the selection of *The Best American Sports Writing* demanded a thorough survey of a variety of publications. Sports writing appears everywhere. More than two hundred magazines published in the United States and Canada were scrutinized, issue by issue, story by story, to select those sports stories that were not just examples of good sportswriting but of good writing. Similarly, more than one hundred major newspapers were queried for submissions, and another fifty screened on a weekly basis. I am no mathematician, but judging from my deteriorating vision and the funny looks I get at the post office every day, I estimate that during this process no fewer than ten thousand separate stories were read and considered. From this multitude, perhaps one percent were delivered to the guest editor. David Halberstam's final twenty-four selections were culled from the best of this grouping for the inaugural volume of *The Best American Sports Writing*. Publications that want to make certain their contributions will be considered for the next edition should include the series on their subscription list (Glenn Stout, *The Best American Sports Writing*, P.O. Box 963, Back Bay Annex, Boston, Massachusetts 02117).

The criteria for selection were relatively simple. A story must have been published during 1990, be more than one thousand words long, and must have convinced me, after reading it once, to read it again and again. Those stories that demanded another look, at the expense of the numerous new publications that had just come in the mail, selected themselves.

I'd like to thank the staff of the Boston Public Library for their kindness and assistance in this project. I am also grateful to Doe Coover, Steven Lewers, Alan Andres, and Larry Cooper for their confidence. David Halberstam's thoughtful selections as guest editor demonstrate, I believe, that a collection of sports writing can be as artful, entertaining, and necessary as the collections of other genres.

GLENN STOUT

Introduction

I GREW UP as a semi-red-blooded all-American boy. That is, I loved sports, and like most true-blue American boys I followed almost all sports faithfully. This meant following baseball in the summer, football in the fall, and basketball in the winter; my only exemption was professional hockey, a sport I simply did not get then and do not get now. Following all sports was not as time-consuming an avocation in the forties, for those were the arid years of American sports, before the arrival of television and before the coming of the contemporary sports glut. As I write today in the spring of 1991, I can watch some eight professional basketball playoff games on the weekend, an equal number, it seems to me, of professional baseball games, as well as college baseball championships, a summer football league with teams from Europe, golf championships, and for those who feel that a summer football league is an inadequate substitute for professional football, some six hours of live coverage of the first round of the professional football draft. Less generous people might speak of this as an addiction.

As a worthy and rather typical member of my tribal species, North American, male, middle twentieth century (roots in radio sports rather than television sports), I did then, and still do, duly open the paper each day and turn first to the sports page; in the instance of tabloids, the first love of the tribe, this of course means reading from back to front. Cultural anthropologists may make of this what they wish. As an all-American boy, therefore, so far so good. Where I failed in my youth as a prototype of the species was in a number of things: I was not big and strong, at least not then; I wore glasses, which in the forties and fifties was a sign of nonathleticism; and worst of all, I displayed a premature and clearly unhealthy interest in that day's sportswriters, as well as the athletes. Even at the age of ten and eleven I checked out by-lines, and I came to know and recognize certain ones. I loved the early, feisty work of Dick Young, whose reporting semed to burn with a toughness and candor unmatched elsewhere (as he turned meaner and more bitter in his later years as a columnist, I came to detest his work), and I was fascinated by Red Smith and Jimmy Cannon and Leonard Gross: Smith because he wrote so beautifully, indeed so delicately; Cannon because he provided a rare sense of immediacy in an age before television when cameras did not do that — a Cannon story always seemed to take the reader right into the clubhouse; and Gross because of his unusual sensitivity to the athletes themselves, and because he instinctively understood that sports was the first showcase of a broader Civil Rights revolution which was just beginning in this country.

When I was young there was no *Sports Illustrated,* which eventually became the most serious bastion of sportswriting as literature, but like a lot of my colleagues who later made our reputations in the great breakthrough in nonfiction letters of the sixties, I read the old *Sport* magazine carefully and I loved it. There was some very good writing in it, it was one of the first places where the writing seemed more serious, and one could sense the beginning of a literary touch, and an attempt to break out of the routine format of magazine writing of the day. (I was hardly the only young teenager affected by it; Dick Schaap, who went on to become one of the preeminent print and television journalists of this generation, likes to recall that there was a letter to the editor of *Sport* published years ago from a teenage boy named Gay Talese, singling out a piece he enjoyed and asking for more articles like it.)

If *Sport* was the monthly bonus, then I devoured every day if I could Smith, Cannon, and Gross. Smith, of course, was the great sportswriter of the time, the acknowledged champion, because of the fresh, graceful way he wrote, because it simply was not in him to offer up anything clichéd. I can remember, as a freshman in college, taking one of Red Smith's early collections, *Out of the*

Red, from Harvard's Lamont Library and keeping it so long that I had to pay $13 in library fees, no small sum in 1951 dollars (the equivalent of four or five meals in Boston's Chinatown with my fellow editors of the *Harvard Crimson*). I can also remember a piece by W. C. Heinz, who was one of my favorite writers and who never quite got the acclaim I thought he deserved (it was his misfortune to work for a paper that was in faster decline than the tabloids I favored); it was about Pete Reiser, the great Dodger player known equally well for his extraordinary talent and for his penchant for crashing into outfield walls and thereby prematurely ending otherwise promising seasons. The piece was done, I believe, for the old *True* magazine, and it contained a memorable scene: it was spring training and a few Dodger players were sitting around talking about the season ahead. "Where you think you'll end up?" they were asked. Most said first place, a few said second. Finally it was Reiser's turn. "Brooklyn Memorial Hospital," he answered. In retrospect, told some forty years later in a time of endless breakthroughs in nonfiction writing, it does not seem so world shattering a bit of writing, but the important thing is that four decades later I still remember it, remember that it was Heinz's way of saying that he was there, that he was going to quote these men as they actually spoke, not as writers thought they should speak, and I also remember that I wanted to be able to write like that.

I was not the only one who loved the work of Bill Heinz. Al Silverman, who edited *Sport* in the sixties and later became the editor of the Book-of-the-Month Club (and is one of the nicest men in this business), tells the story of being at a bar in New York in the sixties when Jimmy Breslin, by then a star columnist with the *Daily News,* was proclaiming that a piece by Heinz in *Sport,* on a fighter named Bummy Davis, was the best sports story of all time. Breslin was making this point with considerable enthusiasm and decided he needed some final bit of proof. "Hey, Rosemary," he yelled to his wife, who was at the other end of the bar, "what's the best sports magazine piece of all time?" "Bummy Davis by Bill Heinz," she immediately answered back. Wonderful, thought Silverman, but too bad it was *True,* not *Sport,* that published it.

When I think of the early influences on me and many of my

contemporaries, I think of men like Smith, Cannon, and Heinz. They were the writers who we as young boys turned to every day, and they were the ones experimenting with form. They were all very different, they were all very good, and what made reading them exciting for a generation of young men and women wanting to go into reporting was that they were changing the rules, not accepting the bland, rigid, constricting form of journalism. They gave the reader a sense of what really had happened, what an important sports event had felt like to those most deeply involved, what the jocks had really said. In truth, they were all in different ways the children of Hemingway, profoundly influenced by him, trying to apply the lessons learned from him — the modernization of the language and the use of realistic dialogue — to the small piece of territory given to them each day on the sports page. Hemingway, in turn, so admired Cannon, who was, of course, the purest of the Hemingway disciples, that he had Cannon's paper, the *New York Post,* flown in every day to his home in Cuba. Since Cannon was very close to DiMaggio, and since Hemingway was a major DiMaggio fan, and since DiMaggio was the Hemingway hero incarnate, reading Cannon allowed Hemingway to keep up with his favorite baseball player.

If writers like that were my first heroes, for a time I did not emulate them. Instead, I went straight, finished college, went off to the South and busied myself reporting on the beginnings of the Civil Rights revolution. I covered very little in the way of sports, although at least once I covered opening day of the Nashville Volunteers, in the Southern Association. The Nashville Vols played at a wondrous old ballpark called Sulphur Dell. There where right field should have been were the old L&N railroad tracks, in effect decapitating right field and making it, as I recall, about 250 feet at the foul pole. In order to give the right fielder a chance, the architects of the park had *landscaped* right field so that it rose ever higher, and the fielder, not unlike a Swiss mountain climber, had to play on an incline. It was a disaster for some young left-handed Nashville hitters who, because of the temptation posed by the wall, developed what became known as the Sulphur Dell chop, a quick, controlled upswing at an unusually sharp angle, which, if the hitter connected, almost guaranteed a home run, but which finished the hitter forever with line drives.

So my life in my early twenties had very little to do with sports. Perhaps, my family hoped, I had finally grown up. A few years later I arrived in New York as a newly minted *New York Times* reporter (first to be a Washington bureau reporter and soon afterward a foreign correspondent) and I met Jimmy Cannon, then in his early sixties, and spent a pleasant evening with him. He after all had been a hero of mine and had covered my other heroes: the great DiMaggio, the sturdy Henrich, the powerful Keller. I was stunned by the almost unbearable quality of his loneliness. If there is such a thing as the beginning of the end of innocence for a young man, then it comes at moments like that, of seeing someone who had been a hero, indeed perhaps a role model, and knowing instantly that there is something dreadfully wrong with the way he has lived, that the price was too great.

In the unofficial pecking order of the *Times,* foreign correspondents ranked above national correspondents, who ranked above city-side reporters, who ranked above sportswriters. In those days, the *Times* did not pay much attention to its sports page. It was mostly an afterthought, and the predecessors of today's fine columnists — Dave Anderson, Ira Berkow, and George Vecsey, and now once again Bob Lipsyte — were not, to be as generous as I can, very good. The transcendent skills of Red Smith in the rival *Trib* were a source of constant embarrassment, if not to the editors of the paper, then at least to most of the reporters who worked there. That being said, there was nonetheless at the *Times* a magnetic attraction that pulled some of the best-known journalists of our age back to the sports department to talk to the sportswriters. I can remember Homer Bigart, the great reporter of two generations in American journalism, a Pulitzer Prize winner as a war correspondent in World War II, a Pulitzer Prize winner as a war correspondent in Korea, almost a Pulitzer Prize winner in Vietnam, a Ruthian figure, sidling back to the sports desk to talk to the beat men who covered the Yankees and the National League teams, and I could sense in him and others, and indeed in myself, a certain envy. We did what we did, and were duly honored for it, we were the paper's stars, but there was an undeclared and gnawing sense that the sportswriters had more fun, and also that they were allowed to earn a living and remain — as most people in the city room, for all of their fame, could not — little boys.

At that time, sportswriters, the good ones on the good newspapers anyway, seemed to have had more freedom to *write,* and generally the best writing in most metropolitan papers during the fifties and sixties was done on the sports pages. That freedom reflected in part the curious double standard of American journalism: because the editors of most important papers did not take their sports departments or the lives of athletes very seriously, and because the sports page therefore was not deemed a serious place, writers who worked there could experiment, they could be irreverent, they could tell stories about athletes they could never tell about, say, a mayor or a congressman. Sportswriters could write more realistically and with more candor than their colleagues in the city room or on the national desk. After all, the sports department was still known on major papers as the toy department.

There was a reason only sportswriters enjoyed this freedom: the more highly regarded the paper, the more reverential its tone toward important political, social, and cultural figures of the day. A good example are stories about Yogi Berra that appeared in the *New York Times.* Certainly there were, in New York politics in the fifties, politicians as colorful as Yogi who used the language with almost equal skill, but the *Times* did not write about them as it wrote about Yogi. As the paper became more influential in the sixties and seventies, it became even more reverential. The problem, of course, is that good writing demands irreverence, skepticism, a certain *edge.* It was all right for a reporter to be irreverent about what he had discovered at a baseball park or a football field on a given day, because he wasn't writing about serious people (athletes were perceived as entertainers), but it was not acceptable for him to be equally skeptical about politicians. The world of politics clearly was not viewed as entertainment, though that strikes me as increasingly debatable.

Another reason that the writing on the sports page tended to be livelier was the drama inherent in the world of sports: the action and flow of a contest, the obvious winners and losers. It was and remains a world in which the value system, the purpose, and the pain are all comprehensible, and comprehensible even to relatively young reporters. Most other journalistic assignments are mundane and by their nature resistant to almost any instinct to indulge in literary tendencies. The one exception is war, which is graphic and can be readily and movingly described, and to which ambitious young journalists have always been pulled. The drama of war, like the drama of sports, is self-evident. The reporter not only set out to move his readers; he was moved himself.

The drama of the rest of life is a great deal more subtle, less easily revealed, and more resistant to the quick assaults of deadline-propelled journalists. The real world is more unruly and complicated; the increments of victory and defeat in ordinary people's lives are infinitely smaller and lend themselves more to the eye and talent of a skilled novelist than a young and eager sportswriter in his or her twenties. In addition, sports reporting is easier to master, so it is easier to add authority to the writer's voice, which is also important. Good writing is first and foremost authoritative; the writer must be sure of the terrain.

It is not surprising, therefore, that so many of the writers who became part of the flowering of nonfiction letters in the sixties, called the New Journalism, had some roots in sportswriting. There, writers could experiment, find their voice, and be rewarded for breaking out of form (after all, a beat writer who covered 154 baseball games using the same form every day was not only boring his readers, he was boring himself). When I think of the pioneers of New Journalism, I think first of the trinity of my early heroes: Red Smith, Jimmy Cannon, and Bill Heinz.

If those early pioneers influenced some of the more important nonfiction writers of the sixties and seventies, then the circle was unbroken; these nonfiction writers continued to experiment with form, to write books, and as they did, they influenced younger writers still working on newspapers. It struck me, as I put this collection together with Glenn Stout, that sportswriting is alive and well in magazines and newspapers, that the coming of television has changed the role of the print reporter and made the good writers ever more nimble. After all, the day when print was the prime carrier and the fastest carrier of news is long over. The job of the skilled sportswriter is to go where the cameras can't go, to find out exactly what hungry readers who already know the outcome need to know, and to beat television at a story it thinks it has already covered.

Some people bemoan the fact that we don't have a Red Smith

anymore, and believe that because he is gone, sportswriting is in decline. I do not agree. There may not be one or two writers who stand out among the pack, as Smith and Cannon did in their time, but one reason is simply that there are so many other sportswriters on so many papers who are writing well, who have learned to break out of the old-fashioned form, slip inside the locker room, and give the reader an extra dimension of what has happened in a sport just witnessed by millions, and to do it with some measure of literary grace.

DAVID HALBERSTAM

The Best
AMERICAN
SPORTS
WRITING
1991

WILLIAM NACK

Pure Heart

FROM SPORTS ILLUSTRATED

JUST BEFORE NOON the horse was led haltingly into a van next to the stallion barn, and there a concentrated barbiturate was injected into his jugular. Forty-five seconds later there was a crash as the stallion collapsed. His body was trucked immediately to Lexington, Kentucky, where Dr. Thomas Swerczek, a professor of veterinary science at the University of Kentucky, performed the necropsy. All of the horse's vital organs were normal in size except for the heart.

"We were all shocked," Swerczek said. "I've seen and done thousands of autopsies on horses, and nothing I'd ever seen compared to it. The heart of the average horse weighs about nine pounds. This was almost twice the average size, and a third larger than any equine heart I'd ever seen. And it wasn't pathologically enlarged. All the chambers and the valves were normal. It was just larger. I think it told us why he was able to do what he did."

In the late afternoon of Monday, October 2, 1989, as I headed my car from the driveway of Arthur Hancock's Stone Farm onto Winchester Road outside of Paris, Kentucky, I was seized by an impulse as beckoning as the wind that strums through the trees there, mingling the scents of new grass and old history.

For reasons as obscure to me then as now, I felt compelled to see Lawrence Robinson. For almost thirty years, until he suffered a stroke in March of 1983, Robinson was the head caretaker of stallions at Claiborne Farm. I had not seen him since his illness, but I knew he still lived on the farm, in a small white frame house set on a hill overlooking the lush stallion paddocks and the main stallion barn. In the first stall of that barn, in the same space that was once home to the great Bold Ruler, lived Secretariat, Bold Ruler's greatest son.

It was through Secretariat that I had met Robinson. On the bright, cold afternoon of November 12, 1973, he was one of several hundred people gathered at Blue Grass Airport in Lexington to greet the horse on his flight from New York into retirement in Kentucky. I flew with the horse that day, and as the plane banked over the field, a voice from the tower crackled over the airplane radio: "There's more people out here to meet Secretariat than there was to greet the governor."

"Well, he's won more races than the governor," pilot Dan Neff replied.

An hour later, after a van ride out the Paris Pike behind a police escort with blue lights flashing, Robinson led Secretariat onto a ramp at Claiborne and toward his sire's old stall — out of racing and into history. For me, that final walk beneath a grove of trees, with the colt slanting like a buck through the autumn gloaming, brought to a melancholy close the richest, grandest, damnedest, most exhilarating time of my life. For eight months, first as the racing writer for Long Island, New York's *Newsday* and then as the designated chronicler of the horse's career, I had a daily front-row seat to watch Secretariat. I was at the barn in the morning and the racetrack in the afternoon for what turned out to be the year's greatest show in sports, at the heart of which lay a Triple Crown performance unmatched in the history of American racing.

Sixteen years had come and gone since then, and I had never attended a Kentucky Derby or a yearling sale at Keeneland without driving out to Claiborne to visit Secretariat, often in the company of friends who had never seen him. On the long ride from Louisville, I would regale them with stories about the horse — how on that early morning in March of 1973 he had materialized out of the quickening blue darkness in the upper stretch at Belmont Park, his ears pinned back, running as fast as horses run; how he had lost the Wood Memorial and won the Derby, and how he had been bothered by a pigeon feather at Pimlico on the eve of the Preakness (at the end of this tale I would pluck the delicate, mashed feather out of my wallet, like a picture of my kids, to pass around the car); how on the morning of the Belmont Stakes he had burst from the barn like a stud horse going to the breeding shed and had walked around the outdoor ring on his hind legs, pawing at the sky; how he had once grabbed my notebook and refused to give it back, and how he had seized a rake in his teeth and begun raking the shed; and, finally, I told about that magical, unforgettable instant, frozen now in time, when he had turned for home, appearing out of a dark drizzle at Woodbine, near Toronto, in the last race of his career, twelve in front and steam puffing from his nostrils as from a factory whistle, bounding like some mythical beast out of Greek lore.

Oh, I knew all the stories, knew them well, had crushed and rolled them in my hand until their quaint musk lay in the saddle of my palm. Knew them as I knew the stories of my children. Knew them as I knew the stories of my own life. Told them at dinner parties, swapped them with horseplayers as if they were trading cards, argued over them with old men and blind fools who had seen the show but missed the message. Dreamed them and turned them over like pillows in my rubbery sleep. Woke up with them, brushed my aging teeth with them, grinned at them in the mirror. Horses have a way of getting inside of you, and so it was that Secretariat became like a fifth child in our house, the older boy who was off at school and never around but who was as loved and true a part of the family as Muffin, our shaggy, epileptic dog.

The story I now tell begins on that Monday afternoon last October on the macadam outside of Stone Farm. I had never been to Paris, Kentucky, in the early fall, and I only happened to be there that day to begin an article about the Hancock family, the owners of Claiborne and Stone farms. There wasn't a soul on the road to point the way to Robinson's place, so I swung in and out of several empty driveways until I saw a man on a tractor cutting the lawn in front of Marchmont, Dell Hancock's mansion. He yelled back to me: "Take a right out the drive. Go down to Claiborne House. Then a right at the driveway across the road. Go up a hill to the big black barn. Turn left and go down to the end. Lawrence had a stroke a few years back, y'know."

The house was right where he said. I knocked on the front door, then walked behind and knocked on the back, and called through a side window into a room where music was playing. No one answered. But I had time to kill, so I wandered over to the stallion paddock, just a few yards from the house. The stud Ogygian, a son of Damascus, lifted his head inquiringly. He started walking toward me, and I put my elbows on the top of the fence and looked down the gentle slope toward the stallion barn.

And suddenly there he was, Secretariat, standing outside the barn and grazing at the end of a lead shank held by groom Bobby Anderson, who was sitting on a bucket in the sun. Even from a hundred yards away, the horse appeared lighter than I had seen him in years. It struck me as curious that he was not running free in his paddock — why was Bobby grazing him? — but his bronze coat reflected the October light, and it never occurred to me that something might be wrong. But something was terribly wrong. On Labor Day, Secretariat had come down with laminitis, a life-threatening hoof disease, and here, a month later, he was still suffering from its aftershocks.

Secretariat was dying. In fact, he would be gone within forty-eight hours.

I briefly considered slipping around Ogygian's paddock and dropping down to visit, but I had never entered Claiborne through the back door, and so I thought better of it. Instead, for a full half hour I stood by the paddock waiting for Robinson and gazing in the distance at Secretariat. The gift of reverie is a blessing divine, and it is conferred most abundantly on those who lie in hammocks or drive alone in cars. Or lean on hillside fences in Kentucky. The mind swims, binding itself to whatever flotsam comes along, to old driftwood faces and voices of the past, to places and scenes once visited, to things not seen or done but only dreamed.

It was July 4, 1972, and I was sitting in the press box at Aqueduct with Clem Florio, a former prizefighter turned Baltimore handicapper, when I glanced at the *Daily Racing Form*'s past performances for the second race, a 5½-furlong buzz for maiden two-year-olds. As I scanned the pedigrees, three names leaped out: By Bold Ruler–Somethingroyal, by Princequillo. Bold Ruler was the nation's preeminent sire, and Somethingroyal was the dam of several stakes winners, including the fleet Sir Gaylord. It was a match of royalty. Even the baby's name seemed faintly familiar: Secretariat. Where had I heard it before? But of course! Lucien Laurin was training the colt at Belmont Park for Penny Chenery Tweedy's Meadow Stable, making Secretariat a stablemate of that year's Kentucky Derby and Belmont Stakes winner, Riva Ridge.

I had seen Secretariat just a week before. I had been at the Meadow Stable barn one morning, checking on Riva, when exercise rider Jimmy Gaffney took me aside and said, "You wanna see the best-lookin' two-year-old you've ever seen?"

We padded up the shed to the colt's stall. Gaffney stepped inside. "What do you think?" he asked. The horse looked magnificent, to be sure, a bright red chestnut with three white feet and a tapered white marking down his face. "He's gettin' ready," Gaffney said. "Don't forget the name: Secretariat. He can run." And then, conspiratorially, Gaffney whispered, "Don't quote me, but this horse will make them all forget Riva Ridge."

So that is where I had first seen him, and here he was in the second at Aqueduct. I rarely bet in those days, but Secretariat was 3–1, so I put $10 on his nose. Florio and I fixed our binoculars on him and watched it all. Watched him as he was shoved sideways at the break, dropping almost to his knees, when a colt named Quebec turned left out of the gate and crashed into him. Saw him blocked in traffic down the back side and shut off again on the turn for home. Saw him cut off a second time deep in the stretch as he was making a final run. Saw him finish fourth, obviously much the best horse, beaten by only 1¼ lengths after really running but an eighth of a mile.

You should have seen Clem. Smashing his binoculars down on his desk, he leaped to his feet, banged his chair against the wall behind him, threw a few punches in the air, and bellowed, "Secretariat! That's my Derby horse for next year!"

Two weeks later, when the colt raced to his first victory by six, Florio announced to all the world, "Secretariat will win the Triple Crown next year." He nearly got into a fistfight in the Aqueduct press box that day when Mannie Kalish, a New York handicapper, chided him for making such an outrageously bold assertion: "Ah, you Maryland guys, you come to New York and see a horse break his maiden and think he's another Citation. We see horses like Secretariat all the time. I bet he don't even *run* in the Derby." Stung by the put-down "you Maryland guys," Florio came forward and stuck his finger into Kalish's chest, but two writers jumped between them and they never came to blows.

The Secretariat phenomenon, with all the theater and passion that would attend it, had begun. Florio was right, of course, and by the end of Secretariat's two-year-old season, everyone else who had seen him perform knew it. All you had to do was watch the Hopeful Stakes at Saratoga. I was at the races that August afternoon with Arthur Kennedy, an old-time racetracker and handicapper who had been around the horses since the 1920s, and even he had never seen anything quite like it. Dropping back to dead last out of the gate, Secretariat trailed eight horses into the far turn, where jockey Ron Turcotte swung him to the outside. Three jumps past the half-mile pole the colt exploded. "Now he's runnin'!" Kennedy said.

You could see the blue-and-white silks as they disappeared behind one horse, reappeared in a gap between horses, dropped out of sight again, and finally reemerged as Secretariat powered to the lead off the turn. He dashed from last to first in 290 yards, blazing through a quarter in :22, and galloped home in a laugher to win by six. It was a performance with style, touched by art. "I've never seen a two-year-old do that," Kennedy said quietly. "He looked like a four-year-old out there."

So that was when I knew. The rest of Secretariat's two-year-old campaign — in which he lost only once, in the Champagne Stakes when he was disqualified from first to second after bumping Stop the Music at the top of the stretch — was simply a mopping-up operation. At year's end, so dominant had he been that he became the first two-year-old to be unanimously voted Horse of the Year.

Secretariat wintered at Hialeah, preparing for the Triple Crown, while I shoveled snow in Huntington, New York, waiting for him to race again. In February, twenty-three-year-old Seth Hancock, the new president of Claiborne Farm, announced that he had syndicated the colt as a future breeding stallion for a then world record $6.08 million, in thirty-two shares at $190,000 a share, making the 1,154-pound horse worth more than three times his weight in gold. (Bullion was selling at the time for $90 an ounce.) Like everyone else, I thought Secretariat would surely begin his

campaign in Florida, and I did not expect to see him again until
the week before the Kentucky Derby. I was browsing through a
newspaper over breakfast one day when I saw a news dispatch
whose message went through me like a current. Secretariat would
be arriving soon to begin his Triple Crown campaign by way of
the three New York prep races: the Bay Shore, the Gotham, and
the Wood Memorial Stakes.

"Hot damn!" I blurted to my family. "Secretariat is coming to
New York!"

At the time, I had in mind doing a diary about the horse, a
chronicle of the adventures of a Triple Crown contender, which
I thought might one day make a magazine piece. The colt arrived at Belmont Park on March 10, and the next day I was there
at 7 A.M., scribbling notes in a pad. For the next forty days, in
what became a routine, I would fall out of bed at 6 A.M., make a
cup of instant coffee, climb into my rattling green Toyota, and
drive the twenty miles to Belmont Park. I had gotten to know the
Meadow Stable family — Tweedy, Laurin, Gaffney, groom Eddie Sweat, assistant trainer Henny Hoeffner — in my tracking of
Riva Ridge the year before, and I had come to feel at home around
Belmont's Barn 5, particularly around stall 7, Secretariat's place.
I took no days off, except one morning to hide Easter eggs, and
I spent hours sitting on the dusty floor outside Secretariat's stall,
talking to Sweat as he turned a rub rag on the colt, filled his water
bucket, bedded his stall with straw, kept him in hay and oats. I
took notes compulsively, endlessly, feeling for the texture of the
life around the horse.

A typical page of scribblings went like this: "Sweat talks to colt
. . . easy, Red, I'm comin' in here now . . . stop it, Red! You behave now . . . Sweat moves around colt. Brush in hand. Flicks off
dust. Secretariat sidesteps and pushes Sweat. Blue sky. Henny
comes up. 'How's he doin', Eddie?' 'He's gettin' edgy.' . . . Easy
Sunday morning."

Secretariat was an amiable, gentlemanly colt with a poised and
playful nature that at times made him seem as much a pet as the
stable dog was. I was standing in front of his stall one morning,
writing, when he reached out, grabbed my notebook in his teeth,
and sank back inside, looking to see what I would do. "Give the
man his notebook back!" yelled Sweat. As the groom dipped un-

der the webbing, Secretariat dropped the notebook on the bed of straw.

Another time, after raking the shed, Sweat leaned the handle of the rake against the stall webbing and turned to walk away. Secretariat seized the handle in his mouth and began pushing and pulling it across the floor. "Look at him rakin' the shed!" cried Sweat. All up and down the barn, laughter fluttered like the pigeons in the stable eaves as the colt did a passable imitation of his own groom.

By his personality and temperament, Secretariat became the most engaging character in the barn. His own stable pony, a roan named Billy Silver, began an unrequited love affair with him. "He loves Secretariat, but Secretariat don't pay any attention to him," Sweat said one day. "If Billy sees you grazin' Secretariat, he'll go to hollerin' until you bring him out. Secretariat just ignores him. Kind of sad, really." One morning, I was walking beside Hoeffner through the shed, with Gaffney and Secretariat ahead of us, when Billy stuck his head out of his jerry-built stall and nuzzled the colt as he went by.

Hoeffner did a double take. "Jimmy!" he yelled. "Is that pony botherin' the big horse?"

"Nah," said Jimmy. "He's just smellin' him a little."

Hoeffner's eyes widened. Spinning around on his heels, jabbing a finger in the air, he bellowed, "Get the pony out of here! I don't want him smellin' the big horse."

Leaning on his rake, Sweat laughed softly. "Poor Billy Silver. He smelled the wrong horse!"

I remember wishing that those days could breeze on forever — the mornings over coffee and doughnuts at the truck outside the barn, the hours spent watching the red colt walk to the track and gallop once around, the days absorbing the rhythms of the life around the horse. I had been following racehorses since I was twelve, back in the days of Native Dancer, and now I was an observer on an odyssey, a quest for the Triple Crown. It had been twenty-five years since Citation had won racing's holy grail. For me, the adventure really began in the early morning of March 14, when Laurin lifted Turcotte aboard Secretariat and said, "Let him roll, Ronnie."

The colt had filled out substantially since I had last seen him under tack, in the fall, and he looked like some medieval charger — his thick neck bowed and his chin drawn up beneath its mass, his huge shoulders shifting as he strode, his coat radiant and his eyes darting left and right. He was walking to the track for his final workout, a three-eighths-of-a-mile drill designed to light the fire in him for the seven-furlong Bay Shore Stakes three days later. Laurin, Tweedy, and I went to the clubhouse fence near the finish line, where we watched and waited as Turcotte headed toward the pole and let Secretariat rip. Laurin clicked his stopwatch.

The colt was all by himself through the lane, and the sight and sound of him racing toward us is etched forever in memory: Turcotte was bent over him, his coat blown up like a parachute, and the horse was reaching out with his forelegs in that distinctive way he had, raising them high and then, at the top of the lift, snapping them out straight and with tremendous force, the snapping hard as bone, the hooves striking the ground and folding it beneath him. Laurin clicked his watch as Secretariat raced under the wire. "Oh my god!" he cried. "Thirty-three and three fifths!" Horses rarely break thirty-four seconds in three-furlong moves.

Looking ashen, fearing the colt might have gone too fast, Laurin headed for the telephone under the clubhouse to call the upstairs clocker, Jules Watson. "Hello there, Jules. How fast did you get him?"

I watched Laurin's face grow longer as he listened, until he looked thunderstruck: *Thirty-two and three fifths?* A full second faster than Laurin's own clocking, it was the fastest three-furlong workout I had ever heard of. Tweedy smiled cheerily and said, "Well, that ought to open his pipes!"

Oh, it did that. Three days later, blocked by a wall of horses in the Bay Shore, Secretariat plunged through like a fullback, 220 yards from the wire, and bounded off to win the race by 4½ lengths. I could hear a man screaming behind me. I turned and saw Roger Laurin, Lucien's son, raising his arms in the air and shouting, "He's too much horse! They can't stop him. They can't even stop him with a wall of horses!"

I had ridden horses during my youth in Morton Grove, Illinois, and I remember one summer I took a little black bullet of a thoroughbred filly out of the barn and walked her to the track that rimmed the polo field across Golf Road. I had been to the races a few times, had seen the jockeys ride, and I wanted to feel what it was like. So I hitched up my stirrups and galloped her around the east turn, standing straight up. Coming off the turn, I dropped into a crouch and clucked to her. She took off like a sprinter leaving the blocks — swooooosh! — and the wind started whipping in my eyes. I could feel the tears streaming down my face, and then I looked down and saw her knees pumping like pistons. I didn't think she would make the second turn, the woods were looming ahead, big trees coming up, and so I leaned a little to the left and she made the turn before she started pulling up. No car ever took me on a ride like that. And no roller coaster, either. Running loose, without rails, she gave me the wildest, most thrilling ride I had ever had.

And there was nothing like the ride that Secretariat gave me in the twelve weeks from the Bay Shore through the Belmont Stakes. Three weeks after the Bay Shore, Turcotte sent the colt to the lead down the backstretch in the one-mile Gotham. It looked like they were going to get beat when Champagne Charlie drove to within a half length at the top of the stretch — I held my breath — but Turcotte sent Secretariat on, and the colt pulled away to win by three, tying the track record of 1:33⅖.

By then I had begun visiting Charles Hatton, a columnist for the *Daily Racing Form*, who the previous summer had proclaimed Secretariat the finest physical specimen he had ever seen. At sixty-seven, Hatton had seen them all. After my morning work was over, I would trudge up to Hatton's private aerie at Belmont Park and tell him what I had learned. I was his backstretch eyes, he my personal guru. One morning, Hatton told me that Secretariat had galloped a quarter mile past the finish line at the Gotham, and the clockers had timed him pulling up at 1:59⅖, three fifths of a second faster than Northern Dancer's Derby record for 1¼ miles.

"This sucker breaks records pulling up," Hatton said. "He might be the best racehorse I ever saw. Better than Man o' War."

Those were giddy, heady days coming to the nine-furlong Wood Memorial, the colt's last major prep before the Kentucky Derby. On the day of the Wood, I drove directly to Aqueduct and spent the hour before the race in the receiving barn with Sweat, exercise rider Charlie Davis, and Secretariat. When the voice over the loudspeaker asked the grooms to ready their horses, Sweat approached the colt with the bridle. Secretariat always took the bit easily, opening his mouth when Sweat moved to fit it in, but that afternoon it took Sweat a full five minutes to bridle him. Secretariat threw his nose in the air, backed up, shook his head. After a few minutes passed, I asked, "What's wrong with him, Eddie?"

Sweat brushed it off: "He's just edgy."

In fact, just that morning, Dr. Manuel Gilman, the track veterinarian, had lifted the colt's upper lip to check his identity tattoo and had discovered a painful abscess about the size of a quarter. Laurin decided to run Secretariat anyway — the colt needed the race — but he never told anyone else about the boil. Worse than the abscess, though, was the fact that Secretariat had had the feeblest workout of his career four days earlier, when Turcotte, seeing a riderless horse on the track, had slowed the colt to protect him from a collision. Secretariat finished the mile that day in 1:42$\frac{2}{5}$, five seconds slower than Laurin wanted him to go. Thus he came to the Wood doubly compromised.

The race was a disaster. Turcotte held the colt back early, but when he tried to get Secretariat to pick up the bit and run, he got no response. I could see at the far turn that the horse was dead. He never made a race of it, struggling to finish third, beaten by four lengths by his own stablemate, Angle Light, and by Sham. Standing near the owner's box, I saw Laurin turn to Tweedy and yell, "Who won it?"

"You won it!" Tweedy told him.

"Angle Light won it," I said to him.

"Angle Light?" he howled back. But of course! Laurin trained him, too, and so Laurin had just won the Wood, but with the wrong horse.

I was sick. All those hours at the barn, all those early mornings at the shed, all that time and energy for naught. And in the most important race of his career, Secretariat had come up as hollow as a gourd. The next two weeks were among the most agonizing of my life. As great a stallion as he was, Bold Ruler had been essentially a speed sire and had never produced a single winner of a Triple Crown race. I couldn't help but suspect that Secretariat was another Bold Ruler, who ran into walls beyond a mile. In the next two weeks, Churchill Downs became a nest of rumors that Secretariat was unsound. Jimmy (the Greek) Synder caused an uproar when he said the colt had a bum knee that was being treated with ice packs. I *knew* that wasn't true. I had been around him all spring, and the most ice I had seen near him was in a glass of tea.

All I could hope for, in those final days before the Derby, was that the colt had been suffering from a bellyache on the day of the Wood and had not been up to it. I remained ignorant of the abscess for weeks, and I had not yet divined the truth about Secretariat's training: he needed hard, blistering workouts before he ran, and that slow mile before the Wood had been inadequate. The night before the Derby, I made my selections, and the next day, two hours before post time, I climbed the stairs to the Churchill Downs jockeys' room to see Turcotte. He greeted me in an anteroom, looking surprisingly relaxed. Gilman had taken him aside a few days earlier and told him of the abscess. Turcotte saw that the boil had been treated and had disappeared. The news had made him euphoric, telling him all he needed to know about the Wood.

"You nervous?" he asked.

I shrugged. "I don't think you'll win," I said. "I picked My Gallant and Sham one-two, and you third."

"I'll tell you something," Turcotte said. "He'll beat these horses if he runs his race."

"What about the Wood?" I asked.

He shook me off. "I don't believe the Wood," he said. "I'm telling you. Something was wrong. But he's O.K. now. That's all I can tell you."

I shook his hand, wished him luck, and left. Despite what Turcotte had said, I was resigned to the worst, and Secretariat looked hopelessly beaten as the field of thirteen dashed past the finish line the first time. He was dead last. Transfixed, I could not take my eyes off him. In the first turn, Turcotte swung him to the outside and Secretariat began passing horses, and down the back side I watched the jockey move him boldly from eighth to seventh to sixth. Secretariat was fifth around the far turn and gaining fast on the outside. I began chanting: "Ride him, Ronnie! Ride him!" Sham was in front, turning for home, but then there was

Secretariat, joining him at the top of the stretch. Laffit Pincay, on Sham, glanced over and saw Secretariat and went to the whip. Turcotte lashed Secretariat. The two raced head and head for 100 yards, until gradually Secretariat pulled away. He won by 2½ lengths. The crowd roared, and I glanced at the tote board: 1:59⅖! A new track and Derby record.

Throwing decorum to the wind, I vaulted from my seat and dashed madly through the press box, jubilantly throwing a fist in the air. Handicapper Steve Davidowitz came racing toward me from the other end. We clasped arms and spun a jig in front of the copy machine. "Unbelievable!" Davidowitz cried.

I bounded down a staircase, three steps at a time. Turcotte had dismounted and was crossing the racetrack when I reached him. "What a ride!" I yelled.

"What did I tell you, Mr. Bill?" he said.

I had just witnessed the greatest Kentucky Derby performance of all time. Secretariat's quarter-mile splits were unprecedented — :25⅕, :24, :23⅘, :23⅖, and :23. He ran each quarter faster than the preceding one. Not even the most veteran race-tracker could recall a horse who had done this in a mile-and-a-quarter race. As quickly as his legions (I among them) had abandoned him following the Wood, so did they now proclaim Secretariat a superhorse.

We all followed him to Pimlico for the Preakness two weeks later, and he trained as if he couldn't get enough of it. He thrived on work and the racetrack routine. Most every afternoon, long after the crowds of visitors had dispersed, Sweat would graze the colt on a patch of grass outside the shed, then lead him back into his stall and while away the hours doing chores. One afternoon I was folded in a chair outside the colt's stall when Secretariat came to the door shaking his head and stretching his neck, curling his upper lip like a camel does. "What's botherin' you, Red?" Sweat asked. The groom stepped forward, plucked something off the colt's whiskers, and blew it in the air. "Just a pigeon feather itchin' him," said Sweat. The feather floated into the palm of my hand. So it ended up in my wallet, along with the $2 mutuel ticket that I had on Secretariat to win the Preakness.

In its own way, Secretariat's performance in the 1³⁄₁₆-mile Preakness was even more brilliant than his race in the Derby. He dropped back to last out of the gate, but as the field dashed into the first turn, Turcotte nudged his right rein as subtly as a man adjusting his cuff, and the colt took off like a flushed deer. The turns at Pimlico are tight, and it had always been considered suicidal to take the first bend too fast, but Secretariat sprinted full-bore around it, and by the time he turned into the back side, he was racing to the lead. Here Turcotte hit the cruise control. Sham gave chase in vain, and Secretariat coasted home to win by 2½. The electric timer malfunctioned, and Pimlico eventually settled on 1:54⅖ as the official time, but two *Daily Racing Form* clockers caught Secretariat in 1:53⅖, a track record by three fifths of a second.

I can still see Florio shaking his head in disbelief. He had seen thousands of Pimlico races and dozens of Preaknesses over the years, but never anything like this. "Horses don't *do* what he did here today," he kept saying. "They just don't *do* that and win."

Secretariat wasn't just winning. He was performing like an original, making it all up as he went along. And everything was moving so fast, so unexpectedly, that I was having trouble keeping a perspective on it. Not three months before, after less than a year of working as a turf writer, I had started driving to the racetrack to see this one horse. For weeks I was often the only visitor there, and on many afternoons it was just Sweat, the horse, and me, in the fine dust with the pregnant stable cat. And then came the Derby and the Preakness, and two weeks later the colt was on the cover of *Time, Sports Illustrated,* and *Newsweek,* and he was a staple of the morning and evening news. Secretariat suddenly transcended being a racehorse and became a cultural phenomenon, a sort of undeclared national holiday from the tortures of Watergate and the Vietnam War.

I threw myself with a passion into that final week before the Belmont. Out to the barn every morning, home late at night, I became almost manic. The night before the race, I called Laurin at home and we talked for a long while about the horse and the Belmont. I kept wondering, What is Secretariat going to do for an encore? Laurin said, "I think he's going to win by more than he has ever won in his life. I think he'll win by ten."

I slept at the *Newsday* offices that night, and at 2 A.M. I drove to Belmont Park to begin my vigil at the barn. I circled around to the back of the shed, lay down against a tree, and fell asleep. I awoke to the crowing of a cock and watched as the stable workers showed up. At 6:07, Hoeffner strode into the shed, looked at Secretariat, and called out to Sweat, "Get the big horse ready! Let's walk him about fifteen minutes."

Sweat slipped into the stall, put the lead shank on Secretariat and handed it to Davis, who led the colt to the outdoor walking ring. In a small stable not thirty feet away, pony girl Robin Edelstein knocked a water bucket against the wall. Secretariat, normally a docile colt on a shank, rose up on his hind legs, pawing at the sky, and started walking in circles. Davis cowered below, as if beneath a thunderclap, snatching at the chain and begging the horse to come down. Secretariat floated back to earth. He danced around the ring as if on springs, his nostrils flared and snorting, his eyes rimmed in white.

Unaware of the scene she was causing, Edelstein rattled the bucket again, and Secretariat spun in a circle, bucked and leaped in the air, kicking and spraying cinders along the walls of the pony .barn. In a panic, Davis tugged at the shank, and the horse went up again, higher and higher, and Davis bent back yelling, "Come on down! Come on down!"

I stood in awe. I had never seen a horse so fit. The Derby and Preakness had wound him as tight as a watch, and he seemed about to burst out of his coat. I had no idea what to expect that day in the Belmont, with him going a mile and a half, but I sensed we would see more of him than we had ever seen before.

Secretariat ran flat into legend, started running right out of the gate and never stopped, ran poor Sham into defeat around the first turn and down the backstretch and sprinted clear, opening two lengths, four, then five. He dashed to the three-quarter pole in 1:09⅘, the fastest six-furlong clocking in Belmont history. I dropped my head and cursed Turcotte: *What is he thinking about? Has he lost his mind?* The colt raced into the far turn, opening seven lengths past the half-mile pole. The timer flashed his astonishing mile mark: 1:34⅕!

I was seeing it but not believing it. Secretariat was still sprinting. The four horses behind him disappeared. He opened ten. Then twelve. Halfway around the turn, he was fourteen in front . . . fifteen . . . sixteen . . . seventeen. Belmont Park began to shake.

The whole place was on its feet. Turning for home, Secretariat was twenty in front, having run the mile and a quarter in 1:59 flat, faster than his Derby time.

He came home alone. He opened his lead to twenty-five . . . twenty-six . . . twenty-seven . . . twenty-eight. As rhythmic as a rocking horse, he never missed a beat. I remember seeing Turcotte look over to the timer, and I looked over too. It was blinking 2:19, 2:20. The record was 2:26⅗. Turcotte scrubbed on the colt, opening thirty lengths, finally thirty-one. The clock flashed crazily: 2:22 . . . 2:23. The place was one long, deafening roar. The colt seemed to dive for the finish, snipping it clean at 2:24.

I bolted up the press box stairs with exultant shouts and there yielded a part of myself to that horse forever.

I didn't see Lawrence Robinson that day last October. The next morning, I returned to Claiborne to interview Seth Hancock. On my way through the farm's offices, I saw one of the employees crying at her desk. Treading lightly, I passed farm manager John Sosby's office. I stopped, and he called me in. He looked like a chaplain whose duty was to tell the news to the victim's family.

"Have you heard about Secretariat?" he asked quietly.

I felt the skin tighten on the back of my neck. "Heard what?" I asked. "Is he all right?"

"We might lose the horse," Sosby said. "He came down with laminitis last month. We thought we had it under control, but he took a bad turn this morning. He's a very sick horse. He may not make it.

"By the way, why are you here?"

I had thought I knew, but now I wasn't sure.

Down the hall, sitting at his desk, Hancock appeared tired, despairing and anxious, a man facing a decision he didn't want to make. What Sosby had told me was just beginning to sink in. "What's the prognosis?" I asked.

"Ten days to two weeks," Hancock said.

"Two weeks? Are you serious?" I blurted.

"You asked me the question," he said.

I sank back in my chair. "I'm not ready for this," I told him.

"How do you think I feel?" he said. "Ten thousand people come to this farm every year, and all they want to see is Secretariat.

They don't give a hoot about the other studs. You want to know who Secretariat is in human terms? Just imagine the greatest athlete in the world. The greatest. Now make him six foot three, the perfect height. Make him real intelligent and kind. And on top of that, make him the best-lookin' guy ever to come down the pike. He was all those things as a horse. He isn't even a horse anymore. He's a legend. So how do you think I feel?"

Before I left, I asked Hancock to call me in Lexington if he decided to put the horse down. We agreed to meet at his mother's house the next morning. "By the way, can I see him?" I asked.

"I'd rather you not," he said. I told Hancock I had been to Robinson's house the day before and I had seen Secretariat from a distance, grazing. "That's fine," Hancock said. "Remember him how you saw him, that way. He doesn't look good."

I did not know it then, but Secretariat was suffering the intense pain in the hooves that is common to laminitis. That morning, Anderson had risen at dawn to check on the horse, and Secretariat had lifted his head and nickered very loudly. "It was like he was beggin' me for help," Anderson would later recall.

I left Claiborne stunned. That night, I made a dozen phone calls to friends, telling them the news, and I sat up late, dreading the next day. I woke up early and went to breakfast and came back to the room. The message light was dark. It was Wednesday, October 4. I drove out to Waddell Hancock's place in Paris. "It doesn't look good," she said. We had talked for more than an hour when Seth, looking shaken and pale, walked through the front door. "I'm afraid to ask," I said.

"It's very bad," he said. " We're going to have to put him down today."

"When?"

He did not answer. I left the house, and an hour later I was back in my room in Lexington. I had just taken off my coat when I turned and saw it, the red blinking light on my phone. I knew. I walked around the room. Out the door and down the hall. Back into the room. Out the door and around the block. Back into the room. Out the door and down to the lobby. Back into the room. I called sometime after noon. "Claiborne Farm called," said the message operator.

I phoned Annette Covault, an old friend who is the mare booker at Claiborne, and she was crying when she read the message: "Secretariat was euthanized at 11:45 A.M. today to prevent further suffering from an incurable condition. . . ."

The last time I remember really crying was on St. Valentine's Day of 1982, when my wife called to tell me that my father had died. At the moment she called, I was sitting in a purple room in Caesars Palace, in Las Vegas, waiting for an interview with the heavyweight champion, Larry Holmes. Now here I was, in a different hotel room in a different town, suddenly feeling like a very old and tired man of forty-eight, leaning with my back against a wall and sobbing for a long time with my face in my hands.

June 4, 1990

DAVID RACINE

Bo Knows Fiction

FROM THE NEW YORKER

THE CROWD in Madison Square Garden erupts when Bo appears at the mouth of the tunnel leading into the arena. The roar is nothing short of deafening as he makes his way across the floor, enveloped in the thunderous applause. There are sixteen thousand in the Garden, the smallest crowd Bo has performed in front of since a late August doubleheader in Cleveland. But they, make the most of their numbers, this raucous New York bunch — shouting, whooping, and stomping their feet as Bo tips his Raiders cap and waves. This humble act sends the decibel level even higher, and voices call out "Do it!" and "Write on, Bo!" until finally all sixteen thousand are chanting "Bo! Bo! Bo!" in one voice.

At the center of the arena is a raised wooden platform upon which sit a large oak desk and leather-covered chair. On the desk is a Smith-Corona electric, as the bunting draped around the platform announces. Next to the typewriter are several pencils sharpened to fine points, a dictionary, a thesaurus, and three bottles of Evian spring water. As Bo mounts the steps behind the platform and takes his seat, the response is tumultuous. Those in the back can finally see the man. The brothers are there, yelling and whistling and shouting "Yo, Bo!" and "My man!" and giving each other high fives. The professors from St. John's and CCNY are just as loud, clapping their hands to a tomatoey redness. They've all come for the spectacle, the show, and Bo, of course, is the show.

In the press box, Marv Albert describes the scene. He has been hired to do the word-by-word for this event by National Public

Radio. Joining him in the booth to provide the color commentary and expert analysis is Joyce Carol Oates — a noted author in her own right, and an admitted fan of today's center of attention. There is talk of a television special later in the tour if all goes well; undoubtedly it will be pay-per-view.

Marv says, "This building, this venerable structure, has seen its share of glory over the years, but I don't think I've ever seen anything like this, Joyce."

"Neither have I, Marv," Joyce replies. "And I've seen most of the big ones — Updike, Vonnegut, Bellow . . ."

"Let's not have you leave yourself off that list, Joyce," Marv cuts in.

Joyce beams, but of course the radio audience can't see this. Then she says, "I can tell you this, Marv: I've read in a lot of places, but I've never gotten a reception the likes of which Bo is getting now, not even in Iowa City."

But this isn't a reading, as Marv is quick to remind the listeners. Those assembled have come to see Bo write, and to judge for themselves whether the tour, labeled "Bo Knows Fiction" by the media, is appropriately named.

"Is there even any precedent for this kind of hoopla, Joyce?" Marv asks. "For a writer, I mean."

"Well . . ." Joyce ponders. "Dickens, perhaps, on his second trip to the States. But again, that was a reading tour. There's Hardy, of course — some still insist that the opening to *Tess* came during a public appearance in Dorchester — but he would have been performing practically in his own back yard." She pauses, then adds, "Neither compares."

On the platform Bo is ready to start. He has rolled a blank sheet of paper into the machine and now sits poised to begin. He picks up a pencil and chews at the eraser. The crowd has quieted and waits expectantly, as if in awe. Several of the professors are scribbling notes on small pads. Bo sets the pencil down and rests his hands in front of the typewriter. The crowd holds its collective breath. Then Bo sits back, exhales, and unzips his warm-up jacket, which has "Smith-Corona" stitched over one pocket and "JUST TYPE IT" in large letters across his broad back. He pulls off the jacket and drapes it over the back of the chair so that the motto remains prominently displayed. Bo knows endorsements, too.

Those assembled cannot help marveling at the sculpted arms and shoulders. Bo is wearing a yellow T-shirt with "WRITE NA-KED" in oversize purple letters across his massive chest — a gift from the writing program at Louisiana State University, where Bo has recently read. Even though it is an extra large, the shirt is stretched tight across Bo's thickly muscled torso. Marv says, "Certainly Bo is among the strongest of the twentieth-century writers, Joyce. Hemingway comes to mind, and maybe John Irving."

"Irving's not in Bo's class," Joyce answers matter-of-factly. "He's fit, to be sure, but Bo is just flat out the most densely muscled postmodernist we've got right now. It's not even close."

"He looks ready to begin," Marv says, cutting the discussion short. He is the consummate pro behind the mike.

At the desk Bo types, "You know me." The three words run across the scoreboard, and the crowd gasps, then breaks into wild applause before the "Quiet Please" signs used for tennis matches in the Garden begin to flash. Order is quickly restored.

"A-mazing," Marv says. "What's happening here, Joyce?"

"Well, Marv, it's still a bit early to tell."

"Can we trust this voice?" Marv asks. "Has Bo done much in second-person narration?"

"Some, but not a lot," Joyce replies cautiously. "That's pretty much been given over to Rick Barthelme and a few others. I'm thinking we may be looking at some metafiction here."

Bo types, "I'm everywhere." The crowd is frenzied.

"Metafiction it is," Marv announces. "Nice call, Joyce."

"I thought as much," Joyce says, obviously pleased with herself.

On the floor, Bo sits back to think, and Marv takes the opportunity to outline the rest of Bo's itinerary. The New York stop is the second of six that Bo will be able to squeeze in between the end of the football season and spring training with the Kansas City Royals. Additional dates were scrapped when John Wathan, the Royals manager, insisted that Bo arrive in camp on time. "I have nothing against books," Wathan stated. "I've read some myself. But Bo needs to be here. He needs the at-bats."

The dates are spaced a week apart, to allow for rest and the rejuvenation of Bo's creative faculties. At each venue Bo will write a complete piece, with the work to be collected at the end of the tour for publication by E. P. Dutton, which is sponsoring the whole shebang along with the PEN American Center. Bo sold out the Boston Garden to kick off the tour, leaving the crowd limp with a six-page prose poem entitled "Caught Looking." Afterward, Bo noted that working beneath the Celtics' fabled championship banners conjured up images of washday in the Bronx for him.

Dates in Philadelphia, Iowa City, San Francisco, and L.A. round out the tour. The Iowa stop, at Carver-Hawkeye Arena, on the University of Iowa campus, has been sold out for weeks. Marv asks Joyce to put it all in perspective. "This is great for fiction," Joyce says. "It really is. Bo is drawing people in who might otherwise never open a book. And it'll go on all year. Every time Bo takes one deep, or plows into the end zone, the cash registers will start ringing. We'll all benefit from it; there's a trickle-down effect at work here. I mean, he's money in the bank. Just look at the endorsements he gets. Can the rest of us be far behind?"

"Bo is, undoubtedly, the hottest commodity going in fiction right now," Marv notes. Besides Smith-Corona, Bo endorses Parker Pens, Liquid Paper, and Hills Bros. Coffee. Word is out he's about to cut a deal with Apple to lend his name to their newest PC, the Macbo. A poster is in the works as well.

"It's great," Joyce concludes. "I wish more top athletes wrote fiction."

"I am in pieces," Bo types. He has been working steadily and carefully. Marv relays the line to his listeners when Joyce finishes, then comments on some nifty foreshadowing. Anticipating the next line, he wings it: "I sense a metaphor coming here — *yessss!*"

"Exquisite," Joyce says.

Seated beside the platform, Barry Hannah, Bo's mentor, raises a fist. Earlier, Marv had talked with Barry. "I'll tell you, Marv," Barry said, "I'd rather have Bo for six weeks than most of these year-round M.F.A. bums. If he wrote full-time, look out." Barry has touched on a raging debate, and this thinly veiled shot is vintage Hannah. A faction within the Associated Writing Programs has condemned the tour, calling it callow showmanship, a deleterious stunt. Some in the AWP, most notably and vocally a group of M.A. students at Johns Hopkins, have gone so far as to call Bo a sham and a celebrity hack. Picketing has been reported.

"Sour grapes," Joyce says succinctly. "I'm with Barry on this one."

"I am whole," Bo writes, and then proceeds to knock off four quick paragraphs. It's all Marv can do to keep up. The crowd sits back, drained by Bo's prose, oohing and ahing as if they were watching fireworks.

"So what about Bo?" Marv asks Joyce at the next opportunity. "Place him for us, could you?"

"Well, Marv, I think the fact that he goes by one name speaks volumes, no pun intended. Of course, that's relatively common in sports . . ."

Marv interrupts with examples. "Kareem, Reggie, Martina —"

"Right," Joyce cuts in. "But in literature it's almost unheard-of. I suspect you'd have to go back to Dante to find a comparable example."

Bo brings the crowd out of its stupor, dazzling them with two pages of tight dialogue in which the character Bo stands before a mirror, discussing himself with his reflection. Heads spin in the stands and eyes roll as Bo piles on layer after layer of concise phrases and clipped double entendres. They clap incessantly, hooting and calling out as Bo the reflection gets the better of Bo the character. When the real Bo finally pauses, the crowd slumps back again, wondering how he can possibly wrap this up, yet knowing he will.

"Stunning," Joyce says, before Marv can even ask. Her voice is a hoarse whisper. She sounds as if she might cry.

While Bo ponders his ending, Marv cues up a taped interview in which Bo discusses his various careers. As is often the case, Bo refers to himself in the third person. "Writing is just Bo's hobby," Bo says. "Baseball and football are his life's work."

"Still," Marv says, "you've managed to balance them all quite well. You are probably the most athletically talented writer we've ever had. Certainly since Hemingway."

"If you call fishing a sport," Bo answers.

"Stephen Crane played baseball at Syracuse," Marv says. "Were you writing back at Auburn?"

"I was," Bo says. Then he adds, "But Crane was from a different time, so it's pointless to compare us. He was from the realism/dead-ball era. Two different things entirely." Bo goes on. "It's a lot more complex now than in Crane's time, or even since the forties, for that matter. Now we're not only dealing with the writing but with the whole aim and direction of fiction itself. I have to concern myself with that. With what's down the road." He pauses. "And then there's the whole aluminum-bat issue." There are other gems. Bo on Poe: "Edgar couldn't get past the drug testing we have today."

Marv stops the tape when he notices that Bo has begun to punch out an ending. The crowd becomes louder by the word, and Marv allows the cacophony to tell the story. Soon everyone is standing as Bo rapidly pounds the keys, until, with his final sentence, "We are all Bo," the crowd is delirious. Strangers trade elbow bashes in disbelief, marveling at what they have just witnessed, and pound each other on the back in a transcendental moment of unity. Fathers lift their children onto their shoulders. Bic lighters are held high, and a steady chant of "More! More! More!" rains over Bo as he disappears into the tunnel beneath the stands — as if they might be able to call him back for a short-short or a poem. For this crowd, its celebrated toughness and cynicism quashed today, a haiku would be enough. But Bo has already left the building.

"He really came to write today," Joyce says finally.

"Words fail me," Marv admits. "This crowd is saying it all." And again they let the chanting tell the story, wondering if Iowa is ready for Bo.

March 19, 1990

PETER RICHMOND

The Sports Fan

FROM THE NATIONAL SPORTS DAILY

THE FIRST TIME I called Bill Murray to see if he wanted to watch some Cubs games he insisted on reading me the Recipe of the Month from the Cubs newsletter, which was Ryne and Cindy Sandberg's recipe for Chicken Parmesan. It didn't sound particularly appetizing. We never found out what it tasted like, even though we did end up in Chicago, and we did end up eating a lot. We just never ate any of Ryne and Cindy Sandberg's Chicken Parmesan. We did eat Diana Ditka's chicken, which wasn't anything special, especially after Bill picked up this kid who wanted an autograph and lowered his head until it was a few inches from the mashed potatoes. We also ate lamb chops with an orange sauce at a cocktail party for some of the Cubs in a men's store that sold ties for $200, but there was nowhere to put the bones except in the pockets of the silk jackets. We also had eggs Benedict with fresh tomato slices, and some pretty good swordfish, but the most appetizing dish by far was the fruit bowl that looked like a Dutch still life in Mick Fleetwood's hotel suite on the forty-first floor. Unfortunately, he never offered us any, even though Bill was polite enough to read aloud from the unpublished science-fiction manuscripts written by Mick's dad, the late Wing Commander Fleetwood of the RAF, at 3 A.M., while the rest of Fleetwood Mac drank pear brandy down at the bar.

And, of course, we ate Polish sausages. We ate a lot of Polish sausages. In fact, the first thing Bill said when he reached our seats behind home plate in Wrigley Field during the national anthem for a 7:35 start against the Expos was, "I brought you a

Polish," and he held up a brown paper bag. He was wearing a baseball cap with the insignia of the Salt Lake Trappers on the crest. He was wearing baggy blue jeans and a black Adidas jacket with Cyrillic writing on it. Holding the bag in his left hand and his ticket stub in the right, with the brim of the cap pulled down, Bill had moved through the crowd without causing a ripple. He seems to fit in Wrigley Field the way something fits in your glove compartment that's always there, where it belongs.

"Beer?" said the vendor who always brings her coldest case to where Bill's sitting.

"That's what we're here for," Bill said. He was right. We drank Old Style, and kept score, and talked about the 1957 Braves. The day they clinched the pennant, Bill's dad — a lumber salesman, father of nine — drove the family up to Milwaukee and they cruised the streets in celebration, even though they were Cubs fans. He can still recite their starting lineup.

Since then, Bill has spent a lot of time in baseball parks. He had two at-bats with the Grays Harbor Loggers. Now he owns part of the Trappers, the Charleston (S.C.) Rainbows, the Williamsport (Pa.) Bills and the Pompano Beach (Fla.) Miracle, which he recently visited on Gaelic night, and when he was presented with a baked potato, plain, he ate it so as not to offend his hosts.

But you're likely to see him just about anywhere. Last autumn, for instance, in the middle of a pennant race, he leaned over the lip of the Cubs dugout in Shea Stadium in the late innings and tried to hand a Heineken and some Cajun fries to Rick Sutcliffe, who pitches for the Cubs. Sutcliffe tried not to panic. His manager, Don Zimmer, had turned the color of a cherry tomato. "At least take the fries," Bill said, hanging upside down. Sutcliffe didn't even take the fries. Bill ate them. The Cubs won the division.

Bill had remembered to put everything on the Polish dogs, including jalapeños and celery salt. The girl at the Polish place on Waveland Avenue invariably gives him the best Polishes on the grill. Bill isn't very comfortable with being treated specially, but a good Polish and a cold Old Style are two of the perks he'd be foolish to spurn, especially considering all of the drawbacks to trying to watch a Cubs game if you're Bill, which are considerable. In Wrigley Field, for instance, he is seldom granted more than four seconds to himself, which grows quickly annoying to a man who is far more than a casual fan. (How many people do you know who know that Lloyd McLendon once hit five home runs in five at-bats in Little League?)

"Are you Bill Murray or a lookalike?" said a doughy man in the bottom of the second as he walked in front of our seats. Marvel Wynne had just singled. "Are you Duffy Dougherty?" said Bill. He was trying to watch Wynne's lead off first.

Then a guy with maximum-security-prison tattoos came up and said, "I know I shouldn't bother you, so I'm going to." Bill looked at him the way you'd look at a dead fish on the beach. The man left.

Another man came over and shoved a program in his face. "If I miss one pitch, I'm going to kill you," Bill said. The man laughed. "I mean it," Bill said. The man left.

"Hey Bill, I think it's great how you support Chicago sports," said someone else.

"I can't do anything else," Bill said.

Mostly Bill didn't seem to mind, if it was between innings. When a teenage girl skipped in front of us and almost kicked over our beers, he said, "Hey, get those big feet outta here," and when she turned around, blushing, he smiled, and she smiled back and sort of melted right there into a pink puddle. Another girl leaned over in the middle of an inning and he signed her program in mock exasperation.

"I'm only doing this because I like the way you look," he said. She laughed. He was telling the truth. In fact, he was in a particularly good mood. A few days earlier he'd taken batting practice with the Trappers and put a few on the track, and the day before, the Miracle had taken part in the amateur draft and had picked up a couple of definite prospects. Also, Dwight Smith hit a home run in the fifth, and now Wynne hit one in the sixth — "He *hit* it!" Bill said, shooting to his feet, watching the arc of the ball over the ivy. But he regretted having made himself so conspicuous, for the Expos soon knocked Shawn Boskie out, and took a considerable lead, and the crowd started paying more attention to Bill than to the Cubs. A woman tried to pass him a love note on an All-Star ballot, and a man handed him a cellular telephone and said loudly, "Talk to my wife." Bill did. Faceless fans kept sending us beers, even though he kept refusing them. "You can't get too relaxed in a military situation," he said, and he was right: we were under siege.

"Dogs and cats, living together!" wailed someone a few rows back.

"This Ghostbusters thing is not going to go away until someone kills themselves with one of the toys," Bill said.

In the middle innings, Mark Grace, who was suffering through a terrible slump, walked into the on-deck circle. Bill stood up and shouted "I can swing that bat!" so loudly that Grace had to turn around to see what kind of demented loon was sitting in the fifth row, and when he saw it was Bill, he couldn't keep himself from smiling, all the while motioning frantically for him to sit back down before everyone got in trouble. I think Bill was trying to help him out of the slump, but he grounded to first base.

Finally, Nelson Santovenia hit a home run for the Expos.

"Nelson Santovenia?" Bill said softly.

It was all over but the shouting, of which there was a lot, so we ducked out a side door and went downtown for dinner.

As we drove down Lake Shore Drive in my rented Geo, Bill said, "The Cubs seemed sort of cranky."

They had, too.

We found a restaurant that had the White Sox–Angels game from Anaheim on the television. As we found a table, Sammy Sosa threw an Angel out at the plate. It was a good sign. Bill never likes to stray too far from baseball. He keeps close tabs on the game and has many interesting theories about sports in general. One is his Civic Metropolitan Trauma Theory, whereby cities undergoing disasters and strife are likelier to be blessed with sports championships. It is not statistically verifiable, however.

Also, his theory about the National League East this year is that the team that eats the most protein will win. "That bodes well for the Mets," he says, "because in New York, they eat their own, whereas in Pittsburgh they eat pure anthracite."

Bill ordered the swordfish. I had the crab.

"You mind if I smoke?" he asked me. Your mother would like Bill. He has these manners. "Manners are the only thing left," Bill said to me.

We tried to watch the White Sox game but people kept appearing from the dimness. The closer they got to the table, the more they all took on the look of subjects in a Diane Arbus photograph, or a Fellini film cast by Woody Allen.

"I want to talk to you about this idea I have for a theme restaurant — you and Belushi," said a man waving a cigar the size of the Graf Zeppelin. (This is a recurring theme; in Pompano Beach, a woman who wanted Bill to ride on her Harley asked him, "How's Belushi?" "He's dead," said Bill. "Yeah, I know," she said, shaking her head.)

The man with the cigar kept trying to buy us drinks, although Bill was just drinking La Croix water, because it's bottled in La Cross, Wisconsin, and they just turned it into French to sell it. Bill will drink anything made in Wisconsin.

Then another man left his woman friend at the bar to sidle up to Bill and introduce himself as a producer. He had something to do with the camera angles at Wrigley Field. About ten minutes later, when she realized that the man had no intention of summoning her, the woman sidled over, too. She was dressed in a black leotard top, and she had black hair and dark eyes and very white skin. She told us she didn't like baseball as much as she liked hockey, which she said she liked because the athletes beat each other up. Bill and I exchanged glances.

"Are you out on the coast most of the time?" said the producer.

"Yeah," Bill said, "the East Coast."

"Really?" said the man.

"I like the air," Bill said.

"Yeah, but what about the females on the West Coast?" the man said, and he actually winked like Eric Idle used to in Monty Python skits.

"Well, I like to talk to the women I meet," Bill said. The man didn't get it. Bill was trying to watch the White Sox–Angels game. "Did you know," he finally said to the man, "that one out of ten people comes from California? Is that frightening, or what?" The man left. Another one took his place, a much older man.

"I used to know George Raft," he said.

"I dated George Raft," Bill said.

A woman came over to tell Bill that he didn't seem very animated.

"I'm emotionally down because the Cubs lost," he said. "If they'd won I'd be out ripping the antennas off cars."

A woman came over with a glass full of clear liquor. Her eyes swam in her head the way the ice cubes swam in her glass. It apparently hadn't been her first drink. She said she worked for the Illinois secretary of state.

"You look like the kind of person I could go on a kill spree with," Bill said. "Knock over a few gas stations, kill a few people."

She did, too.

"Listen — I've struggled, darling," she said as if she were on-stage. People tend to approach Bill as if they were auditioning for really bad parts in life.

As we left the restaurant, the cigar man tried to pay the check.

Bill wouldn't let him. As we left the guy was yelling, "Hey! Hey! Hey!" as if we'd insulted him or something.

On the street, a man in a wheelchair told Bill he'd been shot in the back because he refused to join a street gang. He asked Bill for enough money to stay in the Y. He had an upper body like Lawrence Taylor's.

"I gotta think you could be applying yourself more, Roger," Bill said, and Roger didn't seem to disagree. Then Bill gave him more than enough money to stay for a night at the Y, and said that he hoped he wouldn't see him back at the same spot on the street later that night. "I mean it," Bill said, and judging from the expression on Roger's face, I don't imagine he's returned to the spot yet.

Back at the bar in Bill's hotel, Fleetwood Mac had a bodyguard named Roman who looked as if he'd sprung from the cellar of David Lynch's imagination. He had a smile like he was being shocked by electrodes. Bill asked the bartender for an aquavit. Everyone in Fleetwood Mac immediately asked for an aquavit. They were wearing a lot of silver jewelry and black clothes. Every few minutes one of them invited Bill to accompany them on their jet the next night to Columbus, Ohio. Bill smiled politely a lot. Mick Fleetwood drank everyone's aquavit before they could, and kept saying profound things in an elegant voice. Then he invited Bill up to his suite to listen to his late father's poetry. Bill could tell it meant a lot to Mick, so he agreed. Besides which, the band's conversation had reached the level of chatter between tree slugs.

The poetry was pretty good. It was on a cassette. There were a couple of dozen beers arranged on ice in a huge silver bowl, like shrimp cocktails, only they were beer bottles. Mick offered us beers but none of the fruit.

Bill had an 8:30 radio appearance the next morning, so we left at 3:15. As Mick saw us to the door, he asked me what he'd said that I'd written down on the corner of my Cubs program while we were at the bar, and so I read it:

"The English, the English," I quoted. "The English are the hushpuppy brigade continuing to trample the world in disgrace."

"You're the only one who has that," Mick Fleetwood said, nodding, with a smile. He's right. I am.

Down on Michigan Avenue, Bill and I were the only people on the street. A very warm wind was buffeting the buildings. For some reason, it carried the scent of newly mowed grass. We agreed to meet on the same corner the next morning. Mike Harkey was starting for the Cubs, and we had good seats again.

On the radio show, someone from Elgin called in to ask him about his movie. Among other things, Elgin houses the Elgin Mental Health Center.

"Did you escape?" Bill said. "Are you one of those guys who climbs the sidewalk and kills people in his car?" The man didn't laugh. The radio host asked Bill about the Cubs.

"I think they need a few laughs," Bill said.

I met him on the street corner. He had a white T-shirt and a blue sweater under his arm. The cabdriver said he'd had a bad day. Bill asked him if he was the kind of cabdriver who said he'd had a bad day to get a big tip. The man insisted he'd had a bad day. Bill gave him grief most of the way. When we reached Wrigley, Bill tipped him $20 and told the man to spend it on an activity that family newspapers are reluctant to talk about, although it's legal between consenting adults in most states.

Then we got more Polish sausage on Waveland Avenue.

A girl in a tank top with a Felix the Cat tattoo on the back of her left shoulder tried to sell him a Bart Simpson T-shirt. We were both feeling the effects of not getting much sleep, and she asked him why he was so crabby. I think he resisted the impulse to plant her upside down in one of the bushes. Instead he said, "That's a nice tattoo. I bet you got one somewhere else." If she did, she didn't show us.

The Cubs had given us good seats again, but the team wasn't playing any better. Our vendor wasn't working, and the beer was never cold. In the top of the sixth the Expos scored three runs. A woman from a television network who had an anchor-apprentice smile asked him to come watch her team play softball that weekend.

"Well," Bill said, "maybe I'll come by and insult you."

"That'd be great," she said.

A teenage girl asked him for an autograph.

"This girl smells really nice," he said to me.

"Thank you," she said. "You're very sweet."

"She really smelled good," he said after she left. Another one took her place. She said her name was Jennifer.

"Jennifer, you're a total babe," he said. "Now go on. Get out of here."

To a lot of people who kept coming up, he said, "You don't understand. There's a baseball game going on." Once he said, "Hey! There's a two-and-one count here!"

It was a strange game that afternoon, error-filled and back-and-forth. Bill likes games with errors. "A rally of a double and an error and another double, that's somehow more exciting to me," he said. "That's the real game. Human error."

In the bottom of the eighth it was tied. Bill had to do Siskel live in twenty minutes, back downtown. We decided to stay anyway. But then Jerry Goff hit a home run for the Expos in the top of the ninth.

"Jerry Goff?" Bill said softly.

We found a cab and Bill said to the driver, "Can you get us to the CBS studios in eight minutes?"

"Sure," the driver said, and I think he thought he was in a movie. He screeched the tires and missed a baby carriage by a foot and a half. We headed down Lake Shore Drive like one of those cars in a video driving game. The driver literally screeched up to the curb at CBS. A woman was holding the doors open, looking at her watch. Bill said, "Excuse me," and ducked into the men's room.

He came out a moment later wearing the clean T-shirt and the blue sweater. He'd stuck his head under the sink and combed all his hair straight back. Siskel was wearing clothes that looked like he'd stepped out of a Brooks Brothers catalogue six minutes ago. The anchorpeople segued into Siskel and Bill.

"Bill Murray's movies," Siskel said, by way of introducing Bill, "average one hundred million dollars gross," as if it had anything to do with anything. Bill didn't get animated until Siskel asked him about the Cubs. When Siskel asked him how the studio had come to let him direct his latest film, Bill said, "Sometimes when it's three-and-oh, they let you swing away."

Outside the studio, back on the street, Bill's studio's publicist had produced a limousine the size of a stretch DC-9. He'd been trying to get Bill to ride in limos for two days. This time Bill acquiesced, as a favor to the publicist, who belongs to the age when publicists knew how to publicize, but liked nothing more than making their stars feel like stars. He'd say things to Bill like, "Need anything? Plane tickets? Money?" And Bill would say, "No thanks." In the back of the limo, the publicist had Paris on the car phone, and so Bill talked to Paris for a minute. There were crystal glasses in the bar, but there wasn't any time to use them because the hotel was about six blocks from the CBS studio. In fact, the limo was so big we probably could have gotten in one end at the studio and gotten out the other at the hotel without the car actually moving.

Bill's hotel room was on the forty-fourth floor, facing north. You could see Greenland. A basketball sat in a window sill, looking north up the shore of the lake like someone pining away for something.

Bill changed into a purple shirt and blue jeans and we crossed the street to the cocktail party introducing the Chicago Cubs calendar. Jerome Walton was wearing enough jewelry to anchor a Japanese supertanker. We took some vodka-and-tonics off the trays that kept arriving on the arms of tuxedoed young men, and lamb chops with orange sauce. I put my bones in my pocket, in their napkins.

Mark Grace introduced Bill to a guy with long hair and a cowboy hat. He was the lead singer of a band called Restless Heart. They are apparently very big in white baseball circles. The Cubs all seemed relieved to have Bill to talk to, instead of having to talk to the other guests at the party, who clearly did their shopping at this store, but were not acting as cool as you're supposed to act when your shirt costs $190. They clotted around Bill so that eventually he had to stand behind the sales counter. A man in a $6,000 suit — I'd guess — asked him what his plans were.

"I'm supposed to be making a movie in the fall," Bill said, "but I'm going to try and get out of it."

"Oh," the man said, and went to look for the bar, which was up near the neckties.

We took a cab to Ditka's. At a stoplight we stopped next to a Mercedes painted the color of mold, driven by a woman in dark glasses with a scarf over her hair. Bill leaned out the window.

"Nice color!" he said. "Hey, I'll bet $10 you just quit smoking and drinking!"

When the light changed, she didn't move. She looked as if someone had just hit her with a cattle prod.

We joined Grace and Sutcliffe and Steve Wilson and the lead singer of Restless Heart at a table in the Hall of Fame Room, where a man played lounge songs on an electric piano with a plaque that read "Myles Green at The Piano." Myles was exactly like the lounge singers Bill used to imitate, and by the size of his smile when he recognized Bill, you'd have thought he sensed the irony of it all, but judging by the music he played, he apparently didn't.

There were about thirty-five televisions up on the walls, all showing a Giants-Cardinals game. Every time Will Clark came up, Mark Grace watched very intently. The Cubs asked Bill about his movies.

Bill steered the conversation back to baseball. He told them they'd probably turn it around on the West Coast trip.

"I'm going to give you guys a joke book," Bill said. He was convinced they weren't having enough fun this year. He was right.

"We need it," Grace said.

"We need something," Sutcliffe said.

Bill ordered Diana Ditka's chicken. It had a sauce with a lot of peas in it. When the kid showed up asking for an autograph, Bill shot out of his chair, grabbed the kid by the lapels of his shirt, picked him up two feet in the air and lowered him onto the table

a few inches from Diana Ditka's peas, and shook him in mock
anger. The kid was laughing. Bill let him up and signed the autograph. Then, just when the kid thought he was safe, Bill grabbed
him and did it again. The Cubs were more or less falling out of
their chairs.

I think Bill was doing it for the Cubs, so they'd start winning.

Then a woman with white-blond hair in a black leather skirt,
black halter top, exposed midriff, and a lot of S&M jewelry came
over and handed Bill a piece of paper to sign.

He wrote, "Judy: Don't Let Them Behead Us. Bill."

"What does it say?" she said, peering at it closely. He read it
aloud. She left.

On the walk back to the hotel, Bill found a baseball hat with
elephants on it in the window of a tie store. He wanted to buy it
for Jerome Walton, but the place was closed. It started to rain
and we ducked into a piano bar in the lobby of a nice hotel. We
each had a Pernod and water. No one recognized him. The pi-
anist was much better than Myles, but since he hadn't pasted a
plaque with his name to the piano, we never found out who it
was.

Back at Bill's hotel, no one was in the bar. Fleetwood Mac had
gone to Columbus, but Bill's family had arrived in the RV. It was
one of the great trades of all time.

At breakfast the next morning, Bill's son Homer brought a baseball to the table and tried to cut it with a knife and fork while we
were waiting for the eggs to come. Homer is a catcher. He once
started a triple play with the bases loaded by grabbing a bunt,
stepping on home, and throwing to first, where the first baseman
threw on to third. He's such a catcher that the thing he loves most
is blocking the plate and getting run into and holding on to the
ball, and he's only eight. Luke, who is five, had the glove he'd
given Bill for Father's Day. It was a beautiful glove. They were
all en route to a vacation. But there was one more Cubs game to
go to.

We took the Geo to Wrigley, up Lake Shore Drive, past picnics
and beachgoers, and got a good parking place in the lot across
the street. Before the game Bill hung out with Zimmer in his office while Grace got bubble gum for Homer and Luke. In the

Cubs weight room, Sutcliffe told us Cubs stories. Sutcliffe asked where the seats were, and Bill said, "Up among the weird and the damned."

But on this day, the crowd was soft and comfortable, and it was a fine day for a baseball game. Someone gave Bill a Twizzler and didn't ask for anything in return, and he took it. All afternoon, Luke's green eyes lit up the whole ballpark, and after he saw everyone asking Bill for autographs, he handed his baseball to Bill, and Bill signed it "Dad" and gave it back to him, and Luke tucked it into the pocket of his glove.

Bill's putting the kid in Diana Ditka's peas to make the Cubs laugh had worked, because on this afternoon, Grace broke out of his slump, and Sandberg hit two home runs — two! — and Jeff Pico won easily. The vendor with the nice smile was back, and all of her beer was cold enough to freeze the roof of your mouth.

In the seventh, Larry Walker hit a home run for the Expos.

Bill said, "Larry Walker?" in a soft voice.

But the Cubs won easily.

Outside in the parking lot we made plans to see the Miracle. Then he went on vacation and I went to Wyoming. On the plane I read a magazine with Bill on the cover. At the beginning of the story about Bill, the writer said that Bill seems like the kind of guy you think you can go to baseball games with, but you can't.

He was wrong. You can. You should try. Really. For one thing, you get the coldest beers.

August 30, 1990

LINDA ROBERTSON

Pride and Poison

FROM THE MIAMI HERALD

THE JANUARY DAY Ted Hendricks was elected to the Pro Football Hall of Fame, he visited his favorite hometown haunts.

He heard the announcement on TV at the Interliner Lounge, a cave of a bar with Eastern Airlines strike posters on the walls. Cheers rose from the smoky darkness. Everybody there knows Ted. Drinks on the house.

Hendricks called his mother, who lives nearby. He called Wisconsin to tell Audrey Matuszak, mother of the late John Matuszak, Hendricks's best friend on the Oakland and Los Angeles Raiders. "I made it, Mom Tooz!"

Then a limousine pulled up at the Interliner. Hendricks and his friends piled in, picked up some gyros, and drove around Miami Springs, celebrating.

It was one of the best days of Hendricks's life, and one of the worst.

The greatest football player to come out of Dade County had reached the pinnacle of his career. And after weeks of being sober, he had started drinking again.

First stop on the limo tour January 27 was the Hurricane Bar and Grill, where there's a painting of All-American Hendricks in his University of Miami uniform, emerging from the surf like some amphibious warrior. Drinks on the house.

Next, Mike's Lounge on Northwest 36th Street. Punches to the shoulder of the linebacker who won fans with his antics. Remember the time he rode into training camp on a horse with an orange traffic cone as his lance? Remember the Halloween he came to practice wearing a pumpkin carved in the shape of a helmet? Drinks on the house.

The limo went to Art Bruns's Executive Club. Hendricks's gruff voice took on a stentorian tone. He loosened molars with slaps on the back, repeated the same double-entendre jokes. Drinks on the house.

Hendricks was headed for another bar when his neighbor, Margie Palmer, decided to go home. She was so happy for him, but she saw the toasts as poison.

"He fell off the wagon that night," Palmer said. "He started doing beers, got into Manhattans, and then, what was it? Blackberry brandy. That was his favorite. I told myself, 'He'll straighten out tomorrow.' But it was one big party all week."

In Miami Springs, Ted Hendricks will always be the favorite son. But he has not made a smooth transition from hero to citizen. For Hendricks, star of Hialeah High, the University of Miami, and the NFL, the laurel has withered. He is living a perpetual anticlimax.

He does not have a job. When asked his occupation, he says "retired." He is divorced. His three children live out west. He lives alone in a small house with sparse furniture.

A recent day was typical. He cleaned the pool, played golf, answered fan mail, programmed the big-screen TV, then went out. He knows he is being pulled by the warm current that winds through his hometown. Does he fight the current or ride with it?

"I've been stagnant," said Hendricks, forty-two. "I'm having trouble with the crossword in the morning. My brain's not deteriorating, it's just been nonfunctional for so long."

Most of his old teammates have weaned themselves off adrenaline. He has not. "I'm still looking for something that would excite me. Sometimes, I drink out of boredom."

Hendricks will be inducted into the Hall of Fame August 4, the six foot seven linebacker with skinny legs nicknamed the Mad Stork. He revolutionized his position by roaming the field — blocking kicks, sacking quarterbacks, intercepting passes.

He was the leader of the Raiders, ferocious, fun-loving misfits who won Super Bowl titles in 1977, 1981, and 1984. He was the personification of the pirate logo on his helmet.

Today, everyone wants to share a moment with the great Ted Hendricks. He just can't say no:

"Hi, Ted, can I have an autograph?"

"Ted, buddy, can you play in a golf tournament for charity?"

"Teddy, have I got a deal for you!"

"Ted, can I buy you a drink?"

They don't see his quiet side, only the gregarious man who always has time for his friends, so many friends.

"When you stop loaning money and buying drinks for your so-called friends, they'll disappear," said Fred Wilcox, who runs a golf-cart business at Ted's defunct Crooked Creek Country Club. "But Ted can't resist. He likes to b.s. with people."

After he had Thanksgiving dinner with his mother and brother last year, an old friend called with an invitation to go out. Hendricks had been in a sober period, but he succumbed that night. He hated himself for it, and dialed his own number. "Hey, asshole, I'm checking on you," he thundered into his answering machine. The message was there when he got home the next morning.

When Margie Palmer's mother, Meta Klein, was alive, she scolded Hendricks about his drinking.

He often went over to play cards with Mrs. Klein, who had lost a foot to diabetes. When she fell out of bed or had trouble moving, Palmer called, "Hey, Crane, I need help." He would come and lift Mrs. Klein back into bed, or onto the toilet.

She died last year at age eighty-three. "Went out on Ted's number," Palmer said.

Hendricks is hard to fathom — scary when he's drunk, humble when he's not, witty almost all the time. He can be kind and generous.

"He is such a gentle giant," Palmer said. "I've had fights with people who have seen Ted out drunk and unpleasant. I tell them they have no idea what he's really like."

The traits that made Hendricks a great player — stubbornness, pride, supreme control of the body, a certain reckless abandon — now make it difficult for him to seek help. He once went through rehabilitation but says he won't do it again.

"The problem is," Hendricks said, "I play as hard off the field as I did on it. I try to reach as far as I can, but I can't reach that high anymore."

Hendricks played in 215 straight NFL games over fifteen seasons. In 1983, his last season, he had abdominal muscle pulls so severe he had to roll out of bed and pull his pants on sideways as he lay on the floor.

"What do you think is the best painkiller in the world?" Hendricks asked. He turned down the shots of cortisone, but not of Jack Daniel's.

Raiders trainer George Anderson said it was "amazing he could play so well despite the liquor and wear and tear. His last season, at age thirty-six, it caught up to him."

Drinking was a staple of NFL life. After a road game, players were handed beers and an ice pack as they got on the plane. After a home game, there were cocktail parties.

Hendricks spent five years in Baltimore and one year in Green Bay, then moved to Oakland, where his drinking accelerated with "the hard-living, hard-drinking Raiders," said his ex-wife, Jane Hartman-Tew.

Training camp was in the Napa Valley, and Hendricks and Matuszak led expeditions to the wineries. "Ted would come in the huddle with purple teeth and tongue from the red wine," said ex-linebacker Phil Villapiano, now New York manager for a shipping company. "His drinking was a joke. Then we tried to talk to him about it. [Owner] Al Davis finally said, 'Teddy, you got to get help or you got to go.' "

He decided to go. Hendricks retired after the 1984 Super Bowl and moved back to Miami Springs.

Audrey Matuszak wants him out of there. "I've offered him my house as sanctuary," she said. Hendricks calls her frequently since John Matuszak died of an accidental overdose of prescription painkillers last June.

"I would like to hide him away here in Wisconsin, where he could walk around and clear his head."

Once Hendricks had the athlete's infrastructure: curfews, rubdowns, playbooks, adoring fans. He had everything done for him. Agents negotiated his contracts.

Inevitably, the cheering stopped. Most pro athletes "have to grind through a tough transition," said ex-kicker Errol Mann, now a stockbroker in South Dakota. "Show me something with the same type of return, emotionally and financially."

Other Raiders found a niche: Art Shell coaches the team, Gene Upshaw heads the players' union. Hendricks still drifts, burdened by a series of bad business deals. His biggest investment, Crooked Creek golf course, has been overgrown and idle since 1983.

There have been other dubious ventures: a limo service, a three-hundred-acre ranch in Florida ("the environmentalists got me"), a gold-mining claim on the Yuba River in California, the former O.J.'s Lounge in West Dade, and a quarter horse whose best finish was tenth. Hendricks traded him in for the feed bill.

He estimates he has lost close to one million dollars in all.

"I figured the world was like a football team," Hendricks said. "You trust the people you play with. I depended on people who just wanted to play with my money. I guess I listen to everybody without doing things on my own."

Hendricks lives day to day. He put off a hernia operation until recently. "I can't plan a vacation. Something better might come along."

His income is from "bits and pieces" of investments. County records paint a bleak picture: about $114,000 in taxes are overdue on the golf course, his house, and a Springs condo he rents out.

Hendricks muses about what to do. He considered becoming an engineer, or working for NASA. He was interested in dentistry, "but would you want these big hands trying to fit into your mouth?"

"I could be a pilot, or a CIA agent," he said. "I had a new one today, going through the list of possibilities — counseling. But I have enough problems of my own."

Wilcox said he has "tried to get Ted interested in different jobs, teach him the golf-cart business. But he's got too much pride to ask for a job, not in a hundred years."

Hendricks has no endorsements, either: "I thought about the Lite Beer commercials," he said, "but I hate to influence kids that way. They might grow up to be like me."

*

Hendricks's favorite poet is William Blake. He quotes Blake as affirmation of his own philosophy that "excess is best": "The cistern contains; the fountain overflows. Sooner murder an infant in its cradle than nurse unacted desires." Hendricks introduced Blake's work to Matuszak.

"There are no in betweens," he said. "Just like with Tooz and I. When you're up, you're way up. When you get depressed, you go way down. We aren't Keats people."

That must have been a sight, a six-seven linebacker and a six-eight defensive end poring over poems. But Theodore Paul Hendricks has never been your typical jock.

He was born in Guatemala. His parents, Angela Bonatti and the late Maurice (Sonny) Hendricks, a native Texan, met there while working for Pan Am.

Hendricks speaks Spanish fluently. He has read books on Mayan culture. He graduated 72nd of 1,400 in his 1965 Hialeah High class.

At UM, he majored in physics and took electromagnetic theory and differential equations, but he never went back to finish twelve hours for his degree.

"He could be anything he wants to be, that's the kind of potential he has," Hendricks's UM coach, Charlie Tate, said once. "Why, he could even be governor."

Hendricks has a copy of Blake's "The Tyger" pasted to the first page of his football scrapbook:

> When the stars threw down their spears,
> And water'd heaven with their tears
> Did he smile his work to see?
> Did he who made the Lamb make thee?
> Tyger! Tyger! burning bright
> In the forests of the night,
> What immortal hand or eye
> Dare frame thy fearful symmetry?

The Lamb in Ted made him the last one out of stadiums because he signed so many autographs. He visits children's hospitals around the country and stops by Miami's Veterans Administration Hospital. He plays an endless string of fund-raising sports events. He has coached Special Olympians.

"He uses his body like a big Jerry Lewis," said Tom Romanik of Cloverleaf Lanes.

Hendricks let Eddie Barwick, who lived in the garage apartment behind his house, skip rent payments when Barwick, an Eastern Airlines mechanic, went on strike. "He has a heart as big as he is," Barwick said.

Ted the Lamb will pick up your tab, open the door for you, kiss the back of your hand, present you with a yellow hibiscus flower from his back yard.

It is 11:45 A.M. on a fall weekday at Mike's Lounge in Miami Springs. Hendricks has agreed to a luncheon interview. The Tiger in Ted is throwing down peppermint schnapps. His breath is like a blowtorch. He mumbles the answer to a question, and is asked to repeat it.

"What, CAN'T YOU HEAR ME?" he roars. "AM I NOT E-NUNCIATING CLEARLY?"

Everyone is staring. "Teddy, people are trying to eat," says a waitress wearily.

"OH, EXCUUUUSE ME."

Another question. He responds with an off-color joke and a spine-jarring pat on the back.

"Let's get OUT OF HERE." Hendricks has decided to continue the interview at his house.

He leads the way, driving his 1972 Mercedes rapidly down a back street, but under control. There are two old newspapers on his front steps. Inside the Florida room, he pops in a Who tape. He turns up the volume until conversation is reduced to shouting. He's singing along, imitating the guitar licks.

The visitor slips out the back door to the patio and walks, at first casually, then quickly, to the car. He's six-seven, the visitor is five-seven. End of interview. He doesn't seem to notice.

Suddenly, Hendricks comes through his front door. The visitor rolls down the window to say goodbye and he reaches in, trying to grab the keys in the ignition.

"DON'T LIKE MY MUSIC?" He is not smiling.

"Ted, please call when you want to talk."

He hesitates, withdraws. He stands in the driveway, with the front door open and the Who playing, shrinking in the rear-view mirror like the fade-out of a movie.

Hendricks has an idea of his behavior when he's drunk. "My mind is still working, but I'm a monster on the outside," he said.

"I've got to learn to tone myself down. I wish I could keep that control and still have a good time."

Hendricks's ex-wife, Hartman-Tew, said there were times she and their two sons were afraid of him when he arrived at their Orinda, California, home after an evening out.

The boys — now seventeen and twenty years old — say they are still concerned about their father's "phases." But when he is inducted into the Hall of Fame in Canton, Ohio, they will be there. So will an eight-year-old half-sister they have never seen; Hendricks had his daughter with another woman after he and his wife split up.

"When he's got his head screwed on, he's a great father and a loving, kind, sensitive man," Hartman-Tew said. "When he drank, I couldn't get in there to touch the person I knew. He'd say, 'It's my life. I'm having a good time.' He didn't recognize what was crumbling around him."

Nothing captures Hendricks's frustration more than his golf course.

At the corner of Southwest 104th Street and 97th Avenue a low brick wall advertises "Open to the public." Below that are chips off letters that once spelled Crooked Creek Country Club. In fact, it hasn't been open since 1983, when Hendricks shut it down for lack of business.

He is here on his tractor to mow fairway 5. The neighbors have complained again about the snake-infested overgrowth. "It's a jungle out there. I call this my estate, all one hundred ten acres of it."

Hendricks estimates he has plowed $600,000 into the golf course.

His makeshift office is the former pro shop. The bar is covered with dust. Next to the unused cash register, a spider web undulates. There are holes in the ceiling, golfing cartoons on the walls. A sign says, "Sorry, no rain checks."

Heavy rains in 1983 finally forced Hendricks to close the course, which had deteriorated under his former business partners while he was in Oakland. He came home one time to find "all the employees out by the pool looking at girls in swimming suits. There was forty-five thousand dollars' worth of carts that turned to junk."

He decided to build houses, but Crooked Creek's neighbors stood behind a deed that requires the land to remain a golf course through 2066. "They didn't want to listen to a solution," he said. "So let them look at my eyesore."

Neighbors filed an injunction when Hendricks started hauling away topsoil to sell it. He says they use it as a dump, and when he finds clippings and old tires, he throws them back into their yards. Said neighbor Gloria Kreider, "A lot of people won't cut one blade of grass if it belongs to Hendricks."

He often says that selling the course will remove a weight holding him down. After many attempts to sell, he hopes to close on a joint venture with a Chicago company. "I just want to finish this deal so I don't have to spend my days in a bar."

Last summer, Hendricks was the life of the party during a charity golf event at ex-Dolphin Earl Morrall's Arrowhead course in Davie.

He was performing a slapstick routine, pretending to whiff his shots, stomping his opponents' balls into the ground, cracking jokes. He and the rest of his foursome had a full stock of beer.

Hendricks took a swig and laughed, and the wet spot on the front of his shorts grew into a patch.

He looked down. "Don't make me laugh," he said. "It'll only get worse."

"Ted is in fine form today," one man said, chuckling.

And so it went, Hendricks in his long-brimmed "Mad Stork" hat and stained shorts, hitting an occasional brilliant shot, his partners lucky to be paired with such an entertaining celebrity.

The charity event represented one of the setbacks since Hendricks got out of rehab.

One morning in spring 1989, after five drinks, he began shaking uncontrollably. He asked his neighbors to take him to South Miami Hospital.

"When he was in the hospital," Raiders trainer Anderson said, "I asked Ted, 'Is *this* enough to scare you?' He said he'd wait and see when he got out."

"I figured they'd give me an injection and I'd calm down," Hendricks said. On the third day, he wanted to leave. Doctors said no.

"I threatened to call the Miami Springs police, which was insane," Hendricks said. "Then they brought in fifteen or twenty interns. I looked at the odds and went back to bed."

His mother called that night. "She said, 'I want you to stay in there — for me — for twenty-eight days,'" Hendricks said. "I did her a favor. But I'll never do it again."

The Interliner is the meeting place for a recent weekday interview. Hendricks is, as usual, fidgety — constantly tugging at his mustache, tapping his fingers together.

He and his golfing partner play joker poker. BIG TED is recognized on the video screen for his high score. "Jokers are wild," he said, "just like the characters in here."

Hendricks orders a Budweiser. Then a Bud Dry. Then three Bud Lights. When he finishes, the bartender taps the empty can on the bar. He nods. In two hours, he drinks nine beers.

He is reminded that at a previous interview here, after a round of golf last fall, he was chugging club sodas.

"That must have been when I was on the wagon, when my tolerance was low. Now, I'm sticking with beer. I can control it.

"I don't want to be some bombed-out guy. My mom asked me, 'Do you crave alcohol?' I said no. It's just fun. To stop, all I have to do is look in the mirror and *think*. Can't brainwash this brain."

Miami Springs Police Lieutenant Robert Miller said that "Ted has made a change for the better — if he makes mistakes, he'll fess up." Hendricks has not been arrested by Springs cops, but they have shown him the door.

"It's always tough to live down a negative reputation," Miller said. "Recognizing you have a problem is half the solution."

Before he died last June, John Matuszak recognized his problem, and was trying to get Hendricks to confront his own. "The last time I saw Tooz, he said, 'I hope you make it,'" Hendricks said.

Hendricks was a pallbearer for Matuszak. He resented the obituaries depicting his friend as a drug- and alcohol-addicted wild man. He remembered him as the six-eight Santa Claus who visited hospitals.

He saw himself in Matuszak, another football player fighting to reconcile the tiger and the lamb.

Audrey Matuszak sees the resemblance, too. "These boys have been idolized since high school. What happens after that?" she said. "They're like children — they need lots of love, real love."

June 24, 1990

DUANE NORIYUKI

Let the Games Begin

FROM THE DETROIT FREE PRESS MAGAZINE

THE CONTESTANTS stand side by side, shuffling tentatively on a crumbling asphalt track. All around them are weeds that climb the chain-link fence and muscle up through cracks in the soft, hot asphalt.

You get so used to seeing weeds in this west-side neighborhood of Detroit, you don't even notice them after a while. They are just there, like the drugs, the abandoned homes, and the tragedy, blending into the wounded landscape.

On the other side of the playground is deserted Condon Middle School, sepulchral and massive, vulnerable to thieves who circle the building in trucks, then move in and peck away like buzzards.

Before they gathered at the starting line, there was talk about a guy named Lyndon Baines Johnson. His street name was Bang, and he considered himself pretty fast. He had planned on being at the race — probably to watch, but perhaps to run. But Bang was gunned down the night before. He was twenty-five.

"That's just the way it is around here," says Joe Elliott, seventeen, a former crack dealer who quit school last year, and now stands in lane 1. In lane 2 is Charles (Snook) Thomas, a twenty-year-old dishwasher. And in lane 3 is Delfon Curlpepper, a conference champion sprinter at Oberlin College in Ohio who runs the 100-meter race in 10.79 seconds. He is twenty-one and wants to be a lawyer. They all grew up in this neighborhood, and once each summer they meet here for a race that means nothing.

And everything.

In years past, there would be hundreds of people here at the playground, not far from the intersection of West Grand and Warren, watching, wagering, waiting to see who would claim title to fastest person in the neighborhood. But today there are only about fifty, and next year there may be fewer than that.

Five years ago, Delfon Curlpepper, then a sixteen-year-old high school kid with a bad attitude, took on the reigning champ, a guy just getting started in the drug trade. The champ was the neighborhood favorite despite his occupation. People would challenge him, and he would race them; but no one could beat him until the day Delfon came along.

Ever since then, people have been chasing Delfon, the new king of the hill. Delfon no longer lives in the neighborhood, but he returns each year to run.

The racers arch their necks from side to side, stretch their arms and legs, more out of nervousness and anticipation than physical preparation. They bounce up and down like boxers awaiting the bell as they glance toward the finish line 100 yards away.

There are no starting blocks, no official timers, no protocol. You show up and you run — first the younger kids, then the older ones, and finally the open race for anybody sixteen and older. There is plenty of speed on the track, most of it raw and untapped.

Watching from the finish line is Erica Wright. She is the reason they are here today, perhaps the reason they are still alive.

Wright watches the racers' faces turn solemn as they crouch motionless and tense at the starting line, holding their breath as they await the starter's commands — coiled like cats ready to pounce.

In the summer of 1974, Erica Wright, a computer operator for the Internal Revenue Service, walked across the street from her house to watch her nine-year-old son practice baseball.

She saw a bunch of kids throwing rocks at the team and asked the coach what was happening. He told her they were troublemakers, incorrigibles. Ignore them and they'll go away, he said.

Wright walked over and asked the rock throwers what the problem was. They said they just wanted to play baseball. So she picked up a ball, a bat, a couple gloves and took them to the other side of the playground.

"Batter up," she said.

The next afternoon, the incorrigibles showed up on her front porch.

"What time's practice?" they wanted to know.

That's how the Westside Cultural & Athletic Club got started. Wright quit her job and went looking for funds to run the program. Sixteen years later, she's still looking.

The club is a grass-roots effort to provide children in the community with something positive, something most of them don't get at home. The older kids get jobs. The younger kids get games. Everyone gets attention.

"When we was little, Erica was all we had," says Dennis Carpenter, twenty-one, who is in his seventh year working with the program. "Now we're giving something back."

Carpenter and most of the other fifty-two workers came to this program as youngsters to play. Now that they are older, they come to work, earning $3.35 an hour for the six-week summer program, volunteering their time the rest of the year.

"Ninety percent of these kids' parents are on crack," says Wright, forty-five, who lives with her parents so she can afford to run the program, funded primarily by a $16,000 grant from New Detroit, Inc.

"The majority of kids in this neighborhood who get involved in selling crack are doing it for their mothers. They think, 'If I sell it, my mother can get it from me, and I won't have to see her goin' out there, doin' these things to get it. I can supply her with it.' "

Sometimes the work is heartbreaking. Most of the time it is thankless. But there are kids in the neighborhood who have no one else to turn to. So she stays, trying not to dwell on the equipment and facilities her program lacks.

"What keeps me here? Two weeks ago a fourteen-year-old youth right across the alley took a gun and shot up a crack house," Wright says. "He was looking for his mother." The boy had saved his money from a job at Wendy's to buy a pair of gym shoes. While he was at school, his mother sold them for crack.

"That's why I'm here," she says. "Kids like that need somebody to care."

It's going to be a typical summer for Wright. She will help some kids, lose a few along the way. She will hear gunshots and rush to hold a dying man's head in her lap. She will watch her program dwindle, and at times she will feel alone.

The damn junkies have stolen the basketball hoops from the outdoor court, and the weeds on the playground are waist tall on the workers, ages fourteen to twenty-five, who arrive at work the day before Wright's summer program begins. Condon Middle School closed last September, so they have no gym, no place to go if it rains.

"We're going to make a tent," Wright tells the workers. "The weeds have not been cut like the school district said. We're going to have to make do. If anybody wants to just sit here and complain, you can leave. And don't come back."

No one leaves.

The tent actually is a blue nylon tarp to be strung up next to the picnic shelter at the playground. It is where children will come to eat their lunches, provided by the city, and where mothers will try to steal food. It is where children will be tutored in reading and math, and where they will discuss drugs. They will dance and laugh. At times, they will sit together quietly and stare off into their own thoughts.

"This program's designed to benefit the kids in this area, and that's what it's going to do," Wright tells her workers. "If you don't like what's happening here, you can leave. Everyone here was chosen because we know you care. Everyone here has done something for this neighborhood from the heart."

There will be no arguing, she says. There will be no tardiness. There will be no profanity or dirty stares. "THERE WILL BE NO UNDERARM ODORS." She doesn't have to tell them there will be no drugs.

"As far as having a headache on me, that's out," she barks. "As far as having a headache on these little kids coming here to enjoy a day, I'm not going to have them getting a cold shoulder. They're getting it at home. Most of these kids here, their mamas are on crack. When they come here, y'all are their mamas and daddies. Serve as role models. We're a family here."

And Wright is the neighborhood mother to all the children — the good and the bad — which means she is to be respected always and tolerated even when her loud, piercing criticism seems misdirected or unwarranted.

"Romel, you're the youngest one here. You got a lot of growing up to do in a hurry. You do not argue and fight with anybody. You have to check that temper. All y'all better check that temper."

There is anger in this neighborhood, Wright says. Some of it is born of frustration and grief. Some of it is fueled by drugs. Some of it is hers.

"It seems that the city, the school district, everyone, is just letting this neighborhood go down, even the people who grew up here and moved out," she says. "That way the rich white folks can come in and buy up the land real cheap and redevelop. It's like they're just waiting for this neighborhood to die, for all of us to move out."

But she says *she* will stay. The program will survive, even if all she has is one ball and one kid who needs her.

The neighborhood is not all bad. There still are good people here who are battling to keep their children in school, away from drugs and free from danger. They are fighting back.

And it's a neighborhood with heroes. Stevie Wonder grew up here and still comes to visit. As a child, Wonder would arrive at a house on 25th Street early in the morning and wait on the front porch for his friend John Glover to awaken so they could play music all day.

There's another local legend who grew up here. His name is Byron Leatherwood, and he is awaiting parole.

The letters *BK* are stamped on the basketball court at the Condon playground. In the late 1970s, they stood for the Buchanan Killers, a neighborhood youth gang. But now they stand for the Ball Kings, Wright's basketball program.

Three of the six original members of the gang are in prison. One is dead and one is a junkie. That leaves Craig McKinley, twenty-six, who earns $6 an hour at an automotive quality-control job and mows lawns on the side.

"I was twelve, thirteen years old at the time," says McKinley, who still lives in the neighborhood. "We weren't a gang like the gangs you read about now, but we had guns. Everybody had guns.

We were one of the first gangs to get our hands on submachine guns."

The BKs were led by Brandon (Byron) Leatherwood, who some people say was the best athlete to ever come out of the neighborhood. Leatherwood was imprisoned in 1985 and is serving time for convictions ranging from larceny to escape. He is eligible for parole next year.

"Byron was the man," says McKinley. "Nobody could touch him in basketball. He could do unbelievable things."

In 1976, there was a rivalry between the BKs and another neighborhood gang, the M&Ms, Money Makers. Erica Wright was scared. "I was caught up in the middle," she says. "Some of the little guys that played on our teams had brothers in the M&Ms, and some had brothers in the BKs. And so when we played games, their brothers would come with attitudes about each other, and I didn't know what was about to happen. So I was telling Byron, 'This can't be.' He said not to worry about it, he'd take care of it."

He came back with a proposal to start a basketball program as a means of getting the two gangs together. Wright was hesitant.

"I told him I didn't know anything about running a basketball program," she says. "I was worried about getting the two gangs together in a closed atmosphere. Byron told me he would handle everything, so I got permission to use Condon's gym."

On the first day of practice, Leatherwood marched in with thirty kids — three age groups, three teams, some of them BKs, some M&Ms, some of them just kids who wanted to play basketball. He coached them all. After mixing it up on the court, the gang members decided to join forces and form a Police Athletic League team. That's when the initials *BK* came to stand for Ball Kings.

"He got us all hooked on basketball," McKinley says. "We'd go all over playing other teams. Most teams wouldn't come to this neighborhood to play us, so we always had to drive out there."

Leatherwood was good enough to play in the pros, Wright says, but he's one of those who got away: Away from Wright. Away from the high school coaches who crawled over one another trying to reel him in when he was in a youth home. Away from everyone except the police.

Craig McKinley narrowly escaped joining his teammates in jail.

While dealing crack on the east side, he got stopped by police with $6,000 in drugs in the car. They never searched, but he suddenly realized the risks involved. He decided he didn't want to be in prison while his two daughters grew up. And he remembered a lesson he learned from Wright as a kid. "We had good basketball teams, but in baseball we was nothing," he says. "But at the end of the season, we'd have a big banquet with lots of food and trophies. She made us feel like something."

His life is simpler, safer now. He brings home a paycheck every week. He doesn't need fancy clothes or jewelry; he needs peace of mind. His daughters are six and four.

"Even though I don't have the best life, I feel I'm doing great. I see a lot of guys I grew up with and a lot of guys younger than me who are making a lot of money, but I know it's only going to last a short time. I don't know nobody who retired from the dope game. I just hope I can."

Even today, as he strolls serenely across the Oberlin campus, Delfon Curlpepper vividly recalls the discomfort he felt when he came here as a freshman in 1987. On the football field, where he played cornerback, he got little playing time. And in the classroom, he was just "another stupid jock from the ghetto."

On September 10, he wrote to his grandmother in Cleveland: "I'm having trouble with these studies. They're asking just too much. I don't know if I can handle it. They give me two to three chapters to read in each class. Then, I've got football. I've busted up one of my fingers. Then work study. I'm going crazy.

"In my classes most of the things we're talking about I've never seen in my life . . . and I hate it when other students can answer the questions and I can't."

He recalls walking back to his dormitory after flunking a final exam. As he was packing to return home for Christmas, he told his best friend he wasn't coming back.

But spring was coming. And for many years now, spring had brought track, and hope.

This wasn't the first time Delfon had thought about quitting school. At Cass Technical and, later, Cody high schools, he spent more time at video arcades than in classrooms. At night, he often stayed with friends and sometimes slept on back porches rather than go home, where he felt unwanted by his mother and step-father.

Delfon's life changed when he was fifteen years old and discovered that a man he had known all his life was in fact his father. James McSpadden was not much of a role model. After graduating from Western High School in 1969, the year Delfon was born, he sold heroin. He was jailed once for carrying a gun.

That's why his mother didn't want Delfon to know him. But Delfon needed a shadow to stand in, someplace where he felt he belonged. He moved in with McSpadden and decided he wanted to go to Western High School, the same school his father had attended.

It was a different school and a new beginning, but his inner turmoil was the same. He often expressed his feelings in obscure letters written to himself. Usually he would throw them away or keep them hidden in a secret folder, but one day McSpadden found one. As Delfon lay sleeping, McSpadden quietly picked up the letter and read how his son wanted to kill himself.

In his search for a solution, McSpadden thought back to his own high school days when he was a sprinter at Western. There was something about running that had always taken his mind off everything, leaving behind only the cleansing sensations of speed and freedom.

He encouraged his son to go out for track at Western. Coach Clifton Grove had heard about Delfon's speed and urged him to come out for the team. Delfon finally agreed. It was spring.

"Running became the biggest thing in my life," he says. When he ran, it felt as though no one could hold him back from anything. And there was no better feeling than winning. But Grove made it clear to him there were conditions.

"He told me if I didn't get the grades, I wasn't going to run on his team. I told him I had a two-point grade average, and he said, 'I'm not talking about a two-point, I'm talking about the honor roll and no absences.' The next report card, I had a three-point-one-four average and one absence."

That summer, Delfon ran one of the most important races of his life. He was with his dog, Princess, one morning when his father came out into the street and issued his usual challenge, a sprint to the corner, about 150 yards away.

McSpadden took pride in his speed. Despite all the mistakes he had made in life, despite his defeats, he could still outrun his teenage son. After each victory, he would taunt Delfon. "The day you can beat me," he'd say whenever they raced, "you'll be good."

All summer, Delfon had warned his father that his day would come. As they prepared to race, he decided this would be the day. "This is it," Delfon said. "Whoever wins, we're gonna leave it at that. There ain't gonna be no more bickering about who's fastest."

They began from a standing start, sprinting shoulder to shoulder for forty yards. Then, midway through the race to the corner, Delfon passed his father, and he never stopped.

Joe Elliott sits on a picnic tabletop under the shelter at the playground. He is surrounded by kids. "Stay away from drugs" is his soft-spoken message. "It's fun because it's fast money, until you go to jail. If you don't want to suffer the consequences, then don't do it."

Joe knows about consequences. He loves to gamble, and he doesn't fold easily. He's never afraid to throw the dice. He says he sold crack for about three months "for something to do," but eventually realized the stakes were too high for him. He threw down his cards before encountering the inevitable.

Four workers at the program have dealt drugs, and now they are telling youngsters in the community why it's wrong and where it leads.

"They know firsthand what's going on in these streets," Wright tells the children. "Everybody here, I know, has a family member or a neighbor or a friend who uses crack. If you didn't, you wouldn't be in this neighborhood. I want to tell you that you don't have to get into that whole thing."

She said the same thing to Joe, but he didn't listen. Now he claims he's out of it for good because there's no future in it. "There's only two places you can end up," he tells the children, "jail or dead."

They are the same words that were spoken to him during the past year, and it's difficult to determine whether they have had time to settle and ferment or if they are merely echoing off him.

Joe never was a leader, says his aunt Jackie Elliott, last year's recipient of the *Sports Illustrated* Joe Louis Award for her work as assistant director of Wright's program. "It didn't surprise me when I found out what he was doing," she says. "It was easy for him to get dragged into things."

Joe was raised mostly by his grandparents because his mother, who lives next door, was too young and too busy trying to earn a living. His grandparents treated him like their own son, always taking him places and doing things. Then, in 1986, his grandfather died.

"Things changed after that," Joe says. "It was like I just didn't care about anything after that. I was feeling a lot of anger and hate toward everybody. In a way, I still feel that."

Joe can't explain how the trouble started except to say he began hanging out with the wrong people. He started selling drugs, getting in fights, and cutting classes until he was booted out of Western High School. Eventually, after a fight with his aunt Jackie, he was booted out of his grandmother's house, too.

Jackie had always been in Joe's corner, cheering him at athletic events, encouraging him in his studies. But her pleas were no match for the lure of drug money.

Delfon Curlpepper was more insistent. When he heard his old friend was dealing, he went to talk to him. "I told him," Delfon recalls, "I didn't want to have to come back home and buy a black suit just to see him in a pine box."

There are two paths, Delfon says, one leading the right way, the other the wrong way. There is a line separating the two, and Joe, like a lot of kids from the neighborhood, is walking a tightrope. He just needs a push in the right direction.

"I told him, 'You'll be sitting here twenty years from now on the same street corner with your same buddies, drinking from the same bottle, just like your four uncles. If you like money as much as you say you do, either you're blind or you're dumb. If you want money, the way to do it is to go to school.' "

Joe says he already knew all that. He just forgot for a while. As he explains the changes he will make in his life, his eyes wander.

Snook Thomas sits above a bucket of soapy water scrubbing a pair of $50 high-top gym shoes he bought with the $4.75 an hour he makes washing dishes at the Plymouth Inn. Now he wants to buy a car, a nice one.

Snook is a quitter. He has quit just about everything he's ever started or said he was going to start. In this neighborhood, that can be good.

He was going to play high school football, but he didn't. He was going to run track, but he didn't. He was going to go to college, but he didn't. He was going to sell crack, but he didn't.

He lives with his mother, west of the old neighborhood. He knows he should be in college now, but maybe he'll give it a try later, maybe community college, maybe vocational school. A lot of things are put off until later.

"I want to go to college, but there's so much stuff that I want that if I go to school, I know I'm not gonna have yet. I want a car, a nice car, with some nice tires on it. I don't want no old car."

He has spent the past few summers working with the program, but when he got around to signing up this year, he was too late. Another deadline missed. So he is washing dishes, keeping an eye on the clock.

"I start things, but I don't finish. I don't know why I'm like that," he says. "I really don't know. It gets me every time. I say I'm gonna do something and I don't do it."

He has settled down from his roughhouse high school days, when he transferred from Redford to Cody in the tenth grade, then finally to Western for his senior year, switching every time he buried himself under a pile of absences and mischief.

"I always get this thing where I start feeling real bad because I was skipping school, but I'm so embarrassed to go to class because you walk in like two months later and sit down and the teacher gets on you. After a while, you want to go to class but you don't want to be embarrassed. So after a while, I decided to leave and go to a new school."

Like just about everyone who grows up in the neighborhood, he has been approached to sell crack, but so far he has refrained. "I had a guy come to my house with all kinds of money. I had just started working, and I thought, 'Dang, they make my paycheck look like nothin'.' So I decided to give it a try. I had a connection and everything, but at the last second I decided it wasn't me. I don't wanna be locked up."

Snook has made a name for himself by winning the 50-yard dash the last three years. This year, he thinks he can get Delfon in the 100. He should have won last year, he says, but he lost the lead when he turned his head to see how far back Delfon was.

Even the race paralyzes him with indecision as he considers the prospects of victory and defeat. "If I beat Delfon, it would break his heart. I'm gonna try to beat him. I want to beat him real bad, but if I do beat him, that's gonna break his heart. I don't wanna lose his friendship over a race. I wanna beat him, though."

The bottom line is that when the starter gives the signal, he will quit thinking, and he will run. And this time, he won't turn his head. He wants to beat Delfon so badly, he says he will work out all summer. He wants to be at his peak on race day. "I'm going to start lifting weights every day. Delfon got a run for his money this year."

Snook's training program lasts one day.

It has been Erica Wright's most difficult summer. Without the gym and with fewer kids, it seems the program is losing its grasp. It makes her want to work harder, do more; and sometimes it all gets to be too much. "That's why I holler at the kids so much. I have to get it out of me, too. I go home and I feel bad, because they're already being hollered at at home and school. It's unfair. It's really unfair."

One steamy day in July, her frustration turns to rage. She is screaming at her workers in criticism and anger, sending some of them home early for not carrying out her impossible commands. The afternoon ends with fire hydrants being turned on so children can cool off and splash around in the street before going home. As they shriek and bob, Wright sits at a table.

"A man died in my arms last week," she says quietly. "When that happens, you want even more to do something to change things. You try harder, and disappointments are harder to take, to understand. I'm tired."

Wright was downtown turning in time sheets at the Michigan Youth Corps office at Trumbull and Holden when she heard gunshots. She went downstairs and saw a man lying on the floor, bleeding. "I went to him and kneeled and picked his head up. He was choking on his own blood. I shoved his head back and he started to breathe a little. He looked at me. That hurt . . . To feel life draining in your hands, that's horrible." Wright slapped his face and screamed, "No, no, no. Don't leave us, don't leave us." But the man, seventeen years old, did not respond. He died later at Henry Ford Hospital.

There have been too many deaths, too many funerals, in Wright's life. Sometimes, when she lies in bed, she can hear voices passing in the darkness outside her house. She recognizes them and worries that something in the night will claim them and she will never hear them again.

"This happens so often I don't know if I feel anything anymore," she says. "Then I look at the pictures and see how happy they were when they were with the program, and how constructive they were and how promising they were. That's when it gets to me, then, to see them lying in a casket."

She lowers her head to her arms resting on the table. Most times, she is strong enough, tough enough, to stand up to anybody, anything. But now she is tired and beat. She cries. "My workers that you see out here now, one of them will not be here next year. That's how it is here. But this tent, these tables, they may all look like nothing to you, but to us it means there's still life in this place. There is life."

"On your mark!

"Get set!

"Go!"

Joe Elliott knows he must get a good jump to win the race, because Delfon will be coming on strong after 50 yards. At the same time, if he pushes off too hard at the start, he will slip on the worn asphalt surface.

Joe's first strides are clean, quick; and he is on the fly like a crisp line drive up the middle. After 20 yards, he is in the lead by half a stride, and it quickly becomes a matter of holding on. There are no short cuts in the 100-yard dash.

The summer has changed Joe. Now he looks you straight in the eyes when he says he will never deal drugs again.

"The main thing I learned this summer," he says, "is to stay away from people who are going the wrong way. I'm going the right way."

When he returns to Western High School in September, he will take a class in leadership. He realizes that following people can lead him to trouble. He wants to lead, to be in front of the pack. He worried before the race that he had lost his edge, but after ending Snook's three-year reign in the 50, he feels strong, confident.

Snook is beat even before he starts. After partying until 4:30 in the morning, he awakened at 8 and remembered he had a race to run. So he drove to the neighborhood in the battered 1978 Malibu he bought from his stepfather for $350, got a haircut so he would at least look good, then reported to the track. Snook stays even with Delfon for the first 30 yards, a half stride behind Joe. At the midway point, Joe is lifting his chin, gritting his teeth, and holding on to the lead, but Delfon is gaining ground steadily, smoothly — and pulling away from Snook.

Delfon has been working out all summer at Oberlin, and of the three, he is the only one physically prepared for the race.

"This race is *very* important to me," he says. "It's a pride race."

His fists and knees are pumping high and hard, and finally he pulls ahead of Joe. Delfon has learned how to hold on. He stayed in school when he felt like quitting. He chose life when he felt like dying.

When he felt lost, he held on and eventually met his father and Jackie Elliott and Erica Wright, missing pieces in his life. And when he met them, he met himself, because they told him who he was and what he should do. Go to school, they said. Run. Hold on.

Delfon wins the race going away. He lifts his fists in triumph. Joe knows he has run the best race of his life. He's never felt faster. Snook collapses on a concrete bench after crossing the finish line.

"It's all that drinking," Wright tells him.

He knows she may be right.

"My legs were just tired today," he says. "It hurt losing the fifty, and I didn't even feel like running the hundred. But you be here next year. I'm gonna work out."

A lot can happen in this neighborhood by next year, most of it bad. More than likely, more homes will be torn down, more kids will die as tragically as they lived.

But some of them will return to the playground to play and learn, and Wright will be there waiting for them, wearing her straw hat, moving ten directions at once. She will watch them play, laughing with joy.

Surrounded by weeds.

October 7, 1990

GARY SMITH

The Fight of His Life

FROM SPORTS ILLUSTRATED

THE TWELVE-YEAR-OLD KID stands in front of his bathroom
mirror. He's checking out his face, deciding who he is. His old
man is out on the road with a wool cap tugged over his head and
combat boots on his feet, pounding four miles to his job at an
auto parts factory, snorting and growling and tearing up the dawn
with punches as he goes.

The kid holds his fists low and bites his bottom lip, the way Ali
does. He watches his reflection flit and feint, watches himself try
to make violence something light-footed and lovely. His old man
enters the factory bathroom. He glares at the mirror, begins to
grunt and throw punches.

The kid stops juking and dancing. A year ago, his father had
passed judgment in a newspaper: My oldest son, he said, is not
violent enough to be a good fighter. The kid reaches for the Band-
Aids in the medicine cabinet, sticks one above each eye. He cocks
his fist, scowls into the mirror, punches harder.

Sweat trickles down the father's chin. In a few weeks he will
have the biggest fight of his career, against Philadelphia mid-
dleweight Bennie Briscoe, for a title shot against Carlos Monzón.
"I want it," he says, "like I want food." He steps closer to the factory bathroom mirror, exploding hooks and uppercuts.

The kid stops scowling and punching at the mirror — that's
not *him*. He backs away from the glass, flinching as he rips the
Band-Aids off. The father moves closer to the mirror and lets
another punch fly.

Crack! For an instant he sees himself break into fragments, then there's a crash. The men in the factory come running through the bathroom door.

It is late June 1990. James (Buster) Douglas is six foot four, 240 pounds, and thirty years old. Heavyweight champ of the world. Bill (Dynamite) Douglas is fifty. He hasn't fought in ten years. Buster walks into the house in Columbus, Ohio, where he used to throw punches in front of the bathroom mirror. His father, now skull-shaved and still big-shouldered, looks up at him and nods. The tension is the kind that's in the air before a fight.

Word has just gotten out: Don King is going to fly Bill Douglas to New York next week, supposedly to testify against his own son as part of King's lawsuit to keep contractual control over Buster. Which of them, the father or son, is going to bring it up first? Which is going to duck, which is going to be a *man?*

Their eyes miss each other. Buster sits on a stool in the living room. A videotape is playing on the TV a few feet away. There's the son on the screen — the one they said would never have his father's heart, the kid not violent enough to be a fighter — doing what he wants with Mike Tyson, beating up the best prizefighter in the world.

Bill, in sweatpants and a T-shirt, sits on the sofa watching the fight. Buster's eyes flicker toward him. This man is why Buster sometimes reached the edge of greatness. This man is why Buster always shrank away. But look what's happening on the screen, listen:

"Douglas still landing the jab! Right hand by Douglas right on Tyson's chin!"

Everything has changed now. Everything has changed.

Buster starts thumbing through a magazine. Let the old man speak up. Let the old man squirm.

His father rises from his seat.

"Another right hand!"

His father walks into the kitchen.

"This is the most trouble Tyson has ever been in!"

His father starts talking about nothing much at all.

Maybe Buster should write the old man off, right here, right now. That's what some people thought the new champ should do, carve his father right out of his life. Those who knew Buster well had this feeling: that at age twenty-nine, in a ring in Tokyo, he had finally *begun* to become a man. And the only way to finish the job, to make certain that what happened against Tyson in February had not been an aberration, was to somehow end this long, uneasy stalemate between father and son.

But no, he couldn't do it. People just didn't understand. "You see, that boy didn't *want* to box," said his grandma Sarah Jones. "Boxing was just the only way he knew of feeling close to his daddy." None of the other psychic pangs that compel men to hit men for a living were Buster's. As a kid, he would drift out of the ring and grab a basketball if he was sparring in a gym with a hoop. At fifteen, he quit boxing altogether. Then one day in 1980, at Mercyhurst College in Erie, Pennsylvania, he bumped into the truth. He wasn't going to be a pro basketball player. He wasn't going to study all night for a test. He couldn't think of anything else to do — so he did it. He called his dad and asked him to help him become a pro fighter.

Hell, Buster wasn't a fighter; he hated it when people called him that. "I'm an *athlete*," he would insist. He was a big, sweet, passive kid, the kind who slept with his dogs and opened the door for you and told you to have a nice weekend. "The most honest, most likable, most Christian, most trustworthy heavyweight champion there has ever been," said Dan O'Malley, who used to train with Buster.

Even arguments, because they carried the faint musk of violence, undid him. As a kid, when his dad came home from a prowl on the streets and his mom screamed and his dad snarled back, Buster would disappear. As a man, when people yelled at him, he would turn up the stereo. He would walk out of the room or out of his skin; he would blank out. He signed his autograph "Love & Peace, James Buster Douglas," then drew a happy face.

But that reflection in the glass — it flitted and feinted and flicked that jab so nice. He was big and quick, and if his dad was with him in the mirror, beside him in the foxhole, Buster could bust you in the face and then bust you again. Hell, it was only every three or four months, just for a few minutes.

Carve the old man out of his life? How could he? No one else knew what it was to sit in the passenger seat when his dad was driving him to one of Buster's early fights, to hear him tell stories in the dashboard's glow, in a voice more gentle than Buster had ever heard it, about the old wars with the middleweights and light heavyweights in Philly. Telling how the crowd went nuts when he laid out Billy Lloyd in the first round in 1972 and did a rain dance backward. How he stood flat-footed, round-hearted, trading bombs with Matthew Franklin in 1977.

Those were the real wars, in smoky arenas against chiseled fighters for a few thousand dollars — not these made-for-TV bouts in front of salon-tanned men taking a breather from blackjack. Buster wrapped his father's fights in romance, rolled them in daydream. The ones he hadn't seen, the ones he knew only from radio broadcasts or photos, were the best of all. Even when Buster found himself in some casino's ring, his belly jiggling because he hadn't really trained, all of that honesty could be his — he could borrow it — *if* his old man was in his corner. Buster could walk into a strange city, a strange arena, enter the locker room, and feel at ease — Bill was there in the mirror, still throwing punches, right behind him.

Yet for years Buster's uncle and current trainer, J. D. Mc-Cauley, and his manager, John Johnson, told the kid that to be a boxer, he needed to get rid of his daddy. Figure out that riddle, Buster: To get your daddy's love, you need to be a fighter. To be a fighter, you need to get rid of your daddy. Go on, Buster, ride around all night in your 1970 Cadillac and unscramble that one. So Buster got rid of the old man three times. And brought him back three times. Tried having him as manager and trainer the first three years of his career, 1981 to 1983, and then tried twice more having him as cotrainer with Uncle J.D. But each time they parted, Buster never really had it out with Bill, never quite confronted him. And each time he saw his dad, Buster hated himself for pretending everything was swell.

The Jesse Ferguson fight, Atlantic City, 1985, was the second time Buster stepped into the ring without his father. A few seconds into each round, he began waiting like a schoolboy to hear the bell. "What's wrong with you?" cried Uncle J.D. after Buster had lost the decision. "You shoulda killed that guy."

"I don't know."

"Would you have fought harder if your dad were here?"

"Probably."

"You want him back?"

"Maybe."

"Why?"

Why? He could hardly find words for why. It wasn't *thought* — it was *feeling*. Only his dad knew what it was to find yourself standing in a locker room three minutes before a fight with your bladder full and your crotch in a cup and your hands tied up inside a pair of eight-ounce gloves. Only his dad could reach down without hesitating and take care of it, the way he had done for Buster before another bout in 1985. Only his dad could tell him what to do when he was tired and hurt and some two-fisted fiend was throwing four-punch combinations at his head. Only his dad had *lived* these things.

"*Hit* him, honey!" Bill would shout to his son during fights. There was a sweetness in that. "Take him *out,* little baby!"

But no, this is the last straw — sidling up to King, consorting with the enemy — something *has* to be done. Buster closes the magazine. He looks at his image on the TV screen.

"He's asking questions of Tyson that Tyson hasn't been asked!"

He opens the magazine again.

"See how easily Douglas is dominating the action!"

He starts reading once more about nothing much at all.

It's hard to believe. This hard-muscled sonofabitch who used to take Buster down to the rag-stuffed navy duffel bag hanging from the cellar rafters and show him how to make it moan, this nail-hungry old hammer who used to shriek and leap onto moving trains when he was running the railroad tracks before a fight — someday he'll die. That's why Buster can't just carve his dad out of his life. He needs to do the opposite, his friend Rodney Rogers urges him. He needs to throw his arms around his father and tell him, "I love you," before it's too late, before the old man dies and maroons Buster with all that . . .

Guilt? What guilt? Let the old man say it first. Buster didn't need this man. Buster *resented* him. Resented everyone's assumption that he had been belched from the same volcano as his old man, resented everyone's disappointment when he fought and they all saw it wasn't so.

Five or six times a year he would watch his father pack up the big red Samsonite suitcase and black gym bag, put on the wide-brimmed derby and the dark shades, and walk out the door alone. Bill would return a few days later with a swollen, purpled head that made it hard to know whether he had won or lost, and Buster's mother, Lula Pearl, would *mmm-mmm* that same *mmm-mmm,* and the house would fill with a silence. Buster would get the winter-green to rub on his father's body, and his younger brother Robert would run the bathwater and get the ice. For a few hours their dad would soak in the tub, and then, for a day or two, he would just lie in bed, staring at the ceiling. Buster would catch a glimpse of him when he walked by the open bedroom door and vow never to become like that — then flush with shame for his thoughts.

Hug this man? The one pacing right now, nervously picking up and putting down the keys, the plastic cup, and sunglasses on the bar in the kitchen? Hell, what for? Buster didn't need him. Tension made Buster shrivel up; this man *breathed* tension. Biggest fight of Buster's life to that point, the 1987 IBF title bout with Tony Tucker, and how had Buster spent the weeks before it? Looking over his shoulder to see if his father and uncle and manager were at one another's throats again. Walking out of the room and out of his skin, blanking out. Dinnertime, the fight four hours away, and what was his dad doing? Screaming at a sparring partner over a few bucks.

Say "I love you" to this man? Who just five years ago, when the clock struck twelve at a New Year's party and the fellas went around kissing the ladies, decked a twenty-eight-year-old for kissing Lula Pearl? God, Buster *loathed* being Bill Douglas's son, and yet, any minute now on that TV screen, Tyson was going to catch Buster with an uppercut, and Buster was going to drop . . . and would he have gotten up if he were the son of another man?

Ever since he was nine or ten, the first thing he would think when he was scared or hurt was, No, this can't be, *I'm Bill Douglas's son.* He would see a rope that dangled from a tree above a ravine and hear a voice inside him say the strangest thing: The championship of the world is on the line — will you swing across?

It made no sense; his childhood had been too soft around the edges to live life on a dare. He was born while his mother was still in high school, spent his first six years as Grandma Sarah's little pet. Cribs, high chairs, they weren't good enough, not for her Buster. The child slept in Sarah's bed, ate on Sarah's knee, and at the age of seven months he could be found sitting like a little lord each morning at the White Castle, gumming coffee-soaked biscuit from Sarah's hand.

"The first grandchild," remembers Uncle J.D., Sarah's son. "Never scolded, never punished. Every obstacle in that boy's path, my family took out of his way." Then Buster turned six, and Sarah's heart broke: Bill and Lula Pearl showed her their marriage certificate and set up house with little James.

It became so confusing, the road to manhood, so cobbled with contradictions. Even in his twenties, Buster would run to his mom with every problem, every bruise. Lulu Pearl was Sarah's daughter. She would hug him and stroke him and fix his dinner. She would go to his apartment to scrub his kitchen. His dad . . .

No, even when Dynamite lay there after a fight staring at the ceiling, his organs mush, his cheeks and eyebrows pulp — even then there was nothing soft about him. In the bathtub one day in 1977, just home from another war in Philly, Dynamite learned that a kid had beaten up Robert with his fists and then had grabbed a baseball bat and scared off seventeen-year-old Buster.

Bill Douglas peered through his puffy eyes at Buster. "Why didn't you do something to that boy?" he said.

"Dad," said Buster, "he had a *bat*."

The bathwater moved. Bill's swollen head shook no. "That's no excuse," he said. "If he got a bat, boy, get you a brick."

Hug him? You almost had to hit a man like that to win his respect, to step out of his shadow. In Buster's early years as a pro, because it was hard to find anyone big enough to spar with him, his dad often climbed into the ring. They sparred hundreds of rounds, Bill would tell people. "And Buster hasn't hit me yet," he would say. "Buster never could hit his daddy."

But sometimes . . .

Sometimes it came back to Buster, that day when he was sixteen years old and he dusted off the stereo that was hardly ever used, took it from the cellar, and set it up in his bedroom, only to hear his old man shout from below, "Bring it back!"

"In a minute," muttered Buster.

A minute passed, and suddenly his old man was all over him,

moving like a boxer, smacking him with open-handed hooks and uppercuts, backing him to the wall with a pressure Buster had never felt from another man. But what he remembered most from that day wasn't the sting or the fear or the shame.

"I saw daylight," he would say, his eyes far off.

"Douglas comes back with a left and a right!"

"There was an opening," he would say.

"Three solid shots right on Tyson's face!"

"I can still see it. I *could've* hit him."

The son's confusion stayed inside him. The son's confusion rippled everywhere. Into his career. Into his family life. Into the fat on the back of his neck. On the mornings in Franklin Park when Buster thought he really wanted to be heavyweight champ of the world — when his legs began to pump and his arms ripped the air and the sweat in his eyes made all the birds and trees he liked to gaze at go away — he would feel something come over him. His legs would stop. He didn't want to be his old man.

"Run, Buster!" Uncle J.D. would scream.

"I've got a headache."

"Run, Buster!"

"I've got a cold."

"Run, Buster!"

"I've got an appointment to get my car fixed."

"Run, Buster!"

"I think I broke my leg."

Over six years there wasn't an excuse that J.D. didn't hear. Finally J.D. would shove him and scream, "You're going to run, goddammit, Buster!" Sometimes Buster would run a few hundred yards and slow down again. If the fat stayed on the back of his neck, if he didn't run and spar like a lunatic, the way his father had before fights, and Buster *still* won — wouldn't that make him something more than his father?

He would hoard his energy all through a fight because he wasn't in shape, lose in the late rounds or, more often, win in a way that made promoters wince. "If you had your father's heart with your ability," Uncle J.D. would snap, "you'd be champion in five minutes."

One day J.D. walked up behind Buster in the gym and squeezed the fat on his neck. "Leave him alone!" snarled Bill. "Do you want to fight me?"

Yes, here was an odd thing, another facet to the riddle: If Buster got rid of the fat, became hard and hungry and heavyweight champion — wouldn't that make Bill something less than his son?

"Funny thing," J.D. would say, "but when it came to training, Bill Douglas was soft on his son. Buster would spar two rounds and start whining, and his dad would call the sparring off."

A week before the Tucker bout, as Buster skipped rope in front of the cameras, his dad grabbed another rope, jumped in beside his son, and started skipping too. On fight night his dad appeared in the corner wearing a T-shirt emblazoned with a boxer's name. The boxer was himself.

"I made that boy, I started him, I taught him everything he knows," Bill would snap at J.D. and Johnson when they yelled advice to Buster during bouts. "Don't open your traps again, or it's going to be bad."

It got bad. Bill slapped J.D. in the face. J.D. went after him with a chair. J.D. went after him with a golf club. J.D. went after him at a family picnic, waving a gun. The family ripped. In the middle of it all, wringing her hands, her health deteriorating, was Lula Pearl, who loved her brother J.D. and loved her husband, Bill. Buster couldn't bear it anymore. Buster broke. In the ninth round of the title fight with Tucker, ahead in points, he did it. He lashed out at his father the only way he could. He went to the ropes.

"Solid right cross by Tyson!"
He bowed his head.
"Douglas wobbled again!"
He quit fighting.

But what are they doing, the father and son, sitting and staring at this videotape as if they haven't watched it a dozen times before, as if they don't know what's going to happen, as if there isn't so much to be said? "Whippin' on that suckah," Bill mumbles. "Whippin' on him."

There was no more Bill in Buster's corner after the Tucker defeat, ever again. There was only Bill in Buster's head. Buster would lie alone in his hotel room before a bout, daydreaming footage from his father's wars, conjuring snapshots. Hoping that the *idea* of his dad would be enough, that he wouldn't need the flesh. He would see Bill charging back into the locker room in 1970 after the Don Fullmer fight, his shiny body snorting and winging punches as if it didn't know the match was over, boxing one more round, two more rounds, three. He would see his dad's trainer, Ed Williams, telling little Buster to stand back, to let this man work out whatever it was that had hold of him. Suddenly, Buster would find himself up off his hotel bed, winging and snorting, feeling the strength rush over him.

So sharply would he envision his father's fights that they were almost like films. Dad throwing that right at Carlos Marks's bloodied mouth in 1972, perfect form, right shoulder just where it should be. Dad throwing that missile at Tom (the Bomb) Bethea at Madison Square Garden in 1976, send the Bomb's mouthpiece flying into the third row. Dad on the scales in his underwear before the Matthew Franklin fight in 1977 in Philly, his shoulders rolling up and down as if filled with some electrical current. Dad waking him up in the hotel room the morning of that bout, smiling at him and asking, "How do you feel, Buster?"

Howdoyoufeel,howdoyoufeel,howdoyoufeel?

Sometimes the film in his mind would snag on some shard of memory. "Yeah, he asked me that morning," recalls Buster. "He lost that day, a brutal fight — they stopped it when they shouldn't have. But I didn't ask him, 'How do you feel?' when it was over. I should've asked him."

It all backed up on Buster in the summer of 1989. All the remorse, the resentment, the ripples. His two-year-old marriage began falling apart — death by silence. He had let little conflicts with his wife, Bertha, build and build; he had never seen his dad open up and talk to Lula Pearl. His mom — the person he telephoned first thing every morning when he woke up — began having seizures and talking about dying. Buster's bank account was drying up; nobody wanted to promise an erratic fighter a big payday. The previous Christmas he had had to borrow to buy gifts, and now he didn't know if he could make the next mortgage payment. His aunts were telling him to forget this boxing nonsense, to get a job. The mother of Lamar, the little boy Buster had fathered in high school, had suffered kidney failure and now needed Buster to take more responsibility for his son. The films in his head didn't help; the projector had suddenly stopped working. All Buster had to do was take care of Oliver McCall on July 21 in Atlantic City, he was told, and he would likely get his dream, a title shot at Tyson. But he just didn't give a damn. He was a couple of dozen pounds overweight and wanted to quit boxing, and it scared him to death knowing that he would have to drag that kind of body and heart into a ring against a heavy-weight.

He was lying in his darkened hotel room the morning of the fight when it came out of nowhere. Rogers and two other friends who had recently turned to God walked into his room. "He loves you, Buster," Rogers said softly. "He has great things in store for you. If you say that you'll accept God into your heart, He'll take all the burdens off your shoulders."

Tears started streaming down Buster's cheeks. A father who would understand. A father who would take away his troubles. "I accept Him," said Buster.

"Mike Tyson's hurt!"

A strange sweet feeling ran through him.

"His eye is closing!"

"Like cool air," Buster would say, "being blown into my chest through a straw."

No. It wouldn't be that easy. Buster beat McCall and came home. Bertha packed up and left. Buster was arrested for drunken driving. The mother of his son was near death. He was told he would fight Tyson on February 10. He stared at the posters of two of his dad's wars in Philly that he had recently framed and hung in his garage. He whispered for God in the night.

His own family thought he was crazy to take on Tyson — he couldn't believe it, his own *mom*. He shouted at her. She started crying. "You're mean," she said.

"Damn right I am," said Buster. "I'm mean. *I'm mean*."

A few weeks later, eight days before he would fly to Tokyo for the bout, he got a call at 4 A.M. He rushed to his mom's house. She had been found dead on the floor, at age forty-seven, of a stroke.

He gazed down at her face in the casket. In his grief, it came to him: Here was the perfect excuse. If he backed out of the Tyson fight or lost it, no one, not even his father, could shake his head. For the first time in his life, he was free of expectation, almost off the hook of being Bill Douglas's son.

He closed his eyes and said goodbye to her. There was no one in the world now for Mama's boy to lean on, no one. But that only made him stronger. He could feel it in his arms and legs. He wasn't going to use the perfect excuse.

Three days before the bout, he came down with a heavy cold. The next morning, he ran six miles. "Let's do it again," he said to J.D. when he finished. The morning of the fight, he spent another zillion yen and called Bill for the fourth time that week. Buster had to hear it in his old man's voice once more, he still *had* to.

"Hit him," Bill told him. "Fight that sissy. Attack him. Be first. Throw cross punches. Get your guns off. He's a psycho. Wish I could fight him. Just hit him."

Buster walked into the ring double-dosed on penicillin. It made no difference. He was relaxed. He was fighting a man who never stopped coming, a man who needed it like he needed food. "That same mentality as my dad," Buster would say. "And you know what?"

"What an uppercut by Douglas!"

"I stood up to it."

"Down goes Tyson!"

"I defeated it."

"It's over! Mike Tyson has been knocked out! Unbelievable!"

"In my *own* way."

Life happens to fathers and sons; that's often how they come together. The father's body begins to sag or a grandchild is born or someone dies whom they both love. But this father has turned fifty and his body's still taut, and this son has long ago made a grandchild, and this father has seen his wife dead on the floor. And none of that has been enough to bring them together, none of it.

Maybe *this* would do it. Look, right there on the screen moments after the bout; listen, the son is saying it: "Dad, this one is for you! I love you!" In front of millions of people, replayable millions of times at the push of a button — doesn't that count?

And on the day after the fight, there was his father on NBC

telling millions more, "James is one of the most outstanding . . ." And he hesitated, his breath coming hard, his eyes filling with tears, and he waved his hand at the camera and shook his head no, no, no and said, "I can't say any more . . . I don't know . . ." Isn't that enough, doesn't that count?

The videotape of Buster's fight against Tyson ends. There's fuzz on the screen. The son puts the magazine down on the table and slowly rises. For the first time, he speaks.

"See you later," he says.

"See you later," says his dad.

Before his father can be called to appear in a New York courtroom as a witness for King, an out-of-court settlement is reached. King is barred from promoting Buster's fight with Evander Holyfield, though he gets nearly $4 million and the right of first refusal on future Douglas fights. That night Bill is seen whooping it up at King's celebration party in Harlem. Buster reads about it the next day and bites his bottom lip.

But Buster says he is free now, at last. Free because he finally knows the hardness and hunger are inside of *him,* not just his father. Free because he finally understands the price he has to pay to dredge them up. He and Bertha are back together, and in January they expect a child. He seems happier and more focused, although one day a few months ago, in the middle of a five-mile jog, the shadow came over him again. "I'm in the snakepit of all snakepits," he mumbled, and stopped running.

Upon winning the title, Buster said he would stay in the snakepit for just two more fights — next week's bout in Las Vegas against Holyfield, for which he will earn a record-breaking $24 million, and a Tyson rematch. But now he's hedging. He says he'll fight George Foreman. His eyes widen a little. And yes, he'll fight Tyson as many times, in as many places, as he has to.

"I know that kind of man," the son says as he rises from the couch in his living room. "You have to kill him to keep him down." He starts throwing punches.

"I'll fight that man forever," he says.

October 22, 1990

FRANZ LIDZ

Wild and Crazy Hombres

FROM SPORTS ILLUSTRATED

YOU BEGIN to suspect something's not quite right when Pascual Perez tells you he's the oldest of "five twin brothers." Never mind that there are really six Perez boys — seven if you count Mario, the Bronx cabbie whom Pascual calls his brother but who "really isn't, because he's my cousin." The Perez clan thrives on contradiction.

As it turns out, there isn't a twin — or even a Twin — in the bunch. But the family is loaded with ballplayers who are already major leaguers — Pascual, thirty-two (New York Yankees), and Melido, twenty-three (Chicago White Sox) — or who are working their way up to the bigs. Like Vladimir — *Vladimir?* — twenty-one (New York Mets organization), Ruben Dario, twenty (Kansas City Royals), and Carlos, eighteen (Montreal Expos). Pascual, who once missed a major league start after getting lost driving to his home ballpark, turned free agent at the end of the season and signed a three-year, $5.7 million deal with the Yanks in November. Melido, whose pet cows back home in the Dominican Republic are named Perez, Perez, Perez, and Perez, was one of the top contenders for 1988 American League Rookie of the Year. The rest of the brothers are minor league hotshots, except for Valerio, twenty-seven, who was in the Royals organization from 1982 through 1984 and now plays for a Taiwanese team called Brother Hotel. Every Perez, save the cows, is a pitcher.

As siblings the Perezes are closer to the Marx brothers than, say, the brothers Karamazov. A case can be made for Pascual as Groucho, Melido as Harpo, and Valerio as Chico. Their specialty may be the forkball, but their predilection is decidedly goof-ball. "The secret is cocoanuts," says Juan Pablo (Chi Cho) Gross, their father. (His children have adopted the last name of their mother, Agripina Perez, as is occasionally the custom in their country.) "I tell them, 'Strike out somebody with cocoanut, and baseball no problem.' Baseball small; cocoanut big. My sons big cocoanuts."

Chi Cho's piglet is supposed to be blessed today by Padre Perez (not a son and not a pitcher for San Diego)."To honor her," says Chi Cho, the family's premier shakedown artist, "you must bring much beer and money."

Chi Cho stands in the living room of his tin-roofed, cinder-block house on the outskirts of Santo Domingo. It's a small place off a dirt road, surrounded by fields of sugarcane. The walls are decorated with religious artifacts: votive candles, crucifixes, and baseball cards.

"Me and my family always live here," says Valerio. "Always, always, forever."

Forever?

"Sure. Eight, maybe nine years."

Melido, Vladimir, Carlos, and Ruben Dario are out back by the pigsty with their uncle Mario and sisters Candida Vicenta and Ivelise, who last year hurled her softball team to a local title. They have gathered together to have their photo taken for this magazine.

Only Pascual is missing. "I won't come to have my picture taken without glue," he had announced.

Duco? Elmer's?

"No, man, glue! Money! *Dinero!* With no glue, I stay in my hotel room."

"Pascual loves room service," says Vladimir.

Uncle Mario, Chi Cho's brother, bird-dogs for several major league teams. He claims the boys got their baseball talent from the Gross side of the family. "The Perezes couldn't hit an orange," he insists. Come to think of it, they still can't. They're pitchers, after all. Pascual hit .037 in 1988 with his previous team, the Expos, but batted a torrid .204 last season and raised his career average to .120.

"Ha, ha, ha!" cackles Chi Cho, who just turned sixty-three. "I bat better than my sons." A trim five foot ten, he has lizardlike features and heavy eyelids that make him look as if he is never far from a nap. Last year he pitched on Sundays for an old-timers' team and had a 3–2 record. "He should win more," says Valerio, "but he only pitch three games."

Five decisions in three games?

"One was a tie."

Oh.

Chi Cho was 9–8 in 1988. "My best start I win one-nothing," he recalls. "I have single, double, two RBI."

Two RBIs in a 1–0 game?

"He good, no?" says Valerio.

Pascual prowls the mound like a restless hyena. Every pitch is accompanied by a flurry of gestures, grimaces, and moans. "He looks like he's pitching at the end of a rubber band," says Joe Torre, who managed Pascual from 1982 to 1984 with the Atlanta Braves.

Pascual wears enough gold to buy Trinidad *and* Tobago, and flashes the sly half smile of a kid in a pet store who has just set all the puppies free. But he can also be mercurial — bored one moment, expansive the next. "Anybody know nothing about Pascual," says his old friend Felix Becena. "He's inpredictable."

After nearly being decapitated by a line drive last August at Wrigley Field, Mr. Inpredictability threw a pitch into the Cubs dugout. "I don't do nothing in particular on purpose," he said afterward. Yet two weeks later, while batting against the Dodgers, he purposely ignored three straight bunt signs and struck out swinging. "I was rockin' and rollin'," he explained.

Pascual was tagged Perimeter Perez in 1982 after he got lost just before a game while driving a borrowed car on the interstate that rings Atlanta. "There's a big radio and the merengue music was real loud," he says. "I forgot my wallet, so I have no money and no license. I pass around the city two times easy, but the car so hot I stop at a gas station. I ask for ten dollars' worth, and the guy say, 'You Pascual Perez? People been waiting for you at the stadium.' I'm twenty minutes away, he tell me. I feel like a heart attack. I think I get fired, maybe. Boss Torre say he fine me one hundred dollars. I say, 'What you say, one hundred?' He smile, say, *'Ciento pesos.'* I smile. Ciento pesos worth only ten bucks."

Pascual won four key games down the stretch that year, and the Braves were champions of their division. He was 15–8 in 1983. The Atlanta fans loved his head fakes and through-the-legs pick-off moves, but opposing batters were not amused. Recalls Yankee pitcher Dave LaPoint, "Guys wanted to bounce balls off Pascual's knees, if not his skull."

He missed the first month of the 1984 campaign after Dominican authorities caught him with cocaine in his possession and jailed him for three months. He returned to the rotation in May and pitched brilliantly until mid-August, when he got into a beanball duel with the Padres' pitchers. After they nearly hit him a few times, he stopped throwing inside and started losing.

His ill fortune continued in 1985, and after a series with the Mets in July, he disappeared for five days in New York in order to consult a Dominican spiritualist. "I see bad spirits all around you," said the good doctor. He was right. Pascual finished the season 1–13 with a 6.14 ERA. The following spring he was cut at the end of camp.

The Expos, who signed Pascual to a minor league contract in February 1987, sent him to their Triple A team in Indianapolis, and he tore up the American Association, going 6–0 with a 1.40 ERA in June. He was called up in August and went 7–0 in September to help keep the Expos in the pennant race. The next season he was 12–8 with a 2.44 ERA, and the Expos rewarded him with a one-year, $850,000 contract for 1989. This time he consulted a psychologist instead of a witch doctor and attended weekly sessions of Alcoholics Anonymous. His flamboyance remained undiminished, however. He added a slow-motion pitch he called the Pascual Ball. Many a Latin-American junta could topple in the time it took the ball to reach the plate.

Unfortunately, Pascual had a relapse before spring training last year and spent two months in drug rehab. (As far as major league baseball is concerned, this was his first offense. If he fails to comply with its aftercare program, he will be suspended for a minimum of a year.) Pascual wound up with a 9–13 record in 1989, a stat the pitching-hungry Yankees figured was worth big money. "Reason I jump to New York simple," he says. "They pay."

Though Pascual can be as sensitive as a Romantic poet at times, he says he won't be cowed by his new boss, George Steinbrenner. "Boss Boss is a lot like me," he says. "He like to win." Nor does Pascual think he'll succumb to the temptations of the Big Apple. "For me, New York like downtown Montreal. I don't need no bodyguard. If something happen, my friends keep me straight. Me and Luis Polonia real tight." Yankee fans may remember Polonia as the left fielder who was convicted on a morals charge in Milwaukee last summer and sentenced to sixty days in jail.

"My daughter in the hospital, she very sick," says Valerio by way of introduction. "I can't get her out unless you give me money."

How long has she been there?

"Five days . . . No, three weeks . . . A couple of months, I think."

How much do you need to spring her?

"Thirty dollar. But I take fifty if that all you have."

Valerio says he refined his pitching style by hurling rocks at cocoanuts. That technique got him as far as Double A before he blew out his arm throwing fastballs. The rest of his repertoire included a forkball, a "spoonball," and a "knifeball" — giving new meaning to the term "setting the table."

"Valerio looked like he should have made the big time," says his former minor league teammate, Royals pitcher Mark Gubicza. "Maybe he patterned himself after Pascual instead of just being himself." Whatever that is.

"The Perezes relax all over the place," says Expo scout Jesus Alou. "I've never seen them feel pressured. They don't understand that stuff."

"There are many, many funny stories about Ruben Dario," says Melido. He chuckles.

"Funny stories about Ruben Dario and chickens," says Vladimir, doubling over in laughter.

"Funny stories about Ruben Dario and goats," says Carlos, tripling over.

Like what?

All three shrug. "So many funny stories," says Valerio, "we can't even remember them."

"What country are you from?" asks the customs official in Toronto.

"The Chicago White Sox," answers Melido.

"No, where is your home?"

"The Chicago White Sox."

"And before that?"

"The Kansas City Royals."

Melido settled in Comiskey Park two years ago and went 12–10. Teammates call him Oil Can Harry because of his slick, Medusa-like locks. "He's the silent type who mostly sits and giggles," says LaPoint, his former teammate. "But put a lighter in his hand and it's open season on shoelaces." Melido is the White Sox's leading perpetrator of the hotfoot. "And he cheats at cards too!" says utilityman Steve Lyons.

Melido, who was a disappointing 11–14 last season, may have the best control, on or off the field, of any Perez. He, too, can be exuberant — often bouncing halfway to the dugout after a third out — but he's nowhere near as wild as Pascual. "Melido will be a better pitcher than Pascual," predicts LaPoint. "He doesn't have nine guys lined up ready to kill him."

"Strikeout. Come on, strike him out."

"I don't feel like it."

"Strikeout, on my mother, Agripina Perez. Strikeout, strikeout, strikeout."

"O.K., O.K., O.K."

That's Vladimir on the mound for the Licey Tigres in the Dominican League, conversing with a ball. He winds up and throws, and the ball takes a little hop as it crosses the plate. "You're out!" yells the ump.

"Vladimir talks to his rosin bag, his glove, and sometimes even his manager," says Julio Bibison, Carlos's manager in the Dominican. "It's like going to the circus. It's like seeing Mark Fidrych." Except that Vladimir not only talks to the ball, the ball talks back.

Vladimir had been an unreliable reliever (0–2 with a 4.50 ERA) two years back with the Little Falls (N.Y.) Mets. But when a spot opened up for him in the rotation, he won his first four starts en route to a 6–5 record. In 1989 he missed most of the season after getting a hernia while pitching.

A hernia? Throwing a baseball?

"Yeah," says Valerio. "He must have had a ton of stuff on the ball."

Through it all, Little Falls pitching coach Al Jackson, who is now with the Orioles, called him Señor. "I didn't know his name," says Jackson. "And then when I found out, I couldn't pronounce it."

"Half the guys in my country named Vladimir," says Vladimir. "What you think a Dominican name is, George Bell?"

"Pascual is crazy," says Bibison, "but Carlos is *crazy*."

Carlos is known to the family as El Astuto (the Smart One), but he prefers his English nickname, Good Times. "He will be the best of us all," says Pascual.

Montreal signed Carlos in 1987, when he was sixteen, after Pascual tipped off Alou that the Royals were about to bag Carlos and Ruben Dario, who was then eighteen. Alou went to the Perez home and pleaded with Agripina. After much deliberation, she finally said, "Kansas City can't have both of them, so let Jesus have the baby."

One afternoon last winter, Agripina's baby put on a show while pitching for the Royals' Dominican affiliate. He fussed and fidgeted and faked a throw to third — though there was no runner there — on a grounder back to the box. At another juncture the plate ump tossed Carlos a ball, and he bounced it back to the catcher. Then, mimicking one of Pascual's moves, he "shot" a strikeout victim with an imaginary gun and blew away the smoke. "It's crazy," said Bibison. "Not wild crazy — Carlos don't hit nobody — but crazy. It's Pascual. It's Perez."

Carlos is the only Perez who's a lefty. He asked Bibison why a southpaw's curveballs break in on right-handed batters. "The earth moves to the right," said Bibison, suddenly grasping what it means to be a Perez. "When a lefty throws, it's against the rotation of the world." He paused. "All you Perezes think with your left hand."

January 8, 1990

KEVIN SHERRINGTON

Ten Days of Torture
in Junction

FROM THE DALLAS MORNING NEWS

JUNCTION, Texas — The color scheme and name are different.
But little else has changed since 1954 at what is now the Texas
Tech University Center. Shades of brown swathed the landscape
thirty-six years ago. Inside the gate last week, a hazy, lime-col-
ored shock of mesquite kept a standing-room-only watch on two
sides of a green, open field. Behind the mesquite, emerald ce-
dars dappled gray-green hills.

Bill Durbon slowly drove through campus, past a sentinel of
pecans and the old barracks, to a gate out back. He removed the
gate's lock. Then he turned the car down a shell path to the center's treasure. Of the four hundred acres, this was the most lush.
A grove of pecan trees made a cool, dark canopy. Foot-high grass
swayed drunkenly in the breeze. To the west of the pecans, the
South Llano slithered over a bed of stones, a gurgling passage
that would take nearly two more miles before joining the North
Llano to give this Hill Country town its name.

No outsiders may venture past the back gate without Durbon,
a jealous guard in his role as coordinator of operations. Only Tech
functions are allowed on the grounds. But, in the spring of 1979,
the center's directors made an exception for two dozen former
Texas A&M football players, staff, and an old coach.

The verdant, serene grove made a nice setting for the twenty-
fifth anniversary of football's most hellish camp.

The story of those ten August days at the former Texas A&M

Adjunct, where at least two thirds of Bear Bryant's first Aggie football team quit, is one of the most famous in college football. The survivors, who include Gene Stallings and Jack Pardee, tell tales of two-a-day workouts in temperatures rarely dipping below 100 degrees; of practicing on fields of rock, sand, and burrs; of playing a nightly game in which, at the slam of a barracks door, they would attempt to identify teammates escaping in the darkness.

"Looking back on Junction," Bryant once said, "there were times when, if you hadn't been so well raised, you would have wished you were dead."

The stories have been recounted so often that any who heard them, without having visited this town halfway between San Antonio and San Angelo, might think it a lunar outpost. Proud natives would seem to have every right to resent the stories, or at least their implications.

"Junction got a bad rap," Pardee concluded.

But locals don't seem to mind. They are slow to combat the image created for them by Aggie history. Lack of pride is not the reason. They have no inferiority complex at all about their scenic little town, which they would prefer to remain as it is.

And they are quick to admit that it *was* miserable in the summer of 1954. Even if it's not now.

"We're certainly not burning desert sand," said city secretary Frederica Wyatt, eyes half closed.

The problem thirty-six years ago was a five-year drought that fried central and west Texas. The area's average annual rainfall over that time period fell to nine inches, a little more than a third the normal average. Any grass that gained a footing in the dusty, rocky soil of the adjunct, a mile and a half southwest of town, ultimately burned up and blew away.

"When we drove in that front gate," Bryant later told reporters, "I wanted to puke."

Several Junction accounts contend Bryant knew nothing of the conditions before the team arrived. But Jones Ramsey, then A&M's sports information director, said Bryant scouted the site along with Willie Zapalac, an assistant and a former A&M student, who knew Bryant was looking for a place far from interfering alumni.

Bryant, who had arrived from Kentucky the previous winter, had another reason for wanting to get away. He was displeased by the play of the Aggies in spring training of 1954. He needed something radical. At Junction, he wrote in his autobiography, he would separate the quitters from the keepers.

His intentions quickly became apparent to Junction officials, said R. P. (Buckshot) James, a local banker. Soon after the team's arrival, a delegation from the chamber of commerce invited the Aggies to a barbecue.

"We didn't come out here to eat," Bryant told them. "We came out here to play football."

By the time the team left, they barely had enough players for two squads. Estimates vary on how many started the camp. Figures range from 80 to as many as 115, the latter based on the number of players at spring training's end.

But, whatever the starting point, the final number was certain. Bryant was forced to call off the camp four days early when his numbers dwindled to 29.

"We went in two buses," Stallings said, in the camp's most famous line, "and came back in one."

The players were slow to leave at first, perhaps because they still had their sense of humor. One of the early visitors was a local five-year-old named Arlen Ashley, who brought a small rubber football to be autographed.

As the last of the players signed, he asked Arlen where he would someday attend college.

"He said 'Baylor,' and then ran and jumped in the car," said Ila Ashley, seventy-six. "Then they chased after him like they were going to get him."

She smiled nervously as she recalled the scene, rocking gently in a living room chair. Then she told it again. Her only son was killed in an automobile accident in 1983. But she still has his football. The signatures of forty players and coaches are legible yet, particularly Bryant's. He signed twice.

A few of the signees included players who would not be among the twenty-nine to break camp. Of those, a few were visible in Wanda Teel's home movie.

The stark, clean film — taken by Teel's father, Elmer Parrott, then manager of the adjunct — lasts only three minutes. But its

impression is vivid. The approximately thirty-five players still remaining were dressed in white game uniforms for picture day.
They wore black high-top shoes to keep dirt out of their socks.
At one point, two players ran toward a cameraman. One swung
his foot in a kicking motion as he made a cut. A spray of brown
dirt nearly obscured them.

The film, taken on press day, coincided with the media's first
look at what Bryant had wrought. The touring group of reporters, fresh from a stop in Austin, were struck by the contrast of
the University of Texas, the preseason favorite, and the Junction
Aggies. Dave Campbell, longtime sports editor of the *Waco Tri-
bune-Herald,* called it the most memorable stop in thirty-one years
on the Southwest Conference (SWC) press tour.

The reporters likely absorbed a more graphic picture of the
story they had been hearing about than they wanted. From their
lunch tables in the cafeteria, they could see players working out
or throwing up, depending on the vantage point.

As players left, the load became worse for the survivors. Pardee, a sophomore, was a fifth-team fullback when camp started.
By camp's end, he had been worked at fullback, tailback, center,
offensive and defensive tackle, and offensive and defensive end.

Needing extra work on a day he was being tried at tackle, Pardee began practice an hour early, at 3 P.M. He left the field at 7
P.M. Players weren't given water breaks in those days, as they are
now. Over the course of those four hours, Pardee dropped from
210 pounds to 190.

"I was lucky it didn't kill me," he said.

Teammates had similar experiences. Bill Schroeder, an offensive tackle from Lockhart, Texas, broke huddle during a scrim-
mage at the rodeo fairgrounds, just south of the adjunct, and
trotted to his position. As he leaned over to go into his stance, he
fell face first into the dirt. A local physician, J. E. Wiedeman,
treated Schroeder for dehydration, packed him in ice, and gave
him water.

"I thought he was the luckiest guy in the world," Pardee said,
"because he got to have a drink."

Wiedeman, now a Dallas resident, cared for most of the stricken
players until parents arrived to take them home. Wiedeman told
Bryant at one point, "I have more players than you do."

Bryant was not amused.

Joe Schero, a punter, defensive back, and later one of the founders of Church's Fried Chicken, said Bryant had little sympathy for the players' physical problems. Schero's roommate, former Sunset High School star Joe Boring, injured a knee, tried to continue, and couldn't. He left the team but stayed in school. He played on the Aggie baseball team, eventually became an assistant at SMU, and coached high school football in Garland.

One of the coaches Boring worked under at SMU was Dave Smith, a former quarterback who also left the Junction team. The most famous exit, however, was made by Fred Broussard, an All-SWC center the previous season but an underachiever by Bryant's standards.

Late in the 1954 camp, Broussard was tried at linebacker with little success. Finally, only ten minutes before the end of practice, he threw down his helmet and walked toward the gate.

"Go through that gate," Bryant called after him, "and you'll regret it the rest of your life."

Broussard hesitated a moment, then kept walking.

One of the spectators he passed on his way out was Rob Roy Spiller, who would enroll at Texas A&M that fall. Spiller knew the Aggies were losing a good player in Broussard, who previously had made a habit of quitting and returning. His absence that fall would be the talk of the A&M campus.

"The team captains went to Bryant that evening and tried to get him reinstated," Spiller said, "but Bryant wouldn't do it."

Spiller witnessed the exit of most of the players, in one way or another. He sold bus tickets to many of them at the old Texaco station on Junction's main thoroughfare. The players, arriving in clusters at first, hitchhiked or walked the two miles to the bus station. Later, they straggled in one by one. Spiller estimated as many as fifty left by bus.

Some mornings he found them waiting for him to open up.

"They were usually exhausted and kind of down," said Spiller, now president of the Junction National Bank. "We'd talk about how hot it was and how tough the camp was. They seemed embarrassed. None of them wanted to quit."

But as the players left, the opportunity for playing time grew greater for those who remained. As a five-eleven, 190-pound sophomore guard, Dennis Goehring thought the roster attrition gave him a chance he ordinarily wouldn't have gotten. He knew what to do with it. He was All-SWC in 1955 and 1956, mostly on heart.

"A lot of the guys didn't have the ability to take the heat and the punishment," said Goehring, now a banker in College Station. "It was an endurance contest."

The emotions and opinions of the players were acted out, for the most part, in the barracks at night. They asked themselves why Bryant was being so tough. Some still wonder. All manner of conversation passed among them as they lay each night in the fifteen-by-thirty-foot rooms with concrete floors. The players, coaches, and staff slept in bunk beds, six to a barracks. They rolled up the canvas flaps at night in an attempt to allow any stray breeze through the screens.

Too tired to go into town, they entertained themselves in the barracks. "We'd play a little game where we'd watch through the screens at night," Pardee said. "You'd see one of the doors slipping open and somebody running. Somebody would whisper, 'Who's that?' and the rest would try to figure it out."

The view from inside the barracks is a panorama because of the screen walls. Ten of the campus's original twenty barracks look much the same as they did in 1954. Corrugated asbestos roofs have replaced the canvas tops. Some have been converted to air-conditioned dormitories. But on this particular day, a breeze sifting through the screens made the old barracks seem pleasant.

A few of Tech's students prefer them, Durbon said. They bunk there while enrolled in summer classes. The area where the Aggies practiced is now a driving range. Physical science and graduate art classes also are taught at the center, which the state awarded to Tech in 1971 after A&M allowed its lease to lapse.

Frederica Wyatt still calls it "the adjunct" out of habit, though. She has lived in the town since 1943 and in the county all of her life. Changes in Junction over that time have been so rare that when they do happen, they're sometimes ignored. For that reason, natives refer visitors to Wyatt, Junction's unofficial historian.

Once Junction was a criminals' hideout because of its cedar brakes, hills, and fresh water, and its native appeal still is fresh.

Kimble County has one of the highest annual deer populations in the state. Hunting and fishing are so popular that nine motels, several boasting "refrigerated air," line the 1½-mile highway through town. As a visitor drove a neighborhood street one night last week, a doe and two bucks casually crossed in front of the car.

The town's natural beauty has made many residents resistant to change for any reason. John Kothmann, manager of the chamber of commerce and a former member of the school board, says he recently found he "made enemies for life" because he pushed construction of a new football stadium. At times, any form of progress might be considered threatening. Junction still doesn't have a traffic light.

The population has remained approximately 2,500 for more than thirty years. Because of the town's decades-long dependence on cedar mills and goat and cattle ranching, the town likely won't grow, either, Wiedeman said.

A movement to attract light industries died in the 1970s. Some action has been taken to draw tourists, but even that has met with some resistance. A few town officials objected to the purchase of two billboards on Interstate 10 — 250 miles apart — that refer to Junction as "The Oasis in the Hill Country."

The Junction Aggies might have objected to the description, too. At least in 1954. But in 1979, when Bryant and twenty of his twenty-nine Aggies finally took up the chamber of commerce on that barbecue, the players were stunned. They couldn't believe how green everything was.

They gave short speeches down in the pecan grove to catch everyone up on their lives. Several have become millionaires or, at the least, successful businessmen and coaches. They reflected on the rise from a 1–9 record in 1954 to a 9–0–1 SWC championship in 1956, although an NCAA probation made them ineligible for the Cotton Bowl. They were a fraternity, they said, the last of its kind. The SWC passed a rule afterward banning any off-campus training camps.

Even Bryant said later he never would do it again. But he held that 1954 season, his only losing season, close to him. Before he died in 1983, he set up a $100,000 scholarship fund at A&M, with the stipulation that it benefit only the descendants of the Junction training camp survivors.

Those players who remained, then, eventually won their reward. Most said it was a positive influence on the rest of their lives.

All the town got out of it was a bad rap. But just try to find someone who feels insulted.

"I never have taken offense to it," Spiller said glibly. "The way I see it, to people from east Texas or the cities, maybe this would seem like a desolate place."

Asked how much longer he would remain in such desolation, he smiled and said, "From now on."

August 5, 1990

CHARLES P. PIERCE

Thieves of Time

FROM THE NATIONAL SPORTS DAILY

THE PRESS CONFERENCE was over, and two men from New Castle, Pennsylvania, named Robert Retort and Ed Grybowski had been charged with interstate transportation of stolen property, which is a federal felony. In the conference room of the FBI field office in Pittsburgh, an agent named Bob Reutter was looking over the stolen property, examining it, not with a G-man's eyes, but with those of a fan. There were baseball uniforms — thick, heavy flannel things with the names of the great, lost teams on them. The Memphis Red Sox. The Kansas City Monarchs. There were autographed baseballs and old, sepia-shrouded pictures of young men wearing the heavy flannel uniforms of the great, lost teams. Looking at them, you could see back through time, all the way to the outskirts of town. Bob Reutter spent a long time looking.

It all belonged to an eighty-six-year-old former security guard at the St. Louis City Hall named James Bell. In 1922, when he and the world were young, James Bell was pitching one hot day for the St. Louis Stars in the Negro League. It was late in the game, and there were men on base, and at the plate was a signifying hitter named Oscar Charleston. If the Negro Leagues had a Babe Ruth, it was Oscar Charleston. The nineteen-year-old pitcher stared down the alley and struck Oscar Charleston out of there, saving the game.

Lord, the other Stars thought, that young man is cool. So that's what they called him. Cool Bell. But Manager Bill Gatewood thought the nickname lacked sufficient dignity for the grave young

man with the thoughtful eyes. He's older than that, thought
Gatewood. Cool Papa, that's who he is.

Cool Papa Bell.

The man had style. Anyone could see that. In the Negro
Leagues, the wardrobes always cut like knives. A player named
Country Jake Stevens told Donn Rogosin, the author of *Invisible
Men*, that he knew he'd made the big club when the owner took
him out and bought him three new suits and two new Stetson
hats. Even in this company, Cool Papa was sharp. When he walked
through Compton Hill in St. Louis, children danced in his wake.

He played for twenty-nine years and for seven different teams.
He was the fastest man anywhere in baseball, so swift and deft on
the base paths that, when it looked like Jackie Robinson was going
to be chosen to shatter the segregation of the major leagues, Cool
Papa once ran wild just to show the young shortstop what kind
of play he could expect when and if Robinson was called up. Jimmy
Crutchfield once told a a baseball historian named Robert Peter-
son that when Cool Papa hit one back to the pitcher, everybody
else in the field yelled, "Hurry!" Satchel Paige claimed that Cool
Papa could hit the light switch in the hotel room and be in bed
before the room got dark. That was the story they always told
about Cool Papa Bell. They even told it when he was inducted
into the Baseball Hall of Fame in 1974.

He is old now, and half blind. For years, he held court in his
house on what is now Cool Papa Bell Avenue in St. Louis. He
would tell stories, and sign autographs, and he would show the
curious everything he had saved from his playing days. The uniforms. The programs. The pictures. He always was an obliging
man, was Cool Papa Bell. Even when his health began to fail, he
always was that.

"He always had all of this memorabilia," says Norman Seay,
Bell's nephew and an administrator at the University of Missouri
at St. Louis. "People came from everywhere, from Timbuktu, to
get autographs from Uncle Bell. It was a normal occurrence
around that house."

Then, on March 22, all that changed. Bell was visited by Grybowski and Retort, who had driven seventeen hours to St. Louis
from New Castle, where Retort owns a company called R. D. Retort Enterprises. It operates within the bull market in what are

called baseball collectibles. By all accounts, Retort is an aggressive collector. "He called here a lot, and you couldn't get him off the phone," says a source at the Baseball Hall of Fame in Cooperstown. "He never quite made it clear what the purpose of his research was, but he made a lot of requests for uniform numbers, and for what teams certain players played for. He didn't seem to have much of a working knowledge of baseball history, but he kept us on the phone a half hour at a time."

Retort has declined comment on the specifics of the case against him, but does say that "when it all comes out, you'll see there's one huge world of difference between what I've been charged with and what really happened. It's a situation where, basically, I was there to get autographs from a Hall of Famer, and I was in the wrong place at the wrong time."

It is possible that Retort and Grybowski were invited to come to St. Louis by Bell, who rarely turned down such a request. The two spent several days there. Bell signed a lot of autographs, but it was a slow process. The FBI says that Retort paid Bell $100 for the various autographed items. That is all that Retort says he did there. The FBI does not agree.

According to investigators, Retort and Grybowski returned on March 25 and began to remove from the Bells' house several cardboard boxes filled with the paraphernalia Cool Papa had collected over the course of his career. Bell and his wife, Clarabelle, told both the local police and the FBI that they had felt "trapped" by the two men, and that they were too intimidated to try and stop them. In fact, the Bells said, they were so intimidated that they didn't even report the incident until their daughter, Connie Brooks, discovered what had happened a week later.

Retort, thirty-eight, and Grybowski, sixty-five, were arrested on April 9. Both are free now, Retort on $25,000 bond and Grybowski on $10,000. They will stand trial this summer in St. Louis. Most of the memorabilia was recovered. Connie Brooks has flown in from New York, and she has spent a month helping investigators identify some of the articles. It is a federal offense to take more than $5,000 worth of stolen merchandise across state lines. The estimated value of everything that was taken from Cool Papa Bell's house is $300,000, which has flatly flabbergasted some people who are close to him.

"I couldn't believe it when they said that," says Norman Seay. "I mean, a half a million dollars? To me, he was just my Uncle Bell, and all that stuff he had, I thought its real value was an internal kind of thing, that its value was intrinsic to him."

But that is not the way the world is today. There are people who would call $300,000 a modest price for what was taken from Cool Papa Bell. These are people who understand a new and unsettlingly volatile marketplace in which the past is raw currency, and what energizes that marketplace is the same feeling that came over Bob Reutter when he looked into the FBI's conference room and saw an exposed vein of pure history stretched across its walls.

"I have to admit that I'm a fan, and I looked the stuff over," admits the agent with a chuckle. "I saw those uniforms and I thought, 'How did they ever play in those heavy things?' It was all really interesting to me."

Perhaps the Fourth Lateran Council had the right idea after all. In the thirteenth century, the Roman Catholic Church was awash in very pricey relics, including not only the purported heads of various saints, but also enough alleged pieces of the True Cross to build duplex homes for half the yeomanry in Western Europe. Embarrassed by this unbridled profiteering in the sacred, the church called the council, which forbade the practice in 1215, whereupon the price of a saint's head crashed all over Christendom.

That sort of naked interference in the free marketplace would not be tolerated today. We live in an acquisitive age, a trend encouraged from the very top of the political and cultural elite for more than a decade now. It manifests itself in everything from the leveraged buyout to the current desire of every cherubic four-year-old to surround himself with replicas of pizza-chomping, hey-dude amphibians who are built like Ben Johnson. Indeed, today we have collectibles the instantly accrued value of which almost totally rests with the immediate demand for them. How much more, then, must genuine relics be worth?

It hit the art world first. In his book *Circus of Ambition,* journalist John Taylor describes the rise of what he calls "the collecting class." Taylor writes that, in the 1980s, "Collectors were returning in droves. One reason was the huge surge in income enjoyed

by the individuals in the higher income brackets." In one telling
anecdote, Taylor overhears a rich young couple at an art auction. The husband complains, "We're unhappy with the Cézanne." His wife responds cheerily, "That's O.K., because we're
going to *trade up!*"

Substitute "Pete Rose" for "Cézanne" in that conversation and
you've pretty much got what happened when this dynamic hit
sports — the only difference being, of course, that unlike Rose,
Cézanne wasn't around to pitch his own paintings on the Home
Shopping Network. It is estimated that the trade in sports collectibles has become a $200 million industry in this country. It is
manifested best by all those things that give the willies to the
baseball purists. These include card shows — and the almost uni-
versally condemned notion of the $15 autograph — as well as the
public auction of old baseball equipment.

When Taylor writes that "many of these collectors were frankly
more interested in art as an investment than as a means of cultural certification," it's hard not to hear the complaint that echoes
across the land every time another one of yesterday's heroes starts
peddling his memories. It's hard not to hear the guy at Cooperstown saying that Robert Retort's "working knowledge of baseball" was lacking.

As is the case with any good capitalist enterprise, if you push it
far enough you find yourself passing through greed and moving
all the way into the criminal. The case of Pete Rose is instructive
here. First came the reports that there were several bats in circu-
lation that were purported to be the one that Rose used to break
Ty Cobb's record on September 11, 1985. Now, accounts of that
historic at-bat indicate that Rose used only one bat. Where the
other three (or four, or eight, or twelve) came from remains a
mystery, especially to the gullible people who bought them. In
this, Pete Rose was lucky he only had to face the late Bart Giamatti. The Fourth Lateran Council would've had him in thumb-
screws.

Now, however, it's been revealed that Rose failed to declare to
the Internal Revenue Service the cash income that he made at
card shows and from the sale of various memorabilia. There is
some symmetry, at least, in the fact that, in the same week, Pete
Rose and Michael Milken, symbols of their age, both faced a federal judge.

Nor is Rose's the only criminal case in which baseball collectibles figure prominently. We have the odd affair involving National League umpire Bob Engel, who is alleged to have attempted to steal 4,180 baseball cards from a store in Bakersfield, California. And, believing that his bats were being lifted by enterprisingly larcenous clubhouse personnel, at least one American League superstar has taken the radical step of having the bats sent directly to his home rather than to the ballpark.

But the case of Cool Papa Bell is far more serious than either of these other two. After all, it involves the alleged intimidation of an eighty-seven-year-old, half-blind, sickly man, and it also involves a federal felony even more serious than the one committed by Pete Rose. There would have to be a huge payoff involved for Retort to have risked such a crime. Experts say that there was, and that it has everything to do with the nature of the memorabilia itself.

In the first place, there is a finite number of Negro League collectibles available. When Jackie Robinson signed with the Dodgers, the Negro Leagues essentially collapsed. Therefore, there's no futures market in Negro League memorabilia.

In addition, the people who played in the Negro Leagues are mainly quite old now — Bell is about the average age for a Negro League veteran — and there are not many left who even played back then. That means there are only limited prospects for the lucrative trade in replicas, in which a retired player will authorize (and autograph) things like duplicate bats and uniforms. The FBI charges that Retort and Grybowski forced Bell to sign a letter authorizing such replicas. Retort denies the charge.

Because Negro League memorabilia is so passing rare, there is no established price scale for any of it. Thus, traders are free to ask whatever price they want because there are no benchmarks by which that price can be measured. "If I saw a ball signed by the 1919 Black Sox, I'd know what that was worth," says Alan Rosen, a New Jersey entrepreneur who's known among memorabilia collectors as Mr. Mint. "But if I saw a ball signed by the original winners of the black World Series, I wouldn't know how to authenticate the signatures. I wouldn't know how to price the thing."

This is not an insignificant admission. Mr. Mint has been known to show up in the living rooms of baseball-card collectors with a briefcase full of cash. Indeed, if you were to skulk around, Colin Clive-ishly, and dig up Christy Mathewson, Mr. Mint probably could price the bones for you. Nevertheless, Negro League memorabilia has brought top dollar at a number of auctions. An authentic poster advertising a Fourth of July doubleheader featuring Satchel Paige once sold for $2,400. A program from an exhibition game between a Negro League All-Star team and Dizzy Dean's barnstorming club went for $700. Intact tickets from the Negro World Series or from the annual East-West All-Star game have fetched up to $500 apiece, and an autographed ball from the 1940 East-West game was sold to a collector for $850. A man named George Lyons even got $1,500 for an authenticated contract between a Cuban League team and one James Bell of St. Louis.

"Nobody really has any independent judgment regarding what to pay for something," explains Herman Kaufman, a collector and auctioneer who specializes in Negro League memorabilia. "I'd say that ninety-nine percent of collecting is pure enjoyment, but that the other one percent is knowing that you have something that nobody else has."

Which brings up the question of how far a collector is willing to go to get what nobody else has. Investigators probing the recent massive art theft at Boston's Isabella Stewart Gardner Museum say privately that, while they're confident that they will apprehend the thieves, most of the actual paintings are probably gone forever, quietly sold to collectors and now hanging in someone's library.

Kaufman dismisses the idea of a memorabilia underground — "Why buy something if you can never show it?" he asks — but others in the field are not as sanguine about the possibility. They think Cool Papa's lucky that the FBI got most of his things back.

"If you're asking if sometimes guys'll come to me and say, 'Look, I got this stuff here, and keep it between me and you where you got it,' and that's the deal, I'd have to say yes, that happens," says Joe Esposito of B & E Collectibles in New York. "You have to remember that you're dealing with collectors. They'll do anything."

Cool Papa was hospitalized shortly after the incident with Retort and Grybowski. "He's at the point of death," says his wife. He's at home now, but other family members wonder whether or not it's time for him to leave the house on Cool Papa Bell Avenue and live out his days in a retirement home. They doubt whether Clarabelle can adequately care for him anymore.

"He's very fragile and he's very weak," says Norman Seay. "I don't know what we're going to do. You know, it's funny, all those years growing up next door to him, I didn't realize that he was a celebrity. He was just Uncle Bell. I never realized how great he really was. You know, as an African-American athlete, he never got the respect he should have. It was kind of a second-class identity for him."

That, perhaps, is the real crime. It's more than a simple threat. It's a kind of crime against history. Because of the entrenched racism of major league baseball, Cool Papa Bell never was able to profit fully from his enormous skills. At the very least, then, he ought to be able to profit fully from the accoutrements of that talent, or he ought to be able to leave it alone, snug in boxes in the basement. If what the FBI says is true, then that is the real crime here, not the mere pilfering of things to meet the demands of a marketplace gone dotty, or to satisfy an acquisitive age. It is the further robbing of a man who's already had too much of himself stolen.

There's a man named Tweed Webb who knows what the crime is. He is the unofficial historian for the Negro Leagues in St. Louis, and he is a friend of Cool Papa Bell's. "I go back to about 1910," he says. "I kept all my records, because if you don't have records, you can't prove nothing happened. It's like nothing ever did happen if you don't have records.

"Cool Papa, he's been sick for eighteen or nineteen years, but we talk, you know? He told me about what happened right when it happened. The FBI come out here to talk to me because, you know, I got valuable stuff myself. I got all my records, all my scorecards. Certain people'd love to get their hands on the stuff I got. But I don't sell none of it. I pass along learning to people, but the records are priceless. At least, they're priceless to me."

Oddly enough, both the investigators and the defendant express concern for Bell's health. "I did a lot of work on this out of loyalty to Cool Papa," says Bob Reutter, G-man and baseball fan. "I heard that he wasn't doing too well, and I wanted to get that stuff back for him. I don't imagine the publicity's going to help much, either. I mean, it probably isn't good for him that people know he's got a quarter-million dollars' worth of stuff in his basement."

"I'm worried about what all this will do to his health," says Robert Retort. "It's got to take a toll on the poor man."

It will come to trial sometime this summer. For now, Connie Brooks stays in St. Louis, identifying pieces of her father's past for the investigators. And Cool Papa Bell stays at home. He doesn't get up much anymore. In the twilight, Cool Papa Bell is already in bed. Someone else turns out the light.

May 10, 1990

(Editor's note: James "Cool Papa" Bell died on March 7, 1991, following a heart attack.)

FRANK CONROY

Running the Table

FROM GQ

WHEN I was fifteen and living in New York City, I was supposed
to be going to Stuyvesant High School and in fact I did actually
show up three or four times a week, full of gloom, anger and
adolescent narcissism. The world was a dark place for me in those
days. I lived in a kind of tunnel of melancholy, constantly in trouble at home, in school and occasionally with the police. (Pitching
pennies, sneaking into movies, jumping the turnstile in the sub-
way, stealing paperback books — fairly serious stuff in that earlier, more innocent time.) I was haunted by a sense of chaos, chaos
within and chaos without. Which is perhaps why the orderliness
of pool, the Euclidean cleanness of it, so appealed to me. The
formality of pool struck me as soothing and reassuring, a sort of
oasis of coolness, utterly rational and yet not without its elegant
little mysteries. But I'm getting ahead of myself.

One day, meandering around 14th Street, I stepped through
the open doors on an impulse and mounted the long, broad
stairway. Halfway up I heard the click of the balls. What a marvelous sound! Precise, sharp, crisp, and yet somehow mellow.
There was an intimacy to the sound that thrilled me. At the top
of the stairs I pushed through saloon-style swinging doors and
entered a vast, hushed, dim hall. Rows of pool tables stretched
away in every direction, almost all of them empty at this early
hour, but here and there in the distance, a pool of light, figures
in silhouette circling, bending, taking shots. Nearby, two old men
were playing a game I would later learn to be billiards on a large
table without pockets. The click of the three balls, two white, one

red, was what I had heard on the stairs. The men played unhur-
riedly, pausing now and then with their cues held like walking
sticks to stare down at the street below. Cigar smoke swirled in
the air.

I had walked into Julian's, little knowing that it was one of the
most important pool halls on the East Coast. I was impressed by
the stark functionality of the place — the absence of decoration
of any kind. It seemed almost institutional in its atmosphere, right
down to the large poster hung on the cashier's cage setting out
the rules and regulations. No drinking, no eating, no sitting on
the edges of the tables, no spitting except in the cuspidors, no
massé shots, etc. Tables were twenty-five cents an hour. Cue sticks
were to be found on racks against the walls. Balls available from
the cashier as he clocked you in.

"How do you play?" I asked.

The cashier was bald and overweight. He wore, for some reason, a green eyeshade. "You from Stuyvesant?"

I nodded, and he grunted, reached down to some hidden shelf
and gave me a small paper pamphlet, pushing it forward across
the worn wooden counter. I scanned it quickly. Basic information about straight pool, eight ball, nine ball, billiards, snooker
and a few other games. "Start with straight pool," he said. "Go
over there and watch those guys on twenty-two for a while. Sit
still, don't talk, and don't move around."

I did as I was told, sitting on a kind of mini-bleachers against
the wall, my chin in my hands. The two men playing were in their
twenties, an Abbott-and-Costello duo, thin Bud wearing a vest
and smoking constantly, pudgy Lou moving delicately around the
table, using the bridge now and then because of his short arms.
They paid no attention to me and played with concentration, silent except for calling combinations.

"Six off the thirteen," Lou said.

Bud nodded. They only called combinations. All straight shots,
no matter how difficult, were presumably obvious. After a while,
with a few discreet glances at my pamphlet, I began to get the
hang of it. All the balls, striped and solid, were fair game. You
simply kept shooting until you missed, and then it was the other
guy's turn. After each run, you moved some beads on a wire
overhead with the tip of your cue, marking up the number of

balls you'd sunk. So much for the rules. What was amazing was the shooting.

Object balls clipped so fine they moved sideways. Bank shots off the cushion into a pocket. Long combinations. Breakout shots in which a whole cluster of balls would explode in all directions while one from the middle would limp into a nearby pocket. And it didn't take long to realize that making a given shot was only part of what was going on. Controlling the position of the cue ball after the shot was equally important, so as to have a makable next shot. I could see that strategy was involved, although how they made the cue ball behave so differently in similar situations seemed nothing short of magical. Lou completed a run of nine or ten balls and reached fifty on the wire overhead. He had won, apparently.

"Double or nothing?"

Bud shook his head. Money changed hands. Lou put the balls in a tray, turned out the light over the table, and both men checked out at the cashier's. I sat for a while, thinking over what I had seen, reading the pamphlet again. I didn't have enough money to play that day, but I knew I was coming back.

Sometime in the late sixties, as an adult, I went to the Botanic Garden in Brooklyn to visit the recently completed Zen rock garden. It was a meticulous re-creation of a particular installation from a particular Japanese monastery. No one else was there. I sat on the bench gazing at the spiral patterns in the sand, looking at the black rocks set like volcanic islands in a white sea. Peace. Tranquility. As absurd as it may sound, I was reminded of my childhood experience of Julian's on a quiet afternoon — a sense of harmony, of an entirely disinterested material world entirely unaffected by one's perception of it.

For me, at fifteen, Julian's was a sort of retreat, a withdrawal from the world. I would shoot for hours at a time, racking up, breaking, shooting, racking up, breaking, shooting, in a solitary trance. Or I would surrender to the ritual of practice — setting up long shots over the length of the table again and again, trying to sink a shot with the same configuration ten times in a row, and then twenty, and then a more difficult configuration to a different pocket three times in a row, and then five, etc. I did not get bored with the repetition. Every time a ball went in the pocket I felt satisfaction. When I missed I simply ignored the fact, reset the shot and tried again. This went on for several weeks at a remote table in a far corner of the hall — table nineteen — which nobody else ever seemed to want. Once in a while I'd play with another kid, usually also from Stuyvesant, and split the time. After a couple of months I would sometimes play for the time — loser pays — against opponents who looked even weaker than myself. But most of the time I played alone.

Late one afternoon, racking up on table nineteen for perhaps the tenth time, I noticed a man sitting in the gloom up against the wall. He was extremely thin, with a narrow face and a protruding brow. He wore a double-breasted suit and two-tone shoes, one leg dangling languidly over the other. He gave me an almost imperceptible nod. I chalked the tip of my cue, went to the head of the table and stroked a clean break. Aware that I was being watched, I studied the lie of the balls for a moment and proceeded to sink seven in a row, everything going according to plan, until I scratched. I pulled up the cue ball and the object ball, recreated the shot and scratched again.

"Why don't you use English?" he asked quietly.

I stared at the table. "What's English?"

A moment's pause. "Set it up again," he said.

I did so.

"Aim, but don't hit. Pretend you're going to shoot."

I made a bridge with my left hand, aimed at the object ball and held the tip of my stick right behind the center of the cue ball.

"All right. All lined up?"

"Yes," I said, almost flat on the table.

"Do not change the line. Are you aiming at the center of the cue ball?"

"Yes."

"Aim a quarter of an inch higher."

"You mean I should . . ." For some reason what he was suggesting seemed almost sacrilegious.

"Yes, yes. Don't hit the cue ball in the center. Strike a quarter of an inch above. Now go ahead. Shoot."

I made my stroke, watched the object ball go in, and watched the cue ball take a different path after impact than it had before.

It didn't scratch this time, but missed the pocket, bounced smartly off the cushion and rolled to a stop near the center of the table for an easy next shot.

"Hey. That's terrific!" I said.

"That's English." He unfolded his legs and stood up. He came over and took the pool cue from my hands. "If a person pays attention," he said, "a person can learn about ninety-five percent of what he needs to know in about ten minutes. Ten minutes for the principles, then who knows how many years for the practice." His dark, deep-set eyes gave his face a vaguely ominous cast. "You want to learn?"

"Absolutely," I said without hesitation. "Yes."

As it turned out, it took about half an hour. The man teaching me was called Smilin' Jack, after the comic-strip character and presumably because of his glum demeanor. He was a Julian's regular, and it was my good luck to have caught him when somebody had stood him up for what was to have been a money game. I could sense that he enjoyed going through the drill — articulate, methodical, explicating on cause and effect with quiet relish, moving the balls around the table with no wasted motion whatsoever, executing the demo shots with a stroke as smooth as powdered silk — it was an elegant dance, with commentary. A sort of offering to the gods of pool.

I cannot possibly recount here what I learned. Follow, draw, left and right English and how they affect the movement of the cue ball after impact. The object ball picking up opposite English from the cue ball. The effectiveness of different kinds of English as a function of distance (between cue ball and object ball) and of speed. *Sliding* the cue ball. Playing the diamond points. Shooting a ball frozen on the cushion. How to read combinations, and on and on. I paid very close attention and jotted down what notes I could. (*Over*shoot bank shots to the side pockets. *Under*shoot bank shots to the corner pockets.) At the end of the half hour my head ached. In addition to trying to grasp the principles, I'd been trying to film the whole thing, to superimpose an eidetic memory on the cells of my brain, so I could retrieve what I'd seen at will. I was exhausted.

He handed me the stick, shot his cuffs and adjusted the front of his jacket with a slight forward movement of his shoulders.

"That should keep you busy for a while." Then he simply walked away.

"Thanks," I called after him.

Without looking back, he raised his hand and gave a laconic little wave.

Practice, practice. Months of practice. It was a delicate business, English, affected by things like the relative roughness of the cue tip and its ability to hold chalk, or the condition of the felt, or infinitesimal degrees of table lean. But it worked. There was no doubt about it, when you got the feel of it you greatly increased your power over the all-important position of the cue ball. There was a word for it — the "leave," as in "good shot, but a tough leave." And of course the more you could control the leave, the more deeply involved was the strategy — planning out how to sink twelve balls in a row, rather than just five or six. Progress was slow, but it was tangible, and very, very satisfying. I began to beat people. I moved off table nineteen up toward the middle of the hall and began to beat almost everybody from Stuyvesant.

The most important hurdle for a straight-pool player involves being able to run into the second rack. You have to sink fourteen balls and leave the fifteenth ball and the cue ball positioned in such a way as to be able to sink the last ball (breaking open the new rack at the same time) and have a good enough leave to start all over again. I achieved this shortly before my sixteenth birthday, with a run of twenty-three.

The owners of Julian's recognized the accomplishment as a significant rite of passage and awarded certain privileges to those who had achieved it. During my last year of high school a cue of my own selection, with my name taped to the handle, was kept in a special rack behind the cashier's cage. No one else could use that particular cue stick. It was reserved, along with thirty or forty others for young players who had distinguished themselves.

I was a nonentity at school, but I could walk up to the cage at Julian's and the cashier would reach back for my stick and say, "Hey, Frank. How's it going?"

What a splendid place it was.

There's a lot to feel in pool, a physical aspect to the game, which means you have to play all the time to stay good. I've lost most of my chops (to borrow a word from jazz), but I still drop down to my local bar, the Foxhead, every now and then to play on the undersize table. It's a challenge arrangement. Put your name on the chalkboard, slip two quarters in the slot when it's your turn, and try to win.

There's a good deal more chance in eight ball, your basic bar game, than in straight pool, but it's fun. We've got some regulars. Jerry, a middle-aged man with a gorgeous stroke (a nationally ranked player in his youth), can beat anybody who walks into the place if he isn't furious at having to play doubles, at kids slopping beer onto the felt, or some other infraction of civilized behavior. There's Doug, a graduate student who always looks as if he'd spent the previous night in a cardboard box in an alley and who hits every shot as hard as he can, leaving the question of where the cue ball is going to end up more or less to the gods, in the hope that they will thus tangibly express the favor in which they hold him. (He is a poet.) We have George, an engineer, who exhausts our patience by approaching each situation with extreme care, circling the table several times, leaning over to stare down at a cluster of balls in what appears to be a hypnotic trance, chalking up with the care of Vermeer at the easel and running through a complicated series of various facial and physical tics before committing himself. There's Henry, who programs the jukebox to play "Brown Sugar" ten times in a row before he racks up. We've got students, working people, teachers, nurses (Yes. Women! Smilin' Jack would be scandalized) and barflies. We've got everybody at the Foxhead.

There are nights when I can hold the table for a couple of hours, but not very often. My touch is mostly gone, and bifocals make things difficult. Still, a bit of Julian's is still with me and, at the very least, I talk a good game.

January 1990

GLENN NELSON

The Comrades of Summer

FROM THE SEATTLE TIMES

ALL THE Soviet Sports Ministry official in Moscow knows is that the national baseball tournament is being held in the capital city of the country's second-largest republic.

The official believes there are three games a day, but doesn't know exactly when or where in Kiev they are being played.

This, after all, is the Soviet equivalent of the World Series, one figures. The people in Kiev will be buzzing about it.

They're buzzing about it, all right. Z-z-z-z-z . . .

"Where is the baseball championship being played?" one asks upon arrival in Kiev.

"What's baseball?" is the oft-repeated counter-query.

Eventually, serious sleuthing by the concierge at Kiev's Dnie-pro Hotel and then by a taxi driver uncovers the beginnings of an answer. In a park amid a maze of housing complexes sits what once was a soccer pitch. The combined forces of nature (a day's rain) and man (four days' labor) have rendered it something more — and less.

This turbid tract of Kiev is affectionately known as Pyanikh Field. Victor Pyanikh, the local baseball coach, assembled a crew of players and fellow coaches four days before the tournament. Together, they built by hand the country's first permanent natural baseball field.

Because there is no grass, what should be the infield diamond blends into the outfield. The field has such unusual touches — by Soviet standards, that is — as an outfield fence, foul poles, and a backstop. Pyanikh Field also features the first pitching mound ever used in a Soviet tournament.

In the Ukraine, spring has not yet completely wrenched itself from winter's icy clench, so the Soviet Union's finest comrades of summer are assailed by numbing winds as they vie for both a national championship and spots on the country's entry to the 1990 Goodwill Games.

Undeterred by the sloppy conditions (one tournament was played in the snow last October), the players manage to slip and slide through a game. It's a wonder they manage. One of the two game balls is so caked with mud it is almost undiscernible in the cloudy twilight.

"Usually, the balls are white," says Igor Kulagin, catcher for a team from Tashkent, the capital of Uzbekistan and Seattle's sister city. "But you get used to the dirty ones."

Baseballs have been a scarce commodity from the start. The first ones actually were tennis balls wrapped heavily with tape. Many players have mastered the art of extracting a baseball's core and sewing on a new leather cover. Once, a player accidentally hit a ball into a nearby river and was forced to wade into the water to retrieve it.

None of this matters much to Vasili Bespalov, another rare aspect of Soviet baseball — the spectator.

Pyanikh Field is flanked by a couple of sets of bleachers, whose occupants are almost exclusively athletes either hanging around after having played the previous game or waiting to play in the next one. A field house overlooking the field is jammed the same day with hundreds viewing a girls' wrestling tournament. The country's national baseball tournament attracts only a handful of people, more curiosity seekers than anything.

"I'm having trouble understanding this," says Bespalov, who wandered over from his nearby home. "Maybe it's because I'm a little sick in the head and don't understand much anyway. I've had a brain tap and I'm very old."

Alexander Grabel, standing just up the first-base line from Bespalov, is slightly less perplexed. "This is an interesting game," he says diplomatically, "but football [soccer] is more comprehendible. We don't have as good a tradition in this baseball. It's easier for everyone to go out for football. Maybe later people will like baseball as well."

First, they'll have to figure it out. One thing missing at Pyanikh field is a scoreboard. And the scorekeepers doggedly guard their scorebooks as if they contain state secrets. The only thing that blares from a loudspeaker-equipped van, manned nearby by tournament officials, is the occasional rock-and-roll ditty.

"People don't even know who's winning," says Dmitry Mazulevich, who had a falling out with Pyanikh and no longer plays. "They just watch."

Alexandra Chomenko and Oksana Popereva wander by. The two *babushkas* (grandmothers), their chunky bodies wrapped in overcoats and their hair veiled in scarves, stop and watch. It isn't long before quizzical looks grip their faces.

They are asked what they think of baseball.

"Oh, this is baseball?" Chomenko replies. She pauses, then adds, "What is baseball?"

Popereva smiles and says, "My first impression is that I like this game very much . . . because the young people are doing something instead of just hanging around."

Soon reaching their curiosity threshold, the two waddle away. A few yards down the road, they turn, peer back at the game and engage in animated discussion, then continue their journey. The sequence is repeated several more times before they disappear from view.

It's not likely the *babushkas* are talking strategy, or even about the game. Their thoughts are more likely occupied by the country's moribund economy or the perils of nearby Chernobyl. As those who follow Soviet baseball like to say, "There are more Americans interested in Soviet baseball than Soviets interested in Soviet baseball."

Bob Protexter is one such American. A couple of months ago, he sold most of his possessions, including his car, left Morningside College in Sioux City, Iowa, and headed for the Soviet Union. By prearrangement, he has been helping coach Moscow's D. I. Mendeleyev Chemical and Technology Institute team.

Mendeleyev is the most Americanized team in the Soviet Union, mainly because Richard Spooner is its mentor. Spooner is a project manager for the U.S.–U.S.S.R. Trade and Economic Council and a former Yale intramural baseball player. Some consider him the American father of Soviet baseball.

Yet, even Spooner's influence has failed to purge Mendeleyev of the idiosyncrasies that befuddle Protexter on an almost daily basis.

The most striking thing to Protexter is the relationship between Soviet players and coaches. Pyanikh, for one, is a notorious tyrant, known not so affectionately to his players as Attila the Hun. He often stops his players between innings to excoriate them with such insults as, "You run like a pregnant cockroach!"

"That's typical," Protexter says. "Here, the biggest problem is that the players don't think the coaches know what they're talking about. The coaches don't think the players know what they're talking about, either. And they're both right."

Such circumstances are understandable. *Beizbol* is just slightly younger than *glasnost*, Mikhail Gorbachev's policy of openness that itself has provoked a prolonged period of adjustment. The Soviet Union officially adopted baseball in 1986, after the International Olympic Committee granted the sport full medal status for the 1992 games in Barcelona.

Literally starting from scratch, the Soviet sports hierarchy's first task was developing a pool of players. It began by drafting athletes on the verge of losing their sanctioned status in other sports. Some attempt was made to match athletes with positions requiring skills already honed in another sport. Pitchers tend to be former javelin throwers, and catchers former soccer goal tenders.

It seems there weren't enough former javelin throwers to arm the country's pitching arsenal, however. Each team has only two pitchers; many double as position players. As a result, Soviet pitchers typically go the distance nearly every time. Early in the season, their arms not yet in shape, they are being shelled in about the fifth inning — with no relief in sight.

"Yes, my arm hurts," says the Central Army's Alexander Dundick, considered the country's best pitcher. "But I am not in the best shape right now. I hope to be in top shape in Seattle."

Dundick, thirty-three, is — what else? — a former javelin thrower. Like many of his comrades, he can't quite put a finger on his attraction to baseball. That is, other than the fact the sport has enlisted him among its many second-chance athletes.

"For a person who already has played another sport, it is hard to go work at a plant," he says. "After sports, anything else is very boring."

Vladimir Bogaterev, the national team's "general manager," says, "Soviet people like sports in general, and baseball is one of the new sports that came with *perestroika*. To us, the game is very interesting. People relate to it because it's played in the fresh air and, really, anybody can play."

After finding players, the next most pressing obstacles in Soviet baseball's evolutionary process were, according to Bogaterev, "equipment and knowledge."

As for the former, the Soviets improvised at first. They made their own bats — out of birch, however, so they had the staying power of toothpicks. The first Soviet catchers used goalie masks and gloves from hockey. First basemen also used hockey mitts. Though Japanese models are starting to proliferate, most gloves used by the Soviets still carry the *Hecho en Cuba* stamp.

Cuba and Nicaragua were their first baseball tutors. Advisers since have been loaned by Canada and Sweden as well. The Japanese provided $3.2 million for the artificial-turf stadium built last year for Moscow University.

But the aid the Soviets cherish most has come from the Americans.

The Soviets have an instructional arrangement with the Eastern League minor league circuit. Peter O'Malley, the Los Angeles Dodgers owner, has provided equipment and offered the use of his coaches in the future. Game films and instructional videos from the United States are considered precious.

American videos, in fact, have become so sacrosanct, players often blow off advice from their Soviet coaches, arguing, "That's not the way (Pete Rose/Wade Boggs/George Brett) does it." One Soviet catcher once vowed to name his firstborn son after Gary Carter, the veteran major leaguer whom the Soviet examined closely on videotape.

This infatuation with U.S. aid stems only partly from the fact that baseball is the American pastime. Several Soviets, in fact, dispute the claim that Americans invented the game. They maintain that *lapta*, a folk game played with a bat and ball which can be traced to the reign of Peter the Great, was actually the inspiration for baseball.

"After World War II, people started to forget *lapta*," Bogaterev says. "Now we are trying to put it back into the schools and hope it helps our baseball development. *Lapta* reminds many of our people of baseball."

One can only imagine what *lapta* must have been like because, well, Soviet baseball might not always remind a lot of Americans of the game to which they've grown accustomed.

Soviet pitchers throw curveballs, for example; but many of them hang like the gag signs youngsters attach to the rump of unsuspecting buddies. Instead of "kick me," they say "hit me." Soviet baseball scores are often in the thirty-run range for each team, but that has just as much to do with the quality of fielding.

The Soviets also have a strange way of leading off base. Many Americans extend a left arm back toward the bag as sort of an imaginary tether in the event of pickoff attempts. Soviet base runners extend their right arm, wave it wildly, and shout obscenities while the opposing pitcher begins his windup.

Who taught them this?

"Nobody," Mazulevich says. "This is our way of putting our own stamp upon the game."

The one thing the Soviets have mastered is the art of *looking* like baseball players. Theirs could be faces straight off Topps baseball cards. They walk like baseball players, talk like baseball players, and spit like baseball players. One, Andrei (Andy) Tselikovsky, even chews tobacco.

"I'm fricking running out," says Tselikovsky, who actually uses the word "fricking" along with its more profane derivative. "Know where I can get some more?" Tselikovsky was dubbed Red Man Dude during a recent stint with a junior-college team in Tennessee.

This resemblance to baseball players — in appearance if not deed — could be linked partly to a cultural tendency to sugarcoat reality. Such inclinations hearken to the days of czarist Russia. Count Potemkin erected mock village fronts along the banks of the Dnieper River to present a touring Catherine the Great the illusion of prosperity.

In contemporary, *glasnost*-inspired times, personal facades such as those fabricated in baseball may be more psychological defense mechanisms.

In little more than a week, the Soviet Union takes the extraordinary step of releasing obviously subordinate talent into a global arena. The Soviets' first taste of international competition will come at the 1990 Goodwill Games baseball tournament in Tacoma. They will begin the tournament against the United States on July 26. Expectations are not high.

"Our hope is not to lose by more than twenty runs," admits Kiev's Alexander Riabikov, another of the country's top pitching prospects.

The Soviets have drastically downgraded their expectations for international success in baseball. Judging by the sport's place in the country's athletic pecking order, they've almost had to. Alexander Kozlovsky, deputy chairman of Goskomsport, the state Committee for Physical Culture and Sports, says, "I don't feel baseball will ever become the most popular sport in the Soviet Union." Which goes to show what kind of support the sport enjoys from the top.

Bogaterev says the Soviets are going to Tacoma "not to win, but to study." The Soviet Union's baseball fathers hope the country improves enough to have a shot at the European championship in 1992. They hope then to qualify for Olympic competition in 1996.

Judging by what is occurring between the Central Army and Kiev, two of the longest-standing teams in the Soviet Union, these are haughty objectives.

Central is batting, with a runner on third and one out. The Kiev pitcher tosses a moonball. The Central batter manages only to tap it to a capless Kiev third baseman, who fields the ball cleanly but slips in the muck. As he scrambles to his feet, the Central runner bolts from third.

The Kiev third baseman winds up to get the out at first but changes his mind. Pyanikh's frantic screams echo throughout the park. The third baseman rifles a throw toward the plate, but the wild heave evades the catcher. Meanwhile, the Central batter chugs into second base.

Dmitry Mazulevich pries his fingers off the chain-link-fence backstop, turns away, and shrugs in resignation. "I'm sure you are used to a higher level of play," he says almost apologetically to an American spectator. "Unfortunately, this is what we have done to your game."

July 15, 1990

JOHNETTE HOWARD

The Making of a Goon

FROM THE NATIONAL SPORTS DAILY

HE WENT FROM nobody to notorious with a cudgel of a fist, and there was no rung of hockey to which it couldn't take him. Once he got to the NHL and stayed, the job then became one of maintaining his niche — even after the bone showed through the sliced skin of his knuckles and he had to soak his punching hand in ice between periods, even after doctors nearly had to amputate his right arm.

Joe Kocur, the Detroit Red Wings enforcer, is sometimes referred to by the rabid cult of fight-video collectors around the league as "the Mike Tyson of the NHL." But earning that reputation was one thing; maintaining it led to a frightening night against Pittsburgh when Kocur's whistling right hand dropped Jim Kyte, a six foot five Penguin defenseman, to the ice unconscious; it led to a night against Quebec when he shattered Terry Karkner's jaw and the shaken Nordique team took a week to recover; and it led to a game last February when Kocur flattened New York Islanders winger Brad Dalgarno with a single wallop, then watched Dalgarno teeter off the ice, only to learn later that he'd fractured Dalgarno's left eye orbit, his cheekbone, and — people now whisper — his resolve to go on.

In the beginning, it wasn't Kocur's idea to fistfight his way to the NHL. His first fight? He was just fourteen, playing in his first exhibition game with a new team, and an older kid cornered him and dared him to go. He says he was just fifteen when his coach was Gerry James, a sort of Bo Jackson of Canada, who had dual careers with the Toronto Maple Leafs and Winnipeg Blue

Bombers. James pulled Kocur aside and told him that if he wanted to make hockey a paying career, he had better start fighting with his fists.

"So I did," Kocur recalls. "I had about ten penalty minutes in the first twenty games. In the last forty games, I had two hundred fifty."

But Kocur's start — his real start — came at age seventeen, the night he knocked out a kid named Bruce Holloway in a Western League game in Kamloops, British Columbia. Not every man can recognize a peek at his destiny when he gets it, and even then, not everyone accepts it. But there was no question in young Joe Kocur's mind that he had done both after he saw Holloway collapse with a suddenness that was astounding.

Word of his savagery preceded him — "like wildfire," Kocur says — in stops at Seattle and Portland, in Swift Current and Moose Jaw and Victoria, too. At every arena, scouts with wizened eyes and sharp pencils secretly began pulling Kocur's Saskatoon coach aside, all wanting to know: "Was it a lucky punch or the real thing? Can the kid really fight? How hard does he throw?"

Holloway's coach, a celebrated tough guy named Bill LaForge, said back then: "Kocur took a couple real tough shots that didn't faze him, then he came back and threw a bomb that, I'm sure, Bruce will remember the rest of his life." The other guys on Kocur's team remarked later how he seemed changed as he lunged after Holloway. At that moment, the Saskatoon kids said, Joey Kocur was someone they did not know.

"I never really remembered this myself — I mean, the other guys had to tell me — but I just clicked . . . I mean, something inside of me just snapped," Kocur says today. "I just remember I was coming across the neutral ice and he high-sticked me. And I remember saying something — screaming — that I was going to get him.

"Up to that point I'd been fighting before, but I never really got mad because I guess I was just enjoying it. But right then, against that guy, I just got mad. After that, it was odd because I didn't really know what had happened to him, didn't know what to do — it was the first time, you know? I just remember standing there, thinking, 'Geez, what do I do? Do I hold him up? Do I hit him again? Should I just keep fighting or let him go?' But the refs jumped in quick and the trainers came out running."

And Kocur's teammates were right — he was changed.

"After that, I just threw caution to the wind," Kocur says. "After that, I just felt that I could fight and not get hurt. That I would never lose."

It was a far cry from his first hockey fight two years earlier. "That one, I didn't throw too many punches but I sure received a lot," Kocur says. "As I skated off I just thought, 'What a way to make a living .' "

When the NHL All-Star game convened in Pittsburgh last month, Joe Kocur was not one of the skaters who glided out for a pre-game bow. In fact, in his six NHL seasons, his name has never even appeared on the ballot. But if you were to take a poll among the NHL's players and coaches, you would certainly find Kocur, twenty-five, mentioned among the league's top five "heavy-weights" — NHL parlance for players whose main role is to po-lice the ice, always ready to punch a nose when the team needs a boost or to mete out retaliatory justice as seems fitting. In his par-ticular case, Kocur says, that especially means "keeping the flies off Stevie" (Yzerman, that is, the Red Wings superstar center and Kocur's sometime line mate).

Any poll would show one other thing, too, says St. Louis Blues center Adam Oates: "No one in our league punches harder. In that regard Joe's the absolute best at what he does."

If any pangs of conscience come with the job, if Kocur feels a measure of regret on those mornings when he wakes up and finds blood on his pillow from his mangled right hand, he will not con-fess them. Doctors have told him to expect arthritis and calcium deposits in his punching fist. "Put it this way," Kocur says drolly, "I'll never play piano."

Detroit General Manager Jimmy Devellano hopes to find Ko-cur a job with the Red Wings after his playing days are through because "he's given his hand for the organization."

Devellano's assessment of Kocur's contribution is closer to the literal truth than perhaps he intended.

Along the back side of Kocur's always bloated right hand, a three-inch red scar carves a crooked path from the middle knuckle toward the wrist. He split the hand open during a 1985 minor league game in Halifax, when he knocked out a six-three, two-hundred-pound Nova Scotia defenseman named Jim Playfair.

In the dressing room later, a doctor needed forty stitches to close the gash. But when the rest of the team came off the ice, Kocur got some good news, too: The Red Wings had called him up to the NHL.

The next morning, Kocur took the first plane out and flew all day. He checked into a hotel in Detroit, then spent an excruciating, sleepless night watching his right arm balloon to three times its normal size. When sunrise finally came, he got to the rink early for the Wings' morning skate. But a trainer noticed the new kid was wearing only one glove. The team doctor was summoned, then a hand surgeon, too.

"This was about two P.M.," Kocur says, "and the next thing I knew, they got me a hospital room, got me an IV. I was in major surgery by five P.M."

Because doctors in Halifax didn't realize Kocur had cut his hand on Playfair's teeth, they sewed the wound shut, preventing it from draining and allowing infection to take hold. Just a day and a half later, the poisoned tendons and tissue between Kocur's third and fourth knuckles had already begun to rot.

When he emerged from a morphine-induced cloud two weeks after surgery, doctors explained what had happened. "If I'd waited even one more day, they might have had to amputate my whole right arm," Kocur says.

And how did that make him feel?

"Well," Kocur says, "it made me realize how bad I want to play hockey."

When asked if he ever dreamed of being a goal scorer — maybe a star center who glided along the ice, protected by guys like him — Kocur won't commit. "Maybe," he says. Then he adds, "I also know what got me here and how I'm going to stay.

"I know the day I start playing a fancy hockey game without hitting anyone, without fighting, is the day I'll either get sent down or released from the game," Kocur says. "It's put food in my belly. It's what has kept me in this game. And I wouldn't give up this lifestyle for anything else in the world. So I'm not about to trade in my boxing gloves for a, for a . . . a wand."

But what about that year in the juniors, that year he scored a career-high forty goals?

"That," Kocur says with a sardonic smile, "was also the year I knocked out Holloway. Guys tend to give you a little more room."

On the surface, the fighting and machismo that abound in hockey may seem like an archaic ritual, the folly of men in oversize shorts. But hockey's insiders — men like Kocur — shake their heads and explain not only why intimidation works but why they believe that policing the ice is necessary. Their reasoning also explains why hockey's tough guys are almost as celebrated as the great scorers.

First remember, they will tell you, that hockey would be a violent game even without fighting. Players wear heavy padding. They carry sticks they're unafraid to use, and their skate blades are so sharp that several NHL players have nearly died from gashes suffered in pileups.

The danger is multiplied even further at the NHL level by the sheer speed of the game and the inevitability of collisions. Today's swiftest skaters hit speeds around thirty miles per hour in rinks just 200 feet long and 85 feet wide. And every hockey trainer's black bag contains a pair of forceps, just in case the impact of a collision causes a player to swallow his tongue.

In a game like this, the indecisive and the fearful cannot survive. On rinks this small, there is nowhere to hide. And perhaps it's no wonder that hockey's past is dotted with instances of players retiring because of "nerves" and goalies who suddenly begin to suffer from agoraphobia. Once the puck starts ricocheting around, says Kocur, "you have to be absolutely fearless out there. You have to think that you can't be hurt and never will."

Then, once you have that conviction, hockey also asks that you hold on to it, even when it doesn't make sense.

"Outsiders look at these guys and marvel at how they keep coming back, coming back, playing with broken noses and their jaws wired shut," Red Wings Coach Jacques Demers says. "But it's funny — as a coach, you almost get used to it. They skate off and take stitches and sometimes they just miss one or two shifts. You look and they're back in there. They're tough."

Like no other sport, hockey celebrates its toughest players. Gone are legends like Detroit's Ted (Scarface) Lindsay and savage Eddie Shore, the Boston defenseman of the 1930s who ended his career with a total of 978 stitches. But inside the current edition of *The Hockey Register,* an annual compilation of NHL players' career stats, there appears below each man's name a sort of living lore, a boldface paragraph recounting calamitous injuries or noteworthy fights.

DEAN CHYNOWETH (October 27, 1988) — Left eye injured by Rick Tocchet vs. Philadelphia and missed nearly two months.

BRUCE DRIVER (December 8, 1988) — Broke right leg in three places when checked by Lou Franceschetti vs. Washington and had surgery to implant a plate and 10 screws.

The *Register*'s grisly cataloguing sometimes includes fetishistic detail. Under Guy LaFleur's name it reads: "(March 24, 1981) — Fell asleep at the wheel of his car, hit a fence and a metal sign post, sliced off the top part of his right ear after the fence post went through his windshield." But there's some unintended humor, too. Take Larry Robinson's entry: "(January 1, 1987) — Broken nose. (November 9, 1988) — Sinus problem."

Though the NHL has taken steps, especially in the last fifteen years, to limit the bench-clearing brawls and dangerous stick-swinging incidents that fatten those boldface paragraphs in the *Register,* no one foresees the game's unique nightly phenomenon — legal, bare-knuckle fistfighting — being banned anytime soon.

Not as long as NHL President John Zeigler, like his predecessors, continues to define fighting as "the spontaneous combat which comes out of the frustrations of the game." Not while league executives are buoyed by modestly increasing attendance and a discernible statistical decline in violent incidents. And not in the absence of any serious uprising among the players.

Before the 1974–75 season, the players' union asked owners to ban fighting for one year and were flatly refused. But in a survey taken last season, players were "divided about fifty-fifty" when asked about abolishing fighting, says Sam Simpson, director of operations for the NHLPA.

Salaries are now the hot issue among NHL players, who see major league baseball's average climbing to $500,000 and the NBA median approaching $1 million a year. Against those numbers, the NHL average of $180,000 seems paltry.

"To be honest," says Cliff Fletcher, general manager of the Stanley Cup champion Calgary Flames, "the only real debate going on about fighting is in a couple of magazines and a few newspapers now and then."

As a result, tough guys remain not only legal but important enough to a team that the Red Wings' Demers candidly admits, "I know we wouldn't trade Joey Kocur for a thirty-goal scorer even though Joey has never scored thirty goals."

Why?

"Intimidation," Demers says, shrugging his shoulders. "It works."

"It works," says New York Rangers General Manager Neil Smith.

"It works," says Calgary's Fletcher.

Evidently, it works.

Fearless hockey fighters, like fearless hockey players, are not so much born as they are made. There's a very good reason for that, too, says Demers: "No one enjoys getting punched in the head."

Though Kocur's father, Joe Senior, is a strong, sturdy man — he's got "a handshake you remember for days," says Demers — Kocur says his dad "never fought in his life." And that was pretty much true of Joe Senior's only boy as young Joey was growing up with two sisters on a Kelvington, Saskatchewan, farm.

Fighting on ice never occurred to Kocur back then. But once he started looking beyond his small town, Kocur also understood that hockey requires players to grow up fast. By age fifteen or sixteen, most Canadian prospects leave home and live with foster families while they play fifty- or sixty-game schedules for traveling teams. These prospects, who often don't finish high school, encounter such concepts as "career advancement" early.

Besides, once Kocur started scuffling, he discovered something unexpected: "After the first couple times I got hit, I just thought, 'This ain't so bad.' "

When he looks at his role now, Kocur says, "I guess I enjoy it. But I don't want to sound like an animal, like my sole intention is to hurt somebody permanently. I just look at it as a job that I'm paid to do. And my job is not to lose. I won't fight dirty. I won't jump someone from behind. But when I go to hit someone, I want to hit him in the face. I'm trying to hit as hard as I can. And a few times it has happened that someone got hurt."

That's partly because fighting on skates changes things. "See, hockey fighting is different than boxing," says Kocur, who once visited the training camp of Detroit's Thomas Hearns — courtesy of Red Wings owner Mike Illitch — to pick up a few tips. "In hockey, fighting is pulling and punching. If you just stand there and hold a guy out and hit him, you won't faze him. But if you can pull him into you and punch at the same time, that's when you start hurting people."

How to hit hard is just one of the lessons an enforcer must learn. There's also an unwritten and often unspoken code of honor that governs who hits whom, and under what circumstances. Kocur also likes to do research of his own; knowing other fighters' tendencies helps him avoid surprises. But nothing, Kocur says, supersedes the most basic fighter's rule: Never, ever lose.

"You've got to understand some things about the fighter's job," says Demers. "Tough guys in this league are under a tremendous amount of pressure. Unfortunately, many of them are untalented except for fighting, and they've gotten here the hard way. And once you're recognized as a tough guy in this league, you go from having targets to becoming one.

"As long as you're beating up somebody, the fans are cheering and shouting your name. But the first time you lose one, everyone gets down on you. You have to be fearless. I've seen guys lose just once, and pretty soon they just sort of fade away."

Though coaches and other players all say that Kocur has good all-around hockey talent and that Demers encourages him to use it, Kocur considers himself a fighter first. He believes that preserving his aura of invincibility is essential because "it pays off down the line. Maybe I'll be going into the corner to get the puck and the guy going with me will think, 'Uh-oh, it's Joe Kocur. This guy's crazy. I won't give him the elbow in the face. I'll give him that extra step and poke at the puck instead of trying to take the body. And then maybe I can make a play, make a good pass. And maybe we'll put the puck in the net.' "

Or maybe, as in Brad Dalgarno's case, Kocur will go after the guy who follows him into the corner anyway.

Dalgarno has heard the explanations of why Kocur stalked him for two shifts during that game last February: that the Red Wings thought the six foot three, 215-pound Dalgarno had earlier put too aggressive a cross-check on Gilbert Delorme, that the penalty Dalgarno received wasn't enough.

"In the first place, I thought the penalty was a rather questionable call," Dalgarno says. "But sure enough, two shifts later, Kocur was out on the ice every time I came out. I was kind of, well, nervous. I knew he was tough, and the guys on my team kept skating by and telling me, 'Be careful, be careful Brad. He's out to get you. He's a dangerous guy.' And sure enough, after two shifts, we were fighting."

Before that single punch from Kocur shattered his cheekbone and eye socket, Dalgarno had always had nagging questions about the ethos of the game and prickly doubts about the coaches who kept trying, futilely, to turn him into a fighter because of his size. After Kocur's punch, that chasm grew deeper.

While recuperating at his parents' home in Hamilton, Ontario, a letter arrived. "Someone sent me a newspaper article from Detroit," Dalgarno says. "In it, Delorme was interviewed after I was hurt, and he made it look like, 'Oh, he deserved it.' And I remember I just thought, 'Wait a minute. Who deserved what?' Where's the justice, the value, in that?

"The doctors had to drill a hole in the side of my head [during surgery]. I could've lost my left eye, or my eye could've sunk into my orbital bone and I would've lost my vision. The nerves in the left side of my face might never have rematerialized. Fortunately they have, or I'd look like I had a stroke. I thought, 'Deserves it, deserves it? Who deserves *that?*' "

Knowing hockey wasn't going to change, Dalgarno decided that he would. He says he holds no grudges toward the game and doesn't blame Kocur for triggering his dissatisfaction. Dalgarno says other players feel "trapped by the game," just as he did.

"Ninety-nine percent of the guys in the NHL have been playing since they were five and have no idea what else they would do, or could do," he says. "It's tough for intelligent men to try to put things in hockey into perspective, because you're never told the answers. Hockey doesn't have them."

And so, for Brad Dalgarno, it all came down to this: On the eve of the 1989–90 regular season, with people whispering that his game wasn't the same, Dalgarno — age twenty-two, a former

number one draft pick, a potential twenty-five-goals-a-year
scorer — officially retired.

There is a TV on in a Red Wings coach's office, and one shelf
below it a VCR whirs and sighs. Joe Kocur, who is pushing but-
tons on a remote control, says he didn't see a small classified ad
in *The Hockey News* touting "The Bruise Brothers," a two-hour
bootleg tape of every fight between 1983 and 1989 involving Kocur and ex-Wing Bob Probert. Kocur can hardly believe there is
such a tape. But, he says, he'd like to see it.

Five days later, courtesy of a reporter, Kocur has the tape. As
he fast forwards past fights he doesn't care to see, the combatants
swirl on the screen at a comic, Keystone Kops pace. At one point
he hits Play, and the announcer suddenly shouts, "Kocur's pulling some hair now!"

"Aw, shaaaaddup," Kocur says, scowling sheepishly, hitting Fast
Forward, then Play again.

Announcer: "If Kocur's going to be a fighter in this league,
he's going to have to avoid turning sideways!"

"Awwwww, what does he know?" Kocur says, restarting the fast-
forward frenzy but hitting the Mute button to kill the voices, too.
In a few seconds it becomes clear that the entire tape consists of
nothing but fights spliced end to end. For $45, there are 170 fights
in all, 84 of them Kocur's.

Most of the time, Kocur watches quietly, looking serious. When
other Red Wings players begin to straggle into the room, their
faces are serious, too. Sometimes they wince.

In time, the crowd grows to nine. And suddenly Kocur pipes
up and says, "Hey, did any of you guys see 'Sports Final Edition'
last night on TV? They had this story about people in sports who've
injured other athletes. And one of the guys was this NFL linebacker that got hurt by Freeman McNeil, this running back for
the Jets who had to block him and blew out the guy's knee."

Eyes remain on the screen. But Kocur continues: The linebacker said McNeil called to apologize later, but he said he felt
sorry for McNeil, too. Once he saw what he'd done, McNeil was
so distraught he could no longer play effectively that day. For
that, Jets Coach Joe Walton publicly criticized McNeil's sensitivity.

"In the end," Kocur says, "this linebacker says that, to him, that makes Freeman McNeil a good guy, you know? A real person."

Later, when the office has cleared and the door is shut, Kocur is asked if the linebacker's story made him think. Reluctantly, Kocur says, "Well, yeah. I thought about it."

There is a long pause. When he doesn't continue he is asked, "Would you like to share what you thought?"

Without looking away from the TV or the silent fighting still going on, Joe Kocur says, "No."

February 18, 1990

JEFF COPLON

The Right Call

FROM THE NEW YORKER

LAST APRIL 6, Earl Strom, a stocky, silver-haired man of sixty-two, stepped onto the court at Madison Square Garden to officiate at a game between the New York Knicks and the Philadelphia 76ers — a group of ambitious young men who were generally half his age and almost half again his size. For Strom, the dean of National Basketball Association referees, this would be the last of more than two hundred nights on the job at the Garden. Over the past thirty-three years, he had seen basketball evolve from a waltz-paced and virtually all-white game played by two-hand set shooters into the gliding, antigravitational, inner-city-inspired version of the sport, which made pro basketball one of the growth industries of the 1980s. Strom had presided over the game's greatest teams and most incandescent players, and had also made a little basketball history himself. Had he been a player of equivalent stature, or even a coach, the evening might have lent itself to sentiment: a heartfelt introduction to spur the fans into a standing ovation; a ceremony at halftime with gifts from the Retirees' Catalogue (a rocking chair, a Lincoln Town Car); a chorus of long goodbyes from the guys who knew him when. But a referee remains isolated even in his valedictory, and not a word about Strom's leave-taking would pass the PA announcer's lips. They would have to miss him after he was gone.

It was a bad time for nostalgia, in any case. The six-month regular season had come down to its last few weeks, and the all-important playoffs — "money time," in Magic Johnson's phrase — loomed. Both the Knicks and the 76ers were playoff-bound, but there all likeness ended. After struggling since February, New York craved what had been depressingly rare of late — a win over a good opponent — to help it regroup for the postseason. The Sixers, meanwhile, had won eight straight games and flown to the top of the Atlantic Division. They were eager to kick a Knick or two while the New Yorkers were down — a desire strengthened, no doubt, by the memory of the 1989 playoffs, when the Knicks had celebrated a three-game sweep against Philadelphia by sweeping the court with a push broom.

From the moment Strom tossed up the ball at center court for the opening tap, it was evident that this game had "playoff intensity," as the sportscasters say. The pace was fast, the errors few, and the physical contact unbridled. Most of this contact was, if not strictly legal, at least within the NBA's usual limits: a crash against an opponent's hip and thigh to carve some turf closer to the basket; a tug at his jersey or waistband, the better to keep him earthbound; even the occasional push (applied discreetly, at the small of the back) to force a man out of the play. But midway through the first quarter, with the Knicks owning a six-point lead and the ball, New York's Patrick Ewing sidled over to cut off the Sixers' Charles Barkley and thereby free a Knick forward on offense. This was a moving pick — technically a foul but often overlooked by the officials. Unhappy with the obstruction, Barkley threw Ewing to the floor.

Ewing is listed at seven feet and 240 pounds, and isn't shy about throwing that weight around. Barkley, six-five and 250, is famous for his raw power, startling speed, and manic flair. Neither man is much good at retreating, and it was no surprise when Ewing jumped up to challenge Barkley. The two shoved each other once, then again, and Ewing went sprawling to the floor a second time. Other players stepped in to intercede, and, just as the incident seemed to be over, into the fray jumped a third large man: Charles Oakley, the Knicks' resident enforcer, who'd been shelved with a broken hand, and was watching from the bench in his street clothes. Glowering, he moved toward Barkley and appeared, as the league office noted when it later fined Oakley $1,500, to be "serving as other than a peacemaker." (Barkley was fined the same amount, for "instigating the altercation," and Ewing was dunned $500 for "adding to the fight.")

Earl Strom had had enough. He had already whistled Barkley for a technical foul, or "T'd him up." Now he did the same for Oakley, and summarily threw him out of the arena; Strom pointed dramatically toward the locker room several times to make sure that Oakley and everyone else got the point. Then he called the players from both teams into a huddle and launched into a pro-fanity-laced scolding, loud enough for their coaches to hear. "I told them that people had paid money to see the greatest players in the world, not to see a bunch of hoodlums out on the floor, punching and shoving," Strom recounted to me after the game. "I told them that I was going to toss the next guy who as much as raised his hand to scratch his head."

It was a classic Strom solution. A less experienced or less con-fident referee might have overreacted and bounced Barkley from the game as well, thereby compromising the 76ers' chances and damaging the show. But Strom had managed to restore order while keeping the teams' stars in action. His masterstroke was the ejection of Oakley — a strong statement with no effect on the game's outcome. And by issuing *two* technicals Strom canceled the free throws that such fouls ordinarily call for, and dodged another potential distortion of the final score. The play resumed with no loss of fervor and no further incidents. The Knicks won, as they deserved to. And Strom packed his black leather uniform bag and moved on to his next assignment, in Charlotte — an-other stop on a mostly unacknowledged farewell tour.

"I like Barkley," Strom told me a few days later. "He has a lot of enthusiasm, and he does a lot of things out of his anxiousness to perform so well — he's not a vicious individual." Many NBA referees privately admire some of their more wayward charges. But in Strom these feelings seemed to run deeper — toward af-fection, even protectiveness.

Though Strom is old enough to be a rookie's grandfather, he has kept a young man's looks, save for a few mild furrows in his forehead and some faint crow's-feet around his eyes: his hair is still thick and bristly; his eyebrows are bushy and black. Strom's complexion reddens when he is provoked or exerting himself, and he has deep-set hazel eyes, which flash in a moment's heat. In civilian life, he frequently wears aviator glasses, which soften his face, but on the court he wore contacts, and his features came at you in waves: fleshy nose, full mouth, large teeth, and, not least, magnificent lantern jaw. When he confronted an obstreperous coach or player, that jaw was a jutting edifice — a target that could never be touched. (He was punched just once in the line of duty: it happened more than twenty years ago, when Richie Guerin, then with New York, swung at an opponent and struck the referee instead.) Strom is spreading slightly about the middle, but his body remains firm and compact, down twenty pounds since he began following a low-cholesterol diet six years ago. He has thick forearms and wrists, large hands, and blunt, untapered fingers — the better to punctuate an unpopular call, something he did more flamboyantly than anyone else.

Strom is not a stylish runner (there is a slight shuffle to his gait, and his elbows flap out from his sides), but his legs, toned by years of off-duty jogging and by the five miles he covered during each game, are lean and sinewy. Over the past several years, those legs charted new ground every time he stepped on the court: no one else had refereed major league basketball for as long as Strom had — more than three thousand games, in five different decades, before he finally retired last June — and no one else had stayed active beyond his sixtieth birthday.

Strom has been called the Kareem Abdul-Jabbar of referees, but the analogy is inexact. While Abdul-Jabbar faded noticeably in the last year or so of his unparalleled career, Strom performed agelessly to the end. This past season, when he might have drawn Social Security, he worked as brilliantly as he had in the past — undaunted by nightly races with some of the fastest young athletes in the world, or by the mental strain of making a hundred instant judgment calls a game, or by an itinerary that exceeded seventy thousand miles of air travel annually. If he lost a step over the years — something that Strom denies ("I was *always* slow," he says) — he compensated with anticipation and positioning, and with an iron will to excel.

Strom's stamina is famous even by NBA standards. In June of 1985, during the fifth game of the Celtic-Laker championship finals, the temperature in Boston Garden reached 97 degrees. Abdul-Jabbar took oxygen from a portable tank and still played miserably. Strom's partner, Hugh Evans, had to be replaced in the second half. Strom, then fifty-seven years old, just chugged on, never missing a beat, his face only slightly pinker than usual. Throughout his long career, Strom missed two games, and one of those came when a granddaughter had meningitis. In 1974, after an off-season knee operation, he came back at full tilt two months earlier than his doctor had projected; in 1977, he worked through the protracted NBA playoffs with a stress fracture in his foot. To this day, his sole concession to age remains a two-hour afternoon nap.

Strom was a star official in the early sixties, the era of Sid Borgia and Mendy Rudolph, celebrity referees who ruled the fledgling NBA with arrogance, theatrics, and impeccable judgment. He was *the* star official of the 1980s, despite the recent vogue for low-profile, by-the-book types — "robots" and "clones" in the eyes of scornful old-timers. Like one of those rare silent-film actors who thrived in the talkies, Strom lasted through six supervisors, five commissioners, three professional leagues, and two generations of players: he reffed Dolph Schayes, a star forward with Syracuse in the 1950s, and Dolph's son, Danny, now with Milwaukee. In 1988, when *USA Today* polled the NBA's players and coaches to choose the league's best referee, Strom won in a landslide, with 83 votes out of 193 cast. (His supporters mostly cited his consistency and his fairness, particularly toward road teams, but one player said he voted for Strom because Strom reminded him of his grandfather.) Finishing second, with 43 votes, was Jake O'Donnell, who had risen to prominence only after Strom jumped from the NBA to the American Basketball Association in 1969. Darell Garretson, Strom's supervisor, placed a distant third.

The results surprised no one. According to a prominent team official, Strom had been perennially rated first by the NBA's coaches and general managers in their reports to the league office. For twenty-five of his last twenty-six years in the league, he worked the NBA finals — the only mark of excellence that mattered to Strom, because it not only translated into national network exposure, not to mention more money (Strom is a free spender and an extravagant tipper, and a bulldog for every check), but reflected his unique and unconditional acceptance among coaches and players — the single overriding criterion for any official's success.

"He was the only ref who was relaxed enough or confident enough or crazy enough to come over a minute before tipoff and tell you his latest dirty joke, or ask you what you were doing after the game," Ted Green, a writer for the sports daily *The National,* said recently. "Most referees approach the business with some kind of fear — a fear of losing control, a fear of not being respected, of showing you're too human, of having anyone perceive you as being biased. Earl seemed to have got beyond all those fears."

In the last phase of Strom's career, his acceptance allowed him unparalleled flexibility in handling the occasional player challenge. Two years ago, in Milwaukee, the hometown Bucks coasted into the fourth quarter with a thirteen-point lead over the Phoenix Suns. But Paul Mokeski, then the Bucks' reserve center, was aggrieved. While boxing out his man and getting ready to rebound a Phoenix shot, Mokeski had been diverted by a forearm to the head. Even though the shot went in, and there wasn't any rebound, Mokeski wanted a call for such presumption, and he didn't get one. As he lurched upcourt toward his own basket, he complained to Strom, loudly enough to be heard at the courtside press table, "You're going to have trouble down there if you don't call that."

A typical NBA referee counters such threats in one of two ways. The first is simply to ignore the protest from behind a wall of authority — to say, in effect, "Don't bother me." The second, used if a player or coach carries on too long or abusively (a standard defined by the official's threshold at that moment), is to sting him with a technical, which brings with it a $100 fine. (In extreme cases, when a player or a coach reacts to a technical with yet more verbal rage or with some other display — throwing a sports jacket on the court, for example — a second technical is called, grounds for automatic ejection and an additional, $150 fine.) There is a third course, a middle road, but it is expressly prohibited by the *National Basketball Association Official's Manual:* "No game is to be stopped while the ball is in play to warn a player or coach regarding his conduct. If any interruption is necessary then call a technical foul. Do not stop the action for a warning!"

That, however, is what Strom proceeded to do. He threw up a hand to freeze the clock, then met Mokeski at a spot near the Milwaukee foul line. "I'll start calling it, but I didn't see that one," he said.

"But it was very obvious," Mokeski insisted.

"It was obvious to you, but not obvious to me, O.K.?" Strom said, his nose nearly scraping the player's collarbone, and with a hint of menace in his voice.

The interruption of play had now stretched to fifteen seconds — an eternity in basketball — and Mokeski squirmed, and said, "Are you done?"

"No, I'm not," Strom replied. "The next time you open your mouth, I'm going to throw your ass out of here." He marched the ball out of bounds and blew his whistle to resume play. Officially, nothing had happened.

"Other guys would probably just call a technical," Mokeski said afterward. "They wouldn't talk to you or try to explain, but we get frustrated, just like the refs. At least, Earl gave me that much respect."

Earl Strom was born on December 15, 1927, in Pottstown, Pennsylvania. His parents were devout Orthodox Jews from Eastern Europe, who had settled on the south side, the "wrong" side, of the Reading Railroad tracks. His father, Max, was a foreman at Prince's Bakery, "the greatest Jewish-rye-bread baker of all time," Strom says. Earl, the last of seven children, was pampered, and encouraged in his passion for sports. He was never fleet or particularly nimble, but by the time he reached high school he was a heady player, the type who sensed game strategies ahead of his mates. In baseball, he was a smooth first baseman — "a major league glove with a ten-cent bat," a big league scout later told him. He started at center for his high school football team, which is still remembered fondly in Pottstown for defeating its archrival, Norristown, in 1944, for the first time in forty-five years, setting off a Strom-led snake dance through the streets of the town.

Basketball was a source of deep frustration for Strom when he was in high school. "I was the greatest practice player in the world," he says. "I'd be very aggressive, I'd fight and scratch, I'd make tremendous passes behind my back — I was ahead of my time with those. But, come the game, I would clam up. I wouldn't attempt the things I could do in practice. I was tentative, afraid of making errors. I never started, though I played a lot off the bench. It was a letdown. I always felt I was better than what I did, and better than what the coach thought I was, and that used to gall me."

"He hated to lose, and he had a temper when things went wrong," Hank Stofko, one of his former teammates, says. "As tough as he is as an official, that's how tough he was on officials as a player. He was always being thrown out of games."

It couldn't have helped that Strom's family was in turmoil. His father had always had a weakness for schnapps, and by the war years he had become an alcoholic, bouncing from one bakery job to another. "All four of my older brothers were gone — enlisted, two in the Marine Corps, two in the Army," Strom told me once. "I'm in the tenth grade, and here I am at home with my mother and two sisters, and we're getting calls from the police station to bring my father home. He was a happy drunk. He wasn't arrogant or abusive — he was always a nice man — but it was humiliating for me to have to go to the tavern to pick him up."

Knowing he would be drafted after graduation, Strom enlisted for an eighteen-month hitch in the Coast Guard on the last day of 1945. He was stationed in Groton, Connecticut, and there his heroics at practice landed him on the base's basketball team and exempted him from onerous duty. When the eighteen months were up, Strom went back to Pottstown and knocked around for a month or two, took business courses at a nearby junior college, and eventually landed a job in quality control at Jacobs Aircraft. Basketball remained his passion, though, and he joined a semipro team called the Erntex Knitters, which was sponsored by an underwear manufacturer. Strom had matured as a player, but he still gave the refs grief. One night in 1949, the Knitters were holding their own against a stronger team, thanks mainly to Strom, who for a change could not miss a shot. In the middle of the second quarter, he jumped into a scrum for a loose ball. The sole referee that night, a respected college official named Pete Lewis, was slow to respond. "I was digging for the ball, and it seemed to go on for *minutes*," Strom told me. "I looked for Pete, and I saw him all the way at the other end of the court, and I said, 'Yo, the game's up here. Get the hell up here!' So he not only came up but he threw me out of the ball game. In those days, the referees dressed with the players, and Pete came over to me after the game — he was an older man who wore long johns and those pinch-nosed glasses — and he said, 'You know, young man, you're never going to make it as a player, but you seem to want to be a referee. Why don't you take up refereeing?' I said, 'You know, after watching your exhibition tonight, I don't know why I shouldn't.' "

Lewis eventually became Strom's mentor, helping him crack the better high school leagues and the college circuit, but from the beginning Strom worked tirelessly on his own. "I felt I had the talent, but I knew I had to be seen," he said. Over the next five years, he officiated anywhere: in church leagues, in YMCAs, in junior high schools. He moonlighted as often as six nights a week from his job at Jacobs, traveling sixty miles or more each way to ref in Pennsylvania towns like Coatesville and Warwick. He worked industrial-league games in empty fire halls, in drained swimming pools, and in one gym where a potbellied stove stood at one end line. He took on rural high school doubleheaders for a package fee of $7.50. And he cherished every minute. "It kept me close to the game I loved, it gave me a sense of accomplishment, and we needed the little bit of money I made," he says. (Strom had married Yvonne Trollinger in 1952, and the first of five children was born to them a year later.) "Basketball refereeing came very easily to me. Pete Lewis used to tell me, 'You were born to referee.' "

If anything, the young Strom was excessively creative. When in doubt, he blew his whistle. "I would crouch down and look for things to happen. I was like a cop, and, for some reason, people liked that," he says. They liked it less when Strom made a tough call against the home team — especially in the fevered industrial-league gyms. Hank Stofko recalls, "People came out on Sundays to see the locals slaughter the opposition. There were egos on the line, and players would tackle someone and not believe they committed a foul. I don't know how many times I had to get between Earl and some guy because they were ready to punch each other." Stofko went on to coach high school ball, and when he drew Strom as a referee he came to rue his old crony's integrity. "I never got a break," Stofko says. "Earl was divorced from everybody on the floor, and he called the game the way he saw it. It became like a religion for him."

In 1956, Strom moved on to a customer-relations job with General Electric's missile-and-space-vehicle department in Philadelphia, an hour's commute from Pottstown. He also began working the college basketball circuit. His schedule, never lei-

surely, became so frenetic that his family would lose track of him
for days at a time. On a typical day, he would get to his desk by
nine. His boss would let him leave early for a two- or three-hour
trek to some outlying arena. After the game, Strom would often
drive straight back to the office and grab four hours' sleep at his
desk or in the visitors' lounge. Then he'd get up, shave, don a
clean shirt, and usher a flock of air force colonels around GE's
latest nose cone.

Officiating paid Strom as much as $85 a night, about a third of
his weekly salary, but he would probably have done it for nothing. When, in 1957, he was assigned to a St. John's–George
Washington game at the old Madison Square Garden, at Eighth
Avenue and 49th Street, he felt like a provincial tenor called to
La Scala. "I was scared to death," he said. "I got to the arena a
couple of hours ahead of time, put down my bags, and went out
and stood in the middle of the floor. I was the only guy there."

That summer, Strom received a letter from Jocko Collins, the
NBA's supervisor of officials, inviting him to attend the league's
preseason camp in October as a candidate referee. Strom leaped
at the chance, though he knew that the pros paid less than the
colleges (only $40 a game) and offered no security and scant ben-
efits. The advent, three years earlier, of the shot clock, which required a team to attempt a shot within twenty-four seconds, had
made the pro game more to Strom's taste — fast-paced, hard-
nosed, athletic. The NBA was only eight years old then and had
just eight teams and minimal television exposure; it used show
business to lure fans from the more established (and more se-
date) college game, and referees were an integral part of the show.
The archetypal vaudevillian was Matthew P. (Pat) Kennedy, an
official so popular that his name was posted on the Madison Square
Garden marquee whenever he was working there. Kennedy cut
an imposing figure on the court: he was six foot one, with slick
black hair, fair skin, and a chest that strained his zebra-striped
shirt. But he is best remembered for a Shakespearean baritone,
and for treating the most innocuous foul as a plot against God
and country. He would sprint to the scene of the crime while
whistling frantically, then whirl, point to the offender, and yell
loud enough to be heard in the farthest mezzanine, "No-no-*no-
no*-NO-NO! You-*you*-YOU-YOU! It's-no-*good-you*-STAY-HERE!" — or,

more simply, "I *caught* you *this* time!" But Kennedy was more than a burlesque act. His flamboyance veiled his competence and the fact that he had set a new standard for professional officials. (He left the NBA in 1952 to play straight man for the Harlem Globetrotters, but soon hated the charade.)

Kennedy was gone by the time Strom reached the pros, but his spirit pervaded an elite corps of eleven referees, including the choleric Sid Borgia; the patrician Mendy Rudolph; Norm Drucker, known for his soothing manner toward outraged partisans; and Arnold Heft, a.k.a. the Growler, who could outyell any coach alive. At the first officials' meeting that fall, Strom was excited but not overawed. He thought he had found his proper level, and he felt at home. He heard Collins and the rest echo his own evolving viewpoint: that a referee must weigh a rule's intent, and not merely its language, before making a call.

After watching Strom work a single exhibition game, Collins offered him a job for the season. Strom agreed, with the understanding that the league would squeeze his NBA schedule around his college and high school assignments and his day job at General Electric. (Moonlighting was then the norm among the NBA's referees, for few could support themselves on its piecework wages.) According to Strom, his transition was seamless: "Other rookie refs were blowing fouls on everything and anything, but I didn't blow myself into trouble. I was almost immediately accepted."

His former colleagues tell a different story. They say that Strom was cursed with "the college disease" during his first two years in the NBA, and was dubbed the Pied Piper for his compulsive whistling. "When Earl Strom started, he wouldn't let a mouse move," Borgia told me. "He blew more than a dozen referees."

The NBA's first commissioner, Maurice Podoloff, who, in 1946, had come to basketball from minor league hockey, knew that physical contact, and even an occasional fight or two, would hardly poison the gate. Since the pros already had the superior talent, and their twenty-four-second clock enforced a brisker rhythm, the officials' duty was to avoid fixing a product that wasn't broken. The commissioner knew that basketball is best when it's played nonstop — when one play builds to the next and a team's hot streak, or temporary confusion, creates surges of scoring. Too many fouls chop up the narrative, drain the game's kinetic energy, fence its flow.

The philosophy of the day, which was generally adhered to into the seventies, was for a referee to call as few fouls as possible while keeping the proceedings reasonably clean, safe, and free from mayhem. Dirty play was frowned upon, because it could injure a player or set off a melee, and also because it favored brute strength at the expense of artistry. Hard, aggressive play, on the other hand ("benign roughness," in one sportswriter's phrase), was to be encouraged, because it made the feats of skill — the bullet pass, the off-balance shot — all the more remarkable. "A good official lets them play to the fullest within the rules," John Nucatola, who supervised Strom in the seventies, says. "You let the players get to where it teeters right on the edge, where it's almost getting out of hand, and you *hold* them there."

The pro rules of the day were somewhat vague about defining a foul, and many top college officials foundered in their NBA tryouts. Pro officials were taught to judge events on the basis of their *relevance*, not their mere occurrence. The pro official allowed a play to develop; he momentarily delayed his call in order to decide whether the contact mattered. Even in today's more whistle-happy game, officials have a three-word motto that tells everything about a referee's ideal relationship to his whistle: "Suck to succeed."

No one has ever mastered the pro call better than Sid Borgia, the raspy-voiced, bald-headed dandy who was Strom's mentor at the start. Though Borgia was famous for his temper, he reigned with surpassing common sense. He used the rule book of the day as his guide, not as his master, and when the book fell short of clarity or elaboration — and that happened often — he gladly filled in the blanks. For all his improvisations, however, Borgia's greatest impact on the game came from the calls he didn't make. He truly believed in the motto "No harm, no foul" (although some say he pushed it to another level: "No blood, no foul"). Borgia delighted in vigorous rebounding and bruising defense, and he refused to penalize their practitioners. If the contact wasn't flagrant, he didn't see it. The book on Borgia was simple — bang first and bang often — and his games were often inspired chaos. (A generation later, Borgia's bias toward the defense was reflected in Strom's pronounced tendency to call a charge — a foul against the offensive player for initiating contact with the defender.)

Unlike his colleagues, Borgia was a full-time NBA referee, with nothing to fall back upon, yet he was widely considered the strongest of a sturdy bunch — the least likely to be intimidated by a badgering coach or a home crowd. When the natives grew restless at his seeming perversity, he shouted his next call all the louder. Once, when an enraged fan ran out of the stands and challenged his courage, Borgia summarily decked him. "A referee has to be hungry or crazy," he has said, "and I was a combination of both."

If Pat Kennedy brought style to the NBA and Borgia brought it courage, then Mendy Rudolph — Strom's other great teacher — added an element of class. Known as Mr. Hollywood by the players and fans, Rudolph was suave, debonair, always above the fray. He was indeed Hollywood handsome, and he lit up many a hotel lounge when he sat down impromptu at the house piano. But Rudolph was most elegant — and most influential — on the court, where his expressive hands and lithe body made every call an event. He knew just how good he was, and how much a strong official added to the game. He was fond of saying, "There are really twelve performers, not ten, out there." In 1972, three years before Rudolph retired and seven years before he died (at the age of fifty-three, from heart failure), Robert Vare offered this depiction of him in the *Village Voice:* "Mendy doesn't just approach the scorer's table to signal a foul. He performs a veritable pas-d'action en route, a successful if hybrid mix of minuet, mazurka, and mambo. When he hands the ball to a player at the foul line, his movement suggests a matador executing a complete arc with his cape."

Rudolph was no less courageous than Borgia. But where Borgia was apoplectic, Rudolph under siege was the image of hauteur. His colleagues admired his judgment, aped his mannerisms, and envied his on-court reserve. Strom was especially close to Rudolph, and he reveres his memory. "Mendy almost danced through a call, he did it so smoothly," he says. "I could never begin to do it the way he did."

In assessing his NBA career today, Strom acknowledges that he never needed to break new ground. He was, rather, the supreme synthesizer of an established tradition. "When I came into the league, everyone had his own idiosyncrasies, his own personality, and I didn't try to emulate any one particular guy," he says.

"I tried to fit in certain things from all of them. I picked a little bit here, a little bit there, and I developed my own style." For all his pride, he was receptive to criticism from the veterans. "I wanted to *learn* to be a good pro referee, and I came in with an open mind," he says. "I knew there was a difference from the college game. Mendy used to say to me, 'Hold up on your whistle, because you're going to see things up here you never dreamed of.' I'd see Elgin Baylor go up right at a man, and I'd *know* it was going to be a charge, but just as I was going to blow my whistle he'd twist around the guy and lay it in, and I'd think, Jesus Christ, I don't have a foul. When I called a play, no matter how right I thought I was, if Mendy came up to me — or Sid or Arnie or Normie — and said, 'That wasn't a good pro call,' I'd say, 'Fine, tell me why.' "

After his first year in the NBA, Strom knew where his future lay, and he dropped his college and high school games. He was a quick study, and by his third season, when he was assigned to the play-offs for the first time, he knew, as Drucker put it, "when to lay off and when to blow, when to let a play ride by." In his fourth year, Strom worked all five games of the championship series with Rudolph, an unprecedented distinction. Still, Strom's growing acceptance didn't mean that his job was easy. The league office (shared by Podoloff and a single secretary) was notoriously weak, and the team owners behaved like feudal lords. In St. Louis, the Hawks' front midcourt seats, known as "murderers' row," were the preserve of the team owner, Ben Kerner, and his general manager, his lawyer, his mother, and various loudmouthed members of his entourage. When Kerner was annoyed by a call, he would scream at the offending official, "You'll never work here again!" Moreover, the NBA of the 1960s was far rougher than it is today. The game was generally slower then, and the big and less mobile men had more time to get their licks in. A cheap-shot maestro like Clyde Lovellette would seize a better position for a rebound with a strategic elbow to the other man's trachea. Almost every team had a "policeman" — a hulking center or forward who would protect the star scorers.

More vicious than the owners and more violent than the players were the people the referees feared most of all: the fans. The atmosphere of an NBA arena in the sixties was somewhere between the blood lust of minor league hockey and the partisan frenzy of World Cup soccer. Though the crowds were smaller than those for baseball or football (in 1960, a typical game might draw seven thousand), they sat much closer to the action, and could target their traditional scapegoats, the officials, with both taunts and projectiles. On different occasions, Strom had to dodge eggs, oranges, an empty whiskey bottle, a dead flounder, and a man's shoe. A hurled coin took a chunk out of one of his contact lenses in Detroit; in Syracuse, a woman reached out from her front-row seat and stuck his rear end with a hatpin.

In the pre-expansion league, a given referee might work twelve games or more in the same town in one season — an arrangement that allowed fans to develop deep-seated grudges. The rooters were wildest in the more provincial cities, like Fort Wayne, Indiana, where spectators would pull the leg hairs of opposing players as they passed; St. Louis, where the typical obscenities became brutally racist after the league was integrated in 1950; and Syracuse, where a "bad" call was a civic affront, and a rare home loss was a call to arms. "The fans were on the edge of violence, and certain things just toppled them over," Drucker says.

Strom took it all in stride. "It was the nature of the job," he says. "When the home team lost, it was always the referees' fault, and you always had to fight your way off the floor." And since a uniformed escort was only an occasional courtesy at the time, the officials had to run a gauntlet to their dressing room. They coped with the assault in various ways. Some undid their belts and wrapped them around their hands, with the buckle protruding as makeshift brass knuckles. Strom refused to wear a lanyard and instead carried his whistle in his hand (a habit that stuck), the better to avoid the likes of the Syracuse Strangler, a husky thug whose ploy was to loiter above the runway to the dressing rooms, then reach down and throttle any official within arm's length. On one occasion, Strom recalls, the Strangler snared a hapless referee named Charlie Eckman — "picked him right up by his neck until Charlie's feet were dangling," he says. "He was actually hanging the fellow."

Many college officials couldn't handle such rough-and-tumble; either they "swallowed" their whistle in clutch situations or they quit after a game or two. But Strom thrived on the challenge — he had always loved to be right, no matter how many people disagreed — and showed from the start that he wouldn't be a "homer." In his very first NBA season, he made the point clear to the Brahmins of Boston Garden. It happened late in the game, when the Celtics were far ahead of Philadelphia and the great Bob Cousy was making one of his patented drives to the basket. "He takes off at the foul line and puts the ball around his back — not once but twice — and Bill Russell's man comes out to check him, so Cousy passes to Russell, who slams it home," Strom recalls. "Now the place goes crazy, until they hear my whistle. I call Cousy for walking, and the place is really going nuts — they're throwing anything that's not nailed down. So Cousy comes up to me and says, 'Hey, Earl, in the Pottstown YMCA that's walking. When I do it here, it's not walking.' So I say, 'Bob, if you don't get away from me I'm going to nail you.' He looks at me and says, 'You don't have the guts.' I call a T. He says, 'You don't have the guts to throw me out.' Now he's really testing me. And before Mendy could get to me and say no, no, *no*, I say, 'You're out of here.' Well, now it really gets bad. Throwing Cousy out of Boston Garden is like telling the pope he's got to leave Rome. Cousy's smiling, and he gets his jacket and walks out. The place goes wild. They win by twenty, and we need extra police to get us out of there. It was a hell of a debut. But you know what? I earned Cousy's respect. And I didn't mind the jeering — that's what you call recognition."

The fracases didn't always end so well. After a playoff game in Baltimore in 1962, Strom broke his thumb while slugging a spectator who had hit him in the face with a paper cup; he worked the rest of the playoffs in a hand cast that was molded to fit a basketball. A few years later, he touched off one of his most celebrated rows at a game between Philadelphia and St. Louis in Memphis, a hotbed of Hawk fans. St. Louis was down a point in the closing seconds, and the Hawks' Richie Guerin stole the ball at midcourt and raced to score what would have been the winning basket. Jerry Gross, a radio broadcaster for St. Louis at the time, remembers the scene vividly. "As Guerin drove to score off the backboard, he was one second late," he says. "Earl could have made a marvelous homer call and allowed the goal, but instead he blew the whistle and disallowed the basket, and the Hawks lost. Earl started to trot off the floor, and suddenly a Hawk executive named Irv Gack — he was a short, squat, very outspoken person — came running down the stairs and yelled, 'You stole it from us! You're nothing but a crook, and you're a lousy ref to boot!' So Earl turned around to chase the guy, and Gack turned back up the aisle, crawling up the stairs like a centipede with Earl in hot pursuit, and all the fans were chasing Earl and throwing peanuts."

It was a scenario for disaster. If Strom had had his way with Gack, he would probably have punched his way into a suspension. If the fans had got to Strom, they might have left him in pieces. Fortunately, the protocol of the day called for visiting players to aid any referee in extremis. That night, Strom's champion was none other than Wilt Chamberlain, Philadelphia's gigantic center: he hurdled the scorer's table, hoisted Strom by the back of his shirt ("He picked me up like a saltshaker," Strom said), and carried him, puppy-dog style, to the door of his dressing room. "You owe me one," Chamberlain told him.

"I was young and impetuous and I did a lot of dumb things," Strom acknowledged years later. "I was just a red-ass. I was an angry person, for what reason I don't know." Nonetheless, incidents like those confirmed Strom's reputation as the greatest "road referee" of his day — the uncommon official who would make certain that the two teams had an equal opportunity for victory. This is no small trick in professional basketball: the home teams win about two of every three games year after year, so consistently that handicappers routinely cede them up to four points a game. Travel fatigue figures in this bias, since a basketball road trip is a series of one-night stands and dawn departures, but no savvy observer underrates the impact of a raucous home crowd on the average official, especially when it comes to making a marginal call in the fourth quarter.

Between his job at General Electric and the interminable flights (from Philadelphia to St. Louis was a five-hour run in those days), Strom had little time for sleep and less for his family. His children, whom he doted on and indulged, teasingly referred to him as Uncle Daddy. They were proud of his fame but were generally embarrassed by his antics on the court. When they attended games he worked, "we'd pretend he wasn't our father, so the other people wouldn't yell at us," Susan, his second daughter, says. "Something always seemed to be happening when he was reffing." (The exception was Strom's eldest, Margie, who would root tirelessly for her father from the stands, and whose loyalty went beyond lip service, as Strom found out after he and Norm Drucker presided over a rare Celtic home loss in the playoffs. "We had to walk across this big lobby at Boston Garden to get back to our dressing room," Strom told me, "and all the people are shouting obscenities and spitting at us. All of a sudden, I hear this commotion behind me, and I turn around to see Norm bashing this guy up against the wall. I go back to break it up, when one of the guy's friends takes a swing at Norm. I catch his hand and I hit him and break his glasses, and now I'm pounding *this* guy against the wall. Then I hear my guy yelling 'Ouch, *ouch!*' and I look down, and there is my eleven-year-old daughter, Margie, in her first pair of wedge high heels, kicking the guy in the shins.")

In times of domestic crisis, Strom was usually away, and the load fell on his wife, Yvonne. She was the full-time tutor, counselor, chauffeur, and disciplinarian, and, like so many women of her generation, she accepted the arrangement, though not without occasional protest. The Stroms live in a five-bedroom colonial stone house, which was built for the family twenty-five years ago in suburban Chester County, about five miles from where Strom grew up. When his grown children (and grandchildren) pay a visit, they tend to settle in the sunny family room, where a stained-glass nature scene, crafted by Yvonne, fills the stone hearth. Strom is very proud of her work. "Yvonne is so bright — she could have been a doctor, a lawyer, anything she wanted," he says.

"At first, his refereeing was just a hobby that brought in a little extra income, and even when he began to travel more, to be away on Christmas and Easter, it didn't matter that much," Yvonne said recently. "He told me he would give it up if I really wanted him to, and I said, 'If you give it up we'll break up, because you won't be able to live with the fact that I asked you.' I got caught in the old web. I know the NBA is a male-dominated organization, but when I think of it I think of a female. You know why? Because it's always been a rival in terms of time and priority."

Strom nodded solemnly, and voiced his own regrets. "I put my career ahead of my family many times, and I paid the supreme price of not seeing my children grow up," he said. "When I look back at it, I was very unfair. I would never do it again."

By 1969, Strom, then forty-one, had reached the top of his profession. He was a special favorite of the commissioner, Walter Kennedy (who never questioned his outlandish expense vouchers), and he was paired with Rudolph for almost every crucial game. A portrait from that period, painted for a hometown dinner in Strom's honor, now hangs in the family room. It shows a man in his prime, resplendent in the referees' old-style, black-and-white zippered shirt. (Strom never approved of the switch to today's plain gray jersey, which, he used to say, "makes us look like gas-station attendants.") Holding a basketball, the subject stares straight ahead, unflinching, his mouth stretched wide in a cocky smile. His self-assurance is almost palpable. It's hard to imagine that within months that man would plummet so low as to question his purpose, and even his sanity.

At that time, the American Basketball Association, a two-year-old venture fighting to survive — and, ultimately, to force a merger with the NBA — was busy pillaging the older league's player stock in a series of celebrated bidding wars. In September of 1969, to gain further credibility, the ABA offered then unheard-of money to five senior NBA referees, Strom among them — a $25,000 signing bonus, a salary of $25,000 per year for three years, and additional guarantees for the playoffs. To Strom the decision seemed obvious. If he reenlisted with the NBA, he stood to make $16,000 that season, and little more for the playoffs; in the ABA, he would make more than $50,000. The NBA supplied no life insurance, no job security, and virtually no health plan; the ABA offered all three. Not least, Strom would finally be able to afford to quit his job at General Electric and resume some semblance of a normal family life.

After a meeting with ABA representatives at a hotel at Washington's National Airport, Strom, Norm Drucker, Joe Gushue, and John Vanak all jumped ship and signed a three-year contract. (Rudolph, the fifth referee, decided to stay with the NBA; rumor had it that he'd received a sweetheart deal.) Kennedy, who had balked at matching the ABA offer, shot off a three-page telegram to the defectors, branding them as ingrates and worse, but

Strom didn't care. He was sure that the jump would eventually improve conditions for all professional officials. "Before that, referees were necessary evils," he says. "This established our value — we had something to sell." Strom's analysis proved to be on the mark; by the time he rejoined the NBA four years later, the senior league had lifted officials' salaries above the ABA levels. (This past season, Strom made $111,000 during the regular season, with $35,000 more for the playoffs.) Nonetheless, he counts his move to the ABA as his worst professional mistake.

In its nine-year existence, the ABA enlisted some brilliant talents, such as Connie Hawkins and Rick Barry, and some big-name coaches, such as Alex Hannum and Bill Sharman. Play was wide open, if undisciplined, and was spiced by innovations like the three-point shot — later adopted by the NBA — and a red-white-and-blue striped ball. The sparkle, however, was essentially cosmetic, and the big money was never there. From the start, the team owners had planned to make a limited investment, and parlay a quick merger with the NBA into a big capital gain. But the new league's impact was diluted because of its exclusion from national television, and many of its franchises were less than stable. (By the time the merger did take place, in 1976, only six ABA teams had survived.) The upstarts played in substandard, even seamy, arenas; Strom's first ABA game was at the Dinner Key Auditorium in Miami, where the urinals overflowed and the handyman slept in the referees' dressing room. The gate was well under a thousand, and the game's highlight came at halftime, when the ball girls stripped to bikinis.

Strom called Drucker after the game that night, and Drucker recalls, "I thought I'd have to commit him to an institution. I spoke to him every single day that season — I was his psychiatrist. He didn't smile that year. You cannot imagine what he went through. His first complaint was 'There were only four hundred people at the game last night.' And my standard reply was 'Did you receive your check last week?' But Earl needed the press and the glamour. He was totally out of it, and he did a lousy job. I used to watch him work, and he wasn't the Earl Strom I knew. He wasn't blowing, he wasn't on top of the plays, and the players were saying things to him that the old Earl Strom would never have allowed."

In reviewing his ABA years, Strom called himself "a walking

nervous breakdown." On off days, he would oppress his family with such constant complaining that Yvonne finally made him see a real psychiatrist. That didn't help. At one point, Strom asked Drucker to convey to the brass his plea for an early release from the contract — he was ready to return his bonus, do anything they wanted — but the ABA was unwilling to give an inch in its struggle with the NBA. Strom was reduced to pumping his friends for the latest word on a possible merger, and, in the end, to serving out his three years. "My heart wasn't in it," he concedes. One of the few pleasant moments came at a 1971 exhibition game between the Virginia Squires and the Kentucky Colonels at which Strom noticed a skinny rookie forward with a modest reputation and a wild Afro. "I'd never seen anything like it," he says. "He'd glide through the air and dunk the ball or dribble behind his back and pass off the dribble, and he was just so fluid. The next day, I ran into a reporter in Philadelphia and told him that Julius Erving was the greatest basketball player I'd ever seen in my life." The ABA commissioner, Jack Dolph, fined Strom a token $50 for voicing an inappropriate opinion, and Strom sent Dolph a check for $100, with a note saying, "Here's an extra fifty, because I'm telling you also that he's the greatest player I've ever seen."

Toward the end of 1971–72 season, Strom began negotiating his reentry into the NBA — a reconciliation strongly pushed by most of the senior league's general managers. Walter Kennedy embraced the prodigal at a meeting and made an oral promise that Strom could come back to work the next fall. But through the spring and summer the league office stalled on a contract. Then Strom heard the bad news from Rudolph: his return was opposed by several second-tier officials who had succeeded to the top spots when Strom and the others had left, and who claimed that Strom's overpowering style would hurt the morale of the corps. Kennedy took the bait, and the word came down: there would be no contract that season.

Strom retained an aggressive Philadelphia lawyer named Richie Phillips, who filed a breach-of-contract suit against the league, and to support his family Strom took a job as a travel agent and later opened a bar in Pottstown, where he would regale the locals with tales of high life in the NBA. At the same time, to keep his hand in, he worked weekend games for the minor Eastern League.

In the summer of 1973, after a year of legal fencing, the NBA finally reinstated Strom, in return for his dropping the suit. But relations between the league and its prodigal referee were never quite the same again. The NBA had been a relatively close, if contentious, family; now it was a growing corporate enterprise, with seventeen teams and a media machine that hyped basketball as "the sport of the seventies." Most of the Borgia-era referees had been replaced by people whom Strom could not trust. His new supervisor, Nucatola, who had come to the NBA after a similar job with the Eastern Collegiate Athletic Conference, found the old ways unseemly. He forbade fraternization between referees and coaches or players at bars or hotels, and discouraged his officials from screaming at anyone during a game. Strom usually followed the first rule (he was fined at least twice, though, for allowing team personnel in his dressing room), and usually ignored the second. His competence, as always, was beyond question. But with his maverick attitude and volatile behavior he became an increasing embarrassment to the league office. So he set off a string of incidents that made him more vulnerable to his enemies than ever. In Seattle in 1975, during the closing minutes of a close game between the hometown Supersonics and the Houston Rockets, a young woman stood behind one basket and yelled curses at Strom. After the game ended — the Supersonics won, despite a controversial "roader" call by Strom — he walked toward the bench to retrieve his jacket and felt someone grab his shoulder from behind. "When they put their hands on me, I react," Strom explained later. "I swung around, and I caught this woman flush in the face with my elbow and drove her into the crowd. I felt bad that it was a girl, but I didn't know who it was." The woman was a friend of a Supersonic named Archie Clark, and another Seattle player, Fred Brown, rushed to her defense and pushed Strom into the crowd. Bill Russell, then the Seattle coach, dispersed the mob and saved Strom from a possible beating, but on the way to the officials' dressing room Strom got a faceful of beer from a fan two rows up. "I went crazy," he said. "I tried to climb the railing, but the guards grabbed him and put cuffs on him. I think I would have killed that guy if I'd got hold of him — that's how angry I was."

The altercation received wide coverage, and played poorly for

a league office striving for sophistication. Kennedy's first incli-
nation was to suspend Strom for the rest of the season, if not for
life. After Strom suggested that he might take legal action, the
commissioner reduced the penalty to a $600 fine. But Strom, who
felt he had acted in self-defense, wasn't mollified, and his indig-
nation grew when he discovered that Fred Brown had been fined
only $100. After the National Association of Basketball Referees
failed to intercede effectively either with Kennedy or, the following fall, with his successor, Lawrence O'Brien, Strom bulldogged
his way to a private hearing with O'Brien. Three weeks later, the
league rescinded his fine, and Strom resigned from the association, telling Darell Garretson (then its president), "You guys never
backed me, and some of you didn't want me back. What I accomplished I accomplished on my own, and I don't need a union."

By 1977, the rift between Strom and his colleagues had widened. The NABR, egged on by its new attorney, Richie Phillips,
was determined to become a full-fledged union and get a three-
year contract. When the league balked, the referees voted to strike,
beginning with the last game of the regular season and continuing into the playoffs. Strom was never a union man ("I always felt you should get paid for what you did and how well
you did it," he says), and he still resented Phillips for charging
what he considered an outrageous fee when they had sued the
NBA. He felt a closer allegiance to O'Brien than to the NABR's
ruling clique, which included Garretson and Jake O'Donnell. He
finally decided to work during the strike, which was settled a few
weeks later; he and Richie Powers were the only refs to break
ranks.

"I can't truly say I was happy with myself when I saw some of
my friends on a picket line and I was crossing to work," Strom
said recently. "I never liked the idea of being called a scab — I
just hate that word. I didn't want to be a strikebreaker. But I didn't
appreciate that Richie Phillips was pulling the strings and everyone was jumping to his tune." When the strikers returned to work,
Strom was unrepentant; he baited them by boasting about how
much extra playoff money he had earned in their absence.

Some of Strom's friends in the business understood. "It upset
me at the time," says Gushue, a longtime union carpenter who
had rejoined Strom in the NBA, "but Earl was absolutely his own

man and no one dictated to him about anything." For Phillips
and Garretson, however, it was a betrayal they could not forget.
Their chance for revenge came after a game between the Celtics
and the Denver Nuggets in Boston Garden on November 28, 1979.

Strom worked the game with Richard Bavetta, a younger referee, whom he had tutored and befriended before the strike. At
halftime, Strom criticized some of his partner's foul calls during
the first half. Bavetta later charged that in an ensuing argument
Strom grabbed him and tried to strangle him — a story supported by red marks on Bavetta's neck when he returned for the
second half. Strom maintained that he had merely grabbed Bavetta's jacket after his partner spewed obscenities at him, and
guessed that Bavetta had manufactured the marks by rubbing a
towel across his neck. O'Brien fined Strom $2,500. More than a
year later, Strom repeated his side of the story in an interview in
Referee magazine, and the NABR responded with a telegram drive
(joined by everyone except Vanak, Ed Middleton, and Gushue,
who by this time was retired) in which the referees asked that
O'Brien not assign them to work with Strom in the coming playoffs.

At about the same time, Bavetta filed a formal grievance against
Strom, alleging that the latter had tried to destroy his "effectiveness as a referee," and had caused him and his family "severe
emotional strain." After a hearing that September, the NABR's
executive board placed Strom on probation for three years, bar-
ring him from union meetings. Once again, Strom sued, and this
time he won outright: a federal-district-court judge nullified the
probation, noting that Phillips and the union had failed to supply Strom with a specific written charge before the hearing. The
decision was upheld on appeal in 1984, and the matter was finally dropped.

While Strom's adversaries couldn't bury him, they certainly
damaged his equilibrium. After Garretson succeeded Drucker as
Strom's boss in 1981, Strom was fined repeatedly for minor vio-
lations. He was more thin-skinned than ever, more apt to pro-
voke a player into a technical or to make a bizarre call against a
vocal home crowd. It reached the point, Bob Ryan, a sports columnist for the *Boston Globe,* has said, where Strom's appearance
came to be dreaded through much of the league: "He had a

growing reputation of being highly arbitrary and cantankerous. He was too determined to show who was in charge — the Judge Roy Bean approach — and he had taken it too far."

One of the great virtues of longevity is that you can outlast your enemies' anger, and even your own. As Strom approached his sixtieth birthday, he evolved from an aging bad boy into a hallowed, if eccentric, institution, and tempers and jealousies abated. Phillips left the NABR in 1983 and was replaced by Richard Markowitz, Strom's personal attorney. (Strom finally joined the union when it became a closed shop, and actually walked a picket line during a brief strike shortly after Phillips's departure.) Garretson seemed to realize that Strom wasn't after his job as supervisor, and the two even learned to tolerate each other. Rod Thorn, the new vice president for operations, came to appreciate the nonconformist's value; as the Gushues and Vanaks retired, and the younger veterans failed to approach the same level of public acceptance, Strom became particularly prized for the authority he brought to big games. As Nucatola noted, "Earl has so many pluses that you could forgive an occasional minus."

No longer under siege, Strom undeniably mellowed. He says that the transformation was sealed in 1987, when two of his brothers died within a month. "That shook me into reality," he told me. "I finally realized that my job is just a means to an end, and I don't want to worry about it. I'm going to worry about my wife and my family, and I'm going to enjoy my life."

Others took notice of the change. Three decades after being ejected in Strom's debut, Cousy, now a Celtic television broadcaster, said, "Earl maintains his sense of perspective about the whole thing. He knows what he does is extremely meaningful to the people involved — the players and coaches and general managers — and yet it's not the end of the world. It's still a child's game."

Strom had nothing to prove anymore, no wars to wage. In his last seasons, he called fewer technical fouls (only ten or twelve a year, by his estimate), preferring to douse an offender's ire with a stern avuncular warning. He no longer stole a partner's calls from afar, as he once had, although he would occasionally expropriate a tough one to spare a junior colleague from excessive pressure.

"He's a throwback, but he's right in line with what's going on today," Ronnie Nunn, a younger referee, said after working a game with Strom in Houston in 1988. "He's a griot, like in Alex Haley — the wise man who had the information. He can tell you something that no one else can. I always feel secure when I work with him because he allows you to grow. You can make some mistakes, and yet the game is very much in check because of his presence."

It might seem logical that Strom should pass along his wisdom to the next generation, including eighteen rookie NBA officials — more than a third of the total staff — who were hired two seasons ago, when the league shifted from two-man to three-man game crews. But after the NBA's coaches and general managers recommended that Strom be used as an instructor, the administration vetoed their proposal. At a staff meeting three years ago, according to Strom, Garretson told the assembly, "Let me explain about Earl. He's a very competent official, and his ratings are very high, but he has a unique way of handling a game — and it's so unique that I can't teach it." Nor, went the not so subtle implication, could Strom. "I have the highest regard for him," Garretson told me before declining a longer interview. "Unfortunately, we can't use him with our youngest officials, who could learn so much from him. It's a shame, but we can't use him, because he's such a renegade type. Earl thrives on controversy, and we're trying so hard to go the other way, to avoid controversy — or, at least, keep it to a loud roar."

Rod Thorn says, "I don't think Earl can impart what he does, because so much of it is instinct and feel and innate judgment. It's like Mickey Mantle hitting baseballs from both sides of the plate — how do you impart that?"

"They say you can't teach judgment, but I don't believe that, because judgment is nothing more than philosophy," Strom has said. "Garretson likes to say there's no such thing as a pro philosophy, and that's a bunch of bull. If you teach a guy when to blow the whistle, and what's important and what isn't, that dictates your judgment. That's how I learned — Mendy and Sid taught me their philosophy, and I'm no Phi Beta Kappa."

Strom's teaching ability aside, the real dispute is over the content of his curriculum. "In the old days," Thorn told me, "referees called all over the floor and did virtually whatever they wanted to do — they were stars." Now, he said, it's different: "I don't want star referees. I don't know what star referees do." The league is so allergic to publicity for its officials that it allowed Strom to talk to me only on the condition that the story be published after his retirement; it also blocked Strom from publishing his autobiography until after he had left the game. (Simon and Schuster will bring it out later this fall.)

For Thorn the magic word is "uniformity." "We like to have as much uniformity as possible in our signaling mechanics, so people know what to expect from night to night," he said, and he added, "The players are the game, not the referees. The officials are there as policemen, to enforce the rules of the game. They're not there to inject their personalities into the game." (According to the NBA *Official's Manual*, "authorized NBA signals . . . are dignified and understandable," and "officials using unauthorized signals . . . do a disservice to themselves and to the game.")

Strom's signals were like the man himself: blunt, pugnacious, confident, and original. Calling a foul on a drive to the basket (always a dramatic moment, since the fouled player now has a chance at a three-point play), he would shoot his right arm straight up (with the second and third fingers pointing skyward), blow his whistle (*beep*), then lower his arm and clap his open right hand to his left forearm (to simulate the contact), with the left fist in the air. Then he would shift his weight with a small hop step, lower his left arm, and sweep it forward and upward in an arc of about 270 degrees. (That was known as "the wheel.") At the end of the sweep, he would jerk his left wrist, again with two fingers extended, as if he'd touched a steam iron, to signify "and one": a foul shot, in basketball parlance. This finale was punctuated by Strom's trademark: a second, double blast (*beep-beep*) — an eccentricity he adopted from Rudolph many years ago and one that was savored by modern players. ("That little extra tweet in the whistle gets everyone excited," the Mavericks' Lafayette Lever said recently.)

At his best, Strom would absorb the energy of the past play, then feed it back to the crowd. When he signaled a push, he looked as though he were forcing open a rusty barn door. If a player stepped out of bounds, Strom would kneel and point at the spot, his head bowed, and hold the pose for an extra beat. To disallow a score for goaltending, he would charge toward the opposite basket, his arms flapping outward like the wings of a swan protecting the brood. His signals for traveling were especially colorful, and often mimicked the offender. Once, after the oafish Pat Cummings (then with the Knicks) nearly fell down while mishandling the ball, Strom began with the standard call (a rapid rotation of the forearms around each other), then slowed his hands, tilted his torso, and took five stumbling steps, his face dragging with a drunk's confusion. At other times, he would frown or shrug while making a call, as if to regret canceling a good play. On a technical foul, he was all majesty and defiance as he built a *T* with his arms, the thrust of his windup leading to a left-footed hop. Strom's gesticulations provided nuance and spectacle, and something more: the ability to "sell" a tough call to a restive home crowd.

In recent years, Strom became a hard man to set off; he was no longer a red-ass. At a game at Madison Square Garden last February between the division-leading New York Knicks and the lowly Miami Heat, the visitors kept it close into the fourth quarter, thanks both to a sluggish effort by the Knicks and to Strom's passionate neutrality. Just behind the scorer's table, in the choice seats reserved for guests of the team, a beefy man of about forty loudly scorned Strom's calls; as the score grew tighter, he was echoed by a stylishly dressed woman down the row. During a time-out, while standing by the scorer, Strom called over to the woman, "I don't mind him getting on me, because he's an idiot, but *you* I mind." The banter contained none of the heat or malice that Strom might have projected ten years before. (He even made up with the man toward the end of the game, to make sure no feelings had been hurt.)

In this period, Strom's most serious deviation, in the eyes of his bosses, was his allegiance to the old-school philosophy of letting the players play — his conviction that "some of the best calls are the ones you don't make," and that contact was "not a bad thing" unless it was flagrant. "A lot of times two guys get to the same spot at the same time — it's a tie," Strom says. "So if nothing happens, why call anything?" Strom likes to say that he could gauge the "tempo" of a game — the level of roughness and how players and coaches are reacting to it — within five minutes and adjust his whistle accordingly. "I always had the self-confidence that I could grab the game and stop the nonsense at any time, and get them back to the point where I could let them play," he told me. "I felt I had complete control, so I didn't have to worry about whether somebody was going to get hurt. But Garretson wanted the teams to know who's boss, and for officials to blow-blow-blow so this stuff couldn't happen. He wanted you to stay tight."

Thorn freely acknowledged Strom's "terrific judgment," but claimed that the average referee would founder with so much latitude, and that fewer whistles could lead to the league's worst nightmare — a fight-related injury. "The commissioner's feeling is that we are programming and packaging a very talented group of athletes performing at a high level, and that we don't want the contact to get out of control," Thorn has said. "In the old days, when I played, there was a fight almost every night, but the players weren't as big. Now you have huge, quick people in small arenas. Basketball players do not wear shoulder pads, they're not on skates, they don't have helmets on, so fights in our game are much more serious. Over all, I would say the game is being called a little more closely than it was ten or fifteen years ago."

The question remains, however, whether play-it-safe officials will shrink the game's action until they bottle its flow. It's one thing for a Garretson or an O'Donnell to call a conservative but reliable game. It's another for a rookie to blindly follow the *Manual*'s dictum: "Look for the play that *must* be called." The irony is that as a referee makes more calls for less contact he is more likely to miss a few, and the resulting frustration has led many a player to land a cheap shot. And if a player knows he will be called for even minor contact, he may hit harder — to make certain that his opponent will miss, and perhaps to make the shooter hesitate the next time.

"The young referees are overreacting," Strom said after a recent game. "They're calling things they shouldn't be looking at to begin with. If you're forty feet away from a play and I'm two feet away, no one's going to yell at me if I let it go, so why would you call it from out there? You're cutting down your percentages. And once you're stamped as a bad referee it's hard to live that down."

At bottom, the question of philosophy is also one of competence. The issue is discussed in muted tones and mostly in private, since the league shields itself from public attack on its officials with the threat of five-figure fines. Nonetheless, there is a widespread conviction among insiders that too many referees are mediocre, or worse. Even Thorn concedes that most league officials "are not great, great referees." Bob Ryan considers at least one of three officials to be "N.C. guys" — referees who have No Clue. "There are so many of them in this league that it is frightening," he says. "They haven't kept pace with the changing physical reality of the game, which is that these players are bigger and stronger and faster and they're still confined by a court of ninety-four by fifty feet. You just can't call every bump and touch at this level."

The problem is not limited to the new crop of novices. Many veteran officials "make calls that don't get them in trouble," Drucker says. "They always move to the middle stream, they never take a chance, they worry about what people will say. They don't make the tough calls, the unhappy calls."

Strom lays the responsibility for this safety-first syndrome at Garretson's door. He grants that his ex-supervisor is "a solid senior referee" and "a compulsive worker" who has greatly clarified the *Manual* and the NBA's rule book. But he also contends that Garretson recruits too many incoming officials by college reputation rather than by judgment or professional aptitude, and that he fails to give them the tools they need to improve. "I was taught how to handle an irate coach, how to handle certain players, how you handle fights, and this isn't taught today to young referees," he says. "You don't give crowds a chance to boo and scream. If you make a controversial call against the home team, you take the ball and get it in play right away, or you give it to the shooter at the foul line and say 'Shoot it.' Sid and Mendy used to say that fans aren't going to keep booing when there's a play in progress, because they're going to be intent on watching it. It's common sense, so why can't you teach it?"

In Strom's view, the uniformity campaign is a doomed effort to mask deficiencies — to keep inexperienced and less able referees from standing out. He views with similar disdain the league's 1988 move from two- to three-man officiating crews, which Thorn and Garretson have endorsed as both an infusion of youth and a check on off-the-ball (or "weak side") player contact. In fact, according to Strom, the expanded officiating corps is poorer than ever, since it contains a higher percentage of inadequately trained refs with no feel for the pro call. (Of twenty-four referees added over the last two years, seventeen were chosen from the college ranks, compared with only seven from the minor league Continental Basketball Association, which the NBA subsidizes to develop pro officials.) "They're calling off-the-ball contact more, but they're not necessarily calling it right. I never thought it was a problem in the first place," Strom says. Because of inevitable inconsistencies between by-the-book, college-trained refs and NBA veterans on the same crew, he adds, "coaches get upset, players get upset." At the same time, he acknowledges that the three-man system could prolong the careers of officials whose legs are less bionic than his own.

Unlike baseball, a game of measured pauses, or football, where aggression is a ritual constant, a basketball game streams as unpredictably as Magic Johnson in a three-on-one fast break. Its emotion is wholly of the moment; the physical byplay between two players has little to do with reputation or past grudges and much to do with who pushed whom for the last rebound. The old school of NBA referees rode the flow; they might try to channel or contain it, but they would never ignore it. To Strom and his forebears, a personal style was more than good show business. It was a sort of vantage point, a way to keep track of the game by responding to it directly, with honest emotion. They saw the game from the inside out. "Regardless of what they said about 'No harm, no foul,' we didn't have *half* the problems they're having now," says Borgia, who is still proud and cocksure. "We could *smell* trouble, and we knew when it was going to come. But you have to be a part of the game, and you don't see that anymore."

On an off day toward the end of Strom's officiating career, he and Yvonne took their big Mercedes for an afternoon tour of the deserted streets of downtown Pottstown, where the mills have closed and only the banks are thriving. Yvonne pointed to a bay window above the Woolworth's on High Street, the site of their family's first apartment, and said, "It was a nice town —"

"It *is* a nice town," Strom broke in.

"— that's since gone."

Strom's thatch of hair was slightly disheveled, and he wore his standard leisure uniform: navy blazer, gray Ban-Lon golf shirt, black Italian boots. The trees were still bare on the surrounding brown hills and dairy farms of Chester County, and the landscape was unremarkable, but the sun was out, and Strom seemed to thrive on the familiarity of it all. He is deeply rooted here. The citizens of Pottstown always stood by him, even in his renegade years, and Strom returns their loyalty. He helps out at charity golf tournaments and speaks to local youth groups without a fee. His recent prosperity hasn't changed his tastes: he still plays at the Twin Ponds Golf Club with early retirees from Bethlehem Steel and still haunts the Sunset Pharmacy diner, where patrons drop by his table with stories of their latest grandchild or ailment or business deal.

Strom has never itched to move from Pottstown, but he and Yvonne have been pining of late for a wintertime condominium, a place where they can tee up in February. He's getting off the court with both his health and some money — doing better than Rudolph, who died in his prime and has yet to be anointed by the sport's Hall of Fame, and than Borgia, who gets no NBA pension and needs to replace an arthritic knee. Strom recently audited a communications course at Temple University, and he talks about a second career in sports broadcasting, or about acting as the league's overseas ambassador, for Europe has become a source of both NBA players and lucrative exhibition matches. He surely won't sit lonely and idle, and yet, as his final game approached last June, his friends and professional admirers — including more than a few team owners and general managers — tried to coax him into staying on. "Earl's still very sharp, he's quick, he reacts, he does all the things good referees do," Drucker said before Strom's decision became final. "I told him to referee until he's sixty-five. I don't think he'll quit. I know Earl — he has to be in the limelight." Strom held firm, though not without some moist-eyed nostalgia. At the NBA's All-Star spectacle in Miami last February (the sixth such game that Strom worked), he allowed himself to lapse for a moment into the pure fan's enjoyment he had always kept leashed while he was on the job. "For the first time in thirty-two years of refereeing, I found myself stepping back and watching these guys perform," he told me.

Toward the very end of his career, Strom came to represent a vanishing and coveted resource. In his presence, coaches and players could relax, knowing that they could focus on their own performance without worrying about the calls. Strom still had his weird moments, as when he ejected a vocal fan in Seattle who he thought was a reporter. He still enjoyed making an occasional offbeat call, just to remind people who was in charge, but he became less blatant about it. "Generally, he'd find a way to even things up," Ryan says. "No one knows how to make a game come out right as well as Earl."

As the players grew younger than his sons, Strom took to treating them as colleagues in an allied craft, whether they were journeymen or all-stars. He no longer flaunted his authority. When he picked at them during the fray ("Did you mean to miss that lay-up? Well, I didn't mean to miss that call"), it was the reproach of a harried workman, not of a distant potentate. After a player retired and league protocol was out of the way, a friendship often blossomed; Strom and Julius Erving are now staunch golf and charity buddies. (At Erving's last game, in 1987, Strom ignored a telephoned death threat in order to finish the contest and present Erving with the game ball.)

Last August, the depth and breadth of those relationships were in evidence at a celebrity benefit in Pottstown in Strom's honor. The guest list read like an NBA honor roll from the two-hand-set-shot era to the present: Dolph Schayes and Red Auerbach, Bob Cousy and Oscar Robertson, Connie Hawkins and Erving and Larry Bird. The reclusive Bill Russell flew in on a corporate jet. And Magic Johnson paid $2,000 at a charity auction that night for the satin playoff jacket Strom had worn during his final NBA game — a June 12 championship-round tilt at the Portland Memorial Coliseum between the underdog Trail Blazers and the defending champion Detroit Pistons.

Fittingly, a story came along with the jacket. The Pistons, already up two games to one in the best-of-seven series, had led by sixteen points late in the third quarter before Portland mounted a last-ditch rally. The Trail Blazer fans, frustrated since the Bill Walton glory days of the mid-seventies, were roaring nonstop. With little more than a second to play and his team still down by three, Portland guard Danny Young tore down the right side of the court and, just as the final horn sounded, put up a lunging shot from well behind the three-point line. The shot went in and the fans erupted, presuming that the ball had left Young's hand before the game clock struck zero — that he had tied the score, thrown the game into overtime, and handed the Blazers a chance to scramble back into the series.

But *was* the shot good? The referee closest to the ball — the one responsible for the call, according to Garretson's three-man zone rotations — simply froze on the floor. Strom, meanwhile, was still hustling upcourt from the opposite end line. Nevertheless, he drew his associates into a huddle and shortly emerged with an emphatic decision, the last call of his career: time had expired; the shot was no good. The Pistons had won the game, and two nights later they took the championship.

"A crucial call had to be made, and damn the crowd," Strom told me several days later. "There was no question in my mind — I had that call all the way. There was no way I was going to allow it to count." In the wake of this classic "roader" decision, the Coliseum din turned angry and ominous, but Strom floated through it on the way to his locker room. "I heard some abuse aimed at the other officials," he said. "But no one said anything to me."

October 1, 1990

PAUL PEKIN

A Fling and a Prayer

FROM THE CHICAGO READER

THE WEATHER must cool before salmon leave Lake Michigan to die. In the lingering warmth of late September they lie in wait off Ludington State Park, and fishermen in chest-high waders have to walk out to meet them. Here's a scene you might see along the Atlantic coast when the bluefish are running: the long, graceful rods, the two-handed casts into the surf, the slow walk back to dry sand where the rod is set into a holder to wait, arched, taut, for a strike hundreds of feet away. This is sport. But then the weather breaks and the fish crowd into the Sable River; what happens now is beyond sport and must be experienced to be appreciated.

The Sable River flows through northwestern Michigan, barely visible on the map. It ends once in man-made Lake Hamlin, roughly eight miles north of Ludington proper, and starts up again after the dam on the lake's western border, flowing one final mile through the state park and into Lake Michigan. It's a clean little stream, not especially impressive; the real beauty of the area is in the magnificent dunes and the miles of dazzling sand beach. The sand is everywhere; it drifts, it blows, it creeps, it sneaks into your hair and between your teeth. No visitor to western Michigan departs without a sample of it.

A visitor to Ludington encounters his first salmon in this sand, washed up and drying on the beach, eyes plucked by gulls. The salmon is an impressive thing, long as your leg, just as thick, leather-skinned, hook-jawed, wickedly toothed. You don't have to be told. This is a creature that properly belongs to the sea.

In Michigan the native fish are bass, pike, sunfish, perch, catfish, bowfin, suckers, the rare speckled trout, the even rarer grayling. This salmon is a newcomer, an immigrant. So is its principal forage, the alewife, which arrived with the St. Lawrence Seaway, as did the lamprey eel, a blood-sucking parasite that nearly ended Lake Michigan as a fishing resource. Thanks to the lamprey, there was a time when people spoke of Lake Michigan as a "biological desert," and indeed it was, occupied mainly by tons and tons of inedible alewives that inconveniently died every spring along every beach. If you came to Ludington to fish in those days, it was to fish not in the great lake but in Lake Hamlin. You fished from small boats, you brought your minnow pail, your worm can, your plastic bobber. On lazy summer nights you pulled out bullheads, drank beer, and felt good. People still do it, but not when the salmon arrive.

What distinguishes the Pacific salmon from other Michigan fish is not so much its origins as the cycle of its life and death. In their native Northwest, salmon hatch in the highest reaches of sea-flowing streams where the water is cold, swift, and shallow. As smolts they work their way to the sea; as adults they return once, to spawn, then die. No salmon may live beyond its allotted time. And every salmon must die in the required place. However far they may swim, wherever the water may take them, they must return to the place where first they saw light. Block the stream of the ancestors, you destroy an entire strain of fishes. They will swarm hopelessly; they will uselessly discharge their eggs into silt.

The salmon live no differently in their new midwestern home. Abducted and transported half a continent from the streams and seas of their ancestors, they cannot become other than what they are. It would have been impossible to transplant the adults. What men did instead was take the seed. A new generation, beginning its life in hatchery tanks, has no memories of the ancestral streams. It is a blank page waiting for the word. Released into a new stream, the young salmon accept this place as their home. No matter how unlikely or inappropriate, they will return to it when the cycle ends.

Sportfishing for salmon is not for the poor or uncommitted. Except for spring and fall these fishes run far and deep. It takes big boats to follow them, special gear to reach into their depths.

Charter captains, tracking them with sonar, use trolling rigs
weighted with sinkers the size of cannonballs. They guarantee
their customers fish. No fish, no pay — that's the slogan. The
customers pay two, three, four hundred dollars an outing, split
among a party seldom larger than six.

On a clear blue day in Ludington, boats, chartered and private, file out past the breakwater at dawn, bristling with tackle.
At dusk they are back, circled by gulls. The talk in the restau-
rants and bars is of salmon; you hear it in the next booth, fish
that stripped the line, broke the tackle, secret spots that yielded
up the limit. Salmon have made a new industry on the Michigan
coast.

All summer the salmon belong to the boat people. On shore
the boatless ones crowd the breakwater, cast till arms grow weary,
and eventually surrender their lures to the rocks. From time to
time a whoop goes up, a fish is taken, hope never dies entire. But
the salmon are at sea, a strange and saltless sea their ancestors
never knew, and they are awaiting destiny.

The chinook salmon, also called the king salmon, and its smaller
cousin the coho remain the principal species stocked in the Great
Lakes, although now we also have Atlantic salmon, steelhead trout,
brown trout, and something called a splake, which is a hybrid put
together by the fishery people. The fishery people are constantly
coming up with something new.

The life cycle of the chinook salmon is four years. At full growth
it truly is a king. The record for Michigan is forty-six pounds.
Twenty pounders are common. Thirty pounders are not rare.
For a freshwater fisherman, the sight of such fish is intoxicating,
even unnerving. Coho salmon run smaller, only five, six pounds,
seldom over ten. It takes a little while before one gets to thinking
of such fish as small. It takes a while before one gets to saying,
"It's only a coho." When the snagging starts, it takes, oh, maybe
fifteen minutes.

The first fish enter the river in mid-September. They are very
tentative about it, easily spooked in the clear, shallow water. Even
though snagging season officially opens September 10, it pays to
wait for bad weather. You must understand that the entire class
is schooling up off shore, waiting. They must enter this stream
or die unfulfilled.

Alas, they will die unfulfilled anyway. Few of the salmon stocked
in the Great Lakes successfully propagate their kind. The conditions are almost never right, even in the best of streams. This is
certainly true in the Sable River. At the point where it empties
into Lake Michigan it is a clean but brownish stream that actually
narrows at its sandy mouth. Because this is park land, the river
seems unspoiled, almost natural; you imagine it a thousand years
ago, exactly the same, eternally flowing its forest-stained waters
into the great blue lake. But, of course, one mile upstream there
is that dam. And the dam is what stops the salmon. It is in this
little stretch of river, in most places so narrow a fisherman almost
casts to the opposite bank, that they will meet their end.

As the salmon gather, so do the salmon snaggers. It must be
pointed out that while numerous streams flow to the lake's eastern shore, and salmon run into almost every one, in only a few
designated places are people permitted to snag them. There is
something about the act of snagging that raises the hackles of
high-minded sportsmen. It just doesn't fit with the *Field & Stream*
image of the civilized easterner dropping a carefully chosen royal
coachman at the head of a quiet pool. You might as well, as one
fellow put it, shoot them with guns. Your average salmon snagger might find this a good idea too, if he thought it would work.

The people who come to snag salmon arrive in pickup trucks,
campers, and well-used American passenger sedans. They quickly
fill the campgrounds at Ludington State Park, setting up their
tents and trailers, looking up friends from last year, praying for
bad weather. The out-of-staters come from Pennsylvania, West
Virginia, Indiana, Tennessee, Kentucky, and southern Ohio,
among other places; they speak in down-home accents, play
country music on their radios, and know how to catch fish.

The salmon snaggers are outdoor people. They do not mind a
little rain on their campsites. They would not mind waking to a
thin cover of snow. A gale out of the west, one that sends waves
thundering up on the beaches — that would be best of all. Meanwhile, as the good weather persists, the lovely late midwestern
summer, tourists drive out to the park to watch the sunset and
stand on the bridge over the Sable River, looking down for salmon.
These tourists stay in town, in motels within walking distance of
Lake Michigan. They are couples of an age beyond childbearing,

well dressed, well wheeled. They drive Cadillacs, Lincolns, Chrysler New Yorkers, car-wash clean with Illinois plates. Occasionally a salmon of twenty pounds or so will glide beneath the bridge and these men, elbows on the rail, softly chatting with their wives, will get a certain look and you know the tackle shops will have a new customer come morning.

The tackle for salmon snagging is specific, ugly, and strong. Jack Ferwerda, who owns a resort and bait shop outside the park, will sell you an eight-foot rod of solid fiberglass so tough you could whip a man to death with it. Line? Forty-pound test, too light; fifty-pound test, a little better; sixty-pound, still not too strong. There is no such thing, Ferwerda says, as a line too strong.

Ferwerda also sells the snagging hooks, bullet-shaped lead projectiles with naked treble hooks on both ends. You hold one of these in your hand, you shudder to think what might happen to an innocent bystander stepping into its path.

The successful salmon snaggers know precisely what to carry. Their rods are even longer and heavier than Ferwerda's. Their lines absolutely sixty-pound test or better. They know the right knots that will not slip loose. They carry boxes, heavy boxes, of extra snagging hooks. They are prepared to lose a hundred to the rocks and keep on snagging. They own waders, the kind that pull tight beneath your armpits and fasten with shoulder straps. Most impressive of all are the landing nets the snaggers carry. These are nets that could easily scoop up a full-size dog, any breed up to a German shepherd, and maybe that too. It's almost comical to see a fisherman so confident. Almost, but not after the weather breaks.

Fortunately this gathering army of snaggers is never turned loose en masse on the little Sable River. Mayhem would surely result; at least, that seems to be the view of the Michigan Department of Natural Resources. The first time I visited Ludington they operated a lottery at the field house in the state park. The rules of the lottery were simple, and stern. If you were not seriously interested in salmon snagging, they would soon have had you discouraged. You had to be there at six. No, you could not enter the day before; no, you could not enter by mail. You had to arrive in the dead of night and face the company of several hundred people who by life habit rise early, eat hearty breakfasts, and work hard every day. Four shifts were chosen, two hundred persons each shift, each shift good for two hours of snagging, one shift per person per day. On the stage at the field house were four bins, appropriately marked. You chose one, dropped your name in, and waited for the drawing. The first shift, hitting the river at dawn, was every snagger's first choice, and shift four, which reached the river in midafternoon, was a bit of a joke — good enough for a tourist from Chicago, but not to be seriously considered by a man who had driven all the way from West Virginia. If you went for shift number one and failed, your name automatically moved to the bin for shift number two. Fail again, try for number three. The same for number four. At the height of the run, you could very well be out of bed in the middle of the night and still never reach the river.

Snagging is a blindman's buff kind of game. The technique is to cast into or beyond a likely spot, allow the rig to settle, and then yank it back as hard as you can. Maybe a fish will be swimming by. Maybe your blind jerk will snag it. It seems a shame that one must use such primitive methods, but the plain and simple fact is that salmon embarked on their spawning runs no longer care to engage in such activities as eating. It seems every newcomer must find this out for himself. In Ludington a second and larger river, the Pere Marquette, has its own salmon run, where no snagging is allowed. Morning and evening the banks fill with fishermen, the air fills with flying lures, hidden logs at river bottom fill with lures that will never again fly, and the lesson of the salmon that will not strike is learned and learned again and again. Spawning salmon are occasionally caught on lures, but given the quantity of metal and plastic flashing through the water, one suspects these unfortunate fish may simply have opened their mouths at the wrong time.

Ferwerda's is a good place to get a fix on the salmon run. Part of the service here is a fish-cleaning station where, for one dollar each, you can get your catch skinned and filleted, a dollar you will willingly pay once you have tried this task for yourself. Around ten in the morning, as soon as the first shift has come off the river, successful snaggers begin to pull in, dragging their fish from the beds of pickup trucks, enormous fish, ten, fifteen, twenty pounds, that Al the Fish Cleaning Man, with a few flicks of his knife, turns into the kind of meat that goes for eight dollars a pound at the supermarket. If two or three trucks show up, and the fish they bring have that dead-for-three-hours look, and if the talk is of "this damn weather," meaning the sky is already blue and the air already warm, you might plan on sleeping in the next morning, and spending the afternoon poking around in Lake Hamlin for rock bass. But if the trucks line up one after another, if the fish pile up on the sand, if Al takes the cigarette out of his mouth and really gets to work, you know the run is on.

Al handles the noble king salmon with rural dexterity and no noticeable respect. He is a Ludington resident and this work is extra money, plain and simple. Al will grab a fifteen pounder, toss it up on the cleaning table, and strip away the leathery skin with two strokes of his knife and pliers. Two more strokes and the pinkish white fillets are free. The belly (it's all fat, Al says; don't eat it, the Department of Natural Resources warns), the head, the tail, the entrails, more than half the weight of the fish, are shoved unceremoniously into a Dumpster, and the eggs — the larger fish are almost always female — saved in a separate container. It seems a shame to throw so much of a creature away in order to eat so little.

These salmon eggs are not saved for human consumption. I know of no one who has tried them, although I know of no reason why one should not. Sometimes it is simply best to follow the local customs. What the eggs are used for, Al explains, is bait, bait to catch other salmon. When salmon aren't laying eggs, it seems they are eating them. Salmon eggs are very large for fish eggs, nothing at all like caviar. They are bright orange and several times the size of a BB shot, and a good-size salmon easily yields several pounds of them. To use them as bait, you must sew them into a small mesh sack along with a few Styrofoam pellets to keep them off the bottom. This is what the surf fishermen mostly use, rigged on a slip sinker that allows the salmon to pick up and run without feeling the weight. Al sold me some of these rigs and I tried them with no success. Lacking waders, I simply wasn't getting my cast out into the surf. Almost all of the surfers are locals. A patient and genial lot, they catch maybe a fish or two a day, occasionally the limit, which is three fish of any one species, five overall. One man who had been at it for a month and canned

quite as many salmon as his wife cared to look at was kind enough
to give me a twelve pounder, which I brought back for Al to clean.
I did not have the heart to tell him it had been someone else's
salmon sack that did the trick.

It came to this. I would have to go snagging myself.

Five o'clock in the morning is not my time of day. It is a time
to roll over in a warm bed and clutch a warm woman and gently
hold her to you and slip back into dreams of youth and passion;
nothing that happens at five in the morning can be better than
this.

It is a kind of madness that gets a man out at such a time and
driving north with the great black lake on his left and a couple of
hard Michigan apples in his coat pockets. No one could be awake,
you think, no one, and the parking lot behind the field house is
filled with people who are wide awake and full of party. You jos-
tle inside, show your license, sign your tag, and carry it to the bin
marked FIRST SHIFT. You go downstairs, buy a cup of hot black
coffee, a sweet chocolate doughnut, bring it upstairs, and find a
spot on one of the green wooden benches that line the hall-like
room.

In time snaggers fill every space on every bench and begin to
line the walls. So many people, up so early — almost no one looks
drowsy except for a young woman in the green uniform of the
Department of Natural Resources who waits onstage with two
older men. You watch your competition step to the table, drop
their names into the bin, first shift, everyone gambles on first shift,
they grin, joke with the sleepy DNR girl. Watch where I put it; I
know you're gonna do right by me. In their fisherman's hats, plaid
flannel shirts, and armpit-high waders, the snaggers all seem related. It's a family, a gathering of the clan, all these Kenny Rogers beards, all these down-home accents; you feel an outsider and
carefully scrutinize the faces for another like your own, whatever
kind of face that might be. There are women in the crowd, most
with husbands or boyfriends, and they are ready to go, as wide
awake as the men; there are several blacks, maybe they are from
Tennessee too, and a few clean-cut tourists who no longer feel
this is beneath them. The crowd grows quiet when the senior DNR
officer takes the microphone and reads the rules. Your name will
be called once and once only; fail to answer, your spot will go to

another. Have your license ready when you reach the table. You will be given a badge to wear on the river, and your license will be returned when you return the badge. If your name is not called in the first drawing, a second will be held in one half hour. Good luck.

Two hundred names are drawn from the first bin, which remains discouragingly full. What are your chances? Every single Kenny Rogers beard gets called. Every set of chest-high waders goes. All the regulars you have seen dragging truckloads of fish to Ferwerda's march to the stage and take their badges. If this were Chicago I would have my suspicions, but this is western Michigan, the land of the up-and-up.

Eventually you go in the second shift. A blacktop road follows the river and ends at the dam. Parking there, you meet the first shift, the lucky ones, dragging their stringers of fish too heavy to lift from the ground. Now you see why so many of these pickup trucks from Ohio and West Virginia and Tennessee have a series of metal prongs welded against the front bumpers. People hang salmon, one, two, three, four, five, on these hooks and drive away, displaying their booty to the world. And you wonder, should you get lucky, just where in your little Cavalier you might load such fish, and how in future months you will get rid of the smell.

From the dam to the lake, the Sable River is a shallow, sandy stream never so wide that people casting from opposite banks cannot tangle their lines, if they have not already tangled them with the person at their side. With two hundred snaggers on the river, you are pretty much limited to casting straight forward, none of this upstream or downstream stuff. Now you learn the advantage of the chest-high waders. Ankle-deep stretches alternate with dark and promising pools. It is the people with waders who reach those pools, the people without waders who stand frustrated on the sandy banks.

But the very best spot, the spot most eagerly sought, is below the dam.

It's a surprisingly small dam — on one side, Lake Hamlin, placid, boatless; on the other, the river. For the salmon, this is the end of a journey that never found the sea. You cast into the pool, aiming between the lines of the man on your left and the man on your right. You take care not to catch up the man on the opposite side of the river. You have two hours.

At first it seems odd, casting out unbaited hooks, blindly
snatching them back, trusting all to luck, but it begins to feel like
normal fishing. You cast, you reel, you keep an eye on your companions. A few fish are taken, as always by someone else, and you
grow envious, then discouraged, then bitter. Then, as always
happens when you are not properly prepared, something catches
at the end of your line, and for a moment almost too brief to be
real, you feel a fish pulsing in the current, and just as it rises, just
as you see it in a flash of gold, the line goes slack. Oh, what might
have been!

Let me tell you what it is like to catch a truly big fish. Most
freshwater fishermen only think they have caught big fish. A four-
pound bass is not a big fish. A six-pound northern pike is not a
big fish and neither is a five-pound walleye. No bluegill, crappie,
perch, or rock bass is a big fish. Saltwater fishermen use things
like that for bait. At Pensacola I once saw a man bait up with a
twelve-pound bonito. He was looking to catch a big fish. I saw
people hook onto fish so strong that spectators got bored watching and walked away. I saw one guy hooked onto a fish so strong
even I tired watching. For all I know, that guy and his fish are
still pulling in opposite directions. People who cast colored bits
of plastic into the lily pads do not know about such things.

When it happens, when you at last hook into something truly
large — one time just south of Tampa I snagged a manta ray that
could not be permitted aboard my canoe — your first and immediate reaction goes like this:

My God! My God! I will never land this thing!

The "big one that got away." It's more than a legend, some
mere liar's tale. Big ones really do get away. They smash tackle,
bust lines, gobble up lures and spit out the paint, they swim right
through your landing net and are never seen again.

You do not "play" a truly big fish. You cannot even turn the
reel. In Florida, I saw a man set the rod over his shoulder, turn
his back on the sea, and walk to the opposite end of the pier,
dragging whatever was on the end of the line that much closer.
Then he turned and rushed back, reeling. In this way he finally
brought something with very large teeth up to the pier, where it
promptly cut the line against the barnacled pilings and swam away.
Probably just as well.

The big fish. What else is fishing all about? That moment when the hook is set. That moment when you know this is not a log, not some other fisherman's line, not a passing motorboat, that moment. And you never really believed it would happen. It's the lottery ticket. It's your high school friend's big sister. Some things are too good to come true.

But sometimes they do.

So here is the Pacific salmon at the end of its empty journey — high-tech wildlife with the memory of salt seas and cold flowing coastal streams buried in its cells. Trapped, doomed, it circles, it gropes, and then, bang, the hooks slam home. In a rush of gold it rises to the surface and all the fury of its lost destiny explodes. "Oh! Look at that!" a woman cries. Indeed, look at that! Her man stands waist deep in the water, that guaranteed-never-to-break solid glass rod bent double; he heaves with all his strength and the great fish roars out of the water. This is no time for sportsmanship, people are running from all directions with those oversize landing nets, get this fish to shore before it tangles every line on the river! The struggle is short, brutal, breathtaking. "Oh! He's a beauty!" the woman cries when the fish, dripping eggs, fills the net. A beauty, and you cast out your line, praying, Oh Lord, let it happen for me!

A year later you are back. Suddenly the rules have changed. No more lottery; the state of Michigan has decided to save a little money by streamlining the process. But no, you still do not get to sleep. One way or another, they want you out of bed. Six A.M. seems like a nice civilized hour to the Michigan mind. My mother's brother always told me anyone who slept past six was wasting half the day. Five A.M. That's when they milk the calves and get the chocolate milk they immediately drink up before a sleepy little city kid even has a chance to rub his eyes. Five A.M. That's when they start forming the line outside the park today, and, since it's first come, first served now, maybe you'd better get there a little bit sooner.

No longer do you wait inside a warm field house with hot coffee and doughnuts to comfort you, with good wooden benches to rest your weary bones. Instead, they've got you in a parking lot three miles down the road, waiting for the campsite office to open. You recognize the same crowd as last year, the same Kenny Rogers beards and down-home accents, the same armpit-high waders, the same talk of fish and the weather and the DNR, which is screwing up the fishing. The coffee is now in thermoses, and the wind coming off the lake is cold enough to chill it before it reaches your lips.

In the new system the office opens promptly at six, and each fisherman is given a number corresponding to his position in line. Then we wait again until seven, when we're given badges corresponding to our numbers and are turned loose in that order. It pays to be at the head of this line. All who have been here before know that very well, and yet there is no cheating among these fishers, no attempts to steal ahead of one another. These are courtly, well-mannered people up to and sometimes including the moment when three of them snag on to the same fish at the same time. They stomp around in the cold and tell stories — "Did you see that woman yesterday? She snagged this old boy behind the ear and cast him right out into the river!" — and a visitor from Chicago, joined in conversation, finds himself instinctively dropping a certain familiar F word from his vocabulary.

It is not yet dawn when they issue the badges. The DNR man, same man as last year, walks down the line and announces the new rules. Limit is changed. Three fish, any kind, per person. Only one shift today, as soon as you have your badge you may start, fish till five o'clock if you like. Have your number, your Michigan license, and two dollars ready when you reach the window.

It looks good. Only thirty or forty people ahead of you. Probably got here at three. But you should still get a good spot, and now you know where that good spot is — by the dam. And the fish are going to be there, yes! The wind is like ice and the waves have been thundering up on the beach all night; there are going to be fish in that pool!

The line begins to move. The first fishermen to get their badges run, don't walk, to their cars. Just because you are number one, or ten, or twenty doesn't mean you will reach the water according to your place in line. You still have three miles to drive, and here are all these good old boys from Ohio and Indiana and Pennsylvania, every one of them born behind the wheel, just raring to go. Engines roar, tires squeal, slowpokes are passed at sixty miles an hour. Did I say this wasn't sport? I take every word of it back.

Moments later you reach the dam and the competition is already there, whooping. Fish on! Fish on! Jesus, they'll have everything out before you even get off a cast! Men and wives work together like frontier couples, break a line, break a rod, a reel falls apart, the wife is there with a fresh rig, ready to go, extra rods, extra reels, extra lines, hundreds of extra hooks, not a moment is lost.

The fishermen crowd together, no quarter asked, none given. No sooner a line hits the water, another drops above it. You snag an enormous fish only to see it landed by another who snagged it first. You snag another and that landing net you thought would be plenty large enough might as well be a teaspoon. The others help, not from goodness of the heart, just to get your fish out of the water. They're not in the least disappointed when it snaps your forty-pound line like a thread.

Faster and faster the deadly hooks fly. Only by a miracle is no one maimed. A newcomer bumps you out of position. People step in front of one another. Every fish hooked draws unwelcome company. Weaklings give ground, and having given ground give a little more, and eventually find themselves casting out over a sandbar and bringing back nothing but riverweed. An hour goes by, two, the sun brightens, and you find yourself with two great bloody salmon lying on the bank and the respect of your companions, who by now have become your friends. By God, you held your own. You step back to let a citified gentleman with clean trousers and a brand-new rod take your place. A glorious end for the victors, you grin and compare stories and feel very pleased with yourselves.

It is not a glorious end for the salmon. By hundreds they lie in the sand, dribbling out spawn, turning black, their great hooked jaws agape. Like all dead things, they are ugly, more so since they have been dying now for days and weeks. Except for a woman with her Instamatic camera, nobody even troubles to take a picture. It's cleanup time, lug everything back to the car, a quick trip to the fish-cleaning station, then nothing to carry home but meat.

The state of Michigan warns against eating richly of this meat. With your nonresident fishing license ($20.35 for the year, plus $7.35 for a snagging stamp, plus $9.85 for a trout and salmon stamp if you want to actually fish in the lake) you get a thirty-

page booklet of regulations and a few valuable tips. "For the
freshest tastiest fish, keep them alive until cleaning or on ice."
"Because fish are 85 to 95 per cent digestible they are excellent
food providing well-balanced protein as well as vitamins and
minerals and are very low in sodium."

Lake Michigan fish provide more than that. A few pages later
we read that "organic chemicals, like PCBs, tend to accumulate
to highest levels in fatty fish species such as carp, catfish, large
salmon and lake trout." Consequently, "consumption of some
species should be either restricted or eliminated."

By "restricted," the Michigan Department of Public Health
means no more than one meal a week, and none for children
under fifteen, none for pregnant women. Restricted are all coho
salmon over twenty-six inches and all chinook salmon over twenty-
three inches taken from Lake Michigan waters. By "eliminated,"
the Department of Public Health means all lake trout over twenty-
three inches, all chinook salmon over thirty-two inches, and all
brown trout over twenty-three inches taken from Lake Michigan
waters. Just for good measure, all carp and catfish are eliminated
as well.

None of this greatly troubles the snaggers on the Sable River.
If "they" say something, then it can't really be true, can it? "You'd
have to eat salmon every day for the rest of your life before you'd
get as much as they stick in those damn mice." This guy has three,
his wife has three (actually he caught them all), tomorrow he means
to limit again, before he's done he means to pack his cooler with
as much as two hundred pounds of meat. That's in fillets — no
bones, no skin, no head, tail, or guts. That more than fills a freezer.
That more than takes care of the neighbors.

Shucks. That pays for the trip!

The snagging season officially closes on October 25. What is
left in the Sable River rolls over and dies all by itself. They wash
up on the banks, big black things with horribly hooked jaws. The
gulls descend. Park employees fill Dumpsters. The cold, steady
current washes the last of the eggs back toward the lake. Miles
and miles away, in Beulah and Kalamazoo and Manistique, the
next generation wait in hatcheries for the hand of man to start
them on their journey.

Always busy, the hand of man. Transplanting species from

faraway seas. Creating new hybrids. Giving nature a little help. The fisheries people have been preparing something new for sportsmen. Since Lake Michigan salmon can barely reproduce anyway, why let them spawn at all? Why let them die, as their ancestors have died for thousands and thousands of years, at the peak of their life cycle? Why not zap them in the hatchery, alter their DNA, create a new, improved fish? Such creatures — already they exist — will live and feed and grow in the lake for years and years, grow to one hundred pounds or more. And they'll never come near shore where the snaggers can get them.

These big fish are supposed to be ready around the turn of the century. I see myself, grown old and pale, wheeled aboard one of those sonar-equipped charter boats. I'll be handed a rod chosen by the captain, rigged with a lure fastened by the captain, and it will be lowered to a depth determined by the captain and towed through waters charted by him. I'll sit in my chair watching the rod tip, and when it bends double (a truly big fish!) my heart will race while I watch the captain set the hook and reel in my hundred pounder. Later I'll pose on the dock beside my catch and let the captain take the picture.

Until then, no more snagging for me. I mean to die a sportsman.

September 7, 1990

PETER O. WHITMER

The Unnatural

FROM TROPIC

IT WAS late in the day at the Bucky Dent Baseball School in Del-
ray Beach. Rose and amber bounced off the bellies of the clouds
hanging over Little Fenway Field, a replica of Boston's classic
ballpark. Joe, Steve, Mark, and Larry had been at it for about
four hours and were ready to take it in when a silver-haired man
with a silver mustache billowing clouds of silver smoke appeared
at the on-deck circle.

Joe, who was taking batting practice, thought the man looked
like a manager right out of that movie *The Natural.* He reached
back for whatever energy was left and proceeded to crush four
straight pitches over the left-center-field fence. Neither the silver-haired man nor any of the men in the field had anything to
say about his impressive display of power. They'd seen such things
all their lives.

The man pitching was Larry Brown, a major leaguer for twelve
years. He was fifty years old, but it was impossible to know that
by looking. He had the strong, graceful body of a natural athlete
and an ease on the ball field that made him stand out from men
decades younger. The guy in the infield was Mark Wagner, a
longtime utility infielder for the Detroit Tigers. And the one
standing in the outfield watching Joe's shots rocket over the wall
was Steve Whitaker. Whitaker had once been dubbed "the next
Mickey Mantle," and he might have been, except for the sprin-
kler head in Yankee Stadium that had an unfortunate and permanent impact on his knee.

All these men were bona fide pieces of baseball history, and all were here because they hoped to make some more history before they were through: to become part of the first-ever Senior Professional Baseball League, a winter league made up entirely of former pros over the age of thirty-five.

And then there was Joe Mincberg, the guy slapping line drives over the big green fence. His workout partners had batted the ball around with him for a week without ever inquiring about his pedigree. They must have assumed he was a former minor leaguer, a few of whom would be allowed to fill out Senior League roster slots. At forty-one, Mincberg was a strapping six foot one, just over two hundred pounds. He threw hard, hit harder, hard enough so he blended in with the pros.

But Mincberg knew the truth: he was an oddity, a slugging, running freak show.

He was an *amateur* — a major league criminal defense lawyer who'd played one year of freshman college baseball twenty-three years ago. Now he'd been moved to take a leave from his intense law practice to chase flies and dreams. And it all might have been ascribed to the lunacy that descends on middle-age males, except . . .

Thwok. Another shot over the fence. This guy could hit. Still, nobody said anything. Larry Brown tucked his glove under his arm and jogged off the mound, right by Silver Man. "Hey Dick, how are ya?" Brown said.

Then Mincberg knew. He *was* a manager: the mercurial Dick Williams, who'd led the Boston Red Sox, the Oakland A's, and the San Diego Padres to five World Series, the man Mincberg would have to convince that an aging amateur could play with some of the greats of the game.

Drenched in sweat, Mincberg walked over to Williams and pumped his hand vigorously, saying, "Hi! I'm Joe Mincberg. I'll be trying out for the team."

Dick Williams's mustache curled into a frown. He pulled back his hand from Mincberg's grasp as if it had been thrust into something unexpectedly rancid. It was going to be an uphill struggle.

It already had been.

Mincberg had led the University of Connecticut freshman team in every offensive category as a walk-on in the spring of 1967.

His coach offered him a spot on a summer league semipro team in Cape Cod. Mincberg turned it down; he had to make money to support his widowed mother. When he showed up to play the following year, the coach snubbed him. Mincberg walked off the field and never played organized ball again.

In the next two decades, Mincberg established himself as a criminal lawyer in southern Florida, representing the likes of José Cabrera-Sarmiento, the first *narcotraficante* to be extradited from Colombia, and, in noncriminal matters, Roxanne Pulitzer. In 1983, at the age of thirty-five, he felt the urge to do something other than practice law. He whipped himself into shape and competed in a triathlon. Two years later he joined a ragtag amateur baseball team. They played a seventy-game summer season on evenings and weekends. He was the oldest man out there by about fifteen years, facing young arms that could throw ninety-mile-an-hour fastballs. Still, Joe hit over .350. Soon he was reshaping the team, getting rid of guys who mainly came out for an excuse to drink beer, and attracting real athletes. In no time, the Bulldogs, as he had named the team, were tearing up the league.

In July, late in the 1989 season — Joe was now forty-one — he was on the practice field when one of the players casually mentioned something called Senior League, for ex-pros over thirty-five.

For some reason the "ex-pro" part of it never sank in. From that moment on, Mincberg became obsessed.

A few days later, deep in a news story, Mincberg found a mention of the fact that two roster spots on each Senior League team were to be reserved for non–major leaguers. Of course, the thinking of league organizers was that they were leaving a loophole for guys who had excelled on Triple A minor league teams but never quite made it into the Show.

Mincberg was impervious. In good shape to begin with, he began to train hard. Too hard.

Training camp was set to start in mid-October. On a day in early September, Mincberg had already run down about thirty fly balls when suddenly his knee popped out from beneath him. He could barely walk. The next day he drove down to Miami to see the surgeon who worked with the UM football team, Dr. John Uribe. Uribe confirmed what Mincberg feared. There was major ligament damage. The only treatment: reconstructive surgery. If he had surgery, Mincberg would be out of sports for a year. If he didn't, Uribe said, he might never play sports again.

It was a long drive home. His knee was hot and swollen, barely able to bend. He limped into his house and stayed there. After a week of complete immobility, Mincberg found he could put a little weight on his bad leg but he still couldn't throw on it. After ten days he hobbled into a gym and sat down at a Nautilus leg machine. He got to the gym every morning at six and worked his knee through searing pain. After three weeks he could run, if he didn't cut to either side. Still slightly lame, he started taking batting practice again at the end of September.

Even now, his dream further from reality than ever, Mincberg kept working all the angles. Don Sider, co-owner of the soon-to-be West Palm Beach Tropics, was a lawyer. Mincberg tried to use that tenuous connection to get his attention. When Sider ignored his phone calls, Mincberg faxed him his stats from college and with the amateur team, and offered to play for free.

A few days later, somebody called from Sider's office and invited Mincberg to a Tropics press conference. Mincberg was elated, but there was still the fact that he couldn't walk well. Somehow, he had to hide that fact. He wrapped his knee tight, put on a suit, and tried to walk without a limp.

At the press conference there were numerous former pros: Rollie Fingers, Al Hrabosky, Lee Lacy and Toby Harrah, and others who had already signed contracts to play for the Tropics. Mincberg was introduced as a local lawyer who intended to try out. It was clear that he was no more than some press agent's afterthought. Mincberg was suspended between humiliation and elation. Afterward he introduced himself to Sider, who was noncommittal: "We'll call you."

Still, Mincberg was encouraged. Or he would have been, except for the knee. "Great," he kept thinking to himself. *"Unbelievable!* The opportunity of a lifetime is going to present itself and my f—— knee is going to kill it."

For the first time since he was a little boy, he felt as if he were about to cry.

On October 10, Mincberg got a form letter saying training camp for invited pros would begin the following Monday, the sixteenth. Everyone else was invited to a walk-on tryout — a cattle call. Mincberg thought he'd recovered enough to give it a shot, but he knew that one bad step could take his knee out for good.

It was that night that Larry Brown saw Mincberg work out at Palm Beach Junior College, recognized him from the press conference, and invited him to join other pros working out at Little Fenway, where the Tropics training camp would be.

The day after Mincberg first shook Dick Williams's hand, the Tropics manager appeared at the ball field again. Mincberg was at bat. Larry Brown tipped him off with a discreet nod. A shot off the center field wall. Two shots over the center field wall. Total human silence, just the revolver *pang* off the metal bat.

With each smash the butterflies in Mincberg's gut receded. He kept waiting for a voice over his shoulder to say, *Good shot. Way to hit. Where did you get that power?* Nothing. Finally, he couldn't resist the urge to search Williams for reaction. There he was, back to the plate, chatting casually with the groundskeeper.

"Bring your own equipment; uniforms will be provided." The open tryout seemed more a publicity event. Fat guys. Old guys. Softball guys. One was fifty-eight years old and had driven from Waycross, Georgia. It was a mess, a hundred players, four coaches, one field. Mincberg despaired of ever being seen above the hurly-burly until Don Sider walked over.

"Dick saw you hit the other night," Sider said. "He was very impressed."

The problem was, how do you stand out when there is barely enough room to stand? Mincberg needn't have worried. To pros, it's easy to pick out the real ballplayers: in the field they look relaxed, smooth, not herky-jerky. They throw with authority. They swing like they mean it. One of them was Mincberg.

Still, after Sider's comment, nobody said a word. Mincberg stood in line for a few two-hoppers in the infield, took his five swings with everyone else, and went home.

Day two was supposed to be an intrasquad game, but the umps didn't show up. Dick Williams himself walked out to the mound to call strikes. There he was staring down at Mincberg from behind the pitcher. A called strike. Two called strikes. Mincberg eating his liver.

He would have swung at the next pitch even if it had bounced five feet before the plate. He tagged it for a single.

Larry Brown was there as one of the Tropics' scouts. Every so often, Mincberg would try to make eye contact, but Brown stared straight ahead, poker-faced. The practice game went on for fourteen innings, a Keystone Kops comedy of errors. As the day drew to a close, Mincberg imagined the moment when that fat herd of sweating men would gather around and the names of the lucky few would be called out.

But that was bush league, and these were the bigs. In keeping with the unspoken code of silence that was the soul of the major leagues, the game just ended without anyone in authority saying anything. Mincberg was baffled for a moment, until Larry Brown sauntered over and whispered in his ear, "You're being invited to training camp."

As Mincberg was leaving the field, walking about five inches above the turf, he passed Dick Williams. Mincberg caught his eye and nodded, but Williams just kept walking. For about ten yards. Then he stopped, turned: "Hey. You know you're coming to camp, right?"

Mincberg had a major cocaine-smuggling trial scheduled to begin the same day as training camp. He had filed a formal motion asking for a continuance. Reason: "Counsel has an opportunity to try out for the Tropics professional baseball team."

The motion was granted.

Much later, Larry Brown would tell Mincberg that everyone involved with the Tropics considered his chances of making the team to be the longest of long shots — not necessarily because of lack of ability, but simply because he wasn't one of them. "I didn't say anything," Brown told him. "But I didn't think they were going to consider you at all."

Every morning Mincberg hopped in the Jag at 8:30 and zipped down to the field. He got there at 8:45, even though practice didn't start until 10.

"I just wanted to be there," Mincberg says. "I had been a practicing criminal lawyer since 1973. Never in my wildest dreams did I think I could be playing professional baseball fifteen miles from my home." And he was getting paid! Twenty-two bucks a day. "I've never been more thrilled than when they handed me my first check — it was about eighty dollars for the first four days." In his law practice, Mincberg usually makes $300 an hour.

Mincberg had one advantage over some of the pros. They were coming out of mothballs; he had just completed a summer amateur season. The first day in training camp he felt he was fielding well and throwing hard — in his eagerness to impress, maybe even a little too hard.

Right after the first infield practice, former Montreal Expo Rodney Scott, the Tropics' starting second baseman, walked over to Mincberg. "Wow," he said. "Where did you get that arm?"

The bad news was: Dave Kingman. With 442 career home runs, he is nineteenth on the all-time list, fifth in terms of percentage of home runs as hits, behind Ruth, Kiner, Killebrew, and Williams — players who need no first names. Kingman was a first baseman, Mincberg's position. The good news was that, as Mincberg looked around the first day of camp, he saw only one other first baseman, Gary Gray, a six-year vet who had finished his career with Seattle in 1982. Plus, to Mincberg's eyes, Gray looked a little out of shape.

Baseball is a tight fraternity. As the players arrived, they asked each other about wives and kids and business deals. Mincberg was left out. Then he saw someone he knew, Wayne Krenchicki. Krenchicki, an eight-year pro, had been an All-American third baseman at the University of Miami when Mincberg was a law student there. Mincberg introduced himself and was just about to tell Krenchicki how much he had admired him at UM when Krenchicki unzipped his athletic bag and pulled out a first baseman's glove.

The first intrasquad game came on the fourth day of camp. Gray started at first base for one team, and Krenchicki started for the other. Mincberg rooted against Gray with an unapologetically mean spirit. When Gray made a tremendous play, launching himself blindly and stabbing a hard line drive for an out, Mincberg groaned, and prayed he would make an even more spectacular error on the next play, or even get injured.

In the second intrasquad game, Mincberg got in and lined a

single to right-center. Williams shouted, "Way to go, Joe." He knew his name!

Then, in the field, he stopped a hard grounder and ran to first. Great play. Except he had left the ball sitting in the dirt. He redeemed himself a few minutes later on a sky-high pop-up near the stands. The ball plummeted, missed the dugout roof by inches, and Mincberg, half inside the dugout, stabbed it. As every kid with an imagination has fantasized a million times, the crowd went wild.

After the game, Mincberg saw Krenchicki quietly cleaning out his locker. He had been traded to the Bradenton team. Then, at the end of the week, Gary Gray was cut. That left only two first basemen, Kingman and . . . Mincberg.

The first real exhibition game was at 1 P.M. Joe pulled up four hours early. And there it was on the lineup card: Mincberg, Designated Hitter.

The Tropics were away against the Port St. Lucie Legends, in the New York Mets spring-training complex. There was a crowd. There was a PA system. This was real baseball. He spun with disbelief as he was announced batting seventh, after Rivers, Harrah, Washington, Kingman, Landrum, and Lacy. A weak grounder to the pitcher, a line shot to Felix Millan at second, then a third at bat in the seventh inning with the Tropics down, 4–3, and the bases loaded. A storybook situation — either that or something out of a horror movie. But Mincberg discovered a strange thing: at the plate, he wasn't nervous. Later on, many players would comment that thoughts of faltering careers or nasty divorces were never in their minds when someone like Vida Blue or Jim Bibby was throwing a rock past your head at ninety miles an hour. Many had come to play precisely because of that. Call it fastball therapy.

Joe hit a bullet past a diving Graig Nettles at third, scoring two runs. Mincberg didn't even realize he'd won the game until he got back to the dugout to cheers and back-pounding and a camera crew invading with lights and microphone.

Nobody ever announced a cut or a trade. People simply disappeared when no one was looking. It was like *The Invasion of the*

Body Snatchers. Look out, there goes Rafael Landestoy. Where is Larvell Blanks? He was here yesterday . . . Wasn't Benny Ayala taking infield just five minutes ago? Orlando Gonzalez: gone. Mincberg? Overjoyed. He was holding his own, batting at a .330 clip. And he was getting press.

The *Palm Beach Post,* used to covering some of his more splashy trial work, discovered him on the ball field and prepared a front-page feature: "LAWYER PRACTICING AT 1ST BASE — hopes to erase one of 'life's regrets' — drives a red 1989 Jaguar XJS — just like Jose Canseco!"

It was posted in the locker room, and for the first time many of the other players realized who they were dealing with. A *lawyer.* A *Jag.* It was too perfect, the kind of razzing material any pro player would kill for. And then came a full-grown man into the dugout in the middle of a game. He was well dressed, looking perfectly sane, except he was crying his eyes out, tears clouding his vision, and wailing like a tortured child, "Oh, my God! Where is Mincberg? Where is Joe? I gotta get help!" Recognizing a client whose trial was coming up, Joe went to comfort the man, who continued hovering on the brink of total collapse, whining, "Am I gonna go to jail? Oh, my God, what am I gonna do?" He buried his head in the green and orange palm tree on Joe's Tropics jersey. He sobbed great gobs of air and sounded like a beached manatee.

Diplomatically, Mincberg guided him out of the dugout. When he returned, there was a moment of big-eyed silence, then someone shouted, "Who was that, Mincberg? Another satisfied customer?"

The final exhibition game, the Saturday before Monday's season opener, was in Pompano Beach, against the Gold Coast Suns.

Kingman had a bad ankle. Which meant it was Mincberg starting at first. Now he was nervous. Other than the silent trades and cuts, there had been no coaching, no encouragement, no nothing.

Occasionally someone would say "Looking good." But that was as eloquent as it got. Nobody ever directly addressed his prospects of making the team. In Mincberg's mind, it all came down to this start in the final exhibition. His stomach crawled. Still, he managed to field a pop-up cleanly in the early innings. At bat: a ground out, a called third strike against Mike Kekich. The game was tied, 1–1. The Suns got a man on first, a man on third, and one out. Williams signaled the corners to play in, to stop the man scoring from third.

The ball could have gone anywhere. Where it went was right at Mincberg, lined to the second-base side. Before every play, any serious ballplayer should know exactly what he's going to do in any eventuality. But as he lunged for the ball, Mincberg drew a blank. He should have checked the runner on third. But more important, he should have noticed that the man on first had held up, thinking the drive had been caught for an out. If Mincberg had noticed that, he could have *walked* back to first, tagged the runner, and stepped on the bag for an unassisted inning-ending double play.

Instead, he stumbled onto his wrong foot and clumsily looped the ball in a high arc to the second baseman, who picked it out of his mitt and looked at it as if Mincberg had just tossed him a moon rock.

In the dugout, Williams jumped up as if he had sat on a tarantula. Rigid, fists clenched to his ears, eyes squeezed shut, he looked like he used to during the summer of 1967 when Ken Harrelson would walk into the clubhouse wearing shades, long hair, and a Nehru jacket. "He threw off the wrong foot," Williams stuttered. "He . . . threw . . . just . . . like . . . a . . . girl!"

Standing in front of the world, completely naked at first base, Mincberg could have powered the generators at Turkey Point with his self-loathing.

By the time the game was over, catcher Randy Johnson, who had missed two signs in the early going, was already headed for a plane back to California. Things happen quick. Now was the time the Tropics had to pare back to twenty-five active players and three understudies on the "taxi squad." Mincberg felt the shadow of the ax. He hung his head in a far corner of the dugout, waiting for it to fall, entertaining himself with a dozen different camera angles of his defensive gem. An immense sense of loneliness set in. He could see the darkness at the end of the tunnel. Then the darkness moved toward him. It was Dick Williams. Mincberg couldn't even look up. Williams spoke.

"You're on the taxi squad," Williams said, and started to puff away. Making his second error of the day, Mincberg then proceeded to blurt out the unblurtable, gushing, "Great! Thanks Dick! That was nerves out there," as if Williams had mistaken it for sheer incompetence.

Williams stared at Mincberg's eager face as if he might strike it. "We can't have 'nerves.' "

The Tropics won the opening game by a 9–1 score and proceeded to tear up the league. They won their first nine games, pummeling others by football scores of 18–0 or 23–6. They were never behind in the standings, never looked back.

In the entire Senior League, Mincberg remained the only player signed to a contract ($2,000 a month) without previous professional experience.

Joe didn't play much. He started one game and had a total of eleven at bats. He struck out four times, all swinging. He grounded out six times.

"In retrospect, I enjoyed every day," Mincberg says of his one and only season as a pro. "But while I was living it, the time on the road was a drag. What you find out is that you're in show business. You don't do anything but wait for the curtain to go up. And in my case, when the curtain went up, I could only look forward to a short workout, then I was relegated to the bench."

But there were those eleven at bats, a forty-one-year-old man living out the dream of every little boy, the dream that most men tuck away but never really lose.

True, ten of them were outs. But there was one other.

December 1989 was a record cold month in Florida, and the temperature bottomed out at 38 degrees as the game started with Pete Falcone pitching for the Orlando Juice. It was the first game after Mincberg had been activated from the taxi squad. The stands at Tinker Field, bordered by the Gator Bowl in right-center, held a couple hundred fans, wrapped in blankets. Half were friends of Mincberg's, so the cheering was wild — or as wild as a few dozen half-frozen voices can get — as Joe grounded the second pitch weakly to the shortstop.

The next at bat, working Falcone to a 3 and 2 count, Joe thought "home run" all the way, took a gigantic cut, and struck out. "I can still see the ball, right down the middle. I don't know how I missed it."

The third at bat: Falcone struck him out on three pitches.

In the fourth at bat, another full count. Another strikeout. Mincberg crawled back to the dugout.

The game was high scoring, so he got one more chance. He didn't want to go to bat. He felt miserable and helpless. The Juice brought in Jack Billingham, who had been in three World Series with Cincinnati.

"Going up to the plate for the fifth time, I said to myself, 'Pull yourself together. You can't strike out four times. For God's sakes, do *something*. STICK YOUR HEAD IN THE WAY OF THE BALL!' "

The count went to 3 and 0, and Joe would have been quite pleased to walk, if necessary — anything to avoid a strikeout. Williams gave the take sign, and it came in for a strike. On the next pitch, Mincberg connected, a sharp ground ball to the glove side of the shortstop, who lunged. As Mincberg ran toward first, praying all the way, the ball shot into center field for a base hit. One hundred and fifty frozen voices screamed into the night. Twenty-five Tropics hooted and hollered from the dugout. Dick Williams ran out onto the field to the head umpire, called time out, and retrieved the ball.

Playing first base for the Juice, Tom Paciorek had never seen anything quite like this in his eighteen years in the big leagues. Thoroughly puzzled, he turned to Joe, asking, "What was that all about?"

"That's my first hit."

"Your first hit of the season?" he asked, aware that with one month gone from a three-month season, that could possibly be worth celebrating.

"No, my first professional hit."

"Get the f—— outta here," Paciorek said in disbelief. "What do you mean?"

"I'm a lawyer. I've never played pro ball."

"Get the f—— outta here," Paciorek said again. He looked at the man standing on first base with new interest, then leaned toward the dugout to get a look at the back of his jersey.

"Mincberg!" Paciorek shouted with delight. "What a great baseball name!"

FLORENCE SHINKLE

Fly Away Home

FROM THE ST. LOUIS POST-DISPATCH MAGAZINE

WHEN IT IS seven days old, a homing pigeon gets a band with a number that is registered with the American Pigeon Breeders Union and identifies it for the rest of its life.

Pigeon 0198, owned by William Kamp, is black-gray with an iridescent blue-green sheen at its wing tips, but based on past performance the bird is a lemon. In its last trial toss, it was supposed to fly from a release point in Defiance, Missouri, to Kamp's house in Spanish Lake, an air line of about fifty miles, a little more than an hour's flying time for your average pigeon. Number 0198 arrived so far behind its fellow trainees that Kamp and his wife, Fern, who usually sit under a tree in webbed lawn chairs and chat while they wait for the dilettantes, gave up and went inside for supper.

Kamp: "I said, 'Mom, dark as it is, it doesn't seem possible that we'll get him home this evening.' And then I looked out, and durned if he wasn't coming, right on the edge of night.

"They don't like to fly at night either. I thought, 'Well, he didn't give up and go roost in a tree. He had the desire. Maybe he just needs the navigating experience. Maybe if I keep starting him, he'll get better.'"

Then again, maybe he won't. There are some very particularized squabbles among pigeon fanciers about what factors enhance a racing homer's performance: its lineage, training, diet, color, housing, sex life. There are pigeon fanciers who serve their pigeons only mush before a race. (Kamp: "But heck, I don't think that's right. You wouldn't feed a football player ladyfingers before a game.") There are handlers who insist a bird in love will fly more zealously than one without a romantic interest. There are even breeders who swear that color affects speed, and any homer marked like a lowly "commie" pigeon may roost on the nearest building like one, too.

Kamp himself is an agnostic. He has been raising pigeons for sixty-six years — since he was twelve and the landlord of his north-side St. Louis flat told him he could have birds but no white rats. He isn't sure anything he does or doesn't do will affect the pigeon's estimated time of arrival or alter its keeping faith with its own nature. He takes good care of his birds out of a sense of creaturely obligation: "They do for you and you got to do for them." But he regards all the handlers' hypothesizing about the right feed and the optimum training as just that, theories, erected like shaky scaffolding on top of a phenomenon no one has ever been able to explain.

Kamp: "You're talking about a bird, an ordinary bird, that at three months old can find his way home across three hundred miles he has never flown before. If you raise the bird in a two-by-two-foot box and you release him in Chicago, he'll come home to that box, not just to St. Louis, but to that two-by-two box in your back yard.

"Most of us think training improves a bird. When the young birds are two months old, we start taking them away from home, taking them a little ways farther and a little ways farther and releasing them, giving them an opportunity to develop their navigating ability. I guess that helps, except there's reports of scientists raising pigeons in enclosures with twenty-foot-high ceilings and teaching them to fly indoors. The birds had never seen any landmarks or had any practice flights. But when they were released miles and miles away, here they come home.

"Science never has been able to explain it. Some genius said maybe the birds followed a signal from the earth, but when they wired them to pick up any magnetic pulse, they got nothing. Then someone else said they followed the sun, but then they trained some birds to fly in the dark. No light at all, but here they come home.

"It's instinct with them. It exists inside of them, and it's not connected to radio beams or heat waves or what we feed them. It's direction with a capital D.

"I've had birds come home with a wing partly pulled off from where a hawk got them. I had one bird — I never will forget: I turned him loose in a race, and three years and two months later I walked into the loft, and here's this scroungy, bad-feathered thing, and it's old 640! I never will forget that number, and I've asked myself many a time, 'What made that bird come back after three years?' "

"Well, I hope ol' 0198 doesn't take three years to get back, or this article will never get written," I said.

Number 0198 was starting two days hence in a 120-mile race with a release point at Newburg, Missouri. Kamp was selecting six competitors based on fitness, previous training, and in the case of 0198, unshakable faith in the invincibility of instinct, sovereign instinct, unaffected by human meddling. Direction with a capital D.

Number 0198 was hatched in February and set outside on a landing board six weeks later with this year's other fledglings. All through the late spring and summer, Kamp drove his flock to Defiance or New Melle for rehearsal tosses. On days when he wasn't driving, he and Fern would sit in the lawn chairs while the birds orbited overhead. As long as the two people stayed sitting, the birds knew to stay up. The sound their wings make as they rush overhead is the sound of rain coming through summer trees.

Sometimes Fern will bring out coffee cake. She makes an award-winning cranberry cake from a recipe that preceded cholesterol consciousness. Fern was born in New Salem, Missouri. She met Bill in 1938 at a dance at the Forest Park Highlands, and their courtship had a balladlike simplicity.

Kamp: "She danced by with another guy, and I asked the gal I was dancing with, 'Who is *that*?'

"And boy, did she know how to save money! They talk about the good ol' days, but I don't want to see any more of them. My father died when I was seven months old, and my mother had to work in the damned laundry. When I started at International Shoe, I earned forty dollars a week, and that's how much it was whether I worked weekends or nights or any extra.

"Then later I worked in the steel mills. I had a baby, and I liked the regular paycheck. I'd been selling real estate on the weekends and evenings, and the boss kept telling me to quit and sell full time, but I was scared, breaking off and going on my own. Finally, though, I was doing everything — closing deals, doing promotion, writing insurance — and I thought, 'Heck, I may as well try it.' And it was like marrying Fern: it was what I was supposed to do. And after that everything started to fall into place.

"A couple of years later I started my own company. By then, it was easier for me to read myself, and it just felt right, going on my own. I was in real estate for fifty years, and I never did a deal where afterwards if I saw the person coming down the street, I'd cross over to the other side because I'd be ashamed to meet him. And I made as much as I needed to support my family.

"Our daughter, Judy, is a good girl. She's got the most wonderful arrowhead collection. She even has those tiny bird arrowheads big as an eyelash. When she was little, I used to take her to this gravel quarry near the house and look for rocks. You use your imagination and you'd find one that looked just like a lady with a parasol. Now she's a guide at Cahokia Mounds on the weekends, and yesterday she made a hundred fifty dollars for two hours of teaching. She's going back to college to get her master's degree in environmental science. She figures if she goes ahead and gets ready, pretty soon the school system she's working for will have a job open up that's just what she wants and she'll be home free."

The evening before a race, the pigeons are hauled down to the release point in a specially outfitted trailer in charge of a paid driver called a liberator. The driver has a radio to connect him to the racing secretary so they can talk about the all-important factor: the weather. A bird goes an average of forty miles an hour on a clear, calm day. A tail wind can boost that figure to seventy-five miles an hour, a head wind cut it in half. Obviously, a bird whose loft is downwind of the release point is going to have an advantage over a bird that has to drum its way upwind. But no time concessions are made for that. Life is full of inequities.

The winning bird is the one that flies the most yards per minute. Before the race, a surveyor figures the air line from the release point to each individual loft to the nearest thousandth of a mile. For instance, Bill Kamp's loft is 123.014 miles from the liberation in Newburg. So if Kamp's bird is in the air two hours, fifty-one minutes, and three seconds, how many yards is the bird flying per minute? I asked you first.

On Sunday of the Newburg race, the birds were scheduled to be released at 7:30 A.M. By 6 A.M., Bill was up and had the weather channel tuned in low, droning away as comforting as pigeons purring. It was going to be hot and clear with no breeze, so the pigeons flying in the first race, including ol' 0198, could be expected to start arriving around 10:30 A.M. (If a bird leaving at 7:30 flies forty miles an hour and has to travel about 120 miles, how long does it take, etc.)

Fern was too nervous to make a cranberry cake, so we subsisted on grocery store doughnuts. Bill was fretting that the birds, being young, wouldn't go into the loft after they landed. Nothing is more aggravating than a pigeon that arrives home in expeditious fashion and then moseys up and down the roof, refusing to go inside the loft. On each pigeon's leg is a tiny metal capsule that has to be removed and put in a timer to clock its arrival. Most handlers have trained their birds to coop up at a sound the birds associate with food: sticks clacking or pebbles rattling in a tin can. But a bird that's charged up with the effort of crossing umpteen miles, listening only to its own inner radar, doesn't always react to the familiar rattling or clacking. It may just stay squatting on the roof as the seconds and minutes pass.

This is an extremely tense time for a pigeon handler, I can tell you; it keeps a person on the edge of her webbed lawn chair. Fern and Bill have every movement synchronized at this point. A bird lands on the roof of the loft. Fern rattles the can of pebbles to coax it down to the landing board beside the trapdoor to the coop. Bill grabs a broom to herd it from the landing board into the loft.

Fern says, "Don't scare it back up on the roof with that thing." Bill says, "He's in. Bring the timer, Mom." They charge inside the loft. Bill catches the bird and removes the capsule. Fern puts it in the timer, which makes a noise like a double bolt being shot as it swallows the pellet. We all sag with relief. We go back to the lawn chairs and the doughnuts.

We did this four times, as the first four Newburg-to-Spanish Lake pigeons finished their race. I would like to say that ol' 0198 was one of these front fliers, but journalism has its obligations.

Number 0198 was not in front and not in the middle, and finally it was evident that if this Wrong Way Corrigan was coming at all, it was coming last.

This made me crabby because I thought that these two people, with their decent, unspectacular lives, who raced pigeons instead of thoroughbred horses and got such pleasure from it, should, if there was any justice, have pigeons as well directed as they were.

"Well, I'm going to have to leave pretty soon," I said, relinquishing my lawn chair. It was getting late. Bill had phoned in his fastest times for both races. All the other handlers had reported in, too. Someone was stuck now doing the math to figure the winning bird. "I'm sorry 0198 really did turn out to be a lemon and didn't show direction with a capital D," I said.

"Oh, you're giving up too easily," Kamp said. "I don't never give up on my birds. It's instinct with them. It's a have to, not an ought to. In some of them it's stronger than in others, but it's there in all of them, and I never give up on them."

We started for the car, turning our backs to the loft, seeing a different horizon. Then Bill pointed. "Look there," he said. "There it comes."

And sure enough, there it came. There it came, as certain as divine intention. There it came home.

October 21, 1990

ROGER ANGELL

Tell Me a Story

FROM THE NEW YORKER

GOOD baseball novels are rare, and sometimes we can see why. Imagine you're the highly capable Casey Thackeray ("Mr. Versatility" — *Publishers Weekly*), and that your manuscript of *The Rhinelanders* has been going so well that it may be ready for the spring list after all. Lately, the thing has almost been writing itself. All the hard establishing stuff is behind you — the setting (a proud old Midwest baseball town, lately down on its luck), the older character roles (club owner Midge Schell, the kindly, teetotaling widow and cat lover, who inherited the franchise from her late husband; manager Loopy Miller, a strong-jawed cast-off skipper and former star with the Gotham Millionaires), and your team (the Vermilions, a diverse, talented lineup that at last lived up to its potential this year and has fought all the way into the World Series, against the favored and famous Behemoths, the defending champions). Is this too pat? Have you slipped into melodrama already? Nah, this is baseball, not postmodernist irony; hold on to that *Field of Dreams* flavor. Let's see what flowed onto the floppy disk last night. Hatch Williams, the sunny-tempered little center fielder, a sudden Thor at the plate, has rapped out five successive base hits over two games in the classic. Is five enough? Let's make it seven, what the hey. But he has just taken a pitch right in the sweetbreads, here at the start of game four, and is on his way to the hospital, a cause for deep concern among his double-knitted comrades. Not to worry, though. Out on the hill is smiling Joe Rice, our tall and masterful young right-hander, who is again going head-to-head with the champions' grim-faced ace moundsman, Stew Davis, the winner of eighty-four — c'mon, why not a *hundred* and four? — games over the previous four seasons. Stew looks like death out there, but Joe has a lot going for him, because *he used to pitch for the Behemoths, too,* but was cruelly dealt away in a trade. He is also armed with the wish to bring honor to his famous father-in-law, John Marshall, a legendary Hall of Famer who somehow never did win a Series game. Joe pumps, and flings another slider, struck by a vision of champagne running down old John's pate.

All this is in the book: you can almost see the tasteful Caslon, the classy margins. Why this little chill, then, this creeping doubt? Let's scroll back the text a bit. Here's game two, the teaser tilt that looks as if it might go the wrong way for the Vermilions, as Loopy, counting up the dwindling arms available to him in the late going, notices the absence of sturdy portsider Todd Redding and dispatches the bloodhounds, scarce weening that goodhubby Todd, still in uniform, has hied himself to Kildare Memorial with the missus, there to rendezvous with Mr. Stork. No matter. Mgr. Loopy, tapped on the noggin by the invisible wand of inspiration, dispatches pint-size scrub Willy Waites to the plate as a pinch-hitter in the tenth. The gritty wee chap comes through with a squirming infield chop that he beats out — yes! — for his first base hit ever in Vermilions habiliments. Will Willy now score the winning run? Is Oz a city? In he scoots from second base (need another safe knock in here, to move him up) — wheels churning, chin cleaving the air — across the plate and into the arms of his brawny, weeping teammates, after the batter, the catcher José Oliva, raps the game-winner behind third . . . Hmmm, things are getting away from you here, somehow. And where does that ball land on the old Astroturf? A foot fair? An inch fair? No, it *hits the foul line,* you idiot, and now you gotta rewrite. All this has to go. What got into you, anyway? Baseball is harder than this, and so is baseball fiction, dummy. It could never happen.

Only it did.

The Rhinelanders will never be written — who would believe such stuff? — but its script is in the books, and any alert Ohio fourteen-year-old can work out the dopey transliterations from novel back to baseball history, however unlikely. The Cincinnati Reds, World Series underdogs in everyone's estimation except their own,

defeated the defending world-champion Oakland Athletics in a
shocking four-game sweep that amputated the baseball season at
the moment when laggard October fans, settling down by their
sets for supper, were just beginning to recognize the mannerisms
of the newcomers and to take sides in the long struggles ahead.
The Reds, who had not earned a place in the Series since their
Big Red Machine (the Bench-Rose-Morgan-Perez all-timers)
crushed the Yankees in 1976, had disappointed themselves in recent summers, finishing second in their division for four years
running and a dismal fifth last year, when their manager, Pete
Rose, made more headlines than the team and was at last suspended from baseball for his gambling malfeasances. This season, under a new skipper, Lou Piniella, they burst to the fore
with an opening nine-game streak of victories, and by May 15
stood 8½ games ahead of their nearest pursuer in the National
League West. They cooled off later, but held on when they had
to, and were never out of first place all season — only the second
wire-to-wire winners in the history of the league. The Reds then
prevailed over the Pirates in a crisply played six-game championship series, but almost no one gave them much of a shot against
the enormous and lordly Athletics, who had run up 103 wins while
taking their third consecutive American League West flag, and
then swept the Red Sox — obliterated them, in fact — in the
playoffs. By Series time, the only question at hand — to judge by
the sports media, at least — was whether the Athletics, once they
had disposed of the Cincinnatis, would deserve to be called a
baseball dynasty. That title, vacated for more than a decade, had
become the issue; the World Series was secondary. The Reds'
sweep was startling in every way, then — it took your breath
away — and must now be ranked somewhere among the few absolute upsets in the history of the classic.

The championship playoffs and the World Series are baseball's essential simplifiers, providing a few straightforward closing scenes to the thick summer volume, now that heartbreak and
misadventure have thinned the cast of characters, and then (especially pleasing to beginner readers) allowing a clear hero to step
forward on the final page. We'll give attention to these closing
sobs and conversations (or games and innings) in due course, but
there may be greater pleasure in it if we go back now and leaf

through some of the earlier misunderstandings. Chapter headings, where appropriate, will guide us through the thickets. This year, in any case, some gemlike subplots and pleasing moral tales kept popping up in the text, providing a shorter chapter here and there, and a restful pause in the flow.

The Reds' sustained brilliance in the playoffs and the World Series — they were a flame across the sky — felt particularly fresh and clear, because it came at the end of a spring and summer of repeated lulls and false starts, spurts of hope and then long downslides, that seemed to wear down teams and fans alike. This season was nothing like last year's, when the Pete Rose affair and the death of Commissioner Bart Giamatti and the World Series earthquake hammered the sport in grim succession, but the 1990 campaigns still lacked satisfaction. Clubs with serious pennant plans — the Royals, the Angels, the Padres — went sour so quickly that their seasons had virtually ended before their first full swing around the league. In some quarters the collapse was blamed on the abbreviated spring-training schedule brought on by the labor lockout, but the argument never felt persuasive. Injuries darkened other hopes. The Dodgers lost the services of Orel Hershiser by late April, and Giants manager Roger Craig had to make like Dr. Frankenstein as he tried to sew together a pitching staff from the pitiful assortment of arms and backs and rotator cuffs available to him: twenty-six different pitchers clumped to the mound for the San Franciscos and failed to get the job done. Consistency eluded almost everyone in the end. The Giants and the Dodgers — and the Red Sox, the Blue Jays, the Mets, and even the Pirates — played with zest and dash for days or even weeks at a stretch, but then went dull and flat so quickly (and then sometimes soared again) that you couldn't quite believe how good or how awful they'd looked last Tuesday. The dashing Pirates, who won the National League East and were close to becoming the heroes of this baseball year, one felt, had dizzying game streaks of 6–0, 0–6, and, after a bit, 10–1, all in the month of September. The Mets, mired in fourth place through the spring, fired manager Davey Johnson at the end of May and took off on a glorious 27–5 flight shortly thereafter; they never achieved any stability after the All-Star break, however — unless you count a seven-game winning streak in August and early September, fol-

lowed by five straight losses *twice*. The Red Sox, to the surprise
of all the New England colonies, held a 6½-game lead in their
division on Labor Day, built on an edifice of ten straight wins, but
bounced themselves back into second in less than three weeks;
they won their mini-pennant on the final day, barely beating out
the Blue Jays — a team that once again proved its particular genius for losing when it matters most. The Reds themselves, although never knocked out of first, still managed to drop eight in
a row and eleven out of thirteen in July, and suffered embarrass-
ing sweeps by the Giants and the Pirates at different times; they
played so poorly against the Giants, all in all, that Bay Area writers were struck dumb by their steel and fire in October.

No one performed with more poise and balance across the season than the defending-champion Athletics, who churned out
monthly win totals of eighteen, fifteen, seventeen, and eighteen
games from May through August, and twenty-one in September,
with only one four-game losing streak along the way. Before the
World Series, that is. They were nearly matched in their division
by Jeff Torborg's optimistic young White Sox, who snapped at
their heels through the early going and actually held first place
for seven days in late June and early July; Oakland's depth and
quality wore them down late in the summer, but the White Sox's
final 94–68 record would have beaten any other team but the
Pirates. (A full-house 42,849 Southsider fans turned out on the
last home date to say goodbye to Comiskey Park, which is closing
down after eighty years, but the presence of these young Chisox
on the field brought a little sunshine to the obsequies.) Otherwise, you had to look in the opposite direction to find consistency — at the Yankees, say, who took over last place in their division on May 26 and slammed the cellar door, or at the Braves,
whose third successive last-place finish in the National League
West put them a total of forty-seven games behind, over that
stretch — behind the fifth-place club, I mean. As fans, I suppose
we should be grateful for all this competition and disorder, although it is not, in truth, a sign of sporting quality. A lot of the
time, it felt more like bumper cars.

The Story of O

Since I have not quite completed the lab work for my radical theorem that some baseball statistics have no meaning whatsoever, we must scratch about for some explanations for this year's record total of nine no-hit games. The 1989 season did not produce a single no-hitter, and National and American League pitchers, taken together, had brought forth a total of only nine since 1981. Friends of mine who feel at home with math tell me that this year's flood of no-no's is within range of big-numbers theory — it's a predictable statistical glitch, that is — but the pitchers must be given a little credit as well, and the batters some blame. The proliferating split-finger pitch has tilted the ancient hurler-vs.-batter arms race in recent years, and the umpires have lately worsened the imbalance by informally lowering the strike zone to accommodate the hard-to-call, off-the-table splitter that crosses the back of the plate at shoelace level. The pleasingly hittable waist-high delivery is now called a ball, and batters are laying off it as a result. Contemporary hitters (to this old watcher) more and more appear puzzled or cowed by a pitcher who has his stuff together on a given evening and has begun to get the umpire's call on low pitches and on sliders to the far corner. Instead of edging up and trying to slap the ball, or, still better, trying to steer the outside pitch in the easy direction — which is to say, to right field for a right-handed batter — they continue to take their full, manly, button-popping cuts and miss, or simply fail to offer at the far-side strike that punches them out once again. Not my night, you can almost see them thinking as they trudge peaceably back to the bench and sit down. One of the nicer rewards of the game used to be watching good hitters adjust to difficulties — sometimes in ways we didn't quite appreciate at first. One evening up at Yankee Stadium, I had a useful conversation with Tony Kubek, who tipped me off about how Rickey Henderson — perhaps the most imaginative and flexible hitter now at work — responds to a pitcher who has been getting the called strike on very low pitches. Next time up, Rickey will stand a bit farther back in the box, and — *oops* — the tip of his bat will graze the catcher's mitt as he cocks for the pitch. The catcher moves

back four or five inches before signaling for the next splitter, and
when the down-dropper arrives he must pry it out of the dirt —
a ball, the ump decides, not a strike. The succeeding delivery will
be more where Rickey wants it — up and *pow!*

The no-hitters, in any case, came in many shapes and forms.
Obscure toilers like Randy Johnson of the Mariners and Terry
Mulholland of the Phillies startled themselves, while Nolan Ryan,
by contrast, came through with his sixth lifetime no-hitter, against
the Athletics. Noblemen Dave Stewart and Fernando Valenzuela
threw no-hitters on the same day, though in different cities (it
was a first ever for each of them), and Dave Stieb, of the Blue
Jays, also turned the trick at last, after giving up ninth-inning hits
in two previous near-perfectos. On July 1, hardworking Andy
Hawkins, the Yankee right-hander, *lost* an 0–4 no-hitter to the
White Sox out in Chicago, when two walks and three abominable
fielding errors let in the ugly little flood of runs in the eighth.
Hawkins, a class act, refused to blame his teammates for the farce.
"This is the greatest day of my life," he insisted. "It just doesn't
feel like it yet."

Class Day

The honor rolls had some missing names this year. Wade Boggs
failed in his quest for an eighth straight two-hundred-hit season
and a sixth American League batting title, and Tony Gwynn, who
finished at .309, missed out on a fifth National League crown.
There was still enough good news to go around. Barry Bonds,
perhaps not absolutely the best of the three remarkable Pirate
outfielders — let's wait a few more seasons before we decide —
won the National League MVP with his splendid summer of thirty-
three homers, fifty-two stolen bases, 114 runs batted in, and a
.565 slugging percentage. His teammate Doug Drabek, a stalwart
hard-game performer for the Pirates all year, was an easy choice
for the Cy Young Award, with a 22–6 won-lost mark. Lenny
Dykstra — twitching and twiddling and bonking — led the NL
batters for most of the season but wore down at last, allowing the
gaunt switcher Willie McGee to take his second batting title, at
.335. Traded from the Cardinals in late August, McGee went over

to the Athletics and wound up in the World Series on the wrong side of the field — a visiting potentate from another land. Further shining work in the National League merits mention: Ryne Sandberg's league-leading forty home runs and hundred runs batted in, for instance, and his skein of 123 chances without an error, a new record for second basemen. Matt Williams, the shy, bald, slick-fielding San Francisco third baseman — a great favorite in this corner — led the league with 122 runs batted in, and, perhaps more notably, batted seventy-nine points above his previous lifetime average of .198. His general manager, Al Rosen, keeps whispering that Williams is headed for Cooperstown, and now I'm beginning to think he may be right.* Serious attention must also be directed toward the Dodgers' wand-width young right-hander Ramon Martinez, who struck out eighteen Braves batters in a game back in June, and went on to a twenty-and-six season, with twelve complete games. Thirteen of those victories were against clubs in his own division — he was 13–0 and 1.92 that way, in fact — which helps explain how Tom Lasorda's Dodgers, although prostrated by injuries, came home second in the West. Martinez is twenty-two years old.

Rickey Henderson — he'll be thirty-two on Christmas Day — enjoyed his best season ever, leading all comers in stolen bases, runs, on-base percentage, and pitcher-aggravation, and slugging a powerful .577. He broke Ty Cobb's American League stolen-base mark this year, and now stands (up on his toes, ready to fly) only two behind Lou Brock's all-time 938 lifetime swipes. Rickey's MVP Award was no surprise, then, but Cecil Fielder, the wide-body Detroit slugger, might have beaten him out, at that, if he had played for a contending club. Fielder, a delightfully unexpected star, whacked fifty-one home runs for the Tigers this year, while driving in 132 runs (and fanning mightily 182 times). George Brett, the Kansas City veteran, led the league with his .329 bat-

---

*Pat Tabler belongs in here somewhere, too: he's a born footnote. A blond, right-hand-hitting, nine-year journeyman, Tabler was signed aboard by the Mets in the late season to beef up their bench — and to keep working on a unique private record. Twice in the middle of September, he came up to bat with the bases loaded and each time stroked a single. He's a .286 hitter but a monster when it matters most — forty hits now, in eighty lifetime at bats with the bases full. Asked one night how he accounted for this stunner-stat, he grinned and threw up his hands. "Luck and unconsciousness helps," he said.

ting average, and became the first player to hold that honor in three different decades. Floods of numbers are inexorably dulling, to be sure, but we should pause now and then and remind ourselves what they represent. George Brett, I mean, can *hit*. Brett is the most successful Lau-school graduate around — a practitioner of the odd, flat-bat, back-to-front, head-down, finishing-swirl hitting technique invented by the late Charlie Lau. Ten years ago, Brett mounted a famous summer-long assault on the .400-level fortress, winding up at last with .390. This season, at the age of thirty-seven, he started slowly but batted a scary .388 after the All-Star break. He hit for the cycle (for the second time in his life) in one game — single, triple, double, home run — and went four-for-four on another evening, with two triples. Frank Funk, a Royals coach, pointed out in late summer that none of Brett's recent burst of hits were flares or chinkers. "Everything he puts his bat on," he said, "goes out of there looking like a stream of milk."

Among the AL pitchers, Nolan Ryan, at the age of sixty-three — no: *forty*-three — struck out 232 batters, which was tops in his league. There was notable competition for the AL Cy Young Award this time around, with the balloters being required to choose between Roger Clemens's twenty-one and six, and 1.93 ERA; Dave Stewart's twenty-two and eleven, with eleven complete games (it was his fourth straight twenty-game season); and Stew's teammate Bob Welch's shining twenty-seven and six. Welch got the honor, but I would have been content if the prize could have been passed around, spending four months at a stretch on three different mantelpieces. And how about two firemen's hats — for Bobby Thigpen (of the White Sox), with his record fifty-seven saves and 1.83 ERA, and Dennis Eckersley, with his forty-eight saves and (think about this) 0.61 ERA.

Enough, but still we must say a little something about this year's rookie stars — about Dave Justice, who hit twenty-eight homers for the Braves; and Frank Thomas, whose .330 effort at the plate was the best among all the White Sox; and about six-foot-seven Ben McDonald's 8–5 summer for the Orioles; and Sandy Alomar, Jr., who burst forth, full-armed, as a complete catcher for the Indians. A little will have to do, but I think we'll be reading about these sprouts and others in this exceptional freshman class (on the Orioles, on the White Sox, and on the Expos, in particular) for many years to come. Keep watching this space.

Goodfellas

Baseball grinds out numbers like M&M's, but, as I've been suggesting here, its storytelling capacity is even more pleasing. Again and again this summer, I felt the game's great narrative powers in full flow and sensed that some master — an Aesop, a Dickens, a Stephen King — was out there somewhere, biting his quill and staring at the ceiling and then diving back into his manuscript. Ken Griffey — Ken the elder — was dropped by the Reds in late August and then quickly signed up by the Mariners, so that he could play in the same outfield as his son, Ken Jr. They hit singles, back-to-back, in their first inning together; later on, in a game against the Angels, they hit back-to-back home runs. Young Ken batted .300 for the season, and his pop, over his shorter stretch, .377. Just the other day, I realized I'd failed to appreciate a little flourish or curlicue in this tale, so I went back to a September Mariners box score and found it there:

> G'fey Sr., lf
> G'fey Jr., cf

Another first.

Carlton Fisk warms you, too — although that's not quite the temperature that flows from him on the field. I talked to him early this summer, renewing acquaintance, and watched him play, of course, relishing the mannerisms: that close inspection of his bat surface, as if checking for aphids, just before he steps into the box; and the pitcher confabulations, when he stands with his helmet cocked up on top of his head and his glove arm akimbo. Lately, he reminds me of a wind-weathered granite statue of some Civil War general up on a pedestal above a New Hampshire village green, with one gauntleted hand at his hip. This was Carlton's twenty-first year in the majors; in August, his 328th home run as a catcher (he has 354, all told) put him ahead of Johnny Bench and all other catchers in that category. He'll be forty-three next summer, but has promised he'll be back. He'd *better*.

Nolan Ryan isn't a statue; he's more like the Fourth of July. Each summer, some new feat of his turns up along with the hot weather — last year, his five-thousandth lifetime strikeout; this year, his three-hundredth victory and then the sixth no-hitter — and inspires the same ancient encomiums, the same front-page shots of Ryan holding up a baseball (with some startling new figure inscribed between the seams), the same editorials extolling his down-home ways, his modesty, and his All-American heater. In August this year, I happened on a column in the *Bangor Daily News* that called Ryan "a true sports hero ... without a spike haircut, shades, pumped-up sneakers, garishly colored clothing, or loud and trendy manner of speech," and went on to point out, "The kids love him even though he's not a rap singer (if that is indeed singing), a movie star, or the member of a rock band."

All true, I guess, but it pleases me to know that there's a darker side to Nolan Ryan. Out on the field, he is true blue but also wants baseball played on his terms. A year or two ago, when he was with the Astros, he watched one day as Lenny Dykstra went back to the other dugout (I can't remember whether this was when Dykstra was exuberating for the Mets or with his later team, the Phillies) after driving in a go-ahead run, or some such, and high-fived his way up and down the bench, spitting and grinning, waving his fist in the air, and scattering batting helmets about in his glee. "That young man —" Ryan murmured at last. "Well, he needs a bow tie."

Nolan pitched the next day, and, sure enough, Lenny got his present. Right up under the chin.

Cecil Fielder was a story that could have been written by John R. Tunis. Two years ago, he was a second-string first baseman with the Blue Jays — a backup to the redoubtable Fred McGriff. Sensibly concluding that his long-term Toronto job prospects were limited, he went off to Japan and found employment with the Hanshin Tigers, where he got to play every day, honed his stroke — he *kills* anything low and inside — and smacked thirty-eight home runs. Home again, he signed on (for a handsome $1.5 million salary) with Detroit and immediately began knocking the ball out of sight. (I saw him waft one into greater downtown Lakeland, Florida, last March, but of course I had no idea it would become such a habit with him.) He hit seven homers in April and then three on the same afternoon against the Blue Jays, on May 6. Early in June, he enjoyed another triple-homer outburst (in real life, it's a once-in-a-career sort of thing), this time in Cleveland. Indians pitcher Greg Swindell, who was the victim of all three shots, stared at the ground for a bit after number three went out, and then asked, "Where'd it go — Lake Erie?" Fielder kept on hitting as well as slugging, it should be said; he was up among the AL batting leaders most of the way, and wound up at .277. The homers came along with pleasing regularity — twenty-eight by All-Star game time, forty by August 25 — but some of them tended to linger longer in mind: number forty-one, which cleared the left-field roof of Tiger Stadium. Only Frank Howard and Harmon Killebrew had ever done *that* before.

No one enjoyed all this more than Fielder himself. "I don't understand what's going on," he said at one point. "I'm basically thrilled." His teammates were thrilled, too. "The important thing to know about Cecil," one of them said, "is that he's nicer than he is big."

Fielder, who is twenty-seven, is both ample and streamlined, with a lot of ballplayer packed in astern between the hip pockets. His face is narrow and alert, which may account for the impression he sometimes gives me of a brand-new Madison Avenue bus swinging in at my stop with a cheerful fifteen-year-old driver at the wheel. He was a great hometown story all summer, of course. Late in May, the *Free Press* mounted a contest asking readers to guess how many homers Cecil (it's "*Sess*-il") would hit by the end of the season; 4,386 readers replied, and the top estimate was 250.

Not unexpectedly, Fielder ran into the doldrums in mid-September, at a time when the sports media were abuzz with talk about his chances of gaining admission to the hallowed fifty-homer club, where only ten sluggers had gone before him (but seventeen times in all). No one had hit that many since George Foster turned the trick, back in 1977. It almost didn't happen this time, for Cecil had stuck fast at forty-nine as the last week of the season ran down. His swing, normally brusque and businesslike, had become tilted and uppercutting there at the end, but on the final evening, up at Yankee Stadium, he was himself again. Number fifty — a soaring, no-doubt-about-it poke in the fourth inning, which struck the upper-deck facade in deep left-center — made the story complete. Number fifty-one, four innings later, was an early Christmas present for Cecil and for the 13,380 true believers in the stands who had cared enough to make the trip. How I wish it had been 13,381.

Two Out

George Steinbrenner missed that game, too, but he had no choice in the matter. In midsummer, it will be recalled, Commissioner Fay Vincent ruled that Steinbrenner's relations with a known gambler, Howard Spira, had not been in the best interests of baseball (as the game's lordly language has it), and that he would thenceforth be permitted no further say in the day-to-day operations of the club: he was permanently suspended from the sport, that is. It was an enormous relief, perhaps even to Mr. Steinbrenner himself, who always looked so impatient and angrily ill at ease within the game. My Steinbrenner folders — in my files and my head — are full to overflowing not just with the clips from this case and its earlier statements and maneuverings but with the rest of the long, loud story: the twelve managers hired and fired (or dropped or rehired and then fired again, or something); the Billy Martin hugger-mugger; the thirteen or fourteen general managers out again and in again; the countless talented young players angrily bounced back to Columbus (and whimsically recalled days later) and made less in the process; the eleven hardworking PR men — friends of mine, many of them — who said they could take whatever came with the job and then found that they couldn't; and the pervasive bluster and suspicion and patronizing good-fellowship (George was a world-class patronizer) that you could taste in the air around the Yankee offices. "This whole place is like a minimum-security prison," a well-placed minion murmured to me one evening, and when I laughed he put a warning finger to his lips. "He's here tonight," he said. None of this would matter much, perhaps, except for the larger results: the players degraded, the rosters deforested by wrongheaded or impulsive trades, the fans depressed and driven away, and the franchise, once the proudest in the sports world, humiliated.

I went back up to the Stadium again in September, and discovered that all this had suddenly lifted and drifted away somewhere; it was over, and I didn't have to think about George Steinbrenner anymore. The Yankees on the field that evening didn't give me much to put into my scorecard or my notebook — it was a very young team out there, with perhaps only Roberto Kelly exuding that twinkle or nova-sheen of coming things — but they were giving it their best shot, and the new manager, Stump Merrill, had won a few lately: give him credit. I grew up in Yankee Stadium, I should explain, like hundreds of thousands of other New York men and women, and, sitting in the press box that evening, I could almost remember how I'd felt coming up to the Bronx years ago, when I could hardly wait for the subway-car doors to open (we were outside in the sudden daylight) so I could rocket down the stairs and hurry along under the El and past the high gray Stadium walls, and (my ticket torn and given back) scoot up the ramps and along the cavernous corridors and so down to my seat, wherever it was, from which I could look out across that electric plain and find Lou Gehrig or Joe D. or Whitey or Mickey, and so many others still shining-clear in my mind's eye: Bill Dickey, Tommy Henrich, Steady Eddie Lopat, Cliff Mapes, Tommy Byrne, Ellie and Moose, Yogi and Sparky and Clete, and the rest. That feeling is gone, and players look less tall to me now, of course, but the Stadium feels like my sort of place again, and not George Steinbrenner's. It feels like home.

I think Cincinnati fans understand this feeling very well. The Reds are world champions, but even if the Series had gone the other way it would have had a particular purpose — to wash away the stains and oppressive shadows of the Pete Rose scandals and so restore the team to the local fans and their families. Pete Rose was the most famous Red of all, and to see him cast down and banned from baseball, and now serving out a prison sentence for tax evasion, left painfully conflicting emotions and resentments. (The street signs identifying a major access road in front of Riverfront Stadium as Pete Rose Way remain in place, unchanged in every respect except in meaning.) The Reds' attainment of the Series and their wonderful play in it became a great stroke of baseball luck, a change of weather that felt liberating and deserved. The Pete Rose case and the George Steinbrenner case weren't much alike, except that they both came out of the commissioner's office, which at times had looked to be on the point of breaking down under the imposed burdens of evidence and opprobrium and rumor and crushing publicity. The resolutions, in both cases, were hard, but no one in baseball (or no one I've heard) now says that they were unfair somehow or not essential to the game's good character. Quite the contrary, in fact. All this was part of Commissioner Vincent's job, to be sure, but he and his colleagues and his late friend Bart Giamatti deserve honor for it just the same, and our thanks.

Pete Rose will finish the prison part of his sentence in January, and many fans and writers and followers of baseball will then want him restored to the full sunshine of fame and affection. The means of this, of course, would be his election to the Hall of Fame when he becomes eligible, in 1992. This issue has been hovering in the air, in fact, ever since the first charges against Pete came out almost two years ago, and the question — which I was asked, yes or no, ten times a day in October — is a serious one, for it has to do with our innermost wishes about our sports heroes and their place in our minds. My own answer (if anyone wants to know) is unsatisfying, for it leads to an impossible script. Pete plainly belongs in the Hall on the basis of his record — he would be a unanimous first-round choice under better circumstances — but if he gets in now I think his plaque should tell the truth: down below the bronze likeness and the laurel leaves and the many rows of shining type — first in hits, first in games played, first in at bats, first in winning games, and so forth — there would be the line "Banned from baseball for life for alleged gambling activities and conduct damaging to the game."

If this is hard to envision, think of the rest of it — Pete up there at Cooperstown, under the old trees, tearful on the platform as he accepts the plaque and the accolade and finds himself once more honored and cheered and smiled upon by the fellowship of baseball, the great company from which he is otherwise enjoined and probably forever banned. I can't see that. My answer, however elusive it may look, is no. Much as we want to, we can't take Pete in.

The answer to the other question — did Pete Rose bet on base-ball? — is much easier: yes, he did. Anyone who doubts this or isn't quite sure is here referred to a new book, *Hustle: The Myth, Life, and Lies of Pete Rose,* by Michael Y. Sokolove, a first-class work of sound reporting and balanced, piece-by-piece evidence and inescapable conclusions. It's the baseball book we've been awaiting.

We need to get back on the field here, and I will be brief in saying that the worst baseball news of the year, although entirely ex-pected, was the official announcement that the National League would admit two new expansion teams in the 1993 season, thereby bringing the circuit up to the same fourteen-team level as the American League. The site of the new franchises has not yet been determined, but blueprints and boosterism are rampant in Den-ver, Buffalo, Washington, D.C., St. Petersburg, Phoenix, and Orlando, and sometime next year the citizens of the two blessed burgs will be reveling late into the night, celebrating the birth of their pushovers. The rest of us should be forgiven our restraint when we get the news, for it will mean that fifty present-day or arriving major leaguers will have been amputated from the exist-ing twenty-five-man rosters and given new uniforms: a mild dis-placement except to fans who have lately noticed that only three or four (or perhaps two or three) current teams can be said to be fully manned by competent big leaguers, that basic training in the fundamentals of the game is now habitually conducted (or badly needed) at the major league level, and that the third and fourth starters on about half of our teams are incapable of sus-tained respectable work. The only upside of this expansion is the clear evidence that the leagues don't want it to go any further, no matter what pressure is brought on the game by Sun Belt legis-lators and other fervent supporters of athletic democracy. The commissioner announced that no further increases will be con-sidered in this century — not a very long time, come to think of it, unless you're watching the Smogs or the Filibusters try to play ball.

Old Flames

By the time September came along, my long affair with the Mets was over. It really was — I kept telling myself I didn't even *like* them anymore — but they kept after me, smiling and cajoling, stirring up feelings that were better left alone, making my heart beat faster even when I knew that this couldn't last, that it wasn't good for me. They behaved abominably whenever I turned my back, losing again and again on the road, blowing leads or doing shameful things on the base paths, falling asleep at the plate. Then they'd come home again and everything would change. Back from a vacation, I ventured a trial date at Shea in late August, which turned into a raucous party: Darryl Strawberry hit a grand slam, and Sid Fernandez struck out twelve Giants in a 12–2 walkover. The next night, the mood was sultry, tentative — had I *said* something? — but then abruptly different, suddenly wild: down 3–1, with two outs and no one on base in the ninth, the Mets came on and grabbed it, with Howard Johnson driving in the game-winner with a bloop down the right-field line. They went into first place the next afternoon, and won again on Sunday, sweeping the Giants. Six straight wins now.

There was a funny little sidebar to the Saturday game, when the veteran second baseman Tom Herr, appearing for the very first time as a Met, hit a solo home run in the fifth inning. (He had just been picked up from the Phillies as late-season infield insurance.) This was Herr's twelfth year in the majors — a span in which he has established a strong image as a rock-solid fielder, a dangerous hitter with men on base (in 1985, he startled the record keepers by driving in 110 runs for the Cardinals while hitting but eight home runs), and a man of few words, a classicist. He has a long, thoughtful face, and back in the days when the Mets and Cardinals always seemed to be at each other's throats in September, he perfectly personified the old-school, midlands sort of ballplayer who did his work without fuss or emotion, disdaining publicity and standing O's: not a Met, that is. Much of this had rushed into my mind before Herr reached second base in his home-run circuit — and into his as well, it turned out. "All those years, I'd scowled at the curtain calls here," he said after the game, "so I was thinking, '*Uh-oh*, now I'm going to have to do something after all.' " When he crossed the plate, he shook hands with three or four welcoming Mets — he hadn't learned the local fist-bumping rituals — and ducked hastily into the dugout under the pelting waves of our cheers. Then — I kept watching — he executed a little bent-over dart back onto the first step and shyly lifted his cap a millimeter or two before disappearing once again: an act of perfect politeness.

All was forgiven (well, almost all) as I kissed my Mets goodbye for a little road trip. I wasn't surprised by what happened next, but I can't say that it didn't hurt. A win over the Cards was followed by five ugly losses, with my old inamorata again offering but a sickly smile of surrender as one left-hander after another ("Don't be mad at me honey, I have this *weakness* . . .") came to call. There was a numbing sweep by the Pirates in there, and first place rolled away somewhere under the hotel bed. No letters, no calls, not even a postcard in all this time. Then the phone rang: "Hi, there — it's me! I'm home and I was wondering if — " I hung up. It was over, only . . .

The Mets were not a particularly stable or admirable team this year. Their extended spells of passivity at the plate felt inexplicable on some evenings, infuriating on others. They led the league in home runs and enemy strikeouts but did less well in the more demanding disciplines: fourth in earned-run average, seventh in batting, tenth in fielding. They lost twenty-eight one-run games, and thirteen out of twenty-two two-run games. In September, they lost ten games in which they faced a left-handed starter. All this, I understand, is meat and drink to millions of fans out west of the George Washington Bridge, who look upon a disappointing year by the Mets as a parable of the vanities: too much money, Straw can't play, they're spoiled, and they take those curtain calls, and you can get *killed* in New York. These Mets played under their customary burden of fame and expectation (everybody picked them to win this time), but they did not, in fact, much resemble their immediate predecessors. Only eight of the 1986 champions were still on hand this season, and some of the better news came from unexpected quarters: Mackey Sasser's catching and hitting (he batted .307); the Mark Carreon–Daryl Boston platoon in center; Hojo's strong play at shortstop after Kevin Elster went down with a bad shoulder. Dave Magadan removed all doubts about his day-to-day capabilities with a handsomely sustained .328 year at the plate. (He has a unique, poised-in-midair stance that reminds you of a man just getting up out of an armchair.) Doc Gooden went 19–7, proving particularly tough in the second half, and Frank Viola, although he had fits holding leads in September, wound up at 20–12. John Franco clocked thirty-three saves, and David Cone struck out 233 batters, the most in the league. So why couldn't the Mets win? Was it their weak bench? Their middling middle relief? Was it the poor seasons of Ron Darling and Bobby Ojeda, who pitched unevenly (Darling was in need of surgical repairs, it turned out) and showed great unhappiness over the way they were handled? Nobody could quite say, particularly in the clubhouse — a murmurous, unhappy hall on many evenings, where people seemed disinclined to talk much baseball anymore. Something had gone out of the club; it was missing all year. Bud Harrelson, the manager, was defensive and irritable on the bad nights, but of course he was new at the job and not accustomed to answering questions about the old, deep-burning mystery of the game, which is losing. The Mets' demi-pennant, in any case, disappeared when the Pirates put together seven straight wins late in September, and finished up four games to the good. That outcome was already clear to me — and to the players as well, I believe — after an excruciating doubleheader at Shea against the Expos on the twentieth, when Viola and Franco blew a two-run lead in the eighth inning of the opener, and a very tall rookie named Chris Nabholz (yes, a left-hander) shut them out in the nightcap, on one hit.

Next year's Mets will have a very different look now that Darryl Strawberry, a free agent, has gone off to play for the Dodgers, for a five-year salary of $20.25 million. When the news came, many baseball friends of mine said, "Ahh, let him go!" — and some threw in harsher words as well. My own feelings are closer to those of a woman who called me at home and said, "But who in the world can we look forward to in the batting order now?" The Mets front office can offer impeccable business logic to justify the loss of Strawberry — his lifetime .263 average and his average of thirty-one home runs per year don't look worth all that loot — but, as is often the case with the Mets, such accounting leaves out the fans, whose bottom line is emotion. The implacable Straw-doubters in the stands (*"Darr-ylll! Darr-ylll!"*) always questioned his desire and his glove, and kept bringing up those weeks-long sleepwalking trips up to the plate and back again (in midseason, he had successive five-week sectors of batting that went .248, .379, .207). I know all that — I know, I *know* — but my strongest memory of these particular Mets is of the Straw Man doing something large and sudden in September, and the fans riding high. With the team tied in the ninth inning of a drawn-out, disheveled contest against the Cardinals, he sailed a Lee Smith fastball to the back of the bullpen — a noisy quietus that kept the home winning streak alive. Two nights later, against the Pirates, he threw out Barry Bonds at the plate in the fourth and, minutes later, mashed a three-run job into the right-field loges, against Doug Drabek, putting the Mets in front for the evening. In a game that was later lost, he fired an eighth-inning shot that wiped out a three-run Expos lead. And so on. Straw is gone, but his after-image has not quite disappeared — those amazing arms, and the flicking scimitar stroke, and the way he had to bend double going back down the steps into the dugout — and it's hard to imagine a Mets summer without him.

My thing with the Mets is pathetic, but, as somebody once explained, it's never over till it's over. Our best evening together was a September quickie that began when Dave Magadan stroked a single against the Pirates' John Smiley in the very first inning, driving in the only home tallies of the game. The two runs held up, just barely, because Dave Cone was in terrific form (Magadan told him after the second inning that his fastball was the best he'd ever seen) and kept winning the private battles with the dangerous Pittsburgh sluggers. "Head-to-head was my best pitch all evening," he said later. With the game at 2–1 in the eighth and the tying run on second, it all came down to a thrilling at bat by Bobby Bonilla: a terrifying line drive to the right-field wall, *just* foul; a swinging strike; and another fiery fastball for the K. Cone, exalted, rushed to the dugout and slapped hands and helmets and heads indiscriminately. Then he beat up on the dugout wall. "I was screaming and yelling," he said. "I was in the euphoric state of just going beserk." So were we all.

My other common-law team, the Red Sox, made it into the play-offs in the end, while persistently trying to convince their fans that it could never happen. Their trip through mid-September, while they got rid of that 6½-game lead, was like an old gent coming along Chestnut Street (a straight schuss down Beacon Hill) in a snowstorm: *Whoops! Yow! Look out! Sorry!* This was their third championship in the past five years — the total startles me, for some reason — and it's still not easy to see how they got there. Three of the Sox's early-season starting pitchers fell by the wayside; one of their famous relievers (Lee Smith) was traded, and the other (Jeff Reardon) had to have spinal surgery. Their best hitter, Mike Greenwell, was hopeless in the early going (he had a bad ankle), and their lack of speed and power was an endemic problem. They wound up eleventh in the league in homers, last in stolen bases, and first by a mile in ground-ball double plays (turned by the other guys, I mean). But some obscure pitchers — Dana Kiecker, Tom Bolton, Jeff Gray — absolutely outdid themselves, and Reardon made it back into the pen in September. They also won because Jody Reed had a great season at second base, and because their new catcher, Tony Peña, kept *saying* they'd win, insisted on it, and stayed cheerful all summer. (No optimist had been given a locker in the Sox clubhouse since Luis Tiant took his leave in 1978.) They beat the Twins one night despite hitting into two triple plays, and later startled the Tigers by smacking twelve doubles in a game: two new records that no one had even thought of before. Weird stuff. And they got into the playoffs, of course, because of Roger Clemens.

The Sox won a ghastly, astounding late-September 7–6 game against the Blue Jays (this was the opener of a three-game Fenway series, with first place in the balance) when an obscure pinch-runner, Jeff Stone, was allowed to bat for himself in the ninth (don't ask) and delivered the winning run with a single. "A typical win for this year," Ned Martin, the veteran Sox announcer, told me the next day. "Badly played and badly managed, and a hell of a game."

Clemens pitched that afternoon, his first work since he'd damaged the shoulder of his pitching arm just after Labor Day, in an outing against Dave Stewart and the Athletics. It seemed unlikely for a time that he'd make it back into action at all this year, and the cluster of Red Sox pitching coaches and trainers around him as he warmed up in the center-field bullpen now was suggestive of Rembrandt's *The Anatomy Lesson.* Then Rocket walked in through the late sunshine (great theater, great stuff) to go to work, and got a teary standing O, and he did the difficult, expected thing again, shutting down the Jays through his six innings. Up by a lone run when he left, the Bosox swiftly tacked on five more, insuring Roger's win, as Tom Brunansky came through with his second homer of the game. (He hit a third a bit later on.) Clemens's pitching coach, Bill Fischer, said, "As far as I'm concerned, he can do anything he wants now. If he says he can walk on water, he can walk on water." Joe Morgan said, "It's like Babe Ruth coming through. That's what Roger did for us today."

The pennant itself was postponed until the very last night of the season. I was watching at home by then, with a radio next to me, tuned to a sliver of dial where I could pick up the Blue Jays game down in Baltimore. My nerves were shot, and I may have snarled at my wife a couple of times, and I think the dog as well, but of course it's not right to distract a man at his work. The White Sox played the Bostons very tough (the way they had played all year against all comers), and the thing was won on a trifle, as such games often are: a ball thrown away by the Chicago pitcher during a rundown between third and home. Carlton Fisk, a long-lost Boston hero, had two hits for the Chisox but couldn't quite deliver the killing blow, and when his former teammate Dwight Evans went back to the bench for the last time, the two old Romans embraced on the field.

Curses

As we know, the Red Sox swiftly expired in the American League Championship Series, going down before the mighty A's in four straight games. They had lost in the same fashion to the same club two years ago, but that series had far less effect on this club, in my estimation, than Oakland's suffocating three-game sweep at Fenway Park early this September. Stewart bested Clemens in the second game there, but the Bosox played poorly in all three, committing six errors and suffering an ugly 10–0 blowout in the last one. Back then, and here in October as well, the distance between the two teams seemed enormous. The rivalry between the two starters had begun to feel like something out of King Arthur (the Boston press made a hundred such analogies), for Stewart had now beaten Rocket six straight times, going back to his very first game as a starter for Tony La Russa in July of 1986. (Stewart had not missed a turn in the rotation since that day.) The championship opener, played at Fenway Park, matched up the two nonpareils once again — 319 victories out there, going at it — and for a time it fulfilled all expectation. Clemens, still not at full strength, held a 1–0 lead when he came out after six, but Stew went a full eight, as is his custom, and won it, 9–1, after the Athletics did frightful things to the Sox relievers. The Boston pen was in absolute disarray by this point in the year — Larry Andersen, their best reliever of late, had warmed in twenty straight games — and the Sox in late innings reminded you of Wile E. Coyote running off the rim of a mesa. Suddenly aware that there is nothing firm or sustaining under his feet, he waves a feeble goodbye and drops from view, followed by his eyebrows. "A beautiful game turned into a horrible evening, didn't it?" Manager Morgan said in summation.

This state of affairs was perfectly understood by the next night's Fenway multitudes (the space just behind the long lower grandstand was three or four deep with standees, pole to pole), but their cries and bayings — "Dew-ee! Dew-ee!" — and cascades of clapping contained no bitterness or apprehension that I could detect. Splendidly seated in a downstairs auxiliary press box, I felt at one with the Olde Towne fans surrounding me, and shared their enjoyment of the subtle tempos offered up by the Boston right-hander Dana Kiecker (a UPS driver in the off-season), who eventually handed over a trembling 1–1 tie to his hapless successors. The eventual Oakland 4–1 victory was the tenth in their last eleven ALCS contests. The Fenway mood, if I was reading it correctly, was mostly one of gratitude toward this particular earnest but overmatched Boston nine, which had unexpectedly given the home folks two extra party nights at the very end of the long season. The absence of doom or rage in the soft October air was surprising, because the Sox — as has been noted in this space for a couple of decades now — have been encountering ultimate October disaster, often in gruesome or heartrending fashion, ever since the police-strike era. Four numbers painted on the upper facade of the right-field Fenway stands represent the retired uniform numerals of Bosox Hall of Famers Ted Williams, Bobby Doerr, Joe Cronin, and Carl Yastrzemski, but locals now see them as a mystical 9/4/18, which is the date (or close enough) of the Sox's last world championship, in 1918. The runic reading has been put forward by *Globe* writer Dan Shaughnessy in his engaging book *The Curse of the Bambino,* in which he recounts the celebrated accumulative tragedies — Johnny Pesky's late relay in the 1946 Series, the Reds' seven-game triumph in 1975, the Bucky Dent poke into the screen in the one-game 1978 postseason playoff against the Yankees, and Bill Buckner's fatal muff in the 1986 Mets Series — and blames them all on Harry Frazee's accursed error in selling young Babe Ruth down the river to the Yankees in 1920. The book, a local best seller, inspired any number of exorcisms and voodoo rites among the faithful this summer. A thirteen-year-old New Jersey boy I know, the son of a Sox-bonkers editor, executed one such thaumaturgy, involving a tiny plastic chipmunk and a whiff of leaf smoke, in secret company with a friend. The next night, the friend hit a grand-slam homer in a Little League playoff game — a first ever for him — while up in Fenway Park the Sox, their scalps prickling under their batting helmets, embarked on a six-game winning streak. Maybe the curse has been lifted in another way as well. Absolute publicity is a more deadly force than voodoo, and those noisy, peaceable crowds at the playoffs may have been telling us that they don't give a damn about this stuff anymore.

The great Clemens flap doesn't fit in. Watching game four by television in a Pittsburgh hotel room (I had changed leagues), I was struck dumb, along with the rest of America, when home-plate umpire Terry Cooney, stepping out from behind the plate in the second inning in Oakland, suddenly ejected Clemens from the game. Chaos — but let's back up a bit. Coming home, the Athletics had won the third game, 4–1, in the precise, quietly efficient manner that had characterized their play so far. They weren't hitting much — no big early innings, no monster blows — but they got the job done, and the outcome of the championship was already in view. The Rocket, again matched up against Dave Stewart, was enormously burdened by the cumulative weight of that relationship, by the Sox's evident weakness, and by his gigantic pride. Clemens, I realized once again, looks like nobody else in the world. After seven dominating years in the majors, he has become massive and ageless — he has the body of a great tree — and the impression is abetted by the psychic weight he brings to bear in the Red Sox clubhouse and on the field. Clemens-considerations — his contract, and, more particularly, the day-to-day state of his arm — occupy a unique position in the Sox's strategic thinking, rather like the part that the Pentagon plays in each new Washington administration. He is separately pondered and consulted (Joe Morgan, asked whether Roger's inflamed shoulder would permit him to work against the Athletics in game four, said, "It's his arm and his career"), and in return feels an absolute responsibility to deliver.

Roger's problem on this particular day now included the plain evidence that he didn't have anything left out there. His walk to Randolph had loaded the bases; there were two outs, but he had already given up three hits and a run in the game, and here, glaring in from the rubber and mouthing something we couldn't hear, he was blaming it all on the ump. He'd lost it. The ejection changed everything — not because of the screaming arguments from Joe Morgan and the others, or the debris on the field, or even because of the two additional Oakland runs that came in on Gallego's ensuing double against the succeeding Boston pitcher. What mattered was that an umpire had replaced *all* the players in this game, had become the center of it, and he — not the teams or the way it was played out — would forever be its news.

My own view of the affair is old-fashioned but obdurate. Endless argument of the matter was heard later that day and later that week, with a good deal of revisionism coming to the fore once the replays (and some lip-reading) showed Clemens's contorted features and the uncontrolled foulness of his rage. Cooney's fellow-umps, at the park and elsewhere, supported him all down the line, of course, and pointed out that ejection was automatic once the wrong words were said, and many people in the media also felt that Cooney's swift and irreversible reaction was justified. Umpires have feelings, too, it began to be said, and besides, we've all taken too much from the spoiled, overpaid athletes of our time. Clemens was another John McEnroe, and it was high time something was done. I think something should have been done, too — something different by Terry Cooney. It was later learned that he had called out to Clemens from behind the plate (he kept his mask on, he said, to give Roger a little leeway in the crisis), but this was perhaps the least useful of his options. Certainly he could have walked out and dusted off the plate instead, and murmured to Tony Peña to go out and settle down his pitcher or else. He could have ambled to the mound and asked to examine the ball, and told Roger that the end was very near. He could have beckoned Joe Morgan over and said the same thing, and then walked away if Manager Joe gave him any lip. The walkaway, a classic technique in these ancient quarrels, has fallen into disfavor among today's umpires, who have, with a few exceptions, become ever more visible in the games of late, and sometimes even take an active part in team brawls. Their pride is very evident, especially on television, and they aren't going to take it anymore.

Sam Perlozzo, the Reds third-base coach, was talking about the great stink later that evening at Three Rivers Stadium, and said that it was certainly true that ballplayers sometimes behaved like children these days. The umps, in his view, are parents out there. Now and then, to be sure, they have to say "Go to your room," but only as a last resort. But if they ever lose their tempers, he went on, they lose everything: they've become children, too. The walkaway, I believe, stops all that: a word or two — nose to nose, if need be — and then the stately arbiter departing the scene, headed back for his workplace. The pursuing red-faced player or manager looks small and foolish if he continues his beef to the receding rump, and if he scurries to get around in front again, he's gone. Play ball.

Red Tide

For the second year running, the National League championships provided the autumn's prime entertainment; this time around, it brought high-quality baseball as well. The six-game Reds-Pirates series held almost every ingredient — fine pitching, dazzling defense, home runs and rallies, sudden adventures at some unexpected corner of the ball yard (a play so remarkable that we would peek back later at that base or that particular place along the outfield wall, as if to fix the event in mind with a private plaque), and teams that went at each other with a ferocious tenacity. These were fresh personae for most of the television audience, but friends told me later that it seemed to take no time at all before they began to pick up on the gestures and faces and styles of play so vividly in view: Eric Davis's oddly pursed mouth (and those hotdog booties); Chico Lind's flashing, mini-quick grabs and flips; the icy, impeccable work of Barry Larkin; Lou Piniella standing at ease in midgame, with his arms braced against the dugout roof; Jim Leyland's somber, adult's stare and his small gestures — a finger to his cheek, then to his chin — as he signaled a coach or a catcher; Bobby Bonilla's smile and Barry Bonds's earring; and Rob Dibble hunching his thick, bare arms on the mound and then firing another blazer. As usual, I was forced to watch some of the league-championship games by television (being unable to be in two leagues at the same time), and I was struck by the high quality of the CBS camerawork and by the sensible, expert commentary by both of the teams in the booths. (The compliment does not extend to the network programmers, who had imposed a hiatus on the National League games through one full weekend, and arbitrarily moved another game into a Friday afternoon slot, out of their greed for ratings. The Friday game, in fact, was lost by the Reds when Eric Davis misplayed a fly ball in the late-day CBS sun.)

Successive close games — four of the six were settled by one run — tend to blur in our minds after a few days, especially when they've been played in nearly identical ballparks, but this series left some memorable large canvases. The Reds, to me, kept leaning on their opponents all through these games, shouldering and hip-shoving: in the other guys' faces. They never let them take a deep breath. They scored first in five of the games and permitted the Pirates to hold but one two-run lead in the series, for a total of four innings. Most of all, the Reds played wonderfully well in the field, for once turning defense into drama, showing us why it matters and how it turns games around and breaks the will. The painter Jack Levine has characterized baseball as an aerial game, and, watching the succession of great long-distance throws by Cincinnati outfielders Paul O'Neill and Billy Hatcher and Eric Davis, and the floating footwork and easy acrobatics of shortstop

Barry Larkin, we understood that elusive truth almost for the first time.

The killing pegs from the outfield had a lot to do with the sense of oppression and stifling difficulty that the winners imposed. The Reds *accrued*. Sid Bream singled for the Pirates in the eighth inning of the first game, but was nailed at second, stretching, on a good throw by right fielder Paul O'Neill. Next day, with the Pirates down by a run and with Andy Van Slyke on second and Bonilla on first, O'Neill took Bonds's fly ball in full right field and cleanly threw out the advancing Van Slyke at third — a thriller, as the 9–5 play always is. Even on television (my venue that day) you could see the converging angles of the race, and the ball sailing past Van Slyke's ear as he went into his slide. The play had a dandy little shirttail, for Larkin faked a cutoff at second so convincingly that Bonilla jammed on the brakes and went back to first. The Pirates didn't score. In the ninth, driving the point home, Larkin executed two remarkable plays in succession — a rollover grab and peg from the hole, and then a running stop and throw from way over on the wrong side of second base.

In game four (I was on hand by now), the home-team Pirates scored a tying run in the fourth and seemingly had the go-ahead tally as well, except that Billy Hatcher, fielding Lind's hard single in center, threw out Bream at home plate, shooting the runner and the fan-sounds dead with the same bullet. Bream didn't slide or crash the catcher, and I still don't know why. The Pirates already trailed by a game in the series, and by the eighth were in further difficulties as a result of Sabo's two-run homer — the fourth Cincinnati round-tripper in two games. But Jay Bell, the young Pittsburgh shortstop, here struck a home run of his own, knocking out Reds starter Jose Rijo. Bonilla, now representing the tying run, fought off Randy Myers for ten pitches and then smashed a high drive to left-center — a homer all the way, I thought, except for a late little sag in its flight pattern. It struck three inches below the rim of the left-center-field wall, as Hatcher jumped and missed and fell in a heap. The ball bounced cleanly back onto the field (if it had hit the wall padding, just below, everyone later agreed, it would have dropped straight down and rolled away for an inside-the-park home run), where left fielder Eric Davis gloved it and in the same motion whirled and threw a one-bounce peg to Sabo at third, who cleanly tagged out Bonilla. The tableau was riveting — Sabo sweeping his glove high as he polished off the tag, with third-base ump Harry Wendelstedt piston-pumping the out, and Bonilla and third-base coach Gene Lamont both on their hands and knees in the dirt, while the other Reds around the diamond threw up their fists in chorus.

I couldn't believe any of this, even as it was happening; Davis had come over so swiftly from his place in left that I didn't see him at all, and my first feeling, even as the throw was in flight, was: Who was *that*? It was as if a tenth fielder had been hiding out there, in perfect position for the play. It was a famous play on the instant — Jim Leyland said, "They'll be talking about that play forever," and Lou Piniella said, "Eric Davis has the greatest baseball instincts of any player I've ever seen" — but I'm not sure that its full impact came home to the Pirates (who lost the game, 5–3) right away. Bonds, the next man up, now singled and stole second, but stopped there when Bream struck out. In the inning, the Pirates had put together a homer, a double, a single, and a stolen base, all good for one run.

Even at this juncture, the Pirates may have been brooding more about some of the shorter Cincinnati throwing than the amazing stuff coming out of the outfield: thinking about the pitching, I mean. Except in the third game, when the Reds did odious things to the left-hander Zane Smith, the Pirates had enjoyed a little the better of it from their starters so far, but the vastly publicized "Nasty Boys" relief trio was another story. Norm Charlton had surrendered the winning Bucco run in the first game, but Randy Myers had picked up two saves in his three outings to date, and Rob Dibble had struck out ten of sixteen enemy batters. Despite their identical brawn and sullen chins and the heavy-metal handle, the three are not much alike. Charlton (he has a degree in political science and religion and physical education from Rice) is a left-handed fastball-forkball-slider pitcher, and will probably be moved back into the starting rotation next year. Dibble offers a slider (now and then) and that White Sands heater, which at times clocks in at better than 101 miles an hour. Pedro Guerrero, the veteran Cardinal slugger, took a pitch like that during one at bat this summer, and burst out laughing at the mismatch. Dibble's strikeout ratio (K's per nine innings) was 12.5 this year; last season, it was 12.8, the highest in major league history. Myers, the closer, also throws left, and possesses the full classical repertoire: fastball, curve, slider, change. He has given up the camouflage undies (he still subscribes to *Soldier of Fortune*) that so delighted the writers back when he toiled for the Mets, and now sports a perm. Less of a story, more of a star; more of a pitcher, too.

Dibble will provide copy, in any case. He talked through the playoffs and through the World Series, and on the days in between. He talked on the sidelines, he talked in the dugout, he talked in batting practice and in the interview room and in the postgame clubhouse. He was talking, he sometimes explained, because he felt underpaid and underappreciated on the Reds and wanted his story better known, but I think there was more to him than that. There on the sidelines at these games, he had been magically piped into some vast underground source of natural gas, and any reporter whose notebook was running low could pull in at the pump and fill up. In my own notes I find: "I never ice. I take painkillers — Darvon when I get up, and then Medipren and that Canadian stuff, 2-2-2's. They're all legal. I take them during the day and then I never have to worry about my arm. I come to the park and my arm never hurts at all. I know you're supposed to take food with painkillers, but I never eat breakfast. I throw up blood a lot and then I take a Pepto-Bismol."

And: "I never called myself nasty. Randy, he played in New York and he believes all that hype. I used to be more that way, back when I was in high school. I'd drill those showboaty guys — you know, the ones with sweatbands up and down their arms. When I'm out there, there's no thought between me and the catcher. I've been throwing that way since I was eight years old."

Also: "Everyone thinks I dropped off Mars." He is in fact the son of a radio newscaster in Bridgeport, Connecticut. "I worked five years to get here. I worked forms and foundations for a construction company, which is cold, hard work. It makes a man of you. My sister used to call me a dumb jock, but not anymore. She went to Shea this year and heard everybody yelling over me, and she was flabbergasted."

One of those evenings, Dibble wrapped up his last night-school class in front of his locker and then pulled on a brand-new Mario

Lemieux Pittsburgh Penguins game shirt before heading out to the team bus. Dibble on hockey is another story, but, mercifully, not one that needs telling here.

The Pirates, with winter closing in, played a fine fifth game behind Doug Drabek, holding a lead from the first inning on, for a change, and barely slipping free from exquisite difficulties in the ninth. It was a sweet farewell to the semi-deserving Pittsburgh hometown fans, who did not fill up their ballpark for this or any other of the playoff games, and who somehow never cared enough about Jim Leyland's appealing and spirited young team this year. Back over in Cincinnati two nights later, the Pirates went down before some more terrific Cincinnati pitching (an omen of things to come), achieving but one lone run and one hit. Lou Piniella proved himself a certified genius when he sent up a pinch-hitter, Luis Quinones, to bat for the tough-out O'Neill and Quinones delivered the game-winning single.

The teams appreciated these games most of all, I think. "This was baseball at its best," Jim Leyland said. Billy Hatcher said, "I still can't sleep at times like this. I'll sleep when all this is over."

Andy Van Slyke, standing on the dark and littered turf at Three Rivers an hour after game five wound down, said, "I dream about all this stuff. Out on the field, I fantasize. I want there to be a good fly ball hit to me out there, so I can throw somebody out. I'm thinking, 'Hit it to me! Hit it to me!' Winning this game just gave us two more days of enjoying what we do for a living. That's what I was thinking at the end: I get to play in another baseball game!"

The Freeze

A World Series sweep isn't a satisfying sort of story — you'd make it six or seven games if you were still at work on *The Rhinelanders*, just to make things harder for your lads before they crash through in late innings — but the Reds played so well from first to last in this one that they defeated tedium as well as the Athletics. So many of them got into the act over this short rush of innings that we fans, although we wanted more games and more baseball, never felt cheated of heroes. There was the engaging and clearly self-startled Billy Hatcher, popping a bubble-gum balloon out in center field as he pulled in a fly ball and then stepping back up to the plate and ripping another line drive; his seven consecutive hits and .750 Series average were records of a very special sort — *record* records. Chris Sabo turned game two into a pilot for his own comedy-drama series — "Sluggo," perhaps, with the goggled, buzz-cut, irritable Bart-next-door catching lasers out there and whaling the tar out of the ball, and then stumping angrily down the street when it was over, refusing our smiles and shrugging away our pats on the back. Jose Rijo seemed better prepared for good news. Dave Stewart pitched so poorly in the opening game (his fourth-inning departure was his quickest ever in eleven post-season games with the A's, and he had just been voted the Most Valuable Player in the American League playoffs) that Rijo's businesslike 7–0 shutout didn't get much attention. But when the two went at it again, in the tough and austere fourth game, the Series clincher for the Reds, it was Rijo who came out on top, 2–1. "He outpitched me," Stew said by way of explanation. In the interview room after that game, Rijo kept his right arm around the shoulder of his famous father-in-law, Juan Marichal (who is half a head shorter than he), while holding an unlit fresh cigar in the other hand, and set some sort of nonstop smiling record at the same time. "Why did I throw so many sliders?" he said at one point. "So they can't hit it!" I was pleased about Rijo, whom I remembered from his unhappy first year, with the 1984 Yankees, when George Steinbrenner kept insisting that his rookie fastballer was the equal of that other kid across town, Dwight Gooden. I'd seen Jose work for the Athletics as well — he went west in the first Rickey Henderson trade — when he was still falling a bit short of his potential. Now he'd got it together and then some: he was the World Series MVP.

Lou Piniella was a Boy Edison in these games — everything he tried worked — and his success this fall was very popular with the New York beat writers, who remembered his two stints as manager of the Yankees a few years back, and the class he'd brought to that toilsome post. I can still see him standing on the Stadium sidelines at batting practice, with his chin in the air and his cap (which always looked as if he'd taken it fresh out of the box that day) tipped up above his bangs, while he paused and tried to think of something diplomatic but unevasive to say about the latest odorous bit of news from the boss. I remember him as a Yankee player too, of course, and the great swings on the ball he unfailingly produced in the hard games. All that and the famous rages — the hat on the ground, the arms upraised, something flying though the air. After he lost it out there one night while managing the Yankees, his wife, Anita, said, "I'm forty-three years old and I'm married to a five-year-old." His Reds were way up for this Series, both icy and incandescent, but Lou was never at a loss to explain that. He pointed out that the close, hard-fought playoff games with the Pirates had been wonderful sharpeners, and that being in first place all year had put the Reds "under scrutiny" from first to last. "Our ball club is basically defense and pitching," he said, "and with that you play a lot of close games. We weren't intimidated at all."

Notable to me as well was the fact that he always spoke of his players as if they and he were the same age. The Reds are youthful but not brand-new; the great majority are in their mid to upper twenties, with three to four major league seasons under their belts. They are remarkably athletic — it is not a quality one can attribute to every team — and when Piniella, an old pro but a new one for them, came aboard he found a bunch that was dying to win. Ron Schueler (just the other day, he took the post of general manager with the White Sox) scouted Cincinnati for the Athletics in the late season, and noticed how tight and tentative the Reds were before they clinched the National League West — and how relaxed and dangerous thereafter. They came into the postseason as underdogs, with no burden of expectation on their backs, and one of the first pleasures of the 1991 season will be to see how they play when that is turned around and they have to go out there and be great every day. I think they'll thrive on it.

Beyond all this, the Reds were *hot* in October — in the zone where line drives fly off your bat more often than pop-ups, where the slider always shaves the final eighth of an inch off the outer border of the plate, where the enemy one-bounce screamer comes up in your glove, and where your own half-hit turf-hopper goes over the third baseman's head and hits the line, winning the game. There is no explanation for this when it comes along — players who are hot and those in the deep freeze both throw up their hands and shrug when you ask about it: enjoy it when it comes, they say, because it sure won't last. But, hot or cold, the Reds would have won this one (it says here) — in four games or seven. They were not to be beaten. After game three, Tony La Russa said, "I've pitched them up and down and in and out, and they still rough us up. We throw them off-speed pitches up in the strike zone, and they hit them. We throw them down and away, and they hit them. We stopped them for the last six innings tonight, but it was a seven-run inning too late. All in all, they've beaten the shit out of us."

Game two has appeared more than once in this account, but it deserves a little more buffing. Rickey Henderson led it off with a patented single and stolen base, and came home on a sacrifice, but, tellingly, it was one of the few moments in postseason play when the Cincinnatis failed to put up the first score. This was by *plan*, if such a thing is possible, for the Cincinnati strategists had agreed that keeping the A's behind in the Series was the only way to keep Rickey in check: he would be a mite more careful out on the base paths with his club down a run or two. The Reds now responded with an instant pair of their own, still in the first, but Oakland went back on top with three more runs in the third, one of them a home run by Jose Canseco (it was his only hit in the Series). The catch-up seemed to take forever, and waiting for it wrung out the Riverfront Stadium crowd, but even before those Capra touches at the end — the little-known speedster Billy Bates legging out a single in the tenth and then coming home on Joe Oliver's bouncer over Lansford's reach — you had the feeling that it was the old champions who were bending and wincing under the strain. Canseco got a late start on Hatcher's leadoff drive in the eighth, which eluded his twisting, over-the-head lunge and fell in for a triple, and Hatcher then came in with the tying run on an infield out. Tony La Russa was blunt about it afterward, saying that Canseco's was the kind of play that had to be made if you expected to win. There was also room to doubt Tony's decision to keep his starter, Bob Welch, out there into the eighth, instead of calling on his famous bullpen to hold the lead. As it was, Eckersley came on in the tenth, succeeding Honeycutt but now in the unfamiliar role of trying to hold a tie, and he was racked for three hits and the loss — what he calls a "walk-off piece." All through these games, La Russa was oddly hesitant about going to his relievers; it was as if he were saving them for another demanding series the following week.

I feel uneasy about such second-guessing, which lessens the Reds' accomplishment and also seems to put me in the vociferous company of fans who turned on the Athletics with distaste, almost with scorn, as they lost. "I never liked them" was a popular refrain, and it would be followed with irritable comments about Canseco's ego and Canseco's salary, Mark McGwire's fallibility against inside pitching, La Russa's intellectual hauteur, and so forth. There was also a barely hidden satisfaction among some front-office people in both leagues, which (to me, at least) arose from the brilliant trading and drafting coups executed by Sandy Alderson and his Oakland colleagues over the past five or six years. Just this summer, the A's took a chance when they drafted and then signed Todd Van Poppel, the best high school pitching prospect in the land, whom other clubs had bypassed because it was believed that he would go to college to play ball next year. Then, late in the summer, Oakland traded for the Rangers' Harold Baines (as a badly needed left-handed d.h. bat) and for the Cardinals' Willie McGee (to fill in for the ailing Canseco and Dave Henderson in the outfield) — pennant-insuring moves that several needier teams could have tried as well, if they had thought of them and had been willing to take the risk. This sort of stuff makes for respect if you can go on winning and bashing elbows, but if you win and win and then fall on your face, you will be suddenly popular in a new way.

"From dynasty to travesty in two games," Alderson said wryly on the Oakland bench when the teams went west, and he remained for an hour of reporters' questions about what was happening to the A's and why. Excuses were available to him — the absence of shortstop Walt Weiss, who had torn up a knee in the playoffs (his loss made almost as big a hole in the batting order, I felt, as in the middle of the infield), and Canseco's damaged back, which made it impossible for him to uncock his hips when swinging the bat and thus had made for his new and awkward open stance — but of course he offered none. The A's are a proud, high-class organization, and the pain and shock they felt as they expired in the Series — a colleague of mine who watched the

games by television told me that La Russa's folded arms and fu-
nereal phiz in the dugout reminded him of Dante contemplating
the circles of Hell — should have been plain enough to silence
our carping. "Losing feels worse than people tell me it ought to
feel," Tony said unsmilingly in his office after it was over, and
when somebody asked if all this would leave a scar, he paused
and gave the man that dead-level look of his and said, "There's
nothing wrong with a scar."

The Dynasts

Sudden extraordinary success is very different from sustained
high quality over a long period of time, and this short Series gave
us a chance to consider both of these rarities. For me, the most
impressive aspect of the Reds' victory wasn't what Rijo did or what
Hatcher did, or even what their bullpen went on doing — the A's
scored no runs at all after the third inning in any Series game. It
was the way they hit the ball. In the third inning of the third game,
the Reds scored twice against Mike Moore, going back ahead by
3–2. Up in my press perch in the top grandstand, I entered the
symbols in my scorecard and took stock. Two runs were in, but
there were two out now, and the Reds' advantage looked trifling.
Moore had been knocked about, but the Athletics' bullpen was
up and throwing, and the Cincinnati pitcher, Tom Browning, had
looked no less frail so far. Too much action, but otherwise not a
bad game, and with the Athletics now at home playing on grass
before their vociferous fans, I felt that they still held a little advantage in the night's business. Stew would go again on the mor-
row, and it was possible to think that the teams would be even-up
twenty-six or twenty-seven hours from now, with the best part of
the Series just ahead.
    Well, no. Chris Sabo smashed Moore's third pitch into the left-
field stands. It was his second homer of the game. Benzinger singled, and La Russa came out at last and called in Scott Sanderson, a 17–11 starter with the A's this year. Sanderson threw a
wild pitch and then essayed an off-speed breaking ball to catcher
Joe Oliver, who whacked a double into the left-field corner, driving home the fifth run of the inning. Mariano Duncan singled,

and Barry Larkin, up for the second time in the inning, tripled to the wall in left-center. That was all — seven runs on six hits in the inning — but it would suffice. The Reds won the game, 8–3. The crowd, of course, had gone mute during the onslaught, and all you could hear in the crammed, festive bowl was the droning reverberation of two advertising towplanes circling in the late sunshine overhead. No one said anything, but we understood. Just like that, the Series was over.

I have some experience in these October adventures, but the latter sector of this Reds half-inning — homer, single, double, single, triple — didn't match anything in my memory. It wasn't the scariness of the totals — there have been plenty of other eruptions in Series play — as much as the deadly timing of the assault: very early in a pivotal game that the other team knew it had to win. This sort of hitting comes along sometimes in spring training, and you laugh at it, because you know how freaky it is; you could watch batting practice for a week and never see its like. In a World Series, it feels very different, and the still reverberating echoes of that inning make me believe that these Reds must be ranked very high among the perpetrators of famous upsets in these games — along with the 1914 Braves, let's say, or with the 1954 Giants, who swept a Cleveland Indians team that had won 111 games and had beaten out the Yankees in the process. That 1954 Yankees club won 103 games but finished eight games in arrears, and their failure to make it into the World Series that fall was the only interruption in what would otherwise have been a stretch of ten consecutive pennants, with seven world championships. Now, *there* was a dynasty.

The Athletics are not a dynasty after all — the Ming cracked in the kiln — and the widespread disappointment in this Series seems to arise from that, for some reason. No team has won consecutive World Series since the Yankees did it in 1977 and 1978, while the hairy, green-and-gold, Jackson-Bando-Rudi Oakland A's were the last three-straight champions, earlier in that decade. We want that back — we almost insist on it. You heard "dynasty" all summer, as if it had become the only baseball speculation left to us. Fans I've heard from now speak of the present Athletics with scorn because they lost the World Series in 1988 and now here in 1990, but it's interesting that the veterans among the Reds don't feel that way. "I'll tell you, I'm glad we don't have to play them in the regular season next year," Billy Hatcher said. Why the A's went so flat is something that the Oakland management will be thinking and consulting about all winter, but it's my own feeling that the club will be no less formidable next summer. Winning your division is by far the hardest thing to do in baseball — all the players are in agreement about that — and these Athletics have now done it three times running. Their three-year won-and-lost total comes out to 306–180. (The next-nearest total, for any club, is the Mets' 278–206 in that span, while third-best is the Blue Jays' 262–224 — which puts those teams twenty-eight games and forty-four games to the bad, compared with Oakland.) Down the years, twenty-four different teams have won three hundred games or better over three seasons. The best such record in the modern era is the Orioles' 318 wins in 1969, 1970, and 1971. That Earl Weaver club (how well I remember it!) also lost the World Series in their first October and again in the third — to the upstart Mets and then to the Pirates — but no one mentioned the word "dynasty" back then or mourned the missing of it. Sports mean more to us now, I keep hearing. We demand more — or perhaps it's less.

The baseball story we really want to hear may be a primer. If there is no dynasty, then we must dismiss the old kings and the aging knights from our thoughts and mutter harsh things about them as they leave the hall. They didn't try, they weren't noble after all. We turn our attention to a new tale, with fresh faces and different names in it, and glorious adventures. These are heroes for sure: they are young, and they renew all our hopes. The other story goes on, to be sure, but it is a more demanding sort of reading. Its heroes are grown up and their work is more like our own: a hard year-to-year struggle to find or define quality and to hold on to it, if they can — to do well and to persist in that enormous effort. It's a story of complexity and perhaps also of middle age, but there are some of us who find vivid interest in that, and more lasting rewards.

December 3, 1990

NEAL DONNELLY

Going the Distance

FROM BUFFALO MAGAZINE

"BUFFALO. That's my favorite town," the station attendant blurted when I said I was about to drive there for the weekend.

My battery was low, so I was seeking a quick charge at Lake Amoco on Connecticut Avenue just over the Washington line in Chevy Chase, Maryland.

I replied with a likely assumption: "You must be from Buffalo."

Having lived in six American cities and five world capitals, I have been conditioned to expect trite, derisive comments when my hometown enters the conversation. For this reason, like most western New Yorkers away from home, I have become fiercely loyal to, and protective of, Buffalo.

"Oh, no," he answered. "I'm from here. But I go to Buffalo eight times a year. I'm a Buffalo Bills season-ticket holder. As a matter of fact, I've just received my tickets for next season: section B, aisle 3, row 33, seats 110 and 111."

After I worked my jaw up to normal position from the vicinity of the floor where it had dropped, I asked the obvious question: "How can a man from the home of the Redskins be a Bills season-ticket holder?"

"I hate the Redskins," he said, boldly unafraid of the consequences should such local heresy be overheard. "I've been a Bills fan since 1964. I've never supported any other team."

A series of questions quickly established that his name is Bobby Fox, he is thirty-one years old, recently married, a lifelong Washington resident of sound mind who had seen his first Bills game when he was only six years old.

"A friend visiting my mother was watching the Chargers-Bills AFL championship game on television. The Bills were underdogs, but with Jack Kemp and Cookie Gilchrist they beat the Chargers, 20–7. I still remember the play of the game: Mike Stratton broke Keith Lincoln's ribs. It was a class tackle.

"I just love talking about the Bills," Fox said as I settled into an armchair next to the cash register to listen and take notes between customers.

"How could you remember so much of the game if you were only six years old?" I asked. "I remember the pleasure I got from watching, but the details were lost on me at that age. When I was nine I read the game account on microfilm at the library. But I wanted to relive it, so at one point I considered having myself hypnotized to bring out my memory of the game. I never did."

Talking to Fox is like talking to a man created in a laboratory manned by Buffalo Bills public relations department scientists.

Fox continued: "The Bills and Chargers met again in the 1965 championship game. Curt Gowdy did the game and I recorded it. I still have the tape and listened to it just last year. Both Bills wide receivers were out with injuries. The Chargers were heavy favorites. The Bills won, twenty-three to zip. Humiliated the Chargers in San Diego. Kemp was named MVP. From that time on, I have been a diehard fan.

"The next year, 1966, I was old enough to experience the emotional ups and downs of the entire season and realize how hard it is to win all games and stay on top. They ended with a nine-four-one record, and I felt the pain physically. The Chiefs wasted the Bills in the championship, thirty-one to seven. I cried. I wanted the Bills to go to the first Super Bowl so bad. After that game the Bills went downhill for a long time, but I never gave up on them.

"In 1969 the Bills drafted O. J. Simpson, and I held a party in my room. I put up streamers and balloons and hand lettered banners which said, 'He's Ours' and 'Go O.J.' "

"Who did you invite to the party?" I asked.

"Nobody," Fox answered. "It was just a celebration party for myself."

In 1971 Fox's mother took him to see Niagara Falls. After viewing the cascade, Fox dragged his mother to the Bills training camp, where he photographed practice and talked with some Bills hopefuls. "I was mesmerized by the experience," he recalls.

"Once you get a football team in your system, you can't get it out. In 1980 my passion for the Bills began to dominate my life. I checked off the days on my calendar until the next game," Fox confessed. "I love Joe Ferguson. I like the way he walks, just like a cocky, arrogant quarterback ought to walk. He's got guts and plays hurt — it didn't take twenty million dollars to get him to play. I like Jim Kelly, but Joe Ferguson is tops. Remember when Ferguson was called for an unfair delay-of-game penalty just as the Bills were driving for a score to tie Cincinnati in the closing minutes of the 1981 divisional championship playoff? It was obvious to everyone that the referee was off base. I felt so bad for Joe and was so upset I didn't talk to anyone for a month."

The defection of Chuck Knox, his favorite coach, to Seattle and the failure of Ralph Wilson to sign Tom Cousineau tested Fox's devotion. But Fox kept true to his adopted team through the chaos of the strike season, cocaine allegations, and press reports of bad morale. Like a stern parent willing to see his son punished in order to purge a fault, Fox began to root for Bills losses so they would have the first draft pick.

Fox made his first Bills accessory purchase in 1983, a jacket ordered from Laux Sporting Goods in North Tonawanda. He went on to buy an entire uniform, including a $200 helmet. Once he covered a girlfriend's car with Bills bumper stickers from Laux. "She was upset," he acknowledges with an uncomprehending shake of the head.

Fox put an ad in *Sports Collectors Digest* offering to buy anything connected with the Bills. Buffalonian Budd Bailey responded with bundles of old programs and media guides. "Budd's a great guy," Fox said. "He's not only sent me all this stuff, but gave me inside dope on the Bills locker room. He told me how Joe Cribbs put tape on his locker to resemble prison bars. He hated Buffalo and was traded because of his attitude. But I consider Cribbs to be one of football's greatest running backs. I was sorry to see him leave."

Fox has been a season-ticket holder since 1988. Eight times a year he makes the 456-mile drive from Rockville, Maryland, leaving Saturday morning and arriving eight and a half hours later at the Sheraton Foxhead Inn in Niagara Falls, Ontario, where he and his mother first stayed in 1971. "I always stay there. I think they know me by now," Fox said.

Fox is usually able to coax his mother or his wife, Beverly, to accompany him on the long drive. "My mother is not fond of football, but she likes Niagara Falls. Beverly doesn't care much for football either, but she loves me," Fox said, explaining the basis of his persuasive powers. He tells how once, when getting gasoline in Amherst, Beverly reached into the glove compartment and pulled out a Redskins glass, a premium from a Washington fill-up. A quick talker, she bartered the glass and a full tank for four Bills glasses. "She's a great saleswoman," Fox bragged. "Now I got a set of Bills glasses."

On game day he crosses the Rainbow Bridge, parks at the Niagara Falls bus station, and takes the $6 football shuttle to Rich Stadium. "I got to know some of the shuttle repeaters. They're all friendly, not like Washingtonians. Here in Washington, people look out for themselves and are corked up with tension. Buffalo is a blue-collar town. People work hard for their money. There is something basic and decent about the Buffalonians I know.

"My mother says I should move to Buffalo just for the football season," Fox said with a smile. "Actually my dream is to live in Buffalo. I even subscribe to the *Buffalo News*. It costs me $18.40 a month, but it's one of the best investments I have ever made. Naturally I read the sports section carefully, but I also check out the home finder section on Saturday. The house prices are very attractive compared to Washington," Fox said with a trace of envy.

The December 11, 1988, Raiders-Bills game was the most memorable for Fox. "Buffalo won," he recalled, "but I didn't see all of the last quarter. It was so cold I had to get up and move around the walkways just to keep warm. Cold in Buffalo is not like cold in Washington," Fox claimed, echoing the alien consensus. "At times it gets so cold in that stadium I don't know how people can dig coins out of their pockets to pay vendors. I walked into the men's room once at halftime and could hardly see. All those guys relieving themselves in the cold created a steam which made the place look like London in the fog," he said. Anticipating an objection he added quickly, "No. I mean it."

As we parted, Fox, in a serious tone, said, "There is only one thing that would turn me against the Bills. If they build a domed stadium, I'll transfer my allegiance. Open-air football in Buffalo in December is the way the game was meant to be played."

September 9, 1990

PETER RICHMOND

Death of a Cowboy

FROM THE NATIONAL SPORTS DAILY

SOME DON'T JOIN the diaspora to the cities, to fill up the buildings and prowl the gray streets. Some decide to stay behind and work the land, and to work with the land — to live on it and play on it, dwarfed by its permanence, and secure in it. Because there is always this about the land, about prairie and pond and mountain: they never go away. Beneath a roof of sky, yesterday and tomorrow always have a great deal in common. And to live here, planted on the planet's surface, so that you can sense the roll of the seasons and taste in them time's renewal, is, inevitably, to feel some of that same permanence for yourself.

Perhaps this is why, one full year after Lane Frost died with a bull's horn through his heart in the mud of a rodeo arena, his death is still so tangible and his absence so conspicuous — why his memory is not only unfaded, but growing more substantial: because the permanence has been rended against all reason and expectation, against all of the flows and currents.

Perhaps this is why his parents and widow and best friend still receive letters from people who have written songs about Lane Frost, and poems, and named children after him, and why strangers show up on their doorsteps to talk about him. Perhaps this is why his image now appears in a country music video alongside Martin Luther King and John Wayne. And why thousands of people will visit the memorial display at the Cheyenne Frontier Days this week, to touch the unimaginably soft leather glove, caked with resin, that Lane Frost wore on his last ride, and to caress the heavy blue leather chaps, a few yards from the dirt in which he died.

The thing is, it was not a bad wreck, as wrecks go — and maybe that explains some of the lingering disbelief, the universal disquiet; anyone who's seen any rodeo has seen a hundred worse. There will probably be a few worse today, in the oval arena beneath the sky so wide that the earth feels as if it's been shoved right up into its brilliant blue belly. In fact, it was almost routine: he was tossed off, he got hit by a horn, he fell down, he got up again, and the bull turned away. By then, spectators were heading for the cotton-candy stand, applauding the ride. But then he fell again, face first, into the mud. The horn, or broken rib, had hit an artery, and within a few minutes, or seconds, he was dead.

And so, while it was not a bad wreck, in the realest sense it was the worst wreck in the history of rodeo, the wreck from which the sport, it is now clear, will never recover. Because it was the wreck that claimed Lane Frost.

To catalogue the details of his life in order to effectively convey what he meant, and still means, to the rodeo is like trying to explain the essence of the prairie by describing the color of its grass, and its dirt, and its livestock. In each case, to isolate the individual elements is to come up well short of an understanding of the phenomenon.

But it's as good a starting point as any. First of all, in his twenty-five years, by all accounts Lane Frost lived his life above reproach. As a four-year-old he'd go out and rake the lawn without being asked, and as a twenty-three-year-old, as the world champion bullrider, he'd fix the fence. He'd help out in the stripping chute if a neighbor's help had taken off. He'd pay the way for a paraplegic friend to fly to Reno for the finals, and tell no one. He never said no to a fan. He was a good husband. He resisted the lures of the buckle bunnies who linger late in a rodeo arena, looking to sidle up against the winners. If he'd been given an unfairly low score after a good ride, he'd keep his anger in, and wait until he was out of sight of the crowd to throw his hat. And if he and his wife, Kellie, were arguing, and he was really angry, he'd flip the radio to country and western, because he knew she couldn't stand it.

"He might not have worn a halo, but he was as close as I'd ever been to someone who did," said Richard (Tuff) Hedeman, twice champion bullrider, Lane Frost's closest friend and traveling partner for five years.

"He always cheered people up," said Ty Murray, the best cowboy alive, a good friend. "You coulda drove all night, not had much sleep, not much to eat, see him and be in a good mood in five minutes. He was that way all the time. Around everybody."

Besides all the other things he did, Lane Frost rode bulls, and this requires in a man's makeup something exceptional. Lane's dad, Clyde Frost, a man forged of something unyielding, spent a decade with the rodeo, riding bareback and saddle broncs, but he never put himself on the back of a Brahma bull.

Still, of the 1,050 cowboys entered in the current Frontier Days, 100 ride the bulls, and in the 750 rodeos sanctioned each year by the Professional Rodeo Cowboy Association, there is no shortage of either the fearless or the foolish, all anxious to sit astride an animal that weighs a ton, and that, for eight full seconds, knows nothing but rage.

In 1987, Lane Frost won the championship of bullriding, and won the biggest buckle you can win. Still, there's a new buckle and a different champion crowned every year, almost thirty of them since the PRCA began awarding them. Yes, he'd won some money, more than most of the bullriders, more than $100,000 in 1987. But after expenses he probably grossed no more than $60,000.

Then, in 1988 Lane Frost did something no one had ever done, and his legend began to take strong root. He rode a bull named Red Rock, a bull that no cowboy had been able to stay on in 308 attempts. Lane Frost did. This was the rodeo equivalent of pulling the sword out of the stone. And in five subsequent rides, Frost stayed on the bull twice more, and Red Rock threw him three times.

The King — that's what the other cowboys called Lane. It's a label that, in American folklore, is not pitched around lightly. It's an odd fit, the analogy, but it does fit. Like the other king, Lane was larger than life in life, and now he is much larger than life in death; his Graceland is the whole constellation of rodeo arenas that cover the western landscape.

But the title also does him a disservice, because in its allusion to the corpulent, sopping shell of a man who welded rock and roll to the American soul, it implies a mindless obeisance on the part of a herd of fanatics, worshiping an ideal instead of a person. Whereas Lane Frost more or less lived the life that embodied the ideal. The people who now remember Lane Frost remember him in his true scale and measure, which was only that of a man who lived his life very well and did his work with dedication. And in the land of livestock and grassland and corral and endless highway, that is more or less everything.

And that is why, for all of the temptation to see something profound in the death of a heroic American cowboy, we would do well not to try to analyze the essence of the legend, or take outsize meaning from his death. We would do better to simply note it, and not forget it.

The story of Lane Frost is a simple one. In a world where life is reduced to good and evil, Satan and the Lord, staying on the bull or falling off it, working the ranch or losing it, the death of a great cowboy is as profound as life can get.

That's all it is, a cowboy's death.

That's all, and that's everything.

"Mama, Don't Let Your Babies Grow Up to Be Cowboys" four men were singing in the middle of the Astrodome one night not long ago during the rodeo they call the Houston Fat Show — as if Willie and Waylon and Kris and Johnny really had any idea, as if four men who call themselves the Highwaymen but travel the highway in buses as luxurious as the *Lusitania* have the slightest idea about the modern cowboy.

In fact, the modern rodeo cowboy has the stablest of dreams: earn enough money to put down on his own piece of land, and buy a few head of cattle. En route, for all of the dirt and the muck, for all of the renegade pedigree, it is a clean and exhausting and fulfilling way of spending your time here.

"This is all we live for," Tuff Hedeman was saying on the Astrodome floor, far removed from Willie and his friends. Hedeman has the bullrider's slightly bowed walk, as if gravity is heavier where bullriders stride, and he has the same kick-ass eyes so many bullriders seem to wear. "Our heroes weren't Roger Staubach and Joe Montana," he said. "Where we grew up, cowboys were a way of life. They still are. We're not making millions, but that's not the point. If it wasn't for rodeo, I wouldn't have anything."

For all of its violence, rodeo is a gentle sport, driven by the frontier impulse not to conquer the land or defeat its animals but to simply tame both, to effect a truce: spend eight seconds on an animal's back and flee in safety. It's a sensible kind of victory.

The danger is hardly a surprise. The bullrider is generally a small man, holding on to a rope wound as tightly as possible around the neck of a bull whose only instinct is to rid himself of the irritation on his back, and then, having done so, to search out the rider to give a payback for his audacity. There have been only eleven deaths in PRCA-sanctioned rodeos in the twenty-seven years of its existence, but few bullriders lack scars. Charlie Sampson, one of the best bullriders, has one ear, and the corners of his eyes are crowded with scars the shape of barbed wire. Some get hurt in the chute, which fits the bull like a coffin. Some insist on holding on to the rope even as they're being thrown, and risk being whipped like a yo-yo right back to the horns.

"Rodeo isn't a matter of will you get hurt, it's a matter of when and how hard," Hedeman said. "This is a game of wrecks.

"The scary part," he said, "was that you'd never think it'd happen to Lane. He was a world champion. He was one of the best at what he did. You'd have thought he was the last guy it'd happen to."

He'd had a rough two years after he won the big buckle, starting with the Olympics in Edmonton in the winter of 1988. There was a string of bad scores — the judging in bullriding is as subjective as in any sport, and if a judge thinks the bull isn't bucking hard, which is a difficult thing to tell, he'll lower the score. And Lane's wrecks had started to pile up. In the Olympics he was knocked out for five minutes when his bull bucked him off in front of the chute, then turned around and walked over him — in the idiom, he got stepped on. And one month before his death, he lost his front teeth in Fort Worth when his face hit the back of the bull's head.

"He was still winning," Kellie Frost said one night in their home in Quanah, Texas. She was packing to move to Santa Fe. Lane's National Finals Rodeo jerseys hung on the walls. There was a button that read, I'VE GOT FROST FEVER. "But everything was not going like it usually did. He hadn't won that much last year. He'd come home and say, 'Maybe I need to find somethin' else to do.' "

But things seemed to have turned around in Cheyenne. He'd had a good week, and in the final go-round on Sunday, when the horn sounded after eight seconds, and the scoreboard flashed an 86 — out of 100, but a 90 is virtually unheard-of — he'd officially won more than $10,000. For the briefest of moments, between the time he let the bull buck him off and the time the bull caught him, the entire world of rodeo delighted in his return.

Ten seconds later, it had gone wrong. Everyone knew it, because when the ambulance pulled away from the grandstand, it was not going fast.

"It was a real common-lookin' deal to me," Ty Murray said. "It was stuff you see every day."

The bull was nicknamed Bad to the Bone, but the name was just wishful thinking on its owner's part; it was not a mean bull, not the kind that likes to maul the rider. There are bloodthirsty bulls, but most are not; even Red Rock is the kind of bull you can rub behind the ear when no one's on his back.

At the end of the ride — a good ride, a great ride, he's stayed up on the bull's neck, in total control — he let himself free of the rope and slid down the bull's back, and the bull flipped him off with a flick of its haunches. It was the picture-perfect getaway, textbook stuff. He sailed free, facing the sky, and then, in the air, he turned around like a cat so that he landed on all fours, four or five yards from the bull, in the dirt. But it had been raining all week, and the dirt was muddy, and he had trouble getting up — maybe just a microsecond lost, but a critical one, for the bull had circled around.

Now it dipped its head as Lane braced himself to rise, more as if to investigate the man, certainly not to gore him. In the tape, the bull looks bored, wearing that peculiarly vacuous expression that only cows and bulls can know. And then it looked as if it had decided not to bother and turned its head away. But its horns were huge, and remarkably pointed, and as it turned its head away, the right horn hit Lane on the back of the ribcage on the left side.

Then it walked away. Lane rose, but then he motioned to the

chute, where the other cowboys were sitting astride the fences. There was something wrong in the way he waved. And then he fell in the mud, face down.

"I didn't start worryin' until I seen him lay there," Ty Murray said. "I knew he wouldn't lay there unless he was hurt real bad. There's a million things goin' through your mind."

"I knew something was wrong," Tuff Hedeman said. "First I thought he was knocked out. When we turned him over, he couldn't see me. Someone said he'd stopped breathin', and I knew it was going to be a long road."

From the hospital, Tuff called Kellie at her hotel back in Texas, where she was supervising the stunts for a bullriding movie. It was the first Frontier Days she'd ever missed. Lane was due to come back and do some stunt work.

"Sometimes I feel like tearing out my hair," Kellie Frost said. "Everything was so . . . good. It was the last thing from my mind, that something like that would happen, especially to someone as precious as he was. It makes me mad, because I think, 'He never did anything wrong.' "

"You can't hardly find better people than rodeo people," said Lane's mother, Elsie Frost. "It's a special breed. And God let us have one of the best."

The Frost home in southern Oklahoma features an array of dozens of buckles and saddles won in dozens of cities and towns and states, and many bear Clyde Frost's name. In a room off the living room, saddles lounge everywhere you look, finely tooled leather saddles, things of great weight and heft.

The late Freckles Brown, a famed bullrider, was one of Clyde's closest friends, which goes some of the way toward explaining why Clyde and Elsie Frost's first boy was addicted to bulls. It was a deep pull. Elsie says Lane was five months old when, at a rodeo, he awoke from an infant's sleep when it was time for the bullriding, most likely summoned by the sound of the bull bell. At the age of two, he was seen sleepwalking down a flight of stairs and out the front door, carrying a bull rope on his way to the barn. In the Frosts' earlier home movies, a boy of four is seen astride a calf that is doing everything in its not inconsiderable power to buck the boy, who is bumping up and down with the ferocity of a jackhammer and holding on.

Later, swimming in the irrigation canal behind the family's home in Utah, Lane jumped through the windshield of a submerged car that had been dumped in the water and cut himself under the arm so severely that one hundred stitches were required; on the way to the hospital he spoke once, to ask his mother if the cuts meant that he would never be able to ride bulls. When the family moved to Oklahoma, Lane was the only boy who rode rodeo at Atoka High School, but still, in his junior year, he won the national high school championship in Douglas, Wyoming.

"If anything got in the way of a rodeo, like a ball game, the ball game would have to wait," Clyde Frost said. "Her folks" — he nodded to his wife, sitting on the couch next to him — "was always buyin' Lane little trucks and stuff, but they just sat there. He might use 'em with other kids if they came over, but not for long. He'd always take them out to the corral, and they'd end up doin' somethin' out there."

On a rainy morning, the Frosts were playing Lane's videotape. Beneath the brim of his black hat, even on the television, Lane's spirit was infectious and his demeanor disarmingly friendly. It was Tuff who said Lane could get a wall to talk. On the video, Lane has no difficulty filling sixty minutes talking bulls, but then, as Tuff also once said, Lane should have run for office, he liked to talk so much. Tuff and Tracie and Kellie lost count of the hours they spent waiting on Lane after the rodeos. He'd chat with every fawning fan.

The praise was less easy to find within the Frost home. "Clyde wouldn't slap him on the back," Elsie Frost said. "Even when Lane won, Clyde would try to find somethin' wrong. Once Lane said to me, 'No matter how good I do, I don't do as good as Dad thinks I ought to.' "

Across the room, Clyde Frost does not blink. His is a good, weathered face, set in a permanent expression of no expression at all, the face of a man who expects neither too little nor too much from the lot he has been dealt. It was not Lane's wealth of buckles and saddles and prize money of which Clyde was the proudest. It was the day the mail carrier remarked how stunned he was to see the world's champion bullrider mending a fence, like a common man, a few days after he'd won the title.

"I don't know how people are supposed to feel after a year," Elsie Frost said. "I think we're doing pretty good. Every thirtieth of the month is kind of a hard time. What amazes me is how especially nice everyone has been, and still are. You think they'd think, 'They're gettin' over it by now, don't need attention,' but it seems like people are still givin' it to us. A couple of cowboys came by the other day on their way to Arkansas. Things like that make you feel good."

Outside, oak and hickory and pecan trees dotted the rolling grassland. "Lane done what not many people do," Clyde Frost said in front of his home. Rain was patting the Bermuda grass, and it was the only sound for several miles. "I'd rather live half a life doin' what I want to do than live to be a hundred and not."

"Lane was a born-again Christian," Elsie Frost said, "and this has saved some sinners. If this was going to happen, I've thought, let it happen at the rodeo, where it could make more of an impression than any other rodeo. I don't think God takes lives — the Devil is the one who takes them."

They held the funeral in Atoka, a few dozen miles down the highway from Cheyenne, because it was the closest church that could accommodate 1,200 people.

When they viewed his body, Tuff told Clyde and Elsie that that was exactly the way he'd looked when they'd turned him over.

All of them, Tuff and Kellie and Clyde and Elsie, like to take this wherever they go: He died doing what he wanted to do. He did not die in a head-on, on a back highway — that's the greatest fear by far of all rodeo parents — or in a small plane nosing into a field at 3 A.M. He is not lingering in illness, or crippled, or handicapped. He died at the apex, after one of the best rides of his life, in the oldest rodeo.

"I don't guess too many people can say that they lived their lives to the fullest, every day, and did what they wanted until the last day they did it," a cowboy named Bobby Delvecchio said. "He was glorious when he was alive, and he's glorious now that he's dead. He give back to rodeo more than he got out."

"There isn't a minute goes by," Tuff Hedeman says, "that I don't think of it."

One month after his death at the National Finals Rodeo in 1989, Tuff Hedeman told whomever asked that he wanted to win it all for Lane. Then he went out and did so, won the championship, and then stayed on his final bull for several extra seconds. He had both of their names inscribed on the buckle. And that evening, in tribute, the rodeo organizers turned Red Rock out into the arena alone. The bull looked lost, several people said. Tuff's wife, Tracie, said it seemed as if he were looking for Lane.

July 22, 1990

BRIAN WOOLLEY

The Hands and
Eye of Texas Billy Mays

FROM DALLAS LIFE MAGAZINE

IT COULD easily have turned out wrong, Texas Billy Mays is saying. If he hadn't fallen off that oil derrick on that day so long
ago, if he hadn't been dating that waitress, if Granville Humphrey hadn't come into Sam's Bar, there's no telling whichaway
his life might have gone.

"The way I see it," he says, "every man is born with the ability
to do something better than anybody else can do that thing. The
trouble is, most men never find out what their thing is. I'm one
of the lucky ones. I found the one thing I can do better than anybody."

Billy's sitting at a table in Click's, a bar and game room on
Northwest Highway in Dallas, drinking a beer, explaining.

It was 1958, he says. He was twenty-one and not long off the
family farm up at Emory, near Sulphur Springs. The derrick was
on a rig in the Gulf of Mexico, off Louisiana. Billy's fall broke his
back. While he healed, he hung out at Sam's Bar on Haskell Avenue in Dallas, where his girlfriend worked. "They had a shuffleboard in there," Billy says, "but I didn't pay any attention to it.
Hell, I didn't even know what a shuffleboard was."

Then one day Granville Humphrey walked in. "He came from
Oklahoma City," Billy says. "He had beat everybody in Dallas.
He was the world's champion."

The bar patrons started drawing partners for a shuffleboard
round robin. Thirty-nine players signed up. They needed a for-
tieth. They talked Billy into giving it a try.

"It turned out, me and Granville Humphrey drawed partners," Billy says. "He toted me, I guess you'd say. We won the
round robin. I played the rest of the day and lost the $40 I'd won,
but I'd been hooked. I'd be at Sam's when they opened up in the
morning, and I wouldn't leave till they shut the door at midnight.
At the end of three months, I was the best shuffleboard player in
Dallas. By the time I was twenty-two, I was the best in the world."

In the kind of shuffleboard played by passengers on cruise ships
and senior citizens in St. Petersburg, they shove pucks about the
deck or floor with long sticks. That isn't the kind that Billy Mays
learned in Sam's Bar.

Billy's is the true shuffleboard, the original shuffleboard, the
shuffleboard played in English taverns as early as 1532 and by
early settlers as soon as they had been on the shore of North
America long enough to build taverns of their own.

The modern version of the game is played on a slab of rock
maple that's twenty feet, eight inches long. The slab sits on a table and is surrounded by a padded trough. The players stand at
one end of the table and, taking turns, slide four metal weights
each toward the other end. The board has been sprinkled with
powdered wax to make the weights slide quickly and smoothly.
The player who places a weight closest to the opposite end of the
board without its dropping off scores points. Then the weights
are shot from the other end of the table. In the most commonly
played variety of the game, the first player — or, in the case of
doubles, the first team — to score fifteen points is the winner.

Every beer joint worthy of the name has its shuffleboard, along
with its pool table and its jukebox loaded with country music, and
Billy knows where they all are.

"Just in the state of Texas, I'd say there's five thousand boards
now," he says. "California's got probably six thousand. Washington and Oregon together has got more than California has. They
play a lot in Connecticut and Maine and Massachusetts, but there's
no good players up there. There's a couple of good players in
New York. Pennsylvania's got the best on the East Coast. Michigan, Indiana, and Illinois have a lot of boards, but there's just
five or six places in Iowa to play it. Nebraska's real full of them,
Kansas has got quite a few, and Colorado. There's fifty or one
hundred in Montana, but just a few in Wyoming. North Dakota's

got a couple. South Dakota's got, I'd say, twenty. Idaho don't have very many . . ."

Shuffleboard is a favorite pastime of cowboys, truck drivers, farmers, miners, and construction workers, people who work hard with their hands, but a lot of businessmen and city-slicker professionals play it, too. Shuffleboard players like to bet on their games, and they listen to loud music, drink beer, and smoke cigarettes while they play. Maybe that's why the game looks so much easier than it is. Nobody seems to be straining at it.

"But it's the toughest game in the world," Billy says. "It's a combination of Bobby Fischer–type chess, Arnold Palmer–type golf, and Muhammad Ali–type nerve. There's very little luck in it and a tremendous amount of skill. It's a precision game."

Looking at Billy, you would never peg him for the world's greatest master of the world's toughest game. He's so wiry he could be mistaken for scrawny. He dresses in cowboy boots and satin jackets that advertise beer. His glasses are so thick that his eyes seem outlandishly large. Maybe because of the glasses, his brow is always furrowed horizontally, giving him an air of perpetual bemusement, as if he doesn't know quite where he is, or as if he's trying to find a familiar face in a crowd.

One of the thick lenses isn't very useful. When Billy was nine years old, a rock from his brother's slingshot struck him in the right eye, robbing it of sight. He can distinguish light and dark with it, he says, but nothing else. Then, when he was seventeen, he fought a boxing match in Longview against Donnie Fleeman — who later would KO Ezzard Charles — and was knocked cross-eyed by a blow to the back of his head. "When I get tired, that right eye still wanders a little," Billy says. "I can't hold the thing still."

But it doesn't matter much. "I don't look at the weights when I shoot anyway," he says. "I shoot with my mind. If you turn the weight loose right at your end of the table, it'll go right at the other end. What you've got to do is read the drift, and then you shoot into the drift."

Every shuffleboard is as unique as a fingerprint. Its humps and warps and quirks and curves, its slow spots and fast spots — all undetectable to the eye — make up a board's drift, and the drift is what gives it its character. "The drift is part of the table," Billy says, "but the drift isn't always the same. Weather can change it. Putting a matchbook under one of the table legs can change it.

"When you go play someone on their own table," he says, "it's a bigger advantage to them than when you play a football team on its home field. A guy who plays on a board all the time, he'll know every little drift in it. It's like spotting him three or four points. But in about two games, I'll know the board better than him. I watch. I study what the board does. It's like opening a book and studying it instead of just opening a book and reading."

Billy finishes his beer and walks over to the shuffleboard. It's a board he knows well, for it's a World's Best, his own brand, built by Texas Billy Mays himself at his shop in Seagoville. His signature is on it.

It's what he does for most of his living these days, he says, building and selling shuffleboards for $3,200 to $4,500 each and packaging and selling cans of his special shuffleboard wax, which he says is "the fastest wax on the market," mixed according to his own secret formula. But tonight Click's is paying him $500 to perform trick shots for the customers and then play all challengers.

He starts simple. His wife, Doris, sets two weights on the table at the other end. Billy slides two weights down and knocks them off simultaneously. He repeats the trick using three weights. Then Doris sets two weights on the table and lays a cigarette across them like a rail. Billy slides a weight between them and knocks the cigarette away without touching the two weights supporting it. Then Doris sets a weight near the end of the table and stands a penny against it, on edge. Billy's shot knocks the penny away without touching the weight. Then his grand finale: Billy blindfolds himself with bar napkins, shoves two weights down the board simultaneously, and knocks off two weights at the corners of the other end.

Then for three hours he plays eleven-point games against all comers. He's handicapped by a finger he broke two weeks earlier when he dropped a shuffleboard on it, but he still beats them all. At Click's and other bars where Billy has put on his exhibition over the years, he has played more than three hundred games and has lost only one. "They don't pay me for losing," he says.

But $500 is a far cry from the sums his barroom game used to earn him. In 1962, for instance, when he beat Bob Miles out of $22,000 at the Park Inn Diner in Buena Park, California. That was the match that notified the shuffleboard world that Texas Billy Mays was a force to be feared. Five years later, Billy told *Sports Illustrated* about it:

"We played for thirty hours," Billy says. " 'Let's play for $100,' Bob Miles said. 'Let's play for $200,' I said. 'Make it $300,' he said. 'Make it $400,' I said. There were 120 people in there betting, and only three were betting on me. I won eighteen in a row — nineteen out of twenty-one. He went busted five times and had to go get money. While he was gone, I played $500 freeze-out with Mexican Tommy — he's an interior decorator who has the most beautiful shot in shuffleboard, it's poetry in motion — and K.C. Kid, who's also known as K.C. Chuck. K.C. started betting on me after I busted *him*. Won $4,800. Another boy won $4,000. Some nights you throw those weights up there, looks like someone stop them with a string."

For twenty-five years after he fell off the oil derrick, Billy never worked at what most people would call a regular job. Sometimes he would sell and repair shuffleboards for the National Shuffleboard Co. From time to time he would come back to Dallas and toil awhile as a carpenter. But most of the time he was on the road, playing shuffleboard in glitzy big-city lounges and fly-blown roadside honky-tonks from Philadelphia to Los Angeles and Detroit to Houston for whatever money the locals were willing to bet on their hometown heroes.

He once bet $1,000 a game in Pasco, Washington, and walked out with $10,000. He once won $10,000 in Stockton, California, too, "but that was mostly hot checks," he says.

In the Gay '90s Bar in Hollywood, he played Rock Hudson for $100 a game. "I beat him three games in a row," Billy says. "Then, as I usually did, I tried to jack up the stakes. I said. 'Well, let's play for $200 a game now,' and Rock Hudson said, 'Naw, $100.' And I said, 'Well, if you won't play for $200, I quit.' I was trying to bluff him, see. But he said, 'Damn, I'm sure glad you quit, because I'd hate to have to stay here until I won a game.' "

The best pickings, though, were in the small towns of the West and Midwest, those with five hundred souls, or a thousand, one of whom regularly beat everybody at the local beer joint and thought of himself as God's gift to shuffleboard.

"In those little places, I could always get a game," Billy says, "because the town people would force their local hotshot to play me. They would say, 'Aw, come on, Jimmy,' or whatever the guy's name was, 'I got a hundred dollar bill that says you can beat him.' The longer we play, the more determined the guy is to beat me, and pretty soon I've really got a hustle going."

In the popular mind, a hustler always allows his opponent to win a few games, to set him up for the kill, then raises the stakes and destroys him. But Billy never did it that way.

"I always went in and beat them as bad as I could right off the bat," he says. "That makes them want to play more. See, if you play somebody and let them win, they've got your money in their pocket, and they can quit. A lot of times, that's the reason they'll play you, thinking you're a hustler and you're going to let them win a few. But I just went in and beat them as bad as I could, and then I'd laugh at them a little bit. If you laugh at a man, he's going to want to play you again. His pride makes him do it."

As his reputation grew, he sometimes had to resort to deception to lure someone into a game. "One time I was coming from Canada into Denver," he says, "and I didn't think I would get much action there because I had beat them a couple of months before out of a couple of thousand. So I stopped at a drugstore and bought an Ace bandage and wrapped my right hand in it and put my arm in a sling. Boy, they just jumped on me, and I beat them out of about $1,200. So the next day I wrapped my left hand, just to see if anybody would notice. Not a soul noticed that I had changed hands."

Robbie Gann of Visalia, California, remembers him in those days. "He used to come through the door bragging that he was the greatest shuffleboard player that ever lived," she says. "And if they didn't want to play him, he would say, 'Well, I'll play you one-handed.' And if they said no, then he would say, 'Well, I'll tie one hand behind me and wear a blindfold.' "

"He was the undisputed champion for like fifteen years," says Robbie's sister-in-law, Charlene Goldsmith. "He would step up to the board, and he would play anybody. He never told nobody he wouldn't play them. My husband said the classiest thing about

Billy that's ever been said. He said, 'Billy's talent is surpassed only by his ego.' And after he won, sometimes he would have to fight his way out of a bar, he made everybody so mad."

"I've always been a good loser," Billy says, "but I'm a bad winner. I like to rub their nose in it."

Charlene and her husband, California Bob Goldsmith, own Mr. G's in Visalia. In 1967, their bar was sponsoring a shuffleboard team in a Sacramento tournament and they went to watch.

"I had heard and heard about Billy Mays this and Billy Mays that — world champion, you know — and I was really looking forward to meeting Texas Billy Mays," Charlene says. "But when we got to Sacramento, somebody told us Billy was in the hospital having stomach surgery. He had ulcers, I think. Well, all of a sudden everybody's twittering, you know, saying, 'There's Billy Mays!' and he walks in the door, and he's all bent over. Bent almost double. The doctor wouldn't release him out of the hospital, but he left anyway. And he walks over to a board and starts playing a game for $100 an in. Back in 1967, $100 an in was pretty good money."

Billy remembers that tournament. "I won the triple crown," he says. "I won the singles, I won the doubles, and I won the team event."

He burned up 100,000 miles of highway and three or four used cars a year in those days, getting from bar to bar and tournament to tournament, and sometimes circumstances forced him to depend on the kindness of friends.

"Billy used to come to our house and spend the night," Charlene says. "We never knew who he was going to show up with. One time it was a Canadian. One time it was an Indian. You just never knew with him. It was always " 'Hello, Billy, and who is *she?*' He traveled like a Gypsy all the time, him and whatever wife or woman he was with. A shuffleboard player can resist anything except temptation."

Billy acknowledges that his marital record is smudged. He has had seven wives, four of them before he was twenty-one. "My first wife was Sue," he says, "my second wife was Sybil, my third was Sandra, my fourth wife was Jean, my fifth wife was Myrna . . . Naw, my fifth wife was Sheila, my sixth wife was Myrna, and my seventh is Doris. Me and all my wives but one get along real good."

Billy and Doris have been married five years. Jean lasted fifteen years, Sybil only ninety days. "Sybil was one of them whirlwinds," Billy says. "That was back when I was drinking a little bit, and a bunch of us got drunk, and the next thing I know I was married."

"Sometimes," Charlene says, "Billy would call and say, 'Bobby, can you send me a couple of hundred? I've had a bad run of luck.' And it wasn't that he had shot bad and lost, it was just that things had happened, you know. So Bobby would send him the money. And the very next time we would see him, Billy would come up and pay Bobby that money back. We never failed to send it to him because he always paid it back.

"One time when he was at our house, our little boy wanted to play him. He wanted to play the world champ. So Billy played him. You think he would let that kid win? You know what Billy said to him when they got through? He said, 'You'd better work on your left, kid.' Billy never let anybody win anything."

About seven years ago, Billy gave up the road and came home to Dallas and settled down. "It got to where nobody would play me," he says. "It got to where I couldn't make a living no more."

Billy often calls himself "the world champion shuffleboard player." Other players call him that, too. Still others say he used to be the world champion but isn't anymore. Asked who has replaced him as world champion, some just shrug. Others name another player, but no two are likely to name the same player.

How a player becomes "world champion" isn't clear. Billy used to promote a competition in Las Vegas called the World Championship Shuffleboard Tournament. He won it the last time it was played, in 1984, so maybe he's the reigning champion until another tournament with that name is played.

If the title is based on the number of tournaments won over the years, few would question Billy's right to the title. "I haven't kept a count of them," he says. "I'd say I've won seven or eight hundred. Back when I played all the time, I won about seventy-five out of a hundred."

Or maybe Billy's personal way of determining who has the right to the title is the best. It's certainly the simplest. "If you beat everybody," he says, "you're the world champion."

He still plays some friendly round robins in bars around Dallas, and every now and then he'll enter a tournament in Houston or Austin or Fort Worth, somewhere close at hand, but he admits he's getting rusty. And then there's that broken finger, still bothering him.

But he entered January's Pacific Coast Shuffleboard Association's Shuffleboard Extravaganza II in Las Vegas just to prove that he isn't as far over the hill as rumor is beginning to say.

"You need to play a competitive game every week or two to stay in top form," he says, "and I haven't done that. It's kind of like dancing. You dance a lot, and you keep a real smooth rhythm. But if you don't dance much, you lose that step. I don't have any idea how I'll do in Las Vegas, but I want to give it a try."

He mails in his entry fees — $400 for singles and $200 for doubles competition — but the PCSA notifies him that they weren't received by deadline. His name will be added to a list of alternates who might get a chance to play if some of the entrants don't show up.

Billy is fit to be tied. "Thirty of the best players in the world are going to be there," he says. "It's the biggest tournament there is. There won't be two people in it who aren't capable of winning. But it looks like they don't want to play me."

Nevertheless, a week before the tournament is to begin, he and two friends start toward Las Vegas by car. In Big Spring, they stop to play a little shuffleboard. They win $100. They stop again in Odessa and win $200, and again in Phoenix and come away with $500, more than enough to pay their road expenses. "And the whole town would come out to see us," Billy says.

Billy's room at the Showboat Hotel is free. So are his meals. The PCSA informs him that he won't be allowed to play in the singles competition, but Freddy Thuman of Auburn, California, who has known Billy for years, invites him to partner with him in the doubles.

The Showboat Sports Pavilion, where the tournament is to be played, is a warehouse-size room just upstairs from the bowling alleys, where the Professional Bowlers Association also is playing a tournament. The room has been fitted out with a dozen ordinary barroom shuffleboards — so ordinary that quarters have to be fed into them to activate their scoreboards.

The atmosphere of the pavilion is more akin to a saloon than a sports arena. At tables and in seats around the shuffleboards, players from all over the United States and Canada swap tales about past tournaments, difficult boards they've played, taverns where they spent memorable nights. A blue haze of cigarette smoke lies over the room like smog. Loud music blares. Bars at each end of the room do a steady business.

It's a double-elimination tournament. No one is out until he has lost two matches. A match is two out of three games. Before tournament play begins, the players are sold to "sponsors" in a Calcutta auction, which is similar to an ordinary sports pool except that the players are sold to the highest bidder. At the end of the tournament, the "owners" of the winning players are paid the contents of the Calcutta pot.

One doubles team — Darrol Nelson of Springfield, Oregon, and Jim Allis of Seattle — is sold for $2,800. Billy and Freddy go for $400. "Darrol and Jimmy are probably the best doubles team in the world right now," Billy says.

But he and Freddy get off to a fast start. Halfway into the first game, Billy has memorized the board and starts placing his weights with the precision of a diamond cutter, moving about his end of the board with an easy grace, like a dancer in slow motion. From time to time he meets Freddy at midtable to discuss strategy. Billy always does the talking. Freddy listens and nods.

When he isn't shooting, Billy pays no attention to the game. He walks among the crowd, waving, shaking hands, smoking, exchanging stories with old friends and foes until it's his turn to shoot again.

Freddy, on the other hand, is a wad of nerves wrapped in a bundle of emotion. Every shot to him is exquisite pain or ecstasy. He rants, groans, paces, punches at the air with his fists.

They win the match easily in two games. While most matches in the tournament are requiring two to three hours to complete, Billy and Freddy are finished in an hour and twenty minutes. That afternoon, they win their second match as easily.

The day's third match, the quarter-final round, isn't so easy. Chuck Nooris of Portland, Oregon, and A. Z. Turnbolt of San Jose, California, win the first game, 15–8.

Freddy's face flushes. He moans, he rails. The second game becomes a tedious war of attrition. Two hours and fifteen minutes after it began, Billy and Freddy win, 15–13, then win the third one quickly, 15–8, at 12:30 A.M.

Freddy dashes to the wall where the brackets are posted, to see who their opponents will be in the semifinal round. Billy doesn't bother. "You have to beat them all to win," he says. "It don't matter to me what order they come in."

The semifinal round is to begin at 8 A.M. the next day. At 7:30, Billy breakfasts on M&M's and jogs around an island of cars in the parking lot with Freddy. Then they go inside and demolish their opponents in an hour.

Their next match — the final match of the winners' bracket — is to begin at 6 P.M., against Darrol Nelson and Jim Allis, the $2,800 Calcutta auction babies. To kill the daylight hours, Billy wanders downstairs to the card room for a game of poker.

Darrol and Jim are as good as Billy said. They begin the match with a 6–0 lead. They're very serious, very calm. They play the board like they own it. They win 15–6.

Billy and Freddy manage to win the second, 15–14, but their shooting is erratic, and Freddy is a basket case, screaming and shaking his fists in the air. They lose the final game, 15–3.

They've clinched third place. But to win the championship, they now must beat the winners of the losers' bracket, then beat Darrol and Jim in two matches. They must do it all right now.

"They're saying you're over the hill," someone says to Billy. "Are you?"

"I tell you how you can find out," Billy replies. "Go find somebody that'll play me a game for $500."

The best of the losers — Glen Davidson of Oklahoma City and Sparky Sparkman of San Diego — demolish them, 15–2, in their first game. But Billy and Freddy win two, 15–10 and 15–14.

They've clinched second place. Their two matches against Darrol and Jim are the only matches in the tournaments still to be played. A couple dozen spectators — all that's left of the crowd — are gathered at one table now.

Billy and Freddy win the first game, 15–13.

"I've been trying to explain Billy Mays to my friend here," says a man sitting directly behind Billy, "but I can't. There's no way to explain a Billy Mays. He's the kind of guy you love to hate. He's nothing but a hustler, but if there was a shuffleboard hall of fame, he'd be the first one in it."

Billy and Freddy win the second game, and the match, 15–12.

"I'll guarantee we'll win the next match," Billy mutters to a friend. "Jim's getting drunk, and Darrol's struggling."

Billy and Freddy win the first game, 15–11, and rack up a 4–1 lead in the second.

"Put them out of their misery, Billy!" Freddy shouts.

"Billy Mays has returned!" yells someone in the crowd.

But Darrol and Jim recover and win, 15–14.

At 1:25 A.M., the last game of the tournament begins. The players have been on their feet for almost eight hours without a break. The crowd has dwindled to the hard core, and most of them are drunk.

But Billy seems as fresh as if he were beginning. His movements are silken. His words to Freddy are calming. His shots are sharp and exact.

Finally, at 2:04 A.M., Freddy scores a three-point shot and wins the game, 15–10. He falls to the floor and kicks the air like a dying rabbit.

Billy and Freddy split the $3,105 first-place doubles prize money. Freddy wraps Billy in a hug. "I love you, you old s.o.b.," he says. They shake hands and say goodbye.

Billy also had bought part of himself in the $18,000 Calcutta auction pot. His share of the winnings is $2,785. After the stack of bills is counted into his hand, he announces to the handful of people remaining that this has been his last tournament. "Tournaments are getting to be too much hassle," he says. "I'm getting too old for it. Let somebody else have it."

The people laugh. "Sure, Billy, sure," somebody says.

He sleeps until noon, then begins the long drive home.

March 4, 1990

JACK SMITH

On the Bunny Trail

FROM PHILADELPHIA MAGAZINE

IT RAINED all night, turning the farmland and pasture surrounding the Radnor Hunt into a quagmire. Sunrise failed to improve the morning's sodden mood: the sky remains slate gray; the fields behind the clubhouse are veiled in a mist that intermittently crystallizes into tiny darts of sleet.

The three score men and women who stand chatting outside the clubhouse appear not to mind the chill and the damp. It is a perfect day for beagling.

"The scent will be high today," says L. Stockton Illoway of Newtown Square, looking around. "Some days the scent seems to disappear into the ground, but today the hounds should be able to hunt with their noses." Illoway is in his forties, a tall, wiry man with a guardsman's bushy mustache. As joint master of the Ardrossan Hunt, he will lead this morning's chase.

The hunters' cars are parked beneath the elms between the Radnor Hunt clubhouse, a stark, four-story brick affair, and the stables a hundred yards away. The hood ornaments on some of the cars are miniature cast-iron "shakos" — plumed military helmets signifying membership in Philadelphia's First City Troop, the socially exclusive National Guard unit. Miniature likenesses of beagles adorn the hoods of a few others.

About a dozen of the morning's hunters wear dark green, heavy woolen hunting jackets bearing the blue collars and tan piping of the Ardrossan pack, named for the estate of Edgar and Hope Scott, where the hounds are kenneled. A half-dozen others wear jackets of similar cut, but with the burgundy collars characteristic of the Skycastle pack, headquartered in Chester Springs.

At 10:30 the Ardrossan beagles are released from the rear of a van and come scurrying across the parking grounds, sniffing the ground and the air in a businesslike manner.

None of the beaglers stoops to pet the animals as they mill about, noses to the ground. "They're working animals — they're bred to hunt," says Lorna Forbes of Paoli. "It's a shame, really, when people take an animal that wants to hunt and make a docile pet of him. Oh, sure they're tiny and they're cute and people like them, but they're happiest when they're hunting."

From a few yards away comes the bleat of a bugle, and the hunt is on. The beagles run excitedly down a hill toward the open countryside behind the clubhouse. Sixty or so men and women run and walk behind them.

The sound of Illoway's bugle carries over to the Radnor Hunt kennels, where the hounds used for fox hunting are kept. The larger, rangier hounds race back and forth in their wire enclosure, barking and howling as if asking to come along.

Somewhere in the woods ahead, there is a little bunny rabbit who is about to have the bejesus scared out of him.

The idea of getting out of bed on a Sunday morning and going out in the cold to chase rabbits through the mud — all the while hoping that *you don't actually catch one* — would seem highly unlikely to catch on among sane adults.

But for centuries beagling has been one of the most cherished institutions of the country gentry, here and in England. "It's a lot like fox hunting," says Illoway. "You see a lot of the same people, and the rules of the hunt are similar. But of course, we don't ride horses. We hunt on foot."

There's another important difference between the two. "Other people don't much care about beagling," says Robert Montgomery Scott, president of the Philadelphia Museum of Art and joint master of the Ardrossan pack. "Very few people have even heard about it, and most of them that have tend to think it rather eccentric. People don't aspire to it, socially."

And so, at a time when the Radnor Hunt, the Devon Horse Show, and the Merion Cricket Club have been thoroughly infiltrated by new money, beagling remains pristine.

The beaglers revel in that, as well as in the strangeness of it all. "You see a lot of people get involved in fox hunting and horse shows because they want to show that they have money," suggests Mrs. Forbes, who is founding president of the Delaware Valley Combined Training Association, which stages international-level equestrian events. "And let's face it, the Devon Horse Show is a wonderful place to see and be seen. It's all very impressive for somebody to say they went fox hunting with Radnor Hunt over the weekend.

"But try to impress somebody by saying you were beagling and they'll look at you strangely. Or they'll ask, 'You took your dog for a walk?' "

Its adherents downplay notions of exclusivity, but the sport remains the last bastion of Main Line gentility; from generation to generation the taste for beagling is passed down, along with penchants for old tweeds and mediocre scotch.

At times, claim devotees of the sport, beagling can get downright exciting. "I've never wanted to see a cottontail killed," says Mrs. Forbes, "but when I hear the hounds in full cry, something runs up and down my spine that is absolutely primitive.

"I'm sure it's some primal instinct. To me, the sense of the chase is irresistible. Fox hounds in full cry are even more exciting, but beagling is extremely thrilling in its own way."

But not thrilling enough to become popular, they hope. "If we had too many people tromping across the fields they'd get in the way of the hounds," says Illoway. "And the last thing we want is for this to become a social scene."

Well, there doesn't seem to be much of a fashion competition here today. Nobody is wearing a blazer, an ascot, or riding boots. Dress is either beagling livery or parkas, hiking slacks and sweaters. There's an easygoing camaraderie that stems from the fact that many of the beaglers have known each other since childhood; in some cases, their families have been acquainted for centuries.

Underneath that casual atmosphere, however, there is a strict sense of protocol and ritual. Every pack has a hunt master, who is responsible for the hounds. The field master is the man who keeps the humans from getting too close to the pack, so the hounds can hunt without distraction. The men and women who assist the hunt master are called the whips.

The sport has a lexicon, too. The beagles are not dogs, they're *hounds.* The quarry is not a rabbit, but a *cottontail.* And when a hound is hot on the scent, he doesn't wag his tail; he *feathers* it.

No matter how orderly and civilized a pastime it is, however, there's always the brutal fact that once in a while, the hounds manage to catch a cottontail, with predictable, fatal results. "What a dreadful sport," says one Main Line resident. "You go traipsing across other people's property, knocking down their fences, and the dogs rip your chickens apart and attack your pets. Sure, beagles are tiny and cute, but when they're hunting in a pack, they can be dangerous."

It is hard to imagine the little cuties — oops, hounds — attacking anything much larger than a rabbit, but they will. "We have to keep them off a deer scent," says John Marshall, a member of the Ardrossan hunt. "Otherwise, we could have a very long afternoon."

Marshall is a computer software analyst who began beagling as an eleven-year-old on Nantucket. Keeping the hounds on the proper scent and working together in a disciplined manner involves more than simply running after them, he explains.

"I suppose I spend fifteen, twenty hours a week working with the pack. It takes a lot of time to train a pack."

For beagle puppies, the training goes on from April through July. A younger hound is first teamed with a veteran beagle and taken out three days a week to learn to behave in a pack. In August the puppies join the rest of the hounds, and all begin training.

The hounds frequently go out for a run of three to five miles behind a trainer on a bicycle. During beagling season — from late October through March — they're taken into the field on Saturdays and put through their paces to sharpen them for the next day's hunt.

Though nobody knows where or when the hounds might flush a cottontail — if they do at all — experienced beaglers can predict how the hunt will proceed. "We'll move in a circle the same as in fox hunting or stag hunting," says Marshall. "The cottontail will run away from the hounds until it gets far ahead of them, then it will return to its home. The only difference is that when you're fox hunting or stag hunting, you move in bigger circles."

It was in an effort to make the circles bigger — thus more challenging for both man and hound — that beaglers introduced a new quarry, the Kansas black-tailed jackrabbit, into the Radnor Hunt countryside in the 1930s. "The jackrabbits lasted from the thirties until the seventies," says Marshall. "Now, everything's getting built up — there's not enough open country for them. The jackrabbits used to run like the wind. They'd run for five minutes straight in an open field — you could see everything that was going on. They wouldn't go to ground like these cottontails do. Cottontails prefer briar patches."

Up ahead, the dogs suddenly begin barking, then run into a thicket of trees and underbrush about one hundred yards long. The beaglers spread out, waiting and watching to see if the action is about to begin. After five minutes on the perimeter of the woods, the hunt master decides the dogs have raised a false alarm. Illoway blows two short beeps on the horn, and the dogs' heads lift from the ground, their ears perking up as if they're playing name that tune.

Illoway's bugle is more than a symbol of office; it's the instrument with which the hunt master commands the pack. Two short beeps mean "Listen up!" A series of short beeps means "There's a rabbit over here." An up-and-down wavering sound means "Come back and regroup." A fast tremolo tells the pack that a rabbit has gone to ground, and that they should dig him out.

Marshall moves along behind the pack, scanning the horizon as he goes. "It's a great way to get out of doors and enjoy the countryside," he says. A pair of birds suddenly appear in the sky overhead, soaring and diving. "There's a wood dove," he points out, "and there's a giant blue heron."

Twenty minutes after the dogs have been released, the hunt has wandered into Berwyn, traipsing through the field behind the home of Stephen and Marlie Williams. For some of the beaglers, a rickety bridge of two planks, twenty feet long, provides a moment of adventure, but nobody falls into the creek.

A few hundred yards beyond the creek, the two packs begin baying excitedly, and there is the sound of heavy crashing from a dense patch of woods. Illoway blasts his bugle, and voices begin calling out the names of the hounds.

Two deer bolt from the woods, one almost knocking the field master, Henry Wessells, to the ground in its panicked flight. Wessells, an amateur sports car racer in his late fifties, takes his encounter in stride. "We've thought about going after deer sometime, but it would be an extremely strenuous chase," he observes drily as the deer vanish over the horizon.

An hour into the hunt, it's hard for the novice beaglers to tell just where the chase has led us. The hounds have taken us across streams, through brambles and briar thickets, over an endless series of post-and-rail fences, and we are now rumored to be somewhere on the grounds of the Van Alen estate. The bright-eyed beagles and shaggy bassets mill around between twin rows of hedges, snuffling at the ground, when somebody calls out "Tally-ho!" A tiny rabbit, its eyes wide in panic, darts out and streaks straight down between the hedges, then swerves to the left and disappears into some bushes.

Another rabbit appears, and then a third, with the hounds in hot pursuit. The beaglers stand frozen so as not to frighten the rabbits and turn them back toward the hounds. In a matter of seconds the rabbits have disappeared, and the hounds are backtracking to find their scent. "There were too many rabbits in one spot," Illoway complains. "The scent is confused. It's much better if we have just one rabbit." And off we go again.

Another hour passes. Unlike baseball or tennis, neither innings nor points scored determine how long beagling goes on; a hunt proceeds at the whim of the master of the hunt. The cold has driven the majority of the guest beaglers back to the Radnor Hunt clubhouse, where a Beagle Breakfast is being served.

Even field master Wessells wonders how much longer Illoway plans to keep the hounds in the field. The rain, the baying of the hounds, and the constant beating of bushes suddenly conjure up a vision of Illoway as a landlocked Captain Ahab, abandoning all in his pursuit of the Great White Cottontail. But finally, after the pack has been in the field for close to three hours, Illoway summons the hounds with one last bugle call, and the troupe moves back to Radnor Hunt.

"All in all, a good day," says Marshall, smiling and stomping the mud from his feet at the doorway of the clubhouse. "We saw some geese, a heron and some deer, and chased a few cottontail."

And best of all, not a single rabbit was caught.

Stocky Illoway and his sister, Katherine Schoettle, both of them grimy from the morning's chase, find a table in the clubhouse. A blond woman in a designer sweater comes up to introduce herself. She's new to the Main Line, she explains, and she's interested in joining a beagle hunt. She recites her credentials — schools attended, acquaintances made — and, she concludes, "I *do* ride."

Illoway and his sister listen politely. When the young woman walks away, neither Stocky nor his sister says a word. They don't have to.

February 1990

SHELBY STROTHER

An American Tragedy

FROM THE DETROIT NEWS

THERE ARE five seconds to play. Always. Curtis Jones pushes the rewind button in his head and it returns to that point in time where he is forever stuck. He ignores the butterfly weaving around him. Everyone on the abandoned wood bench in the empty lot with the big shade trees looks up for just an instant. It is the end of another summer. Some of the fellows are having a cold one. So yeah O.K., Curtis, tell us about it one more time. And everyone raises his paper bag to have another sip.

"Four seconds," Jones shouts, holding an imaginary basketball in front of him, shifting his right foot forward, then sideways. "I throw my move. My man falls down, I look at the referee. No foul, no call. Three seconds, two seconds . . ."

Jones's glazed eyes see all the way to a moment that is now twenty-three years old. He leans forward and pushes his bony right arm up and follows through — long, fragile-looking fingers raking at the sky. And he blinks. The shot went in the basket that glorious day in 1967 when a playground legend became king of the city. It has gone in a million times since. Time and space are helpless. Always, five seconds to play. Hit the rewind. Blink.

It was probably the last time Curtis Jones sat on top of the world. It started rolling over on him not so long afterward. And he couldn't stand it. It has to do with seeing something in front of you that makes you flinch. You stop and gasp and discover you're seeing yourself. It's you wandering around the neighborhood, helpless to your own sluggish momentum, and you can't stand it.

So you turn around and go back to where it's safe.

"I was gonna be the best there ever was, you hear me? I should have been a millionaire. Ain't nobody could dribble like me, pass like me. You hear what I'm saying? I'm God. I'm the Lord. I could have put fifteen million dollars in the bank. I made that shot, they carried me off on their shoulders. I could hear them yelling, 'Curtis Jones, you the best ever.' You hear me?"

And everyone nods and has another sip. Jones's tongue splashes out of his mouth, his fingers twitch, his eyes roll. And he reaches for his own bottle of beer. He is breathing hard, excited, nervous. And the eyes, liquid jelly floating in their own stagnancy, have no focus. In a minute he'll jump back up and there will be five seconds left to play once more. All he has to do is blink.

"Curt, you been taking your medicine? Taking the pills like you're supposed to?" asks the shirtless, heavyset man with the roll of skin that hangs over his belt at least a foot. "You're talking so fast, Curt. Slow down. Relax, man."

And Curtis Jones, an American tragedy, closes his eyes. He can't relax. Can't sleep. Can't let loose of that moment. Something became disconnected inside his mind a long time ago. He retreated inside himself, ran all the way back to when it was O.K. to be Curtis Jones. Before everyone knew about his illiteracy and second-grade reading aptitude and 73 IQ, before he was herded off to a foreign land called Idaho, to some junior college five miles from where the neo-Nazi Aryan Nation religious group was founded about the same time. Before he stepped outside of himself and saw what was happening to Curtis Jones. Before he jumped back inside and pulled a nervous breakdown in over him. He lives in his own tunnel now, permanently disabled in the eyes of society, permanently disfigured in his own mind's eye, permanently persecuted in his permanently medicated mind.

Sometimes his mother will get a call to come get him: Mrs. Jones, someone saw your son on the other side of town and he was in an alley, eating mashed potatoes out of a garbage can. Or he might wander into his old high school, the scene of his long-gone glory, not to mention the scene of the crime, stagger through the hall looking for his picture on the Northwestern High Wall of Fame. He'll wear his faded and stretched-out letterman's sweater, carrying a bunch of his old trophies, the rusted and dented artifacts of his faded glory, and scream in those corridors. The echo is loud and pathetic. He'll wail about who he used to be, what he was supposed to be. That's him up there. Yo, world — does anyone remember Curtis Jones?

Only in his mind — inside the cloudy tunnel where a barrage of daily medicines govern his moods and try to fend off the fear that's always so near — he still is that person. Still that smooth, innocent smiling face up on the Wall. And sometimes he makes so much racket the security guard has to be called. Once upon a time, he was carried on the shoulders of fans. Now he gets shoved out the door by beefy sentries, raving at his own shadow. One of the Colts of Northwestern High, maybe the greatest assist man to ever step on its gym floor, could use an assist. What happened to teamwork? They shoot horses, don't they?

A human being either slipped through the cracks of the system or was pushed. The disgrace and the grandeur cast off eerie lights. Guilt is like greed — everywhere. But the system is faceless. It was a crime of grand collaboration and mass complicity. But only one person has been punished.

Wayne County probate court records reveal that Curtis Jones, forty-one, illiterate and unemployed, living on his deceased father's social security benefits, has been committed to the Northville Regional Psychiatric Center eight times since 1970. The diagnosis: acute schizophrenia. He is considered an outpatient now. Doctors say as long as he takes his Prolixin, Cogentin, and heavy-duty B_1 vitamin pills, he doesn't have to be in the hospital.

But he cannot keep the rage from escaping.

"I got too close to my dream and my soul could not bear it," Jones says. "But someone let me get too close, you hear me? I can't read, I can't write. Never could. I knew it would catch up to me. I always had an inferior complex. Man, when you can't read nothing, you can't feel no other way. But I can play ball like a bitch. Still the greatest dribbler of all time. You hear me? Ever see anyone dribble a ball behind his back, 'tween his legs, using just one finger? I invented Larry Bird's shot and he took it from me. Magic's shot — that's mine, too. My passes were stole by Pistol Pete. Isiah took my moves. Earl the Pearl. Damn, ask Jimmy Walker, Dave Bing, what I did to them down at the Y. I was in the eleventh grade and was taking 'em all. I was the Father, the Son, the Holy Spirit. Ice Man George Gervin asked me for my autograph. You hear me? I took the shot that won the city championship for us. Aw man, you see it? Was you there? Aw man, there was five seconds left to play . . ."

And he stops himself this time.

"They say I'm crazy," he says, almost whispering. And he blinks. Pain? What pain?

Spencer Haywood remembers Jones's shot all too well. It beat him and his Pershing High teammates on February 21, 1967. Northwestern won the game, the first prep game in Michigan history to be televised, 63–61, on Jones's nineteen-foot jump shot with three seconds to play, and claimed the Public School League championship. It was the slender junior guard's only field goal of the game.

"Curtis was so far ahead of his time," says Haywood, a former NBA star who has had his own share of personal demons to overcome. "He was Mr. Wizard on the court. A fantastic playmaker. Everything you see the pros do today, Curtis Jones was doing when he was in tenth grade. At one time, there was no doubt in anyone's mind he was going to the NBA and was going to make a lot of money. No doubt whatsoever. That day, that game — I'll never forget it. There were about twenty seconds left to play and Curt got the ball and he just dribbled the clock down and everyone in the gym — man, the state of Michigan stood still for this game — just knew he was going to score the winning basket. Just like he did. It's a shame what's happened to him. A tragedy. But before he got sick, he was the greatest little man on the court there ever was."

Haywood is a recovering addict who regularly attends meetings to help cope with his problem. He also is a major partner in a real estate development company and president of another company that trains computer technicians and places them in the labor force. He shudders when he thinks about the two different paths he and his old rival have traveled.

"I was just like Curtis at one time," Haywood says. "I couldn't read or write in tenth grade. I had no self-esteem anywhere except that court. Just like Curtis. But I got great help from some great people. I got through it. I also went off to a junior college that seemed like Nowheresville, right on the Colorado and New

Mexico border. Curt went to Idaho. But I didn't go to my school alone. I had a friend, a teammate from high school, in fact my best friend, go with me. It was tough and definitely a hard place for a black man from the city to try to adjust to college life. But I made it. Curtis didn't.

"And I don't know who's to blame except maybe all of us. Curtis's failure is America's failure."

Haywood says the last time he saw Jones "was last year when I was giving an antidrug talk at a school on the east side of Detroit. From a distance I saw him as I was walking into the gym. But inside the gymnasium — it was filled with kids — I looked and couldn't find him. I was going to introduce him to the crowd. Then when it was over, I walked out the door and there he was.

"He'd come all that way to ask if he could borrow some money."

Sometimes the lightning crackles inside Jones's head. He feels rumbles and he gets dizzy and, "I'm scared my head's gonna explode. I know something's wrong with me. I just don't know whose fault it is."

One night several years ago, he became convinced a taxi driver was actually an agent of the Ku Klux Klan. It's the reason, said Jones to police, he had to steal the taxi when the driver parked and went inside a party store.

Said the police report filed on the incident, "Subject also claimed to be God."

Henrietta Jones injects herself daily with insulin to control and regulate the diabetes that shoots through her system. There are pills that help keep the blood pressure down. She takes other medicines for the congenital arthritis that forced her to retire from her job with Chrysler eighteen years ago. One of her sons was killed in a barroom fight two blocks from home in 1978. Another son, she says, "has let the street get hold of him. He's messed up with that drug. He's got problems, bad problems."

But Curtis, her baby boy, brings her the most pain. "He just can't stop feeling his dreams were failed," says the sixty-seven-year-old woman, her voice soft as a prayer. "He's not evil. There's so much good inside him. Really there is. But he's so confused what all's happened. We knew he shouldn't go off to college. He was special, went to the special school for years. But he saw something he had to chase after. He tried, and there was just too much pressure. That ability to play ball was God's gift to him, I'm sure. It was compensation.

"I see him cry sometimes, two hours without stopping. He says, 'Mama, I'm no good. I'm no good.' I worry so much. I pray every night for the strength. I'm afraid he's going to kill himself. He just can't let loose and go on with his life. He gets nervous and he can't sleep . . . just walking around, talking to himself, talking about how his life got stolen from him. When he can't sleep, I can't sleep. And when he gets that way, I know pretty soon he's gonna have to go back in the hospital at Northville."

She takes off her glasses to wipe at her eyes. "It hurts me so much to have to go downtown and fill out the court order. It hurts so bad to have to write, 'My son is mentally ill.' I do it because I love him."

A mother sobs for several seconds, shaking her head. The umbilical cord is so frayed and worn. It is a lifeline about to snap, not from apathy, but overuse. She stands up regularly and asks the people in the congregation at Holy Cross Baptist to pray for her son. She is not ashamed; her son is sick and a mother's instincts are to do whatever she can. When she gets calls that Curtis is in trouble, he just got beat up, he's drunk and can't find his way home, she always goes to help him. Get him home.

Rev. James Porter, pastor at Holy Cross Baptist, warned her years ago it would take special prayers, special strength, to pull Curtis through the storms that pass behind his eyes.

"I just want my son to know peace in himself," Henrietta Jones says, swallowing hard. The corned beef on the stove needs turning. She lifts herself up from her chair and walks to the kitchen.

Curtis stays down in the basement, she says. His room — he calls it "my private closet" — is seven by ten feet and consists of a small bed, an ashtray, and a single-bulb light that hangs from the low ceiling.

"He's safe there though," says his mother.

Up the street from the little house on McGraw Street, five blocks from Northwestern High, back at the lot with the sparse grass and thick weeds, Jones licks once again at his thirst. People see him and brand him. Just another drunk. But the beer is only a substitute. When you live in the in-between world — between the gaps where even a streak of light gets bent and twisted, and flowers seem evil and hairbrushes can walk — unable to cope with anything except yesterday, which happened an entire lifetime ago, your thirst is for redemption. Jones wants redemption. He pleads for it. The shame of society he wraps around himself, like some blanket or flap of cardboard he finds in an alley on a cold night when he can't find his way back to his mother's house, is so uncomfortable. He hates the feeling, coarse as burlap; he hates how it irritates him. So he douses it with the beer. It washes away the feeling. Pain? What pain?

He asks constantly if we hear him. Do we? Do we hear Jones's searing anguish? The streets are full of these soft moans. Everyone has a sad story to tell. Jones's is just more complicated than most. Will anyone take the time to hear the story? Redemption's not here just yet.

So he hides behind a sad facade. Jones holds out his palm. Want to see him hold a lit match in his hand? He'll do it for a beer. One time he offered to let someone shoot him in the hand. A gang member laughed.

"He had a gun and I didn't have no money. I told him he could shoot a hole through my hand if he bought me a case of beer. Man, I don't feel that kind of pain. I can hold fire for long as you want me to. Watch this." He reaches into his pants pockets, squirms and feels around. Then curses. "Ain't this a crying shame. I got fifteen million dollars owed me and I ain't got a damn match to my name. Ain't got a damn dime. Greatest player who ever lived and I ain't got the fire to burn my hand off." And he sticks a forefinger to the side of his head and squeezes an imaginary trigger and mouths the word "boom."

Then he reaches for his paper bag and another cigarette. "Smoking cigarettes since I was seven. Smoking made me ambidextrous," he says, laughing as he swallows hard.

There was a time when Jones was considered the finest high school point guard in the United States. Letters from colleges all over the country arrived daily. Scouts were stopping at the service stations on Grand Boulevard regularly, asking directions to Northwestern High, where the great Curtis Jones played. They called him Mr. Wizard. The Magician.

"Before there was Isiah Thomas, there was Curtis Jones," says Wil Robinson, now a chief scout of the Detroit Pistons. "Passer, playmaker, leader, shooter. He was the whole package. But he never should have tried to go to college the way he did. He was doomed to failure. He had no learning skills developed. Somebody should have cared about the person inside the basketball player. The kid is always more important than the final score. I used to tell my players there is a life after the game is over. You must be ready for it."

Robinson was coaching Pershing High that day in 1967. With any kind of luck, Jones could have been playing for Robinson.

"I tried to get him to come to Pershing. He had an aunt or something he could have stayed with. This is all hindsight but I think I could have helped him. Spencer was in the same boat, you know. When you have a deficiency or a disability, it isn't the end of the world. When I used to teach at Miller High, I had a student named Walter Jenkins who also was special ed. But you can reach him today at Northern High. He's the principal there. And it's *Doctor* Jenkins. From special ed to a Ph.D. That's what can happen. But you have to evaluate each one as they come. I think Curtis got special treatment from teachers that he shouldn't have. He got pushed up through the system. All that's doing is prolonging the eventual failure. Most kids, that happens and all they do is flunk out of school. Curtis had a nervous breakdown."

Robinson hasn't seen Jones for years but, "I hear he's still living in the past. That's not good. That one game may have been the crowning glory of the PSL. I've heard people say it was the best game they ever saw. Jones scored the last basket. That was how he played. He'd spend the whole game setting everyone up — he was a very clever, very tricky passer — then he'd take the shot that decided the game. But I also remember something else about that season. We came back and beat Northwestern in the state playoffs. Pershing won the state championship that year."

Robinson then adds, "See what I mean? You gotta let loose of the past."

James Jones was a welder who worked for Chrysler up until the day he started coughing blood into his handkerchief regularly. The lung cancer spread quickly. His youngest son, Curtis, brought all his Little League and rec league trophies to the hospital so his father could have them around him. Then one day he was told: "Daddy died last night."

Curtis was twelve and the loss was devastating. For years his father and mother had tried to work with him about school, reading books to him, trying to teach him how to make his letters. But when his father died, "I took it hard. And I didn't care 'bout much at all for a long time."

One day his mother came home from work and saw clothes from the line strewn all over the floor. Curtis was in the bathroom, sitting on the floor, playing a basketball game in his head, using clothespins as players. There was Wilt Chamberlain and Oscar Robertson and all the stars of the NBA playing a game on the tile. The clothespin with the ball — that was Curtis Jones.

"Basketball was his only interest. You couldn't force a book in his hand. You couldn't take a basketball out of it," his mother says.

On 16th Street, behind a house, through the back yard and into the dirt-road alley is a basketball hoop someone nailed to a pole. Curtis wants to show off. He bounces the basketball that has part of the cover missing on the lumpy road, once, twice, three times. Like a puppy it responds, obeys as he pats it gently, forcefully.

"Bet I make it from here," he says, letting loose with a leaning jumper. Airball. "Come on, bet me, somebody."

The next shot clanks off the back rim.

Then he starts in his relentless replay of that one brief shining moment. Five seconds to play. The ball swishes through the dangling net.

"You lose."

And his laugh is a cackle. And for a moment the glory returns, soaking him, washing away everything else. A small boy walks up, watching. Jones hits four shots in a row. Then he starts dribbling.

"Marques Haynes dreams about handling the ball like this. Curly Neal needs five fingers to do what I do with one," he says, putting the ball between his legs, around his back, twirling around, dropping to a knee.

"Whooee, man," the boys chirp, smiling. "You good. You should be in the NBA, huh? You the next Magic Johnson."

And Jones says, "Man, I was the first Magic Johnson."

Jones and his mother claim Fred Snowden, Northwestern's coach back then, promised a college scholarship to his star guard. Snowden later became an assistant at the University of Michigan, then the University of Arizona, before entering private business.

Jones assumed he would follow his coach to UM. But his high school transcripts were atrocious. His scores on the college entrance exams were even worse. He ranked in the bottom one percentile. Translated, it meant every student in the country theoretically could read better than Curtis Jones.

Jones claims a deal was struck between him, his former coach, and Michigan. Go play for North Idaho Junior College for two years, get your grades up to an acceptable level, then come to Ann Arbor and have two years of eligibility left.

It was 1968 and a troubled, confused, scared teenager from the streets of Detroit left for the wild west of Coeur d'Alene, Idaho.

"From all black to all white," Jones says. "There was maybe six blacks in the whole town, maybe the whole state. There was racial tension. I dated a cheerleader, a white girl. I got in some trouble. One time someone slipped some LSD in my drink at a party. I was messed up. Things got tougher and tougher. I tried. I tried hard. School — nobody cared what I did there. When I had a test, I'd sit there a few minutes, then go to the bathroom. Someone would be there with a test already filled in for me. I was making C's and I still couldn't read a word."

Then one day he missed a class when there was a test. And he had to take a makeup test. And there was nobody waiting in the bathroom with the answers. He asked a girl first to fill in the answers for him. She refused. Then he asked her to read him the questions.

She laughed.

"I couldn't stand it. The word went around like fire. Everyone laughed at me. They called me names. I did more LSD. My girlfriend back home was pregnant with someone else's baby. Friends of mine from Detroit who went to Vietnam and won medals were getting shot and killed. There was riots going on. There was so much blood in the street, so many needles sticking in arms, murderers and killers. I couldn't adjust to Idaho; then I couldn't adjust back to Detroit.

"Since 1970, it seems like I have a friend a year die violently. I think maybe they have it better than me. Their suffering's over."

Shortly after returning to Idaho from summer vacation following his freshman year, the sparks and blank spots began appearing. The short circuits manifested at first in anger and rage, then bizarre behavior, episodes of confrontation with school officials, campus arrests, ordered psychiatric evaluations.

"Then — I don't remember what came then," Jones says.

On February 17, 1970, Dr. Joseph Grismer, a psychiatrist in Idaho, performed a mental evaluation of Jones and suggested immediate help and treatment. On March 23, back home in Detroit, Jones was committed to Northville for the first time.

"I was tied down. I had roaches in my hair, bugs in my mouth," Jones says.

His mother says she's not aware of that ever happening. Sometimes, she adds, "Curtis thinks things he saw when he was in the hospital happened to him, too. He hates the hospital."

On the sidewalk in front of the Jones home, Curtis talks in rambling flurries, raving about cruelty that is everywhere. Then he looks down and points.

"My best friend," he says, looking at his shadow. "Sometimes my only friend. I know I'll never walk alone. I got that shadow. It's stuck with me for life."

Another cackle of laughter. The mind is racing. He says he really is God. He talks about taking "limbs from the octopus and I gave them to the fish. It's reincarnation."

Then he talks in gibberish, unintelligible. Then another big grin.

"Basically, in the tree of life, my plum fell off and rotted."

Jones and his mother walked into an office almost a decade ago and told their story to an attorney, Jerome Quinn. There have been several lawsuits filed on behalf of Jones. A multimillion-dollar suit against the Detroit Board of Education claimed Jones was pushed into college prematurely and ill-equipped, and therefore was exploited, causing his mental breakdown and subsequent problems.

"I took it to the Michigan supreme court, but that's where it is,"

Quinn said. "The court refused to hear it. That doesn't mean you're right or wrong. It means the supreme court refuses to hear it. And that's where it is right now — going nowhere."

Quinn hesitates, then adds, "I'm really amazed. I thought Curtis would get his day in court. I literally worked on that case ten years. It was a good case. And it's a very tragic story."

Roy Allen is director of health and physical education for the Detroit public schools. In 1967 he was a teacher and cross-country coach at Northwestern High. "He may be the greatest talent I ever witnessed," Allen said. "He had unbelievable skill levels, incredible presence and vision. And he probably was the most popular kid in the school. I used to work the gate at the games and usually didn't get to watch until the second half. We turned away crowds. They wanted to see Curtis Jones play. Being truthful, Northwestern was only a little above average, talent-wise. Curtis Jones carried those teams to championships with his unique talents. If you could have seen some of the things he could do. Things that today would amaze you. But back then, well, nobody ever played the game like he did."

Allen says education should be the dominant part of the scholar-athlete's high school experience. He grunts when asked about what happened to Jones. There was no 2.0 minimum grade requirement back then. Bills that required special-education students to be mainstreamed into the general population at schools were still in the future. Tutorial programs had not been developed. There was no Proposition 48 or any of the safeguards that have been instituted to maintain academic standards for college qualification.

"Curtis never should have been sent off to Idaho. He should have been put in an environment where he could become a total person, a functional, literate person. It should have happened in high school and didn't. Then the insult got compounded. He is an American tragedy. I'm not throwing stones at anybody, but he is a true and tragic example, the most tragic I'm aware of."

Two years ago, Jones tried to get a job with the parks and recreation department. He couldn't pass the required test. Last year, he tried to find work as a janitor. He couldn't pass that test, either. He says he's getting tired. And he's crying more and more.

"There are some hot streets in the neighborhood," Jones said.

"Smoke that crack, buy it, sell it. Me, I obey John Law most of the time. Smoke some reefer once in a while is all. Drink my beer. But I'm tired, you hear me. There are contracts out on my life, and I know that. My teeth got knocked out by a gang. I been shot at. A man with an Uzi came in a bar and opened up on everyone. There was a body in the trunk of a car two streets away. This is a hot area and not everyone is my friend. Not everyone knows how great I was. I'm tired. Been walking in a circle for twenty years. Got nothing but time. A big circle. That street to that street to that street. Just me and my friend. The shadow."

Perry Watson remembers the personal duels, the games within the games they enjoyed in high school. Watson played for Southwestern. Today he is the school's head basketball coach. "I took pride in my defense. But Curt made anyone take his game up an extra notch. I remember one game he backed me all the way downcourt, dribbling the ball entirely behind his back. He never brought it in front of him. Nobody could get it from him. He was an amazing player. Truly the best I saw. What you see Earvin Johnson do today, Curt did twenty-five years ago. Only he was six foot and Earvin's six-nine. He should have gone right from tenth grade into the NBA. That's how good Curtis Jones was."

Before his time. How ironic is that? Two months after he suffered his breakdown, Haywood signed a contract with Denver of the American Basketball Association, claiming hardship. It was the first time a player who had started his college career was signed to play pro basketball before his college graduating class arrived.

"If I coulda just held my head together two more months," Jones says.

Lolita Wyanna walks up and hugs him. Friends since he was eight and she was six, they laugh easily around each other. They stare at each other the way old friends do.

"She used to read me my horoscope, tell me what was in store for me," Jones says, smiling. Lolita laughs and pokes him in the arm.

"I couldn't even read what was in my stars. I'm a Virgo. Damn, baby, why didn't you tell me what was going to be? Why didn't you keep me home?"

Lolita's smile fades. While Jones erupts into another version of

The Shot, she sits patiently beside him, patting his leg occasionally.

"I cry still about him," she says. "You see, I know who Curt Jones is supposed to be. I know who he was. I know the whole story from the beginning. He is a victim of modern slavery. He was sold out just like they used to do. And I still cry about what happened to him."

Jones sits up and back down, then back up. Nervous. It's a big circle, all right.

"Maybe five years ago, it was almost dark, it was raining, almost snowing," he says. "I was up on the interstate, dribbling my ball, faking out the cars as they came. I realized where I was and got scared trying to get off the street. I was walking back home and I saw one of my trophies. It done got run over."

Jones blinks. Contact is lost. The tape begins again.

"John Wooden was looking for me. I got letters. The ABA wants me, too. And the NBA. Ask anybody. They all know me. Muhammad Ali one time gave me fifty dollars. I told him we both were the greatest of all time. Ask Ali. Ask Stevie Wonder, I used to ride him around on my bicycle. I used to be somebody great, you hear me? You can ask anybody about that."

September 2, 1990

RICHARD COHEN

Personal Best

FROM THE WASHINGTON POST MAGAZINE

I AWAKE in the morning. On the far wall, opposite the bed, my bookcase is gone. In its place is an electronic scoreboard, smaller than the ones now found in baseball parks but, other than that, precisely the same. I am so surprised, I roll out of bed to my right instead of my left. The board lights up: *This is the first time in 865 days that Richard Cohen has rolled out of bed to the right.*

I am stunned. I glance at the board and then try to pretend it's not there. I pad into the kitchen, make some coffee, and return to the bedroom with a cup — but not the pot of coffee. This happens all the time, but as I start to return to the kitchen, the board lights up: *Richard Cohen has forgotten to bring the coffeepot into the bedroom 11 of the last 13 days.* I stare in disbelief and am about to enter the bathroom for a shower when the board flashes something else: *This is a Northwest Washington record.*

Who knew? I shower, rather proud of myself. Hardly awake, I have nevertheless started the day with a record. It's not a record for all of Washington, and certainly not one for the Washington metropolitan area, but it is a record. In fact, it's a record much like the ones now being flashed on the scoreboards in ballparks, statistics that were not available before computers and that have turned the hallowed hobby of keeping and remembering baseball statistics into a parody of itself, if not a perversion.

I reach for a white shirt while, out of the corner of my eye, watching the scoreboard: *Richard Cohen has worn a white shirt on 3 of the last 6 working days.* Probably true, I concede. I reach for a blue one instead: *Richard Cohen has worn a blue shirt on 23 of the last 48 working days.* True too. But most of my shirts are either blue or white. I reach for a nifty plaid: *Richard Cohen has not worn a plaid shirt since Feb. 6, 1990 — the longest he has gone without wearing a plaid shirt since 1987.* I guess so.

At work, I discover that the bookcase in my office has also been replaced by a scoreboard. By now I am not surprised. I read the papers and then decide what to write. "I . . ." The scoreboard flashes: *Richard Cohen has started a column with the word "I" for 43 days in a row. This is a record for newspaper columnists, excluding the columns Leon Trotsky did for Pravda following the Russian Revolution. It is also a personal best.* No kidding, methinks.

And so the day goes. Almost everything I do is a record, a near-record, an indoor record, a variation of a club record, a modern record, a local record, or my personal best. The truth is that I am not particularly proud of records that are my personal best. I see this category as something akin to grade inflation — excessive praise for insignificant achievements. I pause to wonder if the Japanese have the category of personal best and, if they don't, whether this represents the difference between our two countries. At that very moment, the board lights again: *Richard Cohen has taken a small thing and tried to make something momentous out of it. This, alas, is his personal best.*

It is my luck, I decide, to have a scoreboard like myself: sarcastic. But in due course I begin to cherish the thing. It tells me, for instance, that I spent 3.4 hours just staring out the window that day — no mere personal best, I am informed, but a 15th Street NW modern record. The nineteenth-century record was held by a customs bureau clerk named Franklin, who from 1888 to 1891 did nothing but look out the window. He was a political appointee.

I cannot tell you, nay I will not tell you, what the scoreboard says when I return after — I am electronically informed — my twelfth visit to the men's room. I can only say that while this is a Washington metropolitan area record number of trips, it is nowhere near my personal best and does not approach the world's record held by a man in West Palm Beach, Florida. He's my father.

As the day progresses, my personal scoreboards do for me what those in ballparks do for ballplayers: they convince me of my own uniqueness and value to the organization. I hire an agent, a personal manager, a personal trainer, and a spokesman. I have my spokesman talk to my personal trainer and explain why I'm going to miss my first training session. I become enamored of myself (O.K., even more enamored) and find myself competing not against other columnists but myself. Can I start yet another column with the word "I"? Can I, perchance, use the word "perchance" just one more time? It will be a personal best.

My scoreboards tell me everything. They announce that I write better when the wind is out of the north. I type faster when the humidity is low. I am most thoughtful out of town, and I do best against right-wing columnists on talk shows, although not in August or in St. Louis when it's raining. During cold snaps, I write best on my Zenith portable computer, but once the temperature goes over 70, it's an IBM for me. These are things I sort of knew but couldn't, as it were, prove. Perchance . . . *Richard Cohen has used "perchance" in 15 of his last 17 columns. This breaks the record held by John Maynard Keynes.* I forget what I was going to say.

Returning home in the evening, I find that almost everything I do makes the scoreboard light up. Even in bed, every toss and turn is some sort of record — personal, neighborhood, city, for my age, for my sex. Sleep will not come, and so I rise and write this column. Perchance you may not think much of it, but it is — given the wind and my age — a personal best.

June 17, 1990

STEPHEN KING

Head Down

FROM THE NEW YORKER

"Say, this is some kind of game, isn't it?"
— Pete Rose to Carlton Fisk, game six of the 1975 World Series

"HEAD DOWN! Keep your head *down!*"

It is far from the most difficult feat in sports, but anyone who has ever tried to do it will tell you that it's tough enough: using a round bat to hit a round ball squarely on the button. Tough enough so that the handful of men who do it well become rich, famous, and idolized: the Jose Cansecos, the Mike Greenwells, the Kevin Mitchells. For thousands of boys (and not a few girls), their faces, not the face of Axl Rose or Tone-Lōc, are the ones that matter; their posters hold the positions of honor on bedroom walls and locker doors. Today Ron St. Pierre is teaching some of these boys — boys who will represent Bangor West Side in District 3 Little League tournament play — how to put the round bat on the round ball. Right now he's working with a kid named Fred Moore while my son, Owen, stands nearby, watching closely. He's due in St. Pierre's hot seat next. Fred looks almost painfully slim in his bright green jersey. And he is not making good contact.

"*Head down, Fred!*" St. Pierre shouts. He is halfway between the mound and home plate at one of the two Little League fields behind the Coke plant in Bangor; Fred is almost all the way to the backstop. The day is a hot one, but if the heat bothers either Fred or St. Pierre it does not show. They are intent on what they are doing.

"Keep it *down!*" St. Pierre shouts again, and unloads a fat pitch.

Fred chips under it. There is that chinky aluminum-on-cowhide sound — the sound of someone hitting a tin cup with a spoon. The ball hits the backstop, rebounds, almost bonks him on the helmet. Both of them laugh, and then St. Pierre gets another ball from the red plastic bucket beside him.

"Get ready, Freddy!" he yells, "Head down!"

Maine's District 3 is so large that it is split in two. The Penobscot County teams make up half the division; the teams from Aroostook and Washington counties make up the other half. All-Star kids are selected by merit and drawn from all existing district Little League teams. The dozen teams in District 3 play in simultaneous tournaments. Near the end of July, the two teams left will play off, best two out of three, to decide the district champ. That team represents District 3 in State Championship play, and it has been a long time — eighteen years — since a Bangor team made it into the state tourney.

This year, the State Championship games will be played in Old Town, where they make the canoes. Four of the five teams that play there will go back home. The fifth will go on to represent Maine in the Eastern Regional Tournament, this year to be held in Bristol, Connecticut. Beyond *that,* of course, is Williamsport, Pennsylvania, where the Little League World Series happens. The Bangor West players rarely seem to think of such dizzy heights; they will be happy just to beat Millinocket, their first-round opponent in the Penobscot County race. Coaches, however, are allowed to dream — are, in fact, almost *obligated* to dream.

This time Fred, who is the team joker, *does* get his head down. He hits a weak grounder on the wrong side of the first-base line, foul by about six feet.

"Look," St. Pierre says, taking another ball. He holds it up. It is scuffed, dirty, and grass-stained. It is nevertheless a baseball, and Fred eyes it respectfully. "I'm going to show you a trick. Where's the ball?"

"In your hand," Fred says.

Saint, as Dave Mansfield, the team's head coach, calls him, drops it into his glove. "Now?"

"In your glove."

Saint turns sideways; his pitching hand creeps into his glove. "Now?"

"In your hand. I think."

"You're right. So watch my hand. Watch my hand, Fred Moore, and wait for the ball to come out in it. You're looking for the ball. Nothing else. Just the ball. I should just be a blur to you. Why would you want to see me, anyway? Do you care if I'm smiling? No. You're waiting to see how I'll come — sidearm or three-quarters or over the top. Are you waiting?"

Fred nods.

"Are you watching?"

Fred nods again.

"O.K.," St. Pierre says, and goes into his short-arm batting-practice motion again.

This time Fred drives the ball with real authority: a hard sinking liner to right field.

"All *right!*" Saint cries. "That's *all right,* Fred Moore!" He wipes sweat off his forehead. "Next batter!"

Dave Mansfield, a heavy, bearded man who comes to the park wearing aviator sunglasses and an open-neck College World Series shirt (it's a good-luck charm), brings a paper sack to the Bangor West–Millinocket game. It contains sixteen pennants, in various colors. BANGOR, each one says, the word flanked by a lobster on one side and a pine tree on the other. As each Bangor West player is announced on loudspeakers that have been wired to the chain-link backstop, he takes a pennant from the bag Dave holds out, runs across the infield, and hands it to his opposite number.

Dave is a loud, restless man who happens to love baseball and the kids who play it at this level. He believes there are two purposes to All-Star Little League: to have fun and to win. Both are important, he says, but the most important thing is to keep them in the right order. The pennants are not a sly gambit to unnerve the opposition but just for fun. Dave knows that the boys on both teams will remember this game, and he wants each of the Millinocket kids to have a souvenir. It's as simple as that.

The Millinocket players seem surprised by the gesture, and they don't know exactly what to do with the pennants as someone's tape player begins to warble out the Anita Bryant version of "The Star-Spangled Banner." The Millinocket catcher, almost buried beneath his gear, solves the problem in unique fashion: he holds his Bangor pennant over his heart.

With the amenities taken care of, Bangor West administers a brisk and thorough trouncing; the final score is Bangor West 18, Millinocket 7. The loss does not devalue the souvenirs, however; when Millinocket departs on the team bus, the visitors' dugout is empty save for a few Dixie cups and Popsicle sticks. The pennants — every single one of them — are gone.

"Cut *two!*" Neil Waterman, Bangor West's field coach, shouts. "Cut *two*, cut *two!*"

It's the day after the Millinocket game. Everyone on the team is still showing up for practice, but it's early yet. Attrition will set in. That is a given: parents are not always willing to give up summer plans so their kids can play Little League after the regular, May-June season is over, and sometimes the kids themselves tire of the constant grind of practice. Some would rather be riding their bikes, trying to hang ten on their skateboards, or just hanging around the community pool and checking out the girls.

"Cut *two!*" Waterman yells. He is a small, compact man in khaki shorts and a Joe Coach crew cut. In real life he is a teacher and a college basketball coach, but this summer he is trying to teach these boys that baseball has more in common with chess than many would ever have believed. Know your play, he tells them over and over again. Know who it is you're backing up. Most important of all, know who your cut man is in every situation, and be able to hit him. He works patiently at showing them the truth that hides at the center of the game: that it is played more in the mind than with the body.

Ryan Iarrobino, Bangor West's center fielder, fires a bullet to Casey Kinney at second base. Casey tags an invisible runner, pivots, and throws another bullet to home, where J. J. Fiddler takes the throw and tosses the ball back to Waterman.

"Double-play ball!" Waterman shouts, and hits one to Matt Kinney (not related to Casey). Matt is playing shortstop at practice today. The ball takes a funny hop and appears to be on its way to left center. Matt knocks it down, picks it up, and feeds to Casey at second; Casey pivots and throws to Mike Arnold, who is on first. Mike feeds it home to J.J.

"All right!" Waterman shouts. "Good job, Matt Kinney! *Good job!* One-two-one! You're covering, Mike Pelkey!" The two names. Always the two names, to avoid confusion. The team is lousy with Matts, Mikes, and guys named Kinney.

The throws are executed flawlessly. Mike Pelkey, Bangor West's number two pitcher, is right where he's supposed to be, covering first. It's a move he doesn't always remember to make, but this time he does. He grins and trots back to the mound as Neil Waterman gets ready to hit the next combination.

"This is the best Little League All-Star team I've seen in years," Dave Mansfield says some days after Bangor West's trouncing of Millinocket. He dumps a load of sunflower seeds into his mouth and begins to chew them. He spits hulls casually as he talks. "I don't think they can be beaten — at least not in this division."

He pauses and watches as Mike Arnold breaks toward the plate from first, grabs a practice bunt, and whirls toward the bag. He cocks his arm back — then holds the ball. Mike Pelkey is still on the mound; this time he has forgotten that it is his job to cover, and the bag is undefended. He flashes Dave a quick guilty glance. Then he breaks into a sunny grin and gets ready to do it again. Next time he'll do it right, but will he remember to do it right during a game?

"Of course, we can beat ourselves," Dave says. "That's how it usually happens." And, raising his voice, he bellows, "*Where were you, Mike Pelkey? You're s'posed to be covering first!*"

Mike nods and trots over — better late than never.

"Brewer," Dave says, and shakes his head. "Brewer at their field. That'll be tough. Brewer's *always* tough."

Bangor West does not trounce Brewer, but they win their first "road game" without any real strain. Matt Kinney, the team's number one pitcher, is in good form. He is far from overpowering, but his fastball has a sneaky, snaky little hop, and he also has a modest but effective breaking pitch. Ron St. Pierre is fond of saying that every Little League pitcher in America thinks he's got a killer curveball. "What they think is a curve is usually this big lollipop change," he says. "A batter with a little self-discipline can kill the poor thing."

Matt Kinney's curveball actually curves, however, and tonight he goes the distance and strikes out eight. Probably more important, he walks only four. Walks are the bane of a Little League coach's existence. "They kill you," Neil Waterman says. "The walks kill you every time. Absolutely no exceptions. Sixty percent of batters walked score in Little League games." Not in this game: two of the batters Kinney walks are forced at second; the other two are stranded. Only one Brewer batter gets a hit: Denise Hewes, the center fielder, singles with one out in the fifth, but she is forced at second.

After the game is safely in the bag, Matt Kinney, a solemn and almost eerily self-possessed boy, flashes Dave a rare smile, revealing a set of neat braces. "She could *hit!*" he says, almost reverently.

"Wait until you see Hampden," Dave says dryly. "They *all* hit."

When the Hampden squad shows up at Bangor West's field, behind the Coke plant, on July 17, they quickly prove Dave right. Mike Pelkey has pretty good stuff and better control than he had against Millinocket, but he isn't much of a mystery to the Hampden boys. Mike Tardif, a compact kid with an amazingly fast bat, rips Pelkey's third pitch over the left-field fence, two hundred feet away, for a home run in the first inning. Hampden adds two more runs in the second, and leads Bangor West 3–0.

In the third, however, Bangor West breaks loose. Hampden's pitching is good, Hampden's hitting is awesome, but Hampden's fielding, particularly infielding, leaves something to be desired. Bangor West puts three hits together with five errors and two walks to score seven runs. This is how Little League is most often played, and seven runs should be enough, but they aren't; the opposition chips stubbornly away, getting two in its half of the third and two more in the fifth. When Hampden comes up in the bottom of the sixth, it is trailing by only three, 10–7.

Kyle King, a twelve-year-old who started for Hampden this evening and then went to catcher in the fifth, leads off the bottom of the sixth with a double. Then Mike Pelkey strikes out Mike Tardif. Mike Wentworth, the new Hampden pitcher, singles to deep short. King and Wentworth advance on a passed ball, but are forced to hold when Jeff Carson grounds back to the pitcher. This brings up Josh Jamieson, one of five Hampden home-run threats, with two on and two out. He represents the tying run. Mike, although clearly tired, finds a little extra and strikes him out on a one-two pitch. The game is over.

The kids line up and give each other the custom-ordained high fives, but it's clear that Mike isn't the only kid who is simply exhausted after the match; with their slumped shoulders and lowered heads, they all look like losers. Bangor West is now 3–0 in divisional play, but the win is a fluke, the kind of game that makes Little League such a nerve-racking experience for spectators, coaches, and the players themselves. Usually sure-handed in the field, Bangor West has tonight committed something like nine errors.

"I didn't sleep all night," Dave mutters at practice the next day. "Damn, we were outplayed. We should have lost that game."

Two nights later, he has something else to feel gloomy about. He and Ron St. Pierre make the six-mile trip to Hampden to watch Kyle King and his mates play Brewer. This is no scouting expedition; Bangor has played both clubs, and both men have copious notes. What they are really hoping to see, Dave admits, is Brewer getting lucky and putting Hampden out of the way. It doesn't happen; what they see isn't a baseball game but gunnery practice.

Josh Jamieson, who struck out in the clutch against Mike Pelkey, clouts a home run over everything and into the Hampden practice field. Nor is Jamieson alone. Carson hits one, Wentworth hits one, and Tardif hits a pair. The final score is Hampden 21, Brewer 9.

On the ride back to Bangor, Dave Mansfield chews a lot of sunflower seeds and says little. He rouses himself only once, as he wheels his old green Chevy into the rutted dirt parking lot beside the Coke plant. "We got lucky Tuesday night, and they know it," he says. "When we go down there Thursday, they'll be waiting for us."

The diamonds on which the teams of District 3 play out their six-inning dramas all have the same dimensions, give or take a foot here or an outfield gate there. The coaches all carry the rule book in their back pockets, and they put it to frequent use. Dave likes to say that it never hurts to make sure. The infield is sixty feet on each side, a square standing on the point that is home plate. The backstop, according to the rule book, must be at least twenty feet from home plate, giving both the catcher and a runner at third a fair chance on a passed ball. The fences are supposed to be 200 feet from the plate. At Bangor West's field, it's actually about 210 to dead center. And at Hampden, home of power hitters like Tardif and Jamieson, it's more like 180.

The most inflexible measurement is also the most important: the distance between the pitcher's rubber and the center of the plate. Forty-six feet — no more, no less. When it comes to this one, nobody ever says, "Aw, close enough for government work — let it go." Most Little League teams live and die by what happens in the forty-six feet between those two points.

The fields of District 3 vary considerably in other ways, and a quick look is usually enough to tell you something about the feel any given community has for the game. The Bangor West field is in bad shape — a poor relation that the town regularly ignores in its recreation budget. The undersurface is a sterile clay that turns to soup when the weather is wet and to concrete when the weather is dry, as it has been this summer. Watering has kept most of the outfield reasonably green, but the infield is hopeless. Scruffy grass grows up the lines, but the area between the pitcher's rubber and home plate is almost completely bald. The backstop is rusty; passed balls and wild pitches frequently squirt through a wide gap between the ground and the chain link. Two large, hilly dunes run through short-right and center fields. These dunes have actually become a home-team advantage. Bangor West players learn to play the caroms off them, just as Red Sox left fielders learn to play caroms off the Green Monster. Visiting fielders, on the other hand, often find themselves chasing their mistakes all the way to the fence.

Brewer's field, tucked behind the local IGA grocery and a Marden's Discount Store, has to compete for space with what may be the oldest, rustiest playground equipment in New England; little brothers and sisters watch the game upside down from the swings, their heads down and their feet in the sky.

Bob Beal Field in Machias, with its pebble-pocked-skin infield, is probably the worst of the fields Bangor West will visit this year; Hampden, with its manicured outfield and neat composition infield, is probably the best. With its picnic area beyond the center-field fence and a rest-room-equipped snack bar, Hampden's diamond, behind the local VFW hall, looks like a rich kids' field. But looks can be deceiving. This team is a combination of kids from Newburgh and Hampden, and Newburgh is still small-farm and dairy country. Many of these kids ride to the games in old cars with primer paint around the headlights and mufflers held in place by chicken wire; they wear sunburns they got doing chores, not while they were hanging out at the country-club swimming pool. Town kids and country kids. Once they're in uniform, it doesn't much matter which is which.

Dave is right: the Hampden-Newburgh fans are waiting. Bangor West last won the District 3 Little League title in 1971; Hampden has never won a title, and many local fans continue to hope that this will be the year, despite the earlier loss to Bangor West. For the first time, the Bangor team really feels it is on the road; it is faced with a large hometown rooting section.

Matt Kinney gets the start. Hampden counters with Kyle King, and the game quickly shapes up as that rarest and richest of Little League commodities, a genuine pitchers' duel. At the end of the third inning, the score is Hampden 0, Bangor West 0.

In the bottom of the fourth, Bangor scores two unearned runs when Hampden's infield comes unglued once more. Owen King, Bangor West's first baseman, comes to bat with two on and one out. The two Kings, Kyle on the Hampden team and Owen on the Bangor West team, are not related. You don't need to be told; a single glance is enough. Kyle King is about five foot three. At six foot two, Owen King towers over him. Size differences are so extreme in Little League that it's easy to feel disoriented, the victim of hallucination.

Bangor's King raps a ground ball to short. It's a tailor-made double play, but the Hampden shortstop does not field it cleanly, and King, shucking his two hundred or so pounds down to first at top speed, beats the throw. Mike Pelkey and Mike Arnold scamper home.

Then, in the top of the fifth, Matt Kinney, who has been cruising, hits Chris Witcomb, number eight in Hampden's order. Brett Johnson, the number nine hitter, scorches one at Casey Kinney,

Bangor West's second baseman. Again, it's a tailor-made double-play ball, but Casey gives up on it. His hands, which have been automatically dipping down, freeze about four inches off the ground, and Casey turns his face away to protect it from a possible bad hop. This is the most common of all Little League fielding errors, and the most easily understood; it is an act of naked self-preservation. The stricken look that Casey throws toward Dave and Neil as the ball squirts through into center field completes this part of the ballet.

"It's O.K., Casey! Next time!" Dave bawls in his gravelly, self-assured Yankee voice.

"New batter!" Neil shouts, ignoring Casey's look completely. "New batter! Know your play! We're still ahead! Get an out! Just concentrate on getting an out!"

Casey begins to relax, begins to get back into the game, and then, beyond the outfield fences, the Hampden Horns begin to blow. Some of them belong to late-model cars — Toyotas and Hondas and snappy little Dodge Colts with U.S. OUT OF CENTRAL AMERICA and SPLIT WOOD NOT ATOMS stickers on the bumpers. But most of the Hampden Horns reside within older cars and pickup trucks. Many of the pickups have rusty doors, FM converters wired up beneath the dashboards, and Leer camper caps built over the truck beds. Who is inside these vehicles, blowing the horns? No one seems to know — not for sure. They are not parents or relatives of the Hampden players; the parents and relatives (plus a generous complement of ice-cream-smeared little brothers and sisters) are filling the bleachers and lining the fence on the third-base side of the diamond, where the Hampden dugout is. They may be local guys just off work — guys who have stopped to watch some of the game before having a few brewskis at the VFW hall next door — or they may be the ghosts of Hampden Little Leaguers Past, hungry for that long-denied State Championship flag. It seems at least possible; there is something both eerie and inevitable about the Hampden Horns. They toot in harmony — high horns, low horns, a few foghorns powered by dying batteries. Several Bangor West players look uneasily back toward the sound.

Behind the backstop, a local TV crew is preparing to videotape a story for the sports final on the eleven o'clock news. This causes a stir among some of the spectators, but only a few of the players on the Hampden bench seem to notice it. Matt Kinney certainly doesn't. He is totally intent on the next Hampden batter, Matt Knaide, who taps one turf shoe with his aluminum Worth bat and then steps into the batter's box.

The Hampden Horns fall silent. Matt Kinney goes into his windup. Casey Kinney drops back into position just east of second, glove down. His face says it has no plans to turn away if the ball is hit to him again. The Hampden runners stand expectantly on first and second. (There is no leading away from the bag in Little League.) The spectators along the opposing arms of the diamond watch anxiously. Their conversations die out. Baseball at its best (and this is a very good game indeed, one you would pay money to see) is a game of restful pauses punctuated by short, sharp inhalations. The fans can now sense one of those inhalations coming. Matt Kinney winds and fires.

Knaide lines the first pitch over second for a base hit, and now the score is 2–1. Kyle King, Hampden's pitcher, steps to the plate and sends a low, screeching line drive straight back to the mound. It hits Matt Kinney on the right shin. He makes an instinctive effort to field the ball, which has already squiggled off toward the hole between third and short, before he realizes he is really hurt and folds up. Now the bases are loaded, but for the moment no one cares; the instant the umpire raises his hands, signaling time out, all the Bangor West players converge on Matt Kinney. Beyond center field, the Hampden Horns are blowing triumphantly.

Kinney is white-faced, clearly in pain. An ice pack is brought from the first-aid kit kept in the snack bar, and after a few minutes he is able to rise and limp off the field with his arms around Dave and Neil. The spectators applaud loudly and sympathetically.

Owen King, the erstwhile first baseman, becomes Bangor West's new pitcher, and the first batter he must face is Mike Tardif. The Hampden Horns send up a brief, anticipatory blat as Tardif steps in. King's third pitch goes wild to the backstop. Brett Johnson heads home; King breaks toward the plate from the mound, as he has been taught to do. In the Bangor West dugout, Neil Waterman, his arm still around Matt Kinney's shoulders, chants, *"Cover-cover-COVER!"*

Joe Wilcox, Bangor West's starting catcher, is a foot shorter than King, but very quick. At the beginning of this All-Star season, he did not want to catch, and he still doesn't like it, but he has learned to live with it and to get tough in a position where very few small players survive for long; even in Little League, most catchers resemble human Toby jugs. Earlier in this game he made an amazing one-handed stab of a foul ball. Now he lunges toward the backstop, flinging his mask aside with his bare hand at the same instant he catches the rebounding wild pitch. He turns toward the plate and tosses to King as the Hampden Horns chorus a wild — and premature, as it turns out — bray of triumph.

Johnson has slowed down. On his face is an expression strikingly similar to that worn by Casey Kinney when Casey allowed Johnson's hard-hit grounder to shoot through the hole. It is a look of extreme anxiety and trepidation, the face of a boy who suddenly wishes he was someplace else. *Anyplace* else. The new pitcher is blocking the plate.

Johnson starts a halfhearted slide. King takes the toss from Wilcox, pivots with surprising, winsome grace, and tags the hapless Johnson out easily. He walks back toward the mound, wiping sweat from his forehead, and prepares to face Tardif once more. Behind him, the Hampden Horns have fallen silent again.

Tardif loops one toward third. Kevin Rochefort, Bangor's third baseman, takes a single step backward in response. It's an easy play, but there is an awful look of dismay on his face, and it is only then, as Rochefort starts to freeze up on what is an easy pop fly, that one can see how badly the whole team has been shaken by Matt's injury. The ball goes into Rochefort's glove, and then pops out when Rochefort — dubbed Roach Clip first by Freddy Moore and then by the whole squad — fails to squeeze it. Knaide, who advanced to third while King and Wilcox were dealing with Johnson, has already broken for the plate. Rochefort could have doubled Knaide up easily if he had caught the ball, but here, as in the majors, baseball is a game of ifs and inches. Rochefort doesn't catch the ball. He throws wild to first instead. Mike Arnold has taken over there, and he is one of the best fielders on the team, but no one issued him stilts. Tardif, meanwhile, steams into second. The pitchers' duel has become a typical Little League game, and now the Hampden Horns are a cacophony of joy. The home team has their thumping shoes on, and the final score is

Hampden 9, Bangor West 2. Still, there are two good things to
go home on: Matt Kinney is not seriously hurt, and when Casey
Kinney got another tough chance in the late innings he refused
to choke, and made the play.

After the final out is recorded, the Bangor West players trudge
into their dugout and sit on the bench. This is their first loss, and
most of them are not coping with it very gracefully. Some toss
their gloves disgustedly between their dirty sneakers. Some are
crying, others look close to tears, and no one is talking. Even
Freddy, Bangor's quipmaster general, has nothing to say on this
muggy Thursday evening in Hampden. Beyond the center-field
fence, a few of the Hampden Horns are still tooting happily away.

Neil Waterman is the first person to speak. He tells the boys to
get their heads up and look at him. Three of them already are:
Owen King, Ryan Iarrobino, and Matt Kinney. Now about half
the squad manages to do as he's asked. Several others, however — including Josh Stevens, who made the final out — continue to seem vastly interested in their footgear.

"Get your *heads* up," Waterman says again. He speaks louder
this time, but not unkindly, and now they all manage to look at
him. "You played a pretty good game," he says softly. "You got a
little rattled, and they ended up on top. It happens. It doesn't
mean they're better, though — that's something we're going to
find out on Saturday. Tonight all you lost was a baseball game.
The sun will still come up tomorrow." They begin to stir around
on the bench a little; this old homily has apparently not lost its
power to comfort. "You gave what you had tonight, and that's all
we want. I'm proud of you, and you can be proud of yourselves.
Nothing happened that you have to hang your heads about."

He stands aside for Dave Mansfield, who surveys his team. When
Dave speaks, his usually loud voice is even quieter than Waterman's. "We knew when we came down here that they had to beat
us, didn't we?" he asks. He speaks reflectively, almost as if he were
talking to himself. "If they didn't, they'd be out. They'll be coming to our field on Saturday. That's when *we* have to beat *them*.
Do you want to?"

They are all looking up now.

"I want you to remember what Neil told you," Dave says in that
reflective voice, so unlike his practice-field bellow. "You are a team.

That means you love each other. You love each other — win or lose — because you are a team."

The first time anyone suggested to these boys that they must come to love each other while they were on the field, they laughed uneasily at the idea. Now they don't laugh. After enduring the Hampden Horns together, they seem to understand, at least a little.

Dave surveys them again, then nods. "O.K. Pick up the gear."

They pick up bats, helmets, catching equipment, and stuff everything into canvas duffel bags. By the time they've got it over to Dave's old green pickup truck, some of them are laughing again.

Dave laughs with them, but he doesn't do any laughing on the ride home. Tonight the ride seems long. "I don't know if we can beat them on Saturday," he says on the way back. He is speaking in that same reflective tone of voice. "I want to, and *they* want to, but I just don't know. Hampden's got mo on their side, now."

Mo, of course, is momentum — that mythic force which shapes not only single games but whole seasons. Baseball players are quirky and superstitious at every level of play, and for some reason the Bangor West players have adopted a small plastic sandal — a castoff of some young fan's baby doll — as their mascot. They have named this absurd talisman Mo. They stick it in the chain-link fence of the dugout at every game, and batters often touch it furtively before stepping into the on-deck circle. Nick Trzaskos, who ordinarily plays left field for Bangor West, has been entrusted with Mo between games. Tonight, for the first time, he forgot to bring the talisman.

"Nick better remember Mo on Saturday," Dave says grimly. "But even if he remembers . . ." He shakes his head. "I just don't know."

There is no admission charge to Little League games; the charter expressly forbids it. Instead, a player takes around a hat during the fourth inning, soliciting donations for equipment and field maintenance. On Saturday, when Bangor West and Hampden square off in the year's final Penobscot County Little League game, at Bangor, one can judge the growth of local interest in the team's fortunes by a simple act of comparison. The collection taken up at the Bangor-Millinocket contest was $15.45; when the hat finally comes back in the fifth inning of the Saturday-afternoon game against Hampden, it's overflowing with change and crumpled dollar bills. The total take is $94.25. The bleachers are full; the fences are lined; the parking lot is full. Little League has one thing in common with almost all American sports and business endeavors: nothing succeeds like success.

Things start off well for Bangor — they lead 7–3 at the end of three — and then everything falls apart. In the fourth inning, Hampden scores six runs, most of them honest. Bangor West doesn't fold, as it did after Matt Kinney was hit in the game at Hampden — the players do not drop their heads, to use Neil Waterman's phrase. But when they come to bat in the bottom of the sixth inning they are down by a score of 14–12. Elimination looks very close and very real. Mo is in its accustomed place, but Bangor West is still three outs away from the end of its season.

One kid who did not need to be told to get his head up following Bangor West's 9–2 loss was Ryan Iarrobino. He went two for three in that game, played well, and trotted off the field *knowing* he had played well. He is a tall kid, quiet, with broad shoulders and a shock of dark-brown hair. He is one of two natural athletes on the Bangor West team. Matt Kinney is the other. Although the two boys are physical opposites — Kinney slim and still fairly short, Iarrobino tall and well muscled — they share a quality that is uncommon in boys their age: they trust their bodies. Most of the others on the Bangor West squad, no matter how talented, seem to regard feet, arms, and hands as spies and potential traitors.

Iarrobino is one of those boys who seem somehow more *there* when they are dressed for some sort of competition. He is one of the few kids on either team who can don batting helmets and not look like nerds wearing their mothers' stewpots. When Matt Kinney stands on the mound and throws a baseball, he seems perfect in his place and time. And when Ryan Iarrobino steps into the right-hand batter's box and points the head of his bat out toward the pitcher for an instant before raising it to the cocked position, at his right shoulder, he also seems to be exactly where he belongs. He looks dug in even before he settles himself for the first pitch: you could draw a perfectly straight line from the ball of his shoulder to the ball of his hip and on down to the ball of his an-

kle. Matt Kinney was built to throw baseballs; Ryan Iarrobino was
built to hit them.

Last call for Bangor West. Jeff Carson, whose fourth-inning home
run is really the difference in this game, and who earlier replaced Mike Wentworth on the mound for Hampden, is now replaced by Mike Tardif. He faces Owen King first. King goes three
and two (swinging wildly for the fences at one pitch in the dirt),
then lays off a pitch just inside to work a walk. Roger Fisher follows him to the plate, pinch-hitting for the ever-gregarious Fred
Moore. Roger is a small boy with Indian-dark eyes and hair. He
looks like an easy out, but looks can be deceptive; Roger has good
power. Today, however, he is overmatched. He strikes out.

In the field, the Hampden players shift around and look at each
other. They are close, and they know it. The parking lot is too far
away here for the Hampden Horns to be a factor; their fans settle for simply screaming encouragement. Two women wearing
purple Hampden caps are standing behind the dugout, hugging
each other joyfully. Several other fans look like track runners
waiting for the starter's gun; it is clear they mean to rush onto
the field the moment their boys succeed in putting Bangor West
away for good.

Joe Wilcox, who didn't want to be a catcher and ended up doing
the job anyway, rams a one-out single up the middle and into
left-center field. King stops at second. Up steps Arthur Dorr, the
Bangor right fielder, who wears the world's oldest pair of high-
top sneakers and has not had a hit all day. This time he hits a
shot, but right at the Hampden shortstop, who barely has to move.
The shortstop whips the ball to second, hoping to catch King off
the bag, but he's out of luck. Nevertheless, there are two out.

The Hampden fans scream further encouragement. The
women behind the dugout are jumping up and down. Now there
are a few Hampden Horns tooting away someplace, but they are
a little early, and all one has to do to know it is to look at Mike
Tardif's face as he wipes off his forehead and pounds the baseball into his glove.

Ryan Iarrobino steps into the right-hand batter's box. He has
a fast, almost naturally perfect swing; even Ron St. Pierre will not
fault him on it much.

Ryan swings through Tardif's first pitch, his hardest of the day — it makes a rifle-shot sound as it hits Kyle King's glove. Tardif then wastes one outside. King returns the ball, Tardif meditates briefly, and then throws a low fastball. Ryan looks at it, and the umpire calls strike two. It has caught the outside corner — maybe. The ump says it did, anyway, and that's the end of it.

Now the fans on both sides have fallen quiet, and so have the coaches. They're all out of it. It's only Tardif and Iarrobino now, balanced on the last strike of the last out of the last game one of these teams will play. Forty-six feet between these two faces. Only, Iarrobino is not watching Tardif's *face*. He is watching Tardif's *glove*, and somewhere I can hear Ron St. Pierre telling Fred, *You're waiting to see how I'll come — sidearm, three-quarters, or over the top.*

Iarrobino is waiting to see how Tardif will come. As Tardif moves to the set position, you can faintly hear the *pock-pock, pock-pock* of tennis balls on a nearby court, but here there is only silence and the crisp black shadows of the players, lying on the dirt like silhouettes cut from black construction paper, and Iarrobino is waiting to see how Tardif will come.

He comes over the top. And suddenly Iarrobino is in motion, both knees and the left shoulder dipping slightly, the aluminum bat a blur in the sunlight. That aluminum-on-cowhide sound — *chink*, like someone hitting a tin cup with a spoon — is different this time. A *lot* different. Not *chink* but *crunch* as Ryan connects, and then the ball is in the sky, tracking out to left field — a long shot that is clearly gone, high, wide, and handsome into the summer afternoon. The ball will later be recovered from beneath a car about 275 feet away from home plate.

The expression on twelve-year-old Mike Tardif's face is stunned, thunderstruck disbelief. He takes one quick look into his glove, as if hoping to find the ball still there and discover that Iarrobino's dramatic two-strike, two-out shot was only a hideous momentary dream. The two women behind the backstop look at each other in total amazement. At first, no one makes a sound. In that moment before everyone begins to scream and the Bangor West players rush out of their dugout to await Ryan at home plate and mob him when he arrives, only two people are entirely sure that it did really happen. One is Ryan himself. As he rounds first, he raises both hands to his shoulders in a brief but emphatic gesture of triumph. And, as Owen King crosses the plate with the first of the three runs that will end Hampden's All-Star season, Mike Tardif realizes. Standing on the pitcher's rubber for the last time as a Little Leaguer, he bursts into tears.

"You gotta remember, they're only twelve," each of the three coaches says at one time or another, and each time one of them says it, the listener feels that he — Mansfield, Waterman, or St. Pierre — is really reminding himself.

"When you are on the field, we'll love you and you will love each other," Waterman tells the boys again and again, and in the wake of Bangor's eleventh-hour, 15–14 win over Hampden, when they all did love each other, the boys no longer laugh at this. He continues, "From now on, I'm going to be hard on you — very hard. When you're playing, you'll get nothing but unconditional love from me. But when we're practicing on our home field some of you are going to find out how loud I can yell. If you're goofing off, you're going to sit down. If I tell you to do something and you don't do it, you're going to sit down. Recess is over, guys — everybody out of the pool. This is where the hard work starts."

A few nights later, Waterman hits a shot to right during fielding practice. It almost amputates Arthur Dorr's nose on the way by. Arthur has been busy making sure his fly is zipped. Or inspecting the laces of his Keds. Or some damn thing.

"*Arthur!*" Neil Waterman bellows, and Arthur flinches more at the sound of that voice than he did at the close passage of the baseball. "*Get in here! On the bench! Now!*"

"But —" Arthur begins.

"In here!" Neil yells back. "You're on the pine!"

Arthur trots sullenly in, head down, and J. J. Fiddler takes his place. A few nights later, Nick Trzaskos loses his chance to hit away when he fails to bunt two pitches in five tries or so. He sits on the bench by himself, cheeks flaming.

Machias, the Aroostook County / Washington County winner, is next on the docket — a two-out-of-three series, and the winner will be District 3 champion. The first game is to be played at the Bangor field, behind the Coke plant, the second at Bob Beal Field in Machias. The last game, if needed, will be played on neutral ground between the two towns.

*

As Neil Waterman has promised, the coaching staff is all encouragement once the national anthem has been played and the first game starts.

"That's all right, no damage!" Dave Mansfield cries as Arthur Dorr misjudges a long shot to right and the ball lands behind him. "Get an out, now! Belly play! Let's just get an out!" No one seems to know exactly what "belly play" is, but since it seems to involve winning ball games, the boys are all for it.

No third game against Machias is necessary. Bangor West gets a strong pitching performance from Matt Kinney in the first one and wins 17–5. Winning the second game is a little tougher only because the weather does not cooperate: a drenching summer downpour washes out the first try, and it is necessary for Bangor West to make the 168-mile round trip to Machias twice in order to clinch the division. They finally get the game in, on the twenty-ninth of July. Mike Pelkey's family has spirited Bangor West's number two pitcher off to Disney World in Orlando, making Mike the third player to fade from the team, but Owen King steps quietly in and pitches a five-hitter, striking out eight before tiring and giving way to Mike Arnold in the sixth inning. Bangor West wins, 12–2, and becomes District 3 Little League champ.

At moments like these, the pros retire to their air-conditioned locker rooms and pour champagne over each other's heads. The Bangor West team goes out to Helen's, the best (maybe the only) restaurant in Machias, to celebrate with hot dogs, hamburgers, gallons of Pepsi-Cola, and mountains of French fries. Looking at them as they laugh at each other, razz each other, and blow napkin pellets through their straws at each other, it is impossible not to be aware of how soon they will discover gaudier modes of celebration.

For now, however, this is perfectly O.K. — great, in fact. They are not overwhelmed by what they have done, but they seem tremendously pleased, tremendously content, and entirely *here*. If they have been touched with magic this summer, they do not know it, and no one has as yet been unkind enough to tell them that it may be so. For now they are allowed the deep-fried simplicities of Helen's, and those simplicities are quite enough. They have won their division; the State Championship Tournament, where bigger and better teams from the more heavily populated regions downstate will probably blow them out, is still a week away.

Ryan Iarrobino has changed back into his tank top. Arthur Dorr has a rakish smear of ketchup on one cheek. And Owen King, who struck terror into the hearts of the Machias batters by coming at them with a powerful sidearm fastball on 0–2 counts, is burbling happily into his glass of Pepsi. Nick Trzaskos, who can look unhappier than any boy on earth when things don't break his way, looks supremely happy tonight. And why not? Tonight they're twelve and they're winners.

Not that they don't remind you themselves from time to time. Halfway back from Machias after the first trip, the rainout, J. J. Fiddler begins to wriggle around uneasily in the back seat of the car he is riding in. "I gotta go," he says. He clutches at himself and adds ominously, "Man, I gotta go bad. I mean big time."

"J.J.'s gonna do it!" Joe Wilcox cries gleefully. "Watch this! J.J.'s gonna flood the car!"

"Shut up, Joey," J.J. says, and then begins to wriggle around again.

He has waited until the worst possible moment to make his announcement. The eighty-four-mile trip between Machias and Bangor is, for the most part, an exercise in emptiness. There isn't even a decent stand of trees into which J.J. can disappear for a few moments along this stretch of road — only mile after mile of open hayfields, with Route 1A cutting a winding course through them.

Just as J.J.'s bladder is going to Defcon-1, a providential gas station appears. The assistant coach swings in and tops up his tank while J.J. splits for the men's room. "Boy!" he says, brushing his hair out of his eyes as he jogs back to the car. "That was close!"

"Got some on your pants, J.J.," Joe Wilcox says casually, and everyone goes into spasms of wild laughter as J.J. checks.

On the trip back to Machias the next day, Matt Kinney reveals one of the chief attractions *People* magazine holds for boys of Little League age. "I'm sure there's one in here someplace," he says, leafing slowly through an issue he has found on the back seat. "There almost always is."

"What? What are you looking for?" third baseman Kevin

Rochefort asks, peering over Matt's shoulder as Matt leafs past the week's celebs, barely giving them a look.

"The breast-examination ad," Matt explains. "You can't see everything, but you can see quite a lot. Here it is!" He holds the magazine up triumphantly.

Four other heads, each wearing a red Bangor West baseball cap, immediately cluster around the magazine. For a few minutes, at least, baseball is the farthest thing from these boys' minds.

The 1989 Maine State Little League Championship Tournament begins on August 3, just over four weeks after All-Star play began for the teams involved. The state is divided into five districts, and all five send teams to Old Town, where this year's tourney is to be held. The participants are Yarmouth, Belfast, Lewiston, York, and Bangor West. All the teams but Belfast are bigger than the Bangor West All-Stars, and Belfast is supposed to have a secret weapon. Their number one pitcher is this year's tourney wunderkind.

The naming of the tourney wunderkind is a yearly ceremony, a small tumor that seems to defy all attempts to remove it. This boy, who is anointed Kid Baseball whether he wants the honor or not, finds himself in a heretofore unsuspected spotlight, the object of discussion, speculation, and, inevitably, wagering. He also finds himself in the unenviable position of having to live up to all sorts of pretournament hype. A Little League tournament is a pressure situation for any kid; when you get to Tourney Town and discover you have somehow become an instant legend as well, it's usually too much.

This year's object of myth and discussion is Belfast's southpaw Stanley Sturgis. In his two outings for Belfast he has chalked up thirty strikeouts — fourteen in his first game, sixteen in his second. Thirty K's in two games is an impressive statistic in any league, but to fully understand Sturgis's accomplishment one has to remember that Little League games consist of only six innings. That means that 83 percent of the outs Belfast recorded with Sturgis on the hill came on strikeouts.

Then there is York. All the teams that come to the Knights of Columbus field in Old Town to compete in the tourney have excellent records, but York, which is undefeated, is the clear favorite to win a ticket to the Eastern Regionals. None of their players are giants, but several of them are over five-ten, and their best pitcher, Phil Tarbox, has a fastball that may top seventy miles an hour on some pitches — extravagant by Little League standards. Like Yarmouth and Belfast, the York players come dressed in special All-Star uniforms and matching turf shoes, which make them look like pros.

Only Bangor West and Lewiston come wearing mufti — which is to say, shirts of many colors bearing the names of their regular-season team sponsors. Owen King wears Elks orange, Ryan Iarrobino and Nick Trzaskos wear Bangor Hydro red, Roger Fisher and Fred Moore wear Lions green, and so on. The Lewiston team is dressed in similar fashion, but they have at least been provided with matching shoes and stirrups. Compared with Lewiston, the Bangor team, dressed in a variety of baggy gray sweatpants and nondescript street sneakers, looks eccentric. Next to the other teams, however, they look like out-and-out ragamuffins. No one, with the possible exception of the Bangor West coaches and the players themselves, takes them very seriously. In its first article on the tourney the local newspaper gives more coverage to Sturgis, of Belfast, than it does to the entire Bangor West team.

Dave, Neil, and Saint, the odd but surprisingly effective brain trust that has brought the team this far, watch Belfast take infield and batting practice without saying much. The Belfast kids are resplendent in their new purple-and-white uniforms — uniforms that have not worn so much as a speck of infield dirt until today. At last, Dave says, "Well, we finally got here again. We did that much. Nobody can take that away from us."

Bangor West comes from the district in which the tournament is being held this year, and the team will not have to play until two of the five teams have been eliminated. This is called a first-round bye, and right now it's the biggest, perhaps the only, advantage this team has. In their own district, they looked like champions (except for that one awful game against Hampden), but Dave, Neil, and Saint have been around long enough to know that they are now looking at an entirely different level of baseball. Their silence as they stand by the fence watching Belfast work out acknowledges this eloquently.

In contrast, York has already ordered District 4 pins. Trading

pins is a tradition at the regional tournaments, and the fact that
York has already laid in a supply tells an interesting tale. The
pins say York means to play with the best of the East Coast, in
Bristol. The pins say they don't think Yarmouth can stop them;
or Belfast, with its wunderkind southpaw; or Lewiston, which
clawed its way to the division 2 championship through the losers'
bracket, after dropping their first game 15–12; or, least of all,
fourteen badly dressed pipsqueaks from the west side of Bangor.

"At least we'll get a chance to play," Dave says, "and we'll try to
make them remember we were here."

But first Belfast and Lewiston have *their* chance to play, and
after the Boston Pops has steamed through a recorded version
of the national anthem, and a local writer of some repute has
tossed out the obligatory first pitch (it sails all the way to the backstop), they have at it.

Area sports reporters have spilled a lot of ink on the subject of
Stanley Sturgis, but reporters are not allowed on the field once
the game starts (a situation caused by a mistake in the rules as
they were originally laid out, some of them seem to feel). Once
the umpire has commanded the teams to play ball, Sturgis finds
himself on his own. The writers, the pundits, and the entire Belfast hot-stove league are now all on the other side of the fence.

Baseball is a team sport, but there is only one player with a ball
at the center of each diamond and only one player with a bat at
the diamond's lowest point. The man with the bat keeps changing, but the pitcher remains — unless he can no longer cut it, that
is. Today is Stan Sturgis's day to discover the hard truth of tourney play: sooner or later, every wunderkind meets his match.

Sturgis struck out thirty men in his last pair of games, but that
was District 2. The team Belfast is playing today, a tough bunch
of scrappers out of Lewiston's Elliot Avenue League, is a different plate of beans altogether. They are not as big as the boys from
York and don't field as smoothly as the boys from Yarmouth, but
they are pesky and persistent. The first batter, Carlton Gagnon,
personifies the gnawing, clawing spirit of the team. He singles up
the middle, steals second, is sacrificed to third, then bolts home
on a steal play sent in from the bench. In the third inning, with
the score 1–0, Gagnon reaches base again, this time on a fielder's
choice. Randy Gervais, who follows this pest in the lineup, strikes

out, but before he does, Gagnon has gone to second on a passed ball and stolen third. He scores on a two-out base hit by Bill Paradis, the third baseman.

Belfast comes up with a run in the fourth, briefly making a game of it, but then Lewiston puts them, and Stanley Sturgis, away for good, scoring two in the fifth and four more in the sixth. The final tally is 9–1. Sturgis strikes out eleven, but he also gives up seven hits, while Carlton Gagnon, Lewiston's pitcher, strikes out eight and allows only three hits. When Sturgis leaves the field at the end of the game, he looks both depressed and relieved. For him the hype and hoopla are over. He can quit being a newspaper sidebar and go back to being a kid again. His face suggests that he sees certain advantages in that.

Later, in a battle of the giants, tourney favorite York knocks off Yarmouth. Then everybody goes home (or, in the case of the visiting players, back to their motels or to the homes of their host families). Tomorrow, Friday, it will be Bangor West's turn to play while York waits to meet the winner in the closer.

Friday comes in hot, foggy, and cloudy. Rain threatens from first light, and an hour or so before Bangor West and Lewiston are scheduled to square off the rain comes — a deluge of rain. When this sort of weather struck in Machias, the game was quickly canceled. Not here. This is a different field — one with a grass infield instead of dirt — but that isn't the only factor. The major one is TV. This year, for the first time, two stations have pooled their resources and will telecast the tournament final statewide on Saturday afternoon. If the semifinal between Bangor and Lewiston is postponed, it means trouble with the schedule, and even in Maine, even in this most amateur of amateur sports, the one thing you don't jiggle is the media's schedule.

So the Bangor West and Lewiston teams are not dismissed when they come to the field. Instead, they sit in cars or cluster in little groups beneath the candy-striped canvas of the central concession booth. Then they wait for a break in the weather. And wait. And wait. Restlessness sets in, of course. Many of these kids will play in bigger games before their athletic careers end, but this is the biggest to date for all of them; they are pumped to the max.

Someone eventually has a brainstorm. After a few quick phone calls, two Old Town school buses, gleaming bright yellow in the drenching rain, pull up to the nearby Elks Club, and the players are whisked off on a tour of the Old Town Canoe Company factory and the local James River paper mill. (The James River Corporation is the prime buyer of ad time on the upcoming championship telecast.) None of the players look particularly happy as they climb aboard the buses; they don't look much happier when they arrive back. Each player is carrying a small canoe paddle, about the right size for a well-built elf. Freebies from the canoe factory. None of the boys seem to know just what they should do with the paddles, but when I check later they're all gone, just like the Bangor pennants after that first game against Millinocket. Free souvenirs — good deal.

And there will be a game after all, it seems. At some point — perhaps while the Little Leaguers were watching the fellows at the James River mill turn trees into toilet paper — the rain stopped. The field has drained well, the pitcher's mound and the batters' boxes have been dusted with Quick-Dry, and now, at just past three in the afternoon, a watery sun takes its first peek through the clouds.

The Bangor West team has come back from the field trip flat and listless. No one has thrown a ball or swung a bat or run a single base so far today, but everybody already seems tired. The players walk toward the practice field without looking at each other; gloves dangle at the ends of arms. They walk like losers, and they talk like losers.

Instead of lecturing them, Dave lines them up and begins playing his version of pepper with them. Soon the Bangor players are razzing each other, catcalling, trying for circus catches, groaning and bitching when Dave calls an error and sends someone to the end of the line. Then, just before Dave is ready to call the workout off and take them over to Neil and Saint for batting practice, Roger Fisher steps out of the line and bends over with his glove against his belly. Dave goes to him at once, his smile becoming an expression of concern. He wants to know if Roger is all right.

"Yes," Roger says. "I just wanted to get this." He bends down a little farther, dark eyes intent, plucks something out of the grass, and hands it to Dave. It is a four-leaf clover.

*

In Little League tournament games, the home team is always decided by a coin toss. Dave has been extremely lucky at winning these, but today he loses, and Bangor West is designated the visiting team. Sometimes even bad luck turns out to be good, though, and this is one of those days. Nick Trzaskos is the reason.

The skills of all the players have improved during their six-week season, but in some cases attitudes have improved as well. Nick started deep on the bench, despite his proven skills as a defensive player and his potential as a hitter; his fear of failure made him unready to play. Little by little, he has begun to trust himself, and now Dave is ready to try starting him. "Nick finally figured out that the other guys weren't going to give him a hard time if he dropped a ball or struck out," St. Pierre says. "For a kid like Nick, that's a big change."

Today, Nick cranks the third pitch of the game to deep center field. It is a hard, rising line drive, over the fence and gone before the center fielder has a chance to turn and look, let alone cruise back and grab it. As Nick Trzaskos rounds second and slows down, breaking into the home-run trot all these boys know so well from TV, the fans behind the backstop are treated to a rare sight: Nick is grinning. As he crosses home plate and his surprised, happy teammates mob him, he actually begins to laugh. As he enters the dugout, Neil claps him on the back, and Dave Mansfield gives him a brief, hard hug.

Nick has also finished what Dave started with his game of pepper: the team is fully awake now, and ready to do some business. Matt Kinney gives up a lead-off single to Carl Gagnon, the pest who began the process of dismantling Stanley Sturgis. Gagnon goes to second on Ryan Stretton's sacrifice, advances to third on a wild pitch, and scores on another wild pitch. It is an almost uncanny repetition of his first at bat against Belfast. Kinney's control is not great this afternoon, but Gagnon's is the only run the team from Lewiston can manage in the early going. This is unfortunate for them, because Bangor comes up hitting in the top of the second.

Owen King leads off with a deep single; Arthur Dorr follows with another; Mike Arnold reaches when Lewiston's catcher, Jason Auger, picks up Arnold's bunt and throws wild to first base. King scores on the error, putting Bangor West back on top, 2–1.

Joe Wilcox, Bangor's catcher, scratches out an infield hit to load the bases. Nick Trzaskos strikes out his second time up, and that brings Ryan Iarrobino to the plate. He struck out his first time up, but not now. He turns Matt Noyes's first pitch into a grand-slam home run, and after an inning and a half the score is Bangor West 6, Lewiston 1.

Up to the sixth, it is an authentic four-leaf-clover day for Bangor West. When Lewiston comes to bat for what the Bangor fans hope will be the last time, they are down by a score of 9–1. The pest, Carlton Gagnon, leads off and reaches on an error. The next batter, Ryan Stretton, also reaches on an error. The Bangor fans, who have been cheering wildly, begin to look a little uneasy. It's hard to choke when you're eight runs ahead, but not impossible. These northern New Englanders are Red Sox fans. They have seen it happen many times.

Bill Paradis makes the jitters worse by singling sharply up the middle. Both Gagnon and Stretton come home. The score is now 9–3, runner on first, nobody out. The Bangor fans shuffle and look at each other uneasily. *It can't really get away from us this late in the game, can it?* their looks ask. The answer is, Of course, you bet it can. In Little League, anything can and often does happen.

But not this time. Lewiston scores one more time, and that's it. Noyes, who fanned three times against Sturgis, fans for the third time today, and there is finally one out. Auger, Lewiston's catcher, hits the first pitch hard to the shortstop, Roger Fisher. Roger booted Carl Gagnon's ball earlier in the inning to open the door, but he picks this one up easily and shovels it to Mike Arnold, who feeds it on to Owen King at first. Auger is slow, and King's reach is long. The result is a game-ending 6–4–3 double play. You don't often see around-the-horn d.p.s in the scaled-down world of Little League, where the base paths are only sixty feet long, but Roger found a four-leaf clover today. If you have to chalk it up to anything, it might as well be that. Whatever you chalk it up to, the boys from Bangor have won another one, 9–4.

Tomorrow, there are the giants from York.

It is August 5, 1989, and in the state of Maine only twenty-nine boys are still playing Little League ball — fourteen on the Bangor West squad and fifteen on York's team. The day is an almost

exact replica of the day before: hot, foggy, and threatening. The
game is scheduled to begin promptly at 12:30, but the skies open
once again, and by 11 it looks as though the game will be — must
be — canceled. The rain comes pouring down in buckets.

Dave, Neil, and Saint are taking no chances, however. None of
them liked the flat mood the kids were in when they returned
from their impromptu tour of the day before, and they have no
intention of allowing a repeat. No one wants to end up counting
on a game of pepper or a four-leaf clover today. If there *is* a
game — and TV is a powerful motivator, no matter how murky
the weather — it will be for all the marbles. The winners go on
to Bristol; the losers go home.

So a makeshift cavalcade of vans and station wagons driven by
coaches and parents is assembled at the field behind the Coke
plant, and the team is ferried the ten miles up to the University
of Maine field house, a barnlike indoor facility where Neil and
Saint rally them through their paces until the boys are soaked
with sweat. Dave has arranged for the York team to use the field
house, too, and as the Bangor team exits into the overcast the
York team, dressed in their natty blue uniforms, troops in.

The rain is down to isolated dribbles by three o'clock, and the
ground crew works frantically to return the field to playable shape.
Five makeshift TV platforms have been constructed on steel
frames around the field. In a nearby parking lot is a huge truck
with MAINE BROADCASTING SYSTEM LIVE REMOTE painted on
the side. Thick bundles of cable, held together with cinches of
electrician's tape, lead from the cameras and the temporary announcer's booth back to this truck. One door stands open, and
many TV monitors glimmer within.

York hasn't arrived from the field house yet. The Bangor West
squad begins throwing outside the left-field fence, mostly to have
something to do and keep the jitters at bay; they certainly don't
need to warm up after the humid hour they just spent at the university. The camerapersons stand on their towers and watch the
ground crew try to get rid of the water.

The outfield is in fair shape, and the skin parts of the infield
have been raked and coated with Quick-Dry. The real problem
is the area between home plate and the pitcher's mound. This
section of the diamond was freshly resodded before the tourna-

ment began, and there has been no time for the roots to take
hold and provide some natural drainage. The result is a swampy
mess in front of home plate — a mess that slops off toward the
third-base line.

Someone has an idea — an inspiration, as it turns out — that
involves actually removing a large section of the wounded infield. While this is being done, a truck arrives from Old Town
High School and two industrial-size Rinsenvacs are off-loaded.
Five minutes later, the ground crew is literally vacuuming the
subsurface of the infield. It works. By 3:25, the groundkeepers
are replacing chunks of sod like pieces in a large green jigsaw
puzzle. By 3:35, a local music teacher, accompanying herself on
an acoustic guitar, is winging her way through a gorgeous rendi-
tion of "The Star-Spangled Banner." And at 3:37 Bangor West's
Roger Fisher, Dave's dark-horse pick to start in place of the ab-
sent Mike Pelkey, is warming up. Did Roger's find of the day before have anything to do with Dave's decision to start him instead
of King or Arnold? Dave only puts his finger on the side of his
nose and smiles wisely.

At 3:40, the umpire steps in. "Send it down, catcher," he says
briskly. Joey does. Mike Arnold makes the sweep tag on the invisible runner, then sends the baseball on its quick journey around
the infield. A TV audience that stretches from New Hampshire
to the Maritime Provinces of Canada watches as Roger fusses
nervously with the sleeves of his green jersey and the gray warm-
up shirt he wears beneath it. Owen King tosses him the ball from
first base. Fisher takes it and holds it against his hip.

"Let's play ball," the umpire invites — an invitation that umpires have been extending to Little League players for fifty years
now — and Dan Bouchard, York's catcher and leadoff hitter, steps
into the box. Roger goes to the set position and prepares to throw
the first pitch of the 1989 State Championship game.

Five days earlier:
Dave and I take the Bangor West pitching staff up to Old Town.
Dave wants them all to know how the mound feels when they
come up here to play for real. With Mike Pelkey gone, the staff
consists of Matt Kinney (his triumph over Lewiston still four days
in the future), Owen King, Roger Fisher, and Mike Arnold. We

get off to a late start, and as the four boys take turns throwing, Dave and I sit in the visitors' dugout, watching the boys as the light slowly leaves the summer sky.

On the mound, Matt Kinney is throwing one hard curve after another to J. J. Fiddler. In the home dugout, across the diamond, the three other pitchers, their workouts finished, are sitting on the bench with a few teammates who have come along for the ride. Although the talk comes to me only in snatches, I can tell it's mostly about school — a subject that comes up with greater and greater frequency during the last month of summer vacation. They talk about teachers past and teachers future, passing on the anecdotes that form an important part of their preadolescent mythology: the teacher who blew her cool during the last month of the school year because her oldest son was in a car accident; the crazy grammar school coach (they make him sound like a lethal combination of Jason, Freddy, and Leatherface); the science teacher who supposedly once threw a kid against his locker so hard the kid was knocked out; the home-room teacher who will give you lunch money if you forget, or if you just say you forgot. It is junior high apocrypha, powerful stuff, and they tell it with great relish as twilight closes in.

Between the two dugouts, the baseball is a white streak as Matt throws it again and again. His rhythm is a kind of hypnosis: Set, wind, and fire. Set, wind, and fire. Set, wind, and fire. J.J.'s mitt cracks with each reception.

"What are they going to take with them?" I ask Dave. "When this is all over, what are they going to take with them? What difference does it make for them, do you think?"

The look on Dave's face is surprised and considering. Then he turns back to look at Matt and smiles. "They're going to take each other," he says.

It is not the answer I have been expecting — far from it. There was an article about Little League in the paper today — one of those think pieces that usually run in the ad-littered wasteland between the obituaries and the horoscopes. This one summarized the findings of a sociologist who spent a season monitoring Little Leaguers, and then followed their progress for a short time thereafter. He wanted to find out if the game did what Little League boosters claim it does — that is, pass on such old-fashioned American values as fair play, hard work, and the virtue of team effort. The fellow who did the study reported that it did, sort of. But he also reported that Little League did little to change the *individual* lives of the players. School troublemakers were still school troublemakers when classes started again in September; good scholars were still good scholars; the class clown (read Fred Moore) who took June and July off to play some serious Little League ball was still the class clown after Labor Day. The sociologist found exceptions; exceptional play sometimes bred exceptional changes. But in the main this fellow found that the boys were about the same coming out as they were going in.

I suppose my confusion at Dave's answer grows out of my knowledge of him — he is an almost fanatic booster of Little League. I'm sure he must have read the article, and I have been expecting him to refute the sociologist's conclusions, using the question as a springboard. Instead, he has delivered one of the hoariest chestnuts of the sports world.

On the mound, Matt continues to throw to J.J., harder than ever now. He has found that mystic place pitchers call "the groove," and even though this is only an informal practice session to familiarize the boys with the field, he is reluctant to quit.

I ask Dave if he can explain a little more fully, but I do so in a gingerly way, half expecting that I am on the verge of hitting a hitherto unsuspected jackpot of clichés: night owls never fly in the daytime; winners never quit and quitters never win; use it, don't lose it. Maybe even, God save us, a little Hummm, baby.

"Look at them," Dave says, still smiling. Something in that smile suggests he may be reading my mind. "Take a good look."

I do. There are perhaps half a dozen of them on the bench, still laughing and telling junior high school war stories. One of them breaks out of the discussion long enough to ask Matt Kinney to throw the curve, and Matt does — one with a particularly nasty break. The boys on the bench all laugh and cheer.

"Look at those two guys," Dave says, pointing. "One of them comes from a good home. The other one, not so good." He tosses some sunflower seeds into his mouth and then indicates another boy. "Or that one. He was born in one of the worst sections of Boston. Do you think he'd know a kid like Matt Kinney or Kevin Rochefort, if it wasn't for Little League? They won't be in the same classes at junior high, wouldn't talk to each other in the halls, wouldn't have the slightest idea the other one was alive."

Matt throws another curve, this one so nasty J.J. can't handle it. It rolls all the way to the backstop, and as J.J. gets up and trots after it the boys on the bench cheer again.

"But this changes all that," Dave says. "These boys have played together and won their district together. Some come from families that are well-to-do, and there's a couple from families as poor as used dishwater, but when they put on the uniform and cross the chalk they leave all that on the other side. Your school grades can't help you between the chalk, or what your parents do, or what they don't do. Between the chalk, what happens is the kids' business. They tend it, too, as well as they can. All the rest —" Dave makes a shooing gesture with one hand. "All left behind. And they know it, too. Just look at them if you don't believe me, because the proof is right there."

I look across the field and see my own kid and one of the boys Dave has mentioned sitting side by side, heads together, talking something over seriously. They look at each other in amazement, then break out laughing.

"They played together," Dave repeats. "They practiced together, day after day, and that's probably even more important than the games. Now they're going into the State Tournament. They've even got a chance to win it. I don't think they will, but that doesn't matter. They're going to be there, and that's enough. Even if Lewiston knocks them out in the first round, that's enough. Because it's something they did together between those chalk lines. They're going to remember that. They're going to remember how that felt."

"Between the chalk," I say, and all at once I get it — the penny drops. Dave Mansfield *believes* this old chestnut. Not only that, he can *afford* to believe it. Such clichés may be hollow in the big leagues, where some player or other tests positive for drugs every week or two and the free agent is God, but this is not the big leagues. This is where Anita Bryant sings the national anthem over battered PA speakers that have been wired to the chain-link behind the dugouts. This is where, instead of paying admission to watch the game, you put something in the hat when it comes around. If you want to, of course. None of these kids are going to spend the off-season playing fantasy baseball in Florida with overweight businessmen, or signing expensive baseball cards at memorabilia shows, or touring the chicken circuit at two thousand bucks a night. When it's all free, Dave's smile suggests, they have to give the clichés back and let you own them again, fair and square. You are once more allowed to believe in Red Barber, John Tunis, and the Kid from Tomkinsville. Dave Mansfield believes what he is saying about how the boys are equal between the chalk, and he has a right to believe, because he and Neil and Saint have patiently led these kids to a point where *they* believe it. They do believe it; I can see it on their faces as they sit in the dugout on the far side of the diamond. It could be why Dave Mansfield and all the other Dave Mansfields across the country keep on doing this, year after year. It's a free pass. Not back into childhood — it doesn't work that way — but back into the dream.

Dave falls silent for a moment, thinking, bouncing a few sunflower seeds up and down in the palm of his hand.

"It's not about winning or losing," he says finally. "That comes later. It's about how they'll pass each other in the corridor this year, or even down the road in high school, and look at each other, and remember. In a way, they're going to be on the team that won the district in 1989 for a long time." Dave glances across into the shadowy first-base dugout, where Fred Moore is now laughing about something with Mike Arnold. Owen King glances from one to the other, grinning. "It's about knowing who your teammates are. The people you had to depend on, whether you wanted to or not."

He watches the boys as they laugh and joke four days before their tournament is scheduled to begin, then raises his voice and tells Matt to throw four or five more and knock off.

Not all coaches who win the coin toss — as Dave Mansfield does on August 5, for the sixth time in nine postseason games — elect to be the home team. Some of them (the coach from Brewer, for instance) believe the so-called "home-team advantage" is a complete fiction, especially in a tournament game, where neither team is actually playing on its home field. The argument for being the visitors in a jackpot game runs like this: At the start of such a game, the kids on both teams are nervous. The way to take advantage of those nerves, the reasoning goes, is to bat first and let the defending team commit enough walks, balks, and errors to put you in the driver's seat. If you bat first and score four runs, these theorists conclude, you own the game before it's barely begun. QED. It's a theory Dave Mansfield has never subscribed to. "I want my lasties," he says, and for him that's the end of it.

Except today is a little different. It is not only a tournament game, it is a *championship* tournament game — a *televised* championship game, in fact. And as Roger Fisher winds and fires his first pitch past everything for ball one, Dave Mansfield's face is that of a man who is fervently hoping he hasn't made a mistake. Roger knows that he is a spot starter — that Mike Pelkey would be out here in his place if Pelkey weren't currently shaking hands with Goofy down in Disney World — but he manages his first-inning jitters as well as one could expect, maybe a little better. He backs off the mound following each return from the catcher, Joe Wilcox, studies the batter, fiddles with his shirtsleeves, and takes all the time he needs. Most important of all, he understands how necessary it is to keep the ball in the lowest quarter of the strike zone. The York lineup is packed with power from top to bottom. If Roger makes a mistake and gets one up in the batter's eyes — especially a batter like Tarbox, who hits as powerfully as he throws — it's going to get lost in a hurry.

He loses the first York batter nevertheless. Bouchard trots down to first, accompanied by the hysterical cheers of the York rooting section. The next batter is Philbrick, the shortstop. He bangs the first pitch back to Fisher. In one of those plays that sometimes decide ball games, Roger elects to go to second and try to force the lead runner. In most Little League games, this turns out to be a bad idea. Either the pitcher throws wild into center field, allowing the lead runner to get to third, or he discovers that his shortstop has not moved over to cover second and the bag is undefended. Today, however, it works. St. Pierre has drilled these boys well on their defensive positions. Matt Kinney, today's shortstop, is right where he's supposed to be. So is Roger's throw. Philbrick reaches first on a fielder's choice, but Bouchard is out. This time, it is the Bangor West fans who roar out their approval.

The play settles most of Bangor West's jitters and gives Roger Fisher some badly needed confidence. Phil Tarbox, York's most consistent hitter as well as their ace pitcher, strikes out on a pitch low and out of the strike zone. "Get him next time, Phil!" a York player calls from the bench. "You're just not used to pitching this slow!"

But speed is not the problem the York batters are having with Roger; it's location. Ron St. Pierre has preached the gospel of the low pitch all season long, and Roger Fisher — Fish, the boys call him — has been a quiet but extremely attentive student during Saint's ball yard seminars. Dave's decisions to pitch Roger and bat last look pretty good as Bangor comes in to bat in the bottom of the first. I see several of the boys touch Mo, the little plastic sandal, as they enter the dugout.

Confidence — of the team, of the fans, of the coaches — is a quality that can be measured in different ways, but whatever yardstick you choose, York comes out on the long side. The hometown cheering section has hung a sign on the lower posts of the scoreboard. YORK IS BRISTOL BOUND, this exuberant Fan-O-Gram reads. And there is the matter of those District 4 pins, all made up and ready for trading. But the clearest indicator of the deep confidence York's coach has in his players is revealed in his starting pitcher. All the other clubs, including Bangor West, pitched their number one starter in their first game, bearing an old playoff axiom in mind: if you don't get a date, you can't dance at the prom. If you can't win your prelim, you don't have to worry about the final. Only the coach from York ran counter to this wisdom, and pitched his number two starter, Ryan Fernald, in the first game, against Yarmouth. He got away with it — by a whisker — as his team outlasted Yarmouth, 9–8. That was a close shave, but today should be the payoff. He has saved Phil Tarbox for the final, and while Tarbox may not be technically as good as Stanley Sturgis, he's got something going for him that Sturgis did not. Phil Tarbox is *scary*.

Nolan Ryan, probably the greatest fastball pitcher ever to play the game of baseball, likes to tell a story about a Babe Ruth League tournament game he pitched in. He hit the opposing team's leadoff batter in the arm, breaking it. He hit the second batter in the head, splitting the boy's helmet in two and knocking him out for a few moments. While this second boy was being attended to, the number three batter, ashen-faced and trembling, went up to his coach and begged the man not to make him hit. "And I didn't blame him," Ryan adds.

Tarbox is no Nolan Ryan, but he throws hard and he is aware that intimidation is the pitcher's secret weapon. Sturgis also threw hard, but he kept the ball low and outside. Sturgis was polite. Tarbox likes to work high and tight. Bangor West has got to where they are today by swinging the bat. If Tarbox can intimidate them, he will take the bats out of their hands, and if he does that Bangor is finished.

Nick Trzaskos doesn't come anywhere near a leadoff home run today. Tarbox strikes him out with an intimate fastball that has Nick ducking out of the box. Nick looks around unbelievingly at the home-plate umpire and opens his mouth to protest. "Don't say a word, Nick!" Dave blares from the dugout. "Just hustle back in there!" Nick does, but his face has resumed its former narrow look. Once inside the dugout, he slings his batting helmet disgustedly under the bench.

Tarbox will try to work everyone but Ryan Iarrobino high and tight today. Word on Iarrobino has got around, and not even Phil Tarbox, confident as he appears to be, will challenge him. He works Ryan low and outside, finally walking him. He also walks Matt Kinney, who follows Ryan, but now he is high and tight again. Matt has superb reflexes, and he needs them to avoid being hit, and hit hard. By the time he is awarded first base, Iarrobino is already at second, courtesy of a wild pitch that came within inches of Matt's face. Then Tarbox settles down a little, striking out Kevin Rochefort and Roger Fisher to end the first inning.

Roger Fisher continues to work slowly and methodically, fiddling with his sleeves between pitches, glancing around at his infield, occasionally even checking the sky, possibly for UFOs. With two on and one out, Estes, who reached on a walk, breaks for third on a pitch that bounces out of Joe Wilcox's glove and lands at his feet. Joe recovers quickly and guns the ball down to Kevin Rochefort at third. The ball is waiting for Estes when he arrives, and he trots back to the dugout. Two out; Fernald has gone to second on the play.

Wyatt, York's number eight hitter, dribbles one up the right side of the infield. The ball's progress is slowed further by the soggy condition of the ground. Fisher goes for the ball. So does King, the first baseman. Roger grabs it, then slips on the wet grass and *crawls* for the bag, ball in hand. Wyatt beats him easily. Fernald comes all the way home on the play to score the first run of the game.

If Roger is going to crack, one would expect it to happen right here. He checks his infield, and examines the ball. He appears ready to pitch, and then steps off the rubber. His sleeves, it seems, are not quite to his liking after all. He takes his time fixing them while Matt Francke, the York batter, grows old and moldy in the batter's box. By the time Fisher finally gets around to throwing, he all but owns Francke, who hits an easy hopper to Kevin Rochefort at third. Rochefort throws on to Matt Kinney, forcing Wyatt. Still, York has drawn first blood and leads, 1–0, at the end of an inning and a half.

Bangor West doesn't put any runs on the board in the second inning, either, but they score against Phil Tarbox just the same. The rangy York pitcher trotted off the mound with his head up at the end of the first inning. Going in after pitching the second, he trudges with his head down, and some of his teammates glance at him uneasily.

Owen King, who bats first in Bangor's half of the second, isn't intimidated by Tarbox, but he is a big boy, much slower than Matt Kinney. After running the count full, Tarbox tries to jam him inside. The fastball runs up and in — too much of both. King is hit hard in the armpit. He falls to the ground, clutching the hurt place, too stunned to cry at first, but obviously in pain. Eventually, the tears do come — not a lot of them, but real tears, for all that. At six foot two and over two hundred pounds, he's as big as a man, but he's still only twelve and not used to being hit by seventy-mile-an-hour inside fastballs. Tarbox immediately rushes off the mound toward him, his face a mask of concern and contrition. The umpire, already bending over the downed player, waves him off impatiently. The on-duty paramedic who hurries out doesn't even give Tarbox a second look. The fans do, however. The fans are giving him all kinds of second looks.

"Take him out before he hits someone else!" one yells.

"Pull him before someone *really* gets hurt!" another adds, as if being hit in the rib cage by a fastball weren't really getting hurt.

"Warn 'im, ump!" a third voice chimes in. "That was a deliberate brushback! Warn 'im what happens if he does it again!"

Tarbox glances toward the fans, and for a moment this boy, who has formerly radiated a kind of serene confidence, looks very young and very uncertain. He looks, in fact, the way Stanley Sturgis did as the Belfast-Lewiston game neared its conclusion. As he goes back to the mound, he slams the ball into his glove in frustration.

King, meanwhile, has been helped to his feet. After making it clear to Neil Waterman, the paramedic, and the umpire that he wants to stay in the game and is capable of doing so, he trots down to first base. Both sets of fans give him a solid round of applause.

Phil Tarbox, who of course had no intention of hitting the leadoff batter in a one-run game, immediately shows how shaken he is by grooving one right down the middle to Arthur Dorr. Arthur, the second-smallest boy in Bangor West's starting lineup, accepts this unexpected but welcome gift by driving it deep to right center.

King is off at the crack of the bat. He rounds third, knowing he can't score but hoping to draw the throw that will assure Arthur of second base, and, as he does, the wet conditions become a factor. The third-base side of the diamond is still damp. When King tries to put on the brakes, his feet go out from under him and he lands on his ass. The relay has come in to Tarbox, and Tarbox will not risk a throw; he charges King, who is making feeble efforts to regain his feet. At the end, Bangor's biggest player just raises his arms in an eloquent, touching gesture: *I surrender.* Thanks to the slippery conditions, Tarbox now has a runner on second with one out instead of runners on second and third with none out. It is a big difference, and Tarbox displays his renewed confidence by striking out Mike Arnold.

Then, on his third pitch to Joe Wilcox, the next batter, he hits him smack in the elbow. This time, the cries of outrage from the Bangor West fans are louder, and tinged with threat. Several of them direct their ire at the home-plate umpire, demanding that Tarbox be taken out. The ump, who understands this situation completely, does not bother even to warn Tarbox. The stricken look on the boy's face as Wilcox jogs shakily down to first undoubtedly tells him it isn't necessary. But York's manager has to come out and settle the pitcher down, to point out the obvious: *You have two outs and first base was open anyway. There's no problem.*

But for Tarbox there *is* a problem. He has hit two boys this inning, hit both of them hard enough to make them cry. If that weren't a problem, he would need a mental examination.

York puts together three singles to score two runs in the top of the third, opening up a 3–0 lead. If these runs, both solidly earned, had come in the top of the first, Bangor would have been in serious trouble, but when the players come in for their raps they look eager and excited. There is no feeling among them that the game is lost, no whiff of failure.

Ryan Iarrobino is Bangor's first batter in the bottom of the third, and Tarbox works him carefully — too carefully. He has begun to aim the ball, and the result is fairly predictable. With the count at 1–2, he plinks Iarrobino on the shoulder. Iarrobino turns and pounds his bat once on the ground — whether in pain, frustration, or anger is impossible to tell. Most probably it is all three. Reading the mood of the crowd is much easier. The Bangor fans are on their feet, yelling angrily at Tarbox and at the ump. On the York side, the fans are silent and bewildered; it is not the game they were expecting. As Ryan trots down to first, he glances over at Tarbox. It is brief, that glance, but it seems clear enough: *That's the third time, you. Make it the last time.*

Tarbox confers briefly with his coach, then faces Matt Kinney. His confidence is in shambles, and his first pitch to Matt, a wild one, suggests that he wants to continue pitching this game about as much as a cat wants a bubble bath. Iarrobino beats York catcher Dan Bouchard's throw to second easily. Tarbox walks Kinney. The next batter is Kevin Rochefort. After two failed bunt attempts, Roach settles back and allows Phil Tarbox the chance to dig his hole a little deeper. He does, walking Kevin after having him 1–1. Tarbox has now thrown more than sixty pitches in less than three innings.

Roger Fisher also goes 3–2 with Tarbox, who is now relying almost exclusively on soft breaking stuff; he seems to have decided that if he does hit another batter he will not hit him hard. There is no place to put Fish; the bases are jammed. Tarbox knows it and takes a calculated risk, grooving another one, believing Fish will lay off in the hope of a walk. Roger snaps hungrily at it instead, bouncing one between first and second for a base hit. Iarrobino trots home with Bangor's first run.

Owen King, the player who was at bat when Phil Tarbox started to self-destruct, is the next batter. The York coach, suspecting his ace will work even less successfully to King this time, has seen enough. Matt Francke comes in to relieve, and Tarbox becomes York's catcher. As he squats behind the plate to warm Francke up, he looks both resigned and relieved. Francke doesn't hit anyone, but he is unable to stop the bleeding. At the end of three innings, Bangor West has only two hits, but they lead York, 5–3.

It is now the fifth inning. The air is full of gray moisture, and the YORK IS BRISTOL BOUND banner tacked to the scoreboard uprights has begun to sag. The fans look a little saggy themselves, and increasingly uneasy. *Is* York Bristol bound? *Well, we're supposed to be,* their faces say, *but it's the fifth inning now, and we're still two runs behind. My God, how did it get so late so early?*

Roger Fisher continues to cruise, and in the bottom of the fifth Bangor West puts what appears to be the final nails in York's coffin. Mike Arnold leads off with a single. Joe Wilcox sacrifices pinch-runner Fred Moore to second, and Iarrobino doubles off Francke, scoring Moore. This brings Matt Kinney to the plate. After a passed ball advances Ryan to third, Kinney hits an easy grounder to short, but it squirts off the infielder's glove and Iarrobino trots home.

Bangor West takes the field jubilantly, owning a 7–3 lead and only needing three more outs.

When Roger Fisher takes the mound to face York in the top of the sixth, he has thrown ninety-seven pitches, and he's a tired boy. He shows it at once by walking pinch-hitter Tim Pollack on a full count. Dave and Neil have seen enough. Fisher goes to second base, and Mike Arnold, who has been warming up between innings, takes over on the mound. He is ordinarily a good reliever, but it's not his day. Tension, maybe, or maybe it's just that the damp dirt of the mound has caused a change in his normal motion. He gets Francke to fly out, but then Bouchard walks, Philbrick doubles and Pollack, the runner charged to Fish, scores, and Bouchard is held up at third; by itself, Pollack's run means nothing. The important thing is that York now has runners on second and third, and the potential tying run is coming to the plate. The potential tying run is someone with a very personal interest in getting a hit, because he is the main reason York is only two outs away from extinction. The potential tying run is Phil Tarbox.

Mike works the count to 1–1, and then throws a fastball right down the middle of the plate. In the Bangor West dugout, Dave Mansfield winces and raises one hand toward his forehead in a warding-off gesture even as Tarbox begins his swing. There is the hard sound of Tarbox accomplishing that most difficult of baseball feats: using the round bat to hit the round ball squarely on the button.

Ryan Iarrobino takes off the instant Tarbox connects, but he runs out of room much too early. The ball clears the fence by twenty feet, bangs off a TV camera, and bounces back onto the field. Ryan looks at it disconsolately as the York fans go mad, and the entire York team boils out of the dugout to greet Tarbox, who has hit a three-run homer and redeemed himself in spectacular fashion. He does not step on home plate but *jumps* on it. His face wears an expression of near-beatific satisfaction. He is mobbed by his ecstatic teammates; on his way back to the dugout, his feet are barely allowed to touch the ground.

The Bangor fans sit in silence, utterly stunned by this awful reversal. Yesterday, against Lewiston, Bangor flirted with disaster; today they have swooned in its arms. Mo has changed sides again, and the fans are clearly afraid that this time it has changed for good. Mike Arnold confers with Dave and Neil. They are telling him to go on back and pitch hard, that the game is only tied, not lost, but Mike is clearly a dejected, unhappy boy.

The next batter, Hutchins, hits an easy two-hopper to Matt Kinney, but Arnold is not the only one who is shaken; the usually dependable Kinney boots the ball, and Hutchins is on. Andy Estes pops out to Rochefort at third, but Hutchins advances to second on a passed ball. King grabs Matt Hoyt's pop-up for the third out, and Bangor West is out of trouble.

The team has a chance to put it away in the bottom of the sixth, except that doesn't quite happen, either. They go one-two-three against Matt Francke, and all at once Bangor West is in its first extra-innings game of postseason play, tied 7–7 with York.

During the game against Lewiston, the muddy weather eventually unraveled. Not today. As Bangor West takes the field in the top of the seventh, the skies grow steadily darker. It's now approaching six o'clock, and even under these conditions the field should still be clear and fairly bright, but fog has begun to creep in. Watching a videotape of the game would make someone who wasn't there believe something was wrong with the TV cameras; everything looks listless, dull, underexposed. Shirtsleeve fans in the center-field bleachers are becoming disembodied heads and hands; in the outfield, Trzaskos, Iarrobino, and Arthur Dorr are discernible chiefly by their shirts.

Just before Mike throws the first pitch of the seventh, Neil elbows Dave and points out to right field. Dave immediately calls time and trots out to see what's the matter with Arthur Dorr, who is standing bent over, with his head almost between his knees.

Arthur looks up at Dave with some surprise as he approaches. "I'm O.K.," he says in answer to the unspoken question.

"Then what in hell are you doing?" Dave asks.

"Looking for four-leaf clovers," Arthur responds.

Dave is too flabbergasted, or too amused, to lecture the boy. He simply tells Arthur it might be more appropriate to look for them after the game is over.

Arthur glances around at the creeping fog before looking back at Dave. "I think by then it's gonna be too dark," he says.

With Arthur set to rights, the game can continue, and Mike Arnold does a creditable job — possibly because he's facing the substitute-riddled bottom of York's order. York does not score, and Bangor comes up in the bottom of the seventh with another chance to win it.

They come close to doing just that. With the bases loaded and two out, Roger Fisher hits one hard up the first-base line. Matt Hoyt is right there to pounce on it, however, and the teams change sides again.

Philbrick flies out to Nick Trzaskos to open the eighth, and then Phil Tarbox steps in. Tarbox is not finished working Bangor West over yet. He has regained his confidence; his face is utterly serene as he takes Mike's first pitch for a called strike. He swings at the next one, a pretty decent changeup that bounces off Joe Wilcox's shin guard. He steps out of the box, squats with the bat between his knees, and concentrates. This is a Zen technique the

York coach has taught these boys — Francke has done it several times on the mound while in tight spots — and it works for Tarbox this time, along with a little help from Mike Arnold.

Arnold's final pitch to Tarbox is a hanging curve up in the batter's eyes, exactly where Dave and Neil hoped no pitch would be today, and Tarbox creams it. It goes deep to left center, high over the fence. There is no camera stanchion to stop this one; it ends up in the woods, and the York fans are on their feet again, chanting "Phil-Phil-Phil" as Tarbox circles third, comes down the line, and jumps high in the air. He doesn't just jump on home plate; he *spikes* it.

Nor, it seems at first, will that be all. Hutchins bangs a single up the middle and gets second on an error. Estes follows this by hitting one to third, and Rochefort throws badly to second. Luckily, Roger Fisher is backed up by Arthur Dorr, saving a second run, but now York has guys at first and second with only one out.

Dave calls Owen King in to pitch, and Mike Arnold moves over to first. Following a wild pitch that moves the runners up to second and third, Matt Hoyt bangs one on the ground to Kevin Rochefort. In the game that Bangor West lost to Hampden, Casey Kinney was able to come back and make the play after committing an error. Rochefort does it today, and in spades. He comes up with the ball, then holds it for a moment, making sure Hutchins isn't going to break for the plate. *Then* he throws across the diamond to Mike, getting the slow-running Matt Hoyt by two steps. Considering the wringer these boys have been through, it is an incredibly canny piece of baseball. Bangor West has recovered itself, and King works Ryan Fernald — who hit a three-run homer against Yarmouth — perfectly, nipping at the corners, using his weirdly effective sidearm delivery to supplement the over-the-top fastball. Fernald pops weakly to first and the inning is over. At the end of seven and a half, York leads Bangor, 8–7. Six of York's RBIs belong to Philip Tarbox.

Matt Francke, York's pitcher, is as tired as Fisher was when Dave finally elected to replace him with Mike Arnold. The difference is that Dave *had* a Mike Arnold and, behind Mike, an Owen King. The York coach has no one; he used Ryan Fernald against Yarmouth, making him ineligible to pitch today, and now it's Francke forever.

He starts off the eighth well enough, striking out King. Arthur Dorr comes up next, one for four on the day (a double off Tarbox). Francke, obviously struggling now but just as obviously determined to finish this game, goes full with Arthur, then serves one up that's way outside. Arthur trots down to first.

Mike Arnold comes up next. It wasn't his day on the mound, but he does well this time at the plate, laying down a perfect bunt. The intent is not to sacrifice; Mike is bunting for the base hit, and almost gets it. But the ball will not quite die in that soggy patch between home and the pitcher's mound. Francke snatches it, glances toward second, and then elects to go to first. Now there are two men out with a runner at second. Bangor West is an out away from the end.

Joe Wilcox, the catcher, is up next. With the count 2–1, he hits a chalk hugger up the first-base line. Matt Hoyt grabs it, but just an instant too late; he takes the ball less than half a foot into foul territory, and the first-base umpire is right there to call it. Hoyt, who has been ready to charge the mound and embrace Matt Francke, instead returns the ball.

Now the count on Joey is 2–2. Francke steps off the rubber, stares straight up into the sky, and concentrates. Then he steps back on and delivers one high and out of the strike zone. Joey goes for it anyway, not even looking, swinging in self-defense. The bat makes contact with the ball — pure luck — and it bounces foul. Francke does the concentration bit again, then throws — just outside. Ball three.

Now comes what may be the pitch of the game. It *appears* to be a high strike, a game-ending strike, but the umpire calls ball four. Joe Wilcox trots down to first base with a faint expression of disbelief on his face. It is only later, watching the slow-motion replay on the TV tape of the game, that one can see how right, and how good, the umpire's call was. Joe Wilcox, so anxious that he is pinwheeling the bat in his hands like a golf club right up to the moment of the pitch, rises on his tiptoes as the ball approaches, and this is the reason it appears to be letter-high to him as it crosses the plate. The umpire, who never moves, discounts all of Joe's nervous tics and makes a major league call. The rules say you cannot shrink the strike zone by crouching; by the same token, you cannot expand it by stretching. If Joe hadn't gone up on his toes, Francke's pitch would have been throat-high instead of letter-high. So, instead of becoming the third out and ending the game, Joe becomes another base runner.

One of the TV cameras was trained on York's Matt Francke as he made the pitch, and it caught a remarkable image. A video replay shows Francke light up as the ball breaks downward just a moment too late to earn the strike. His pitching hand comes up in a victorious fisted salute. At this moment, he begins to move to his right, toward the York dugout, and the umpire blocks him out. When he returns to view a second later, his expression has become one of unhappiness and incredulity. He does not argue with the call — these kids are taught not to do that in their regular seasons, and to never, never, *never* do it in a championship situation — but as he prepares to work the next batter Francke appears to be crying.

Bangor West is still alive, and as Nick Trzaskos approaches the plate they come to their feet and begin to yell. Nick is obviously hoping for a free ride, and he gets one. Francke walks him on five pitches. It is the eleventh walk given up by York pitching today. Nick trots down to first, loading the bases, and Ryan Iarrobino steps in. Again and again, it has been Ryan Iarrobino in these situations, and now it is Ryan once more. The Bangor West fans are on their feet, screaming. The Bangor players crowd the dugout, fingers hooked through the mesh, watching anxiously.

"I can't believe it," one of the TV commentators says. "I can't believe the script of this game."

His partner chips in, "Well, I'll tell you what. Either way, this is how both teams would want the game to end."

As he speaks, the camera offers its own ghastly counterpoint to the comment by focusing on the stricken face of Matt Francke. The image strongly suggests that this is the *last* thing the York lefty wanted. Why would he? Iarrobino has doubled twice, walked twice, and been hit by a pitch. York hasn't retired him a single time. Francke throws high and outside, then low. These are his 135th and 136th pitches. The boy is exhausted. Chuck Bittner, the York manager, calls him over for a brief conference. Iarrobino waits for the conference to end, then steps in again.

Matt Francke concentrates, head back and eyes closed; he looks like a baby bird waiting to be fed. Then he winds up and throws the last pitch of the Maine Little League season.

Iarrobino has not been watching the concentration bit. His head is down; he is only watching to see how Francke will come, and his eyes never leave the ball. It is a fastball, low and tailing toward the outside corner of the plate. Ryan Iarrobino dips a little. The head of the bat whips around. He catches all of this one, really cranks it, and as the ball flies out of the park to deep right-center field, his arms shoot up over his head and he begins to tap-dance deliriously down the first-base line.

On the mound, Matt Francke, who was twice within inches of winning his game, lowers his head, not wanting to look. And as Ryan rounds second and starts back toward home, he seems to finally understand what he has done, and at that point he begins to weep.

The fans are in hysterics; the sports commentators are in hysterics; even Dave and Neil seem close to hysterics as they block the plate, making room for Ryan to touch it. Rounding third, he passes the umpire there, who is still twirling one magisterial finger in the gray air, signaling home run.

Behind the plate, Phil Tarbox takes off his mask and walks away from the celebration. He stamps his foot once, his face clenched with deep frustration. He walks off-camera and out of Little League for good. He will play Babe Ruth ball next year, and probably he will play it well, but there will be no more games like this for Tarbox, or for any of these boys. This one is, as they say, in the books.

Ryan Iarrobino, laughing, crying, holding his helmet on his head with one hand and pointing straight up to the gray sky with the other, leaps high, comes down on home plate, and then leaps again, straight into the arms of his teammates, who bear him away in triumph. The game is over; Bangor West has won, 11–8. They are Maine's 1989 Little League Champions.

I look toward the fence on the first-base side and see a remarkable sight: a forest of waving hands. The parents of the players have crowded against the chain-link and are reaching across the top to touch their sons. Many of the parents are also in tears. The boys all wear identical expressions of happy disbelief, and all these hands — hundreds of them, it seems — wave toward them, wanting to touch, wanting to congratulate, wanting to hug, wanting to *feel*.

The boys ignore them. Later, there will be touches and hugs.

First, however, there is business to take care of. They line up and slap hands with the boys from York, crossing at home plate in the ritual manner. Most of the boys on both teams are crying now, some so hard they can barely walk.

Then, in the instant before the Bangor boys go to the fence, where all those hands are still waving, they surround their coaches and pummel them and each other in joyful triumph. They have held on to win their tournament — Ryan and Matt, Owen and Arthur, Mike and Roger Fisher, finder of four-leaf clovers. At this moment they are cheering each other, and everything else will just have to wait. Then they break for the fence, going toward their crying, cheering, laughing parents, and the world begins to turn in its ordinary course once again.

"How long are we gonna keep on playing, Coach?" J. J. Fiddler asked Neil Waterman after Bangor clinched the division against Machias.

"J.J.," Neil replied, "we're gonna play until someone makes us stop."

The team that finally made Bangor West stop was Westfield, Massachusetts. Bangor West played them in the second round of the Eastern Regional Little League Championship, at Bristol, Connecticut, on August 15, 1989. Matt Kinney pitched for Bangor West and threw the best game of his life, striking out nine, walking five (one intentional), and giving up only three hits. Bangor West, however, got only one hit off Westfield pitcher Tim Laurita, and that one belonged, predictably enough, to Ryan Iarrobino. The final score was 2–1, Westfield. Credit Bangor's one RBI in the game to King, on a bases-loaded walk. Credit the game-winning RBI to Laurita, also on a bases-loaded walk. It was a hell of a game, a purist's game, but it couldn't match the one against York.

In the pro world, it was a bad year for baseball. A future Hall of Famer was banned from the sport for life; a retired pitcher shot his wife and then took his own life; the commissioner suffered a fatal heart attack; the first World Series game to be played at Candlestick Park in over twenty years was postponed when an earthquake shook northern California. But the majors are only a small part of what baseball is about. In other places and in other leagues — Little League, for instance, where there are no free agents, no salaries, and no gate admissions — it was a pretty fine year. The Eastern Regional Tournament winner was Trumbull, Connecticut. On August 26, 1989, Trumbull beat Taiwan to win the Little League World Series. It was the first time an American team had won the Williamsport World Series since 1983, and the first time in fourteen years that the winner had come from the region in which Bangor West plays.

In September, the Maine division of the United States Baseball Federation voted Dave Mansfield amateur coach of the year.

April 16, 1990

Biographical Notes

Notable Sports Writing of 1990

Biographical Notes

ROGER ANGELL defines baseball for *The New Yorker* magazine, where he has worked as an editor since 1956. His essays on the game have been collected in the books *The Summer Game, Five Seasons, Late Innings, Season Ticket,* and, most recently, *Once More Around the Park.*

RICHARD COHEN is a columnist for the *Washington Post.* He is the author, with Jules Witcover, of *A Heartbeat Away: The Investigation and Resignation of Spiro Agnew.*

FRANK CONROY's short stories have appeared in a number of magazines and journals. He is the author of *Stop-Time* and *Midair.* Since 1987 he has been a professor of English at the University of Iowa.

JEFF COPLON is a free-lance sportswriter who lives in Brooklyn. He co-wrote *Speed Trap,* about Canadian sprinter Ben Johnson, with Charlie Francis. His stories have appeared in *The New York Times Magazine, Playboy,* and *Rolling Stone.*

NEAL DONNELLY recently retired after a career with the U.S. Information Agency, for which he worked in Taiwan, Hong Kong, and Washington. He has translated a number of Chinese publications, and is the author of *A Journey Through Chinese Hell.* He is a native of Buffalo.

JOHNETTE HOWARD lives near Detroit and works as a feature writer for *The National Sports Daily.* Prior to that, Howard worked at the *Detroit News.* She is a 1982 graduate of the University of Pittsburgh.

STEPHEN KING is one of America's most popular and prolific authors. His novels, such as *Carrie, The Dead Zone,* and *Pet Sematary,* and his short stories have redefined horror writing. He lives in Maine, and roots for the Red Sox.

FRANZ LIDZ had covered only one sports event in his life before joining the staff of *Sports Illustrated*. His memoir, *Unstrung Heroes: My Improbable Life with Four Impossible Uncles*, is scheduled to be made into a motion picture.

WILLIAM NACK has been a senior writer for *Sports Illustrated* since 1979, covering racing, boxing, basketball, chess, and other sports. A Chicago native, Nack grew up working at the Arlington Race Track in suburban Chicago. He served in General Westmoreland's command headquarters in Vietnam before joining *Newsday* in 1968.

GLENN NELSON was born in Japan and grew up in Seattle. He attended Seattle University and earned a master's degree in political science from Columbia. He has covered sports for the *Seattle Times* since 1982.

DUANE NORIYUKI wrote for a number of Colorado newspapers before joining the *Detroit Free Press*, where he is currently a staff writer for its Sunday magazine.

PAUL PEKIN has worked as a pressman, owned a variety store, taught at Columbia College and the Art Institute of Chicago, and spent ten years as a police officer for the Cook County Forest Preserve. His work has appeared in a number of publications, including *The Chicago Tribune Magazine* and *Kansas Quarterly*.

CHARLES P. PIERCE worked for the *Boston Phoenix*, for whom he covered national politics, and the *Boston Herald* before joining *The National Sports Daily*. A graduate of Marquette University, Pierce once worked on the national organizational staff for Mo Udall's presidential campaign. His work appears in Dan Riley's anthology *The Red Sox Reader*.

DAVID RACINE's short stories have appeared in *CutBank*, *The Mississippi Review*, and *The South Carolina Review*. He grew up in Massilon, Ohio, home of the famous Massilon Tigers high school football dynasty. He lives in Baton Rouge, Louisiana.

PETER RICHMOND's work has appeared in many publications, including *Rolling Stone*, *The New York Times Magazine*, and *Glamour*. In 1988 and 1989 he was a Nieman Fellow at Harvard University. He is working on a book about the building of the new ballpark in Baltimore.

LINDA ROBERTSON has written for the *Miami Herald* since 1983, where she has split her time covering sports, crime, and tourism. She graduated from the University of North Carolina at Chapel Hill, and grew up in Midland, Michigan.

KEVIN SHERRINGTON has been a sportswriter since entering the journalism profession in 1977. In 1985 he joined the *Dallas Morning News,* the fifth Texas newspaper for which he has written.

FLORENCE SHINKLE is a native of St. Louis. She was a free-lance writer before joining *The St. Louis Post-Dispatch Magazine* as a feature writer in 1989.

GARY SMITH saw his first fight, Ali-Frazier I, on closed-circuit TV in 1971. As a reporter for the *Philadelphia Daily News,* he was able to watch boxing up close. A native of Wilmington, Delaware, he is currently a special contributor for *Sports Illustrated.*

JACK SMITH has written for *Town and Country, Newsday,* and the *Philadelphia Inquirer* on the French Foreign Legion, snake hunts and related subjects.

SHELBY STROTHER won more than one hundred awards over his twenty-year career as a journalist. A native of Coral Gables, Florida, Strother enlisted in the air force in 1967 and served thirteen months in Vietnam. Before joining the *Detroit News* in 1985, he worked at the *Melbourne Times* and the *Denver Post.* He died on March 3, 1990.

PETER O. WHITMER is the author of *Aquarius Revisited: Seven Who Created the Counterculture That Changed America.* His writing has appeared in numerous publications, including *The Saturday Review* and the *Boston Globe.* Once the drummer for the rock band The Turtles, Whitmer is now a clinical psychologist. He lives in Princeton, Massachusetts.

BRIAN WOOLLEY is a feature writer for the *Dallas Morning News* and the author of two novels, *Some Sweet Day* and *Time and Place.*

Notable Sports Writing of 1990

SELECTED BY GLENN STOUT